MARTIN SCORSESE

MARTIN SCORSESE

A Biography

Vincent LoBrutto

Westport, Connecticut
London

Library of Congress Cataloging-in-Publication Data

LoBrutto, Vincent.
  Martin Scorsese : a biography / Vincent LoBrutto.
     p.   cm.
  Includes bibliographical references and index.
  ISBN 978-0-275-98705-3 (alk. paper)
  1. Scorsese, Martin.   2. Motion picture producers and directors—United
States—Biography.   I. Title.
  PN1998.3.S39L63   2008
  791.4302′33092—dc22
  [B]   2007029911

British Library Cataloguing in Publication Data is available.

Library of Congress Catalog Card Number: 2007029911
ISBN: 978–0–275–98705–3

First published in 2008

Praeger Publishers, 88 Post Road West, Westport, CT 06881
An imprint of Greenwood Publishing Group, Inc.
www.praeger.com

Printed in the United States of America

The paper used in this book complies with the
Permanent Paper Standard issued by the National
Information Standards Organization (Z39.48–1984).

10 9 8 7 6 5 4 3 2 1

To Vincenzo LoBrutto, Marie LaLomia, Michael Stabile, Lucy LaRosa,
Anthony LoBrutto, and Rose Stabile, Italians, and Italian-Americans,
for giving me the blood of my blood.

To Everett Aison for telling a twenty-year-old Italian-American
kid from Queens that he had cinematic gifts at a time he really needed to hear it.

CONTENTS

ACKNOWLEDGMENTS

This author would first like to thank the subject of this book, Martin Scorsese, for his generosity. This is an unauthorized biography but Mr. Scorsese allowed me to look at selected papers in his archives at The Wesleyan Film Studies Center, granted me an interview in my role as editor of *CinemaEditor* magazine, and gave me an open invitation to contact his office during the writing of this book. His kindness and contribution to film scholarship are most appreciated.

Thanks to Leigh Johnson and the staff at The Wesleyan Film Studies Center, for arranging my viewing of the Scorsese papers; Edgar Burcksen, the Editor-in-Chief of *CinemaEditor*, for his constant support and his assistance in arranging my interview with Mr. Scorsese; Thelma Schoonmaker, for making sure that there was time for "Marty and Vinny" to chat; my chairman, Reeves Lehmann, for his unconditional support for my work; and Sal Petrosino, a friend a *paisan*. Film historians extraordinaire Gene Stavis and Roy Frumkes for perspective, information, and wisdom; Tony Lover and John Gallagher, for their Scorsesian observations; Kristi Zea, Skip Lievsay, Robert Richardson, Tom Rolf, and Michael Ballhaus, for insights into working with Scorsese; Gene Phillips, for his friendship and expert view on all things cinematic; Pat McGilligan, for his reportage on *Taxi Driver*; Peter Tonguette, for countless engaging talks and for perception way beyond his years; Gino, Pino, Paul, Leo, and all the boys at Pelham Pizzeria, for the good Italian food, sustenance, and goodwill; all School of Visual Arts students past and present, especially members of my American Film Mavericks class; Bible scholar Jack Meadows, for his insights into *The Last Temptation of Christ*; Stephen Pizzello, for sharing his reportage on Scorsese at work; and Dr. Jean Miller, for spiritual guidance. At Praeger I want to thank Eric Levy, this book's first editor, and Dan

Harmon, who carefully and expertly saw it and its author to completion. Cineastes Kevin Janner and Nathan Cox, for their enthusiasm and rigorous debates; Jean-Paul Dorchain, Documentation Department, Royal Film Archive of Belgium; and Joe Paradise, for his personal reflections.

To my wife Harriet Morrison who must live through my transformations with each book, this time listening to me say, "What are you bothering me over—a steak?" way too many times; and for keeping our lives together and the author on the straight and narrow path—I love you, Harriet.

INTRODUCTION

This biography is a critical, cultural, and psychological investigation where the work of Martin Scorsese is the spine and soul of the man.

Since the era of auteur criticism, a tradition has been established of mining a director's canon of films for themes, personal artifacts, clues, and codes that would reveal and define the creator. This approach makes for fascinating reading and discussion but is inherently treacherous for a biographer. In my biography of Stanley Kubrick (a filmmaker who greatly inspired and influenced Martin Scorsese), intensive research into the life and work of Kubrick (1928–1998) led me to conclude that the auteur methodology might have provided some answers about Kubrick, the man, but that to purport direct connections between thematic properties of Kubrick's films and the facts and reality of his life would have been an auteurist trap to fall into—by mistakenly assigning attitude, behavior, and personality traits "found" in the films to its maker.

If Kubrick was cool and analytical, Martin Scorsese is red-hot and emotional. Scorsese is a personal filmmaker. Every one of his films contains his DNA in varying degrees. Scorsese's films are informed by the finite areas directly related to his life: Italian and Italian-American culture, Catholicism, New York City, the movies, film history and film grammar, and family—blood relatives and the brotherhood of the cinema. The signposts, autobiographical references, thematic allusions, personal views, and the mirror of film history are there to be identified, read, decoded, and explained.

The genesis of this book began in 1997 when my then literary agent suggested I follow up *Stanley Kubrick: A Biography* with one on Martin

Scorsese. At that time I was considering several directorial subjects; Scorsese had not been on my list for a reason. When "Why don't you do Scorsese?" rang in my ears, the question triggered a number of high-voltage emotions.

I have always admired Martin Scorsese's ferocious talent as a film director. In my estimation Scorsese has ascended to the mantle held by the late Stanley Kubrick as the greatest living-at-work filmmaker. The consideration to write a biography of Martin Scorsese was a weighty one. The first Scorsese film I had seen was *Mean Streets* in its initial 1973 release. I was twenty-three years old and in my third year at the School of Visual Arts Film School. From the opening shot through the final frame, I watched the screen and kept silently repeating, "How can this guy know me so well?" Watching *Mean Streets* was a revelation. The dark secrets Italian-Americans knew about themselves and their culture were exposed like raw nerves. My objectivity was invaded by a truth teller who had the courage and cinematic gifts to put our ethnic culture up on the screen. Decades of stereotyping in film and television were shattered when Scorsese explored his heritage and tribal rights in *Mean Streets*, *GoodFellas*, *Casino*, and *The Last Temptation of Christ*.

For me, viewing these works is an anxiety-provoking albeit liberating sensation as part of my psyche and blood-membership in ethnic and popular culture is exposed. The suggestion to "do Scorsese" tested a sense of commitment that resonated well beyond a sense of professionalism.

As I learned more about Scorsese, the points of connection were startling. A series of similarities have provided me with unique insight into Martin Scorsese. I am an Italian-American, a baby boomer, and a native New Yorker with Sicilian roots. I was an East Coast film student, then independent filmmaker, film editor, filmmaking and cinema studies educator, and have been passionate and obsessive about motion pictures since my first 8mm effort in 1967.

The research for this book began back in 1973 after that screening of *Mean Streets* in its debut run. I clipped and filed all the articles I could find concerning Martin Scorsese, read books as they appeared, saw the movies as they arrived, and followed his career through a particularly close-looking glass.

Direct research began in 1997. I quickly found that the paradigm I used to write *Stanley Kubrick: A Biography* would not get me where I wanted to go. After many outlines and plans, it became crystal clear that it was Scorsese's films that would lead me on a path to reconciliation concerning the nexus between Scorsese's work and life.

For oral history the reader is encouraged to examine *Martin Scorsese: A Journey* by Mary Pat Kelly and *Scorsese on Scorsese*, edited by David Thompson and Ian Christie. These are revealing and valuable books.

This biography is not consistently linear. The films are the spine of the book; the biographical aspects grow out of the making of those films. My aim is to connect the content, aesthetic style, and cultural and autobiographical riches in Scorsese's cinematic career to his physical and spiritual life.

Thus, this is a biography where the life lived and the director's films in all aspects constantly intersect. Focus on the films is not thematic critical interpretation—when there is film analysis it is intended as a reader's guide to Scorsese's work process designed to offer an informed opinion and to illuminate Scorsese's lifebreath as it transforms and absorbs into each Martin Scorsese Picture.

Many Italian-Americans and other immigrant-rooted cultures have lived an outsider's existence. As many Scorsese films document, America is a wondrous melting pot, but also a country of turf designation, tribal structure, and ancestral tradition. As author, I think of my role as an outsider who has been an insider on this endeavor. I am not a friend, colleague, or associate of Martin Scorsese's, but in the true definition of the Italian term, I believe we are *paisans*, brought together by what the noted scholar Richard Gambino calls "the blood of my blood."

PART 1
Turf, 1880–1959

1

My Voyage to Little Italy

Of all the regions in Italy, it is Sicily that reflects the Italian nature and spirit. Sicily is an island where the sun bakes the skin, and passions run deep. It is the fabled home of the Cosa Nostra and of rich food flavored with deep red tomatoes and ripe garlic. Rome, Naples, and Florence brought sophistication to the Italian character, but Sicily exudes the raw emotional intensity that is all we understand to be Italian. Sicilians speak in dialects derivative of Arabic and Greek imported by the civilizations that invaded them throughout history. The Sicilians treasure family and are wary of government. They live by a code of honor known as the *omerta*. The rules of the *omerta* are strict but unwritten, passed down from father to son, and from mother to daughter. They define respect, retribution, redemption, and right and wrong. The Sicilian is born into a closed society; he walks among us but is loyal only to his family and to God. The code is the invisible bible. Trust no one but *la famiglia* and your *paisans*.

Martin Scorsese's paternal grandfather, Francesco Scorsese, was born in Polizzi Generosa, Sicily, around 1880. Polizzi Generosa lies near Palermo, the capital of Sicily. Francesco Scorsese's mother died when he was only six or seven years old, and the boy felt rejected when his father remarried. Francesco was taken in and later adopted by a neighboring farmer. Working in the fields, Francesco began to dream about America, the land of the free, and the land of opportunity. Throughout the Mezzogiorno, the area comprised of the provinces of Abruzzi, Campania, Apulia, Lucania, Calabria, and Sicily, Italians shared the dream of a better life. The citizenry lived in anguish. Taxes were imposed on grain—the staff of life—and suffering from lack of food and life-threatening malaria and cholera caused a pervasive distrust of the government. The stage was set for a mass exodus. Francesco was a *contadino*, a member of the peasant class of farmers, fishermen, and artisans. He worked hard on the land of his adopted father. The farmer had plans for Francesco. He wanted him to work the homestead and marry one of his daughters, but nineteen-year-old Francesco Scorsese was determined. With every swing of the scythe his desire to leave for America grew. Resisting the offer of land and family, he boarded a ship and arrived in America just at the beginning of the twentieth century.

Martin Scorsese's paternal grandmother, Teresa, was also born in Polizzi Generosa. Teresa was an excellent cook who made classic dishes of the region that set the standard for the family's future generations. Teresa's putensa sauce featured oil-cured olives, finely chopped Italian plum tomatoes, fresh basil, and grated locatelli cheese. She made succulent braciole by pounding steak until it was paper thin, then stuffed the meat with toasted bread crumbs, finely chopped salami and hard-boiled eggs, minced garlic and parsley, and freshly grated cheese, topped with her homemade tomato sauce. Her ricotta pie was full of the fresh, textured, creamy cheese and flavored with sugar, vanilla, cinnamon, candied fruit, and chocolate chips. The petite and strong-willed young woman had set out for America in a small boat. After a month battling angry seas, starvation, and disease, Teresa saw the great green lady and the torch—she was in America.

Martin Cappa, Scorsese's maternal grandfather and his namesake, was born in the town of Ciminna, Sicily. Like Francesco, Martin never knew his mother and was cared for by a family who took him in. When he came of age, the tall, dashing, and elegant man with a handsome face and handlebar mustache became a soldier in the cavalry.

Domenica Cappa was also born in Ciminna, Sicily. One day she heard the sound of cavalry horses passing by her house. She ran out onto the low balcony and watched the soldiers as they rode by. Suddenly, the deep-lidded eyes of the regal young woman caught the glance of a handsome cavalry soldier. Martin Cappa rode close to Domenica. He was wearing a blue uniform, and a hat with a large, white plume. They looked deeply into each other's eyes and fell in love.

After a twenty-two day courtship Domenica and Martin were married. Their daughter Sarah was born in 1912. Martin got caught up in the New World fervor and left for America to find a new life for his family. He began writing to Domenica to join him but she feared the trip and continually resisted. Frustrated, Martin wrote a final plea, threatening to leave her if she didn't come immediately. Domenica and Sarah got on the next boat, but only because her brother was by her side. When they were ready to sail, Domenica turned and panicked when she realized that her brother was gone—she had been tricked. The trip was long and arduous.

Francesco, Teresa, Domenica, and Martin made the same trip as thousands of Italian immigrants yearning for a better life; they had the clothes on their backs, a few belongings, and the culture of the old world. The odyssey was a shared experience. They didn't know what it meant to be Italian-American; they were Italian-born and would become the first transplanted generation. Setting foot on the streets of New York was the beginning of their American experience. For a majority of Italians it was a place to lay down roots. The earliest arrivals settled in Lower Manhattan; then there was a surge north to Mulberry Street. The Mulberry District, as it was known, became the largest Italian enclave in the United States. Once an affluent area, by 1845 it had deteriorated into a hub of organized crime. The narrow cobble-stoned streets were dominated by river gangs, with names like Swamp Angels and Slaughter Housers, who robbed and murdered the rich. Police would only patrol the Mulberry District in platoons of six or more. The Brewery was a complex of apartment buildings in the heart of Mulberry where thieves, murderers, pickpockets, beggars, prostitutes, and degenerates of every variety committed mayhem. When the Brewery was torn down in 1853 laborers carried out sacks of unidentified human bones discovered in the walls and infamous cellars. The Bend was a Mulberry section described by immigrant historian Jacob Riis as "a purgatory of unrelieved squalor. An inferno tenanted by the very dregs of humanity." Men, women, and children were crammed into damp basements, leaky garrets, sodden cellars, drafty outhouses, and stables converted into crude dwellings. Mulberry's Bend was eventually torn down by the New York Tenement Housing Commission in 1892. In June 1901 The Bend was converted into Mulberry Park. As Italians arrived in the Mulberry at the turn of the century, conditions were improving. Determined to make a new life as Italian-Americans, the cultures of the *Mezzogiorno* and the underworld history of the District shaped and influenced their immediate situation and the destiny of generations to come.

Italian bastions formed all over the five boroughs of New York. Italian communities developed in the likeness of the region, village, or section of a village in Italy from which the immigrants had migrated. Italian settlements sprung up in Boston, San Francisco, New Orleans, and across America, but the Mulberry District was the Mecca. It surpassed all others in population and business enterprises. Mulberry became synonymous with Italian-American life and was referred to by most as Little Italy.

New York's Little Italy is located on the Lower East Side of Manhattan, delineated by Mulberry, Mott, Prince, and Spring Streets. The Irish had been the first to immigrate to the District. As Italians arrived in large numbers, at first there was resentment, and then, the Irish began to relocate around the borders of the neighborhood. The district truly transformed into a Little Italy. Within this small number of blocks the Italians simulated their homeland by creating a village mentality with sharply drawn boundaries. The Sicilians traveled from the southern tip of Italy's boot to declare Elizabeth Street an American home. The Neapolitans planted their flag on Mulberry Street. Class distinctions were clearly demarcated; the Northern Italians felt superior, the Sicilians were a worker class. Little Italy was ruled by a *capo* system brought over from the old country, rather than a city government or the federal government of the United States. A *capo* is a boss, the chief, a leader, and the man in charge. In Italy the *capo* was a landowner. In America, the Sicilians answered to the *capos* of the neighborhood that controlled their streets. You kept your mouth shut and your eyes open. Everyone answered to the *capo du tutti* who earned his respected position out of fear.

The seeds of Martin Scorsese's destiny were planted by his grandparents when the two families independently settled on Elizabeth Street. Francesco, a proud man with no formal education (but with a strength of character) worked as a laborer. At twenty-one he married Teresa in the old Saint Patrick's Church, which presided over Little Italy on an entire city block. The Scorsese's moved to 241 Elizabeth, and the Cappa's chose the fourth floor of 232 across the street. Martin Scorsese's father, Charles (whose name was really Luciano) was born to Francesco and Teresa in about 1913. Martin Scorsese's mother, Catherine Cappa, was born in about 1912.

At one point fourteen people lived in the three-room Cappa apartment. All nine children resided in the living room. An aunt, uncle, and their son occupied the bedroom, and the kitchen was in the middle. Fanny Scorsese, Charles' older sister, lived beneath the Cappa's. Charles liked to stay at his sister's, and, therefore, was a frequent visitor in Catherine's building.

Martin Cappa was a scaffold worker and traveled to Springfield, New Jersey, to find work. He was away from his family from Monday through Friday, returning only on weekends. His hard labor yielded forty-five dollars a week, a good wage at the time. But the labor took its toll. An arm injury put Martin out of work for an extended period. Domenica was an expert seamstress and began to stitch pants to make up for the lost income. One of her patrons was Daddy Browning, a New York millionaire whose clothes were custom-made at Arnhem's on Ninth Street. Like many Italian-American women, Domenica worked at home doing piecework, trying to survive in a free-enterprise democracy. Domenica taught Catherine and her sister Sarah the craft. The girls watched their mother as she meticulously worked up the seams of high quality pants, while simultaneously watching over her smaller children.

Francesco Scorsese worked in shipyards for the New York Steam Company, and in the fruit and vegetable business. The Italian diet was fortified by fresh fruit and vegetables considered exotic by many Americans of the era. Fennel, broccoli rabe, bulbs of garlic, eggplant, squash, and ruby-red plum tomatoes, which were the staple of Italian cuisine, were sold on carts and in specialty stores. The fruit and vegetable business was a predominantly Italian occupation for the first half of the century. During World War I Francesco did hard labor in the hull of ships. At New York Steam, Francesco had as many as one hundred workers under his supervision. But Francesco wanted to be his own boss. After leaving the job he opened and closed at least ten produce businesses, often losing money on the deal. Italian women would carefully inspect each head of garlic. Everything was sold loose. A *signora* would handpick just enough fresh mushrooms, *efughi*, for the night's dinner.

One of Francesco's business endeavors was a grocery store on the ground level of their Elizabeth Street apartment. His family was infuriated over the decision. New York Steam kept asking him to come back to work, but Francesco refused and remained self-employed.

Teresa Scorsese was a strong-willed woman. Nine people lived in their small four-room apartment. To supplement the income, there were two boarders while Charles was growing up. Teresa cooked for them and hand-washed their clothes. Conditions were spare and there was no real furniture in the household. During the day, beds were upright so family business and chores could be conducted. At night, beds were taken down and there was little room to walk around.

Charles Scorsese and Catherine Cappa grew up in Little Italy—it was their neighborhood and Elizabeth Street was their block. The street was crowded with people, storefronts, and pushcarts. First the neighborhood had been Irish; then Jewish businessmen came in. Every store and basement was taken over for enterprise. In the morning the pushcart peddlers lined up on the shady side of Elizabeth Street. In the afternoon when the sun shifted, the peddlers switched to the other side. The neighborhood had a Five and Dime, a shoe store, a dry goods shop, and many Irish bars. Charles enjoyed going to Schimmel's for potato knishes and coffee. Chinatown was on the other side of Canal Street. Catherine graduated from junior high school but could not continue. The family couldn't afford it, so Catherine sewed in a doll's clothing factory until she was seventeen, when she began working in a dress factory on Second Avenue. There she sewed dresses for twenty-five cents apiece. Later, Charles' brother introduced her to Mr. Silverman, The Jersey King, who manufactured dresses made of Jersey fabric. This was a better job and for more money. Catherine worked for The King for thirty-nine years.

Charles worked as a clothing presser in the days before steam lines made the job simpler. Charles applied his trade with a sixteen-pound iron, a bucket of water, a sponge, and a cloth. He was a top-notch presser. Charles was given samples of dresses and was expected to make each dress look perfect. He found the job a satisfying challenge. Pressing was seasonal work dependent on the garment industry's calendar. Off-season, Charles got unemployment for nineteen weeks. While Charles was collecting his checks, he hung out with friends, all pressers, in a pool room on Elizabeth Street. Charles didn't make much money at first. He was a perfectionist and only the hurried hands made money at piecework. Later his reputation brought him to the International Dress House where he pressed fine gowns for twenty dollars an hour.

Charles and Catherine lived across the street from each other. They often saw one another as they went about their business. Charles became smitten with the teenage Catherine. He began a courting campaign. Charles didn't have a balcony but he turned his fire escape into a veranda, where he serenaded his lady playing a guitar and singing Italian arias. On their first date they strolled by a Second Avenue dress shop window and Charles bought Catherine a brown woolen dress with a leopard collar. This first purchase established a tradition; Charles began to give Catherine samples he got from his boss at International Dress House. Catherine, a size five who weighed ninety-four pounds, would never have to buy a dress for retail again.

Charles and Catherine spent Sundays in Washington Square Park, where Charles and his friends played guitars and ukuleles. Their courtship matured and in June 1934, they married.

The Cappa apartment was too small for a wedding celebration, so the party was held on the roof. To Italian-Americans living in New York City, the roofs of their crowded apartment buildings represented freedom, a tar beach in the warm weather, a place to get air, to be alone, or with a friend, or loved one. Relatives and friends of the Scorsese and Cappa families gathered on the roof, the men in their best suits, the women in their best dresses. Charles and Catherine, now husband and wife, made a grand entrance up the stairwell and through the heavy door and were applauded with cheers and handfuls of rice. It was an urban image—Catherine in her white wedding dress, Charles in his tuxedo—the black tar, Elizabeth Street apartment buildings in the background, and behind those the skyline of New York. This was an Italian football wedding. A long table held stacks of wrapped sandwiches full of Genoa salami, proscuitto, cappocola ham, and mortadella cold cuts. Long streams of pink crape paper flowed from a pole decorating the festive and sacred event. Guests grabbed sandwiches and made trades by calling out, "I've got a cappocola," "I've got a salami," and tossing the specialties like a football. A traditional wedding cake was served. A local priest congratulated the couple. Some guests ate while standing on their feet, and others sat down on the slanted periphery of the roof. Photos were taken of the bride and groom, the women of the family, and the men of the family. All had a great time. Charles and Catherine Scorsese were ready to begin a life and a family together.

2

Corona: *Paradiso*

Martin Scorsese was born on November 17, 1942, in the suburb of Corona, Queens. His parents, Charles and Catherine Scorsese, had moved from Elizabeth Street to escape the oppressive old-world conditions under which they had been raised. Living on Elizabeth Street in a cramped apartment with their oldest son, Frank, had not been much of an improvement over the earlier generation's plight in Sicily. Little Italy was a cement and tenement environment, ruled by the *capo* bosses, and constrained by invisible but impenetrable borders, rigid class distinctions resistant to change, and a suspicion of the outside world.

Charles and Catherine made the weighty decision to venture from New York City to what Little Italy called *the country*. The distance traveled didn't add up to much in miles, but it was a lifestyle change that granted their boys a snippet of the American dream—a house, a yard, and a place to play and grow up without urban fear and the constant exposure to life's realities on the Lower East Side.

Corona was largely inhabited by Italian-Americans. The majority of Italian émigrés were from the southern island of Sicily. The Joseph Lisa/William F. Moore Memorial Square was known as Spaghetti Park. There were bocce courts where old-timers rolled a small *pallino* in the dirt and used skills unknown to American bowlers to land the bocce ball closest to the prize. One Hundred Eighth Street and Corona Avenue were lined with Italian meat markets stocked with fresh handmade sausage and beef for *braciole* and Italian restaurants that served tomato-rich Sicilian specialties long before the more delicate garlic, oil, lemon, and parsley dishes of the North became fashionable.

The Scorseses lived in a two-family house located near the children's aunts and uncles, another aspect of "family," "home," and "neighborhood," which brought harmony to Marty's young life. "I was born in the peace and greenery of Corona, Queens," Scorsese fondly remembers, "and I loved it. I loved Corona, Queens. It was two-family houses. There was a yard at the back, and a little tree."

Land was important to Italian-Americans. Many invested in "lots" they would later use to build homes or sell for profit. Land was turf. Back in Sicily they worked the landowner's soil for survival and never enjoyed or benefited from it. Now, in *L'America* the land could be theirs to do as they wished—it represented power. Even the smallest patch meant freedom and a link with the old country. They could plant tomatoes and basil and feast outdoors. Sausage stuffed with fennel, red pepper, parsley, and cheese could be grilled over the coals and pasta, meatballs, eggplant, and other dishes were cooked in the kitchen and taken outside to be enjoyed in the open air.

In Corona, providence was already at work shaping Martin Scorsese's life. Baby Marty was born with the genetic and biochemical components to develop asthma, an enduring disease that would threaten every breath he took. For Marty, his backyard and his tree were critical theatrical backdrops for his imagination. Like most little boys in the 1940s he loved Westerns. His first professional aspiration was to be a cowboy. He had the entire outfit, including a hat and six guns. The yard was a stage to play out scenarios based on the movies and television shows he had seen. Every boy had an arsenal of toy guns. Shooting them was an expression of nascent masculinity, heroic fantasies of getting the bad guy, of invincibility and the experience of death when shot by a nonexistent bullet. To Marty, the little tree was proof that he was a man of the West. In the quiet of his Corona neighborhood, he could sustain his fantasies, uninterrupted by urban noise pollution and the dangers of the Lower East Side streets.

3

Corona: *Purgatorio*

When Martin Scorsese was three, it was determined that he was suffering from the disease known as asthma. Factors totally out of his control were about to change his inner and outer world, and the direction of his young life.

In 1945 little was known about the cause of this respiratory illness and how to treat it effectively without life-altering results. Members of the working class like Catherine and Charles Scorsese were especially vulnerable to primitive advice and recommendations during this era of treatment for the malady. A physician was at the highest level of their society. The word of the doctor was law and was followed religiously. Italian-Americans especially tended to put doctors on the highest pedestal. They were easily impressed and did not question, challenge, or even seek out other opinions on the health, welfare, and care of the patient: "He's under a doctor's care," and "You know what the doctor said!"

It was conventional wisdom at the time that asthma was primarily a psychologically triggered illness. Asthma sufferers were characterized as sensitive, weak, and sickly. The proclamation was, "It's all in his mind." Treatment included medication, but was guided by a strict directive: "Keep them indoors, don't expose the child to excitement or physical activity. Keep them quiet and calm. They are emotionally charged, 'high-strung' and any exposure to extreme situations could trigger an attack. They must be protected from the dangers in the air they breathe and the uncertainties outside of the controlled environment of their home."

Middle-class Italian-American Roman Catholics had faith in the power of prayer. There is a saint to pray to for deliverance for almost every ailment and human condition. The patron saint invoked against the suffering brought on by asthma is Saint Aldric also known as Elric. Like Charlie in

Mean Streets, Saint Aldric struggled with allegiances to the church and to the street. As if describing the inner struggle between good and evil that is the focus of many Scorsese pictures, Sean Kelly and Rosemary Rogers in *Saints Preserve Us!* concluded: "The connection if any, between his [Saint Aldric] counterfeiting career and his heavenly concern for asthma sufferers is unknown."

The Scorsese family's early perception of Marty was shaped by his asthmatic condition. Marty was given allergy shots practically from birth. As a toddler he began having trouble breathing. In 1946, at age four, his doctors decided to remove his tonsils. Tonsillectomies were subject to debate within the medical community, which was at odds about the advisability of the procedure for children with respiratory weaknesses. Some doctors believed in early removal of these tissues prone to infection, contending that complications increased as children grew older —for an adult a generally simple procedure could become more critical.

Because of their parental anxieties, limited medical understanding, and an unconditional reliance on the doctor's advice, Charles and Catherine decided young Marty should have his tonsils removed. Four is a tender age for an operation and often parents of this period transferred their own fears onto their children. It was decided that the young, sickly, and sensitive boy would not be able to cope emotionally with the reality of surgery. As a consequence Charles and Catherine never discussed the operation with the boy and instead concocted a story that was ultimately more traumatic than the medical procedure itself.

Arrangements for the operation were made. When the moment was upon them, Catherine told Marty they were taking him to a wonderful circus. When the boy arrived at his destination he was confused and eventually angry. Even as an adult Martin Scorsese never understood why he wasn't told or why the operation was necessary. This became further complicated as the asthma worsened, convincing Marty that the tonsillectomy made the asthma more severe, causing increased physical and psychological suffering.

Health decisions on Marty's behalf may have been motivated by love and overprotection, but Scorsese's self-perception was of someone who had to be isolated and watched carefully. Marty was considered too frail to play or spend extended time with the other children in his neighborhood. Although he loved the fresh air, his backyard, and the tree that completed his cowboy image, he spent most of the time inside his Corona home. He played no physical sports or even games like tag. The circumstances of his life set the stage for his attraction to art and the movies and Scorsese would ultimately recognize his future was being formulated.

In 2003 Martin Scorsese received a Special Achievement Award from the Asthma Network Mothers of Asthmatics (AANMA). His videotaped acceptance speech revealed that he understood the destiny formed by his childhood illness, and the attitude toward asthma in the 1940s.

"I've had asthma since I was a child before they started manufacturing the sprays and drugs like Albuterol. Of course I made a lot of trips to the hospital but I still carry my asthma spray with me all the time. Do I wish that I could have lived without it? Yes, but I realized that I would have been a very different person had I never suffered from asthma. I knew very early on that I couldn't let it beat me so I didn't. . . . I focused that more intensely on the things that I could do and that's something I will never regret."

The fear instilled in his family as they watched Marty suffer became his view of the world. At the earliest age he was an observer who was also closely watched. Everyone looked out for Marty. He became hyperintense about what he *could* do—*watch and listen*. His own physical suffering would develop into his religious obsession about paying for sin with crucifixion and ultimately into his cinematic and personal life theme—*redemption*.

The fires of hell dominated Marty's being. The quiet boy tried prayer but was imprisoned in a mid-twentieth-century world of ritual and belief. Marty, the nice Italian-American boy, did as he was told, did what others believed, but the power of his imagination and his passion for what he could see and hear within the boundaries of his circumstances would deliver him.

What can a child with so many physical limitations do? In the early years of the decade, television was not yet the electronic babysitter it would eventually become. There was radio, reading, and comic books—*sequential art*. Marty was open to hearing and watching stories, in a book, in a comic, and in the oral tradition. For the latter there was a wealth of material. Italians are great storytellers; emotional, narrative exaggerators who know their audience and could build a story combining humor, tragedy, excitement, and wonder. But the decision on how to fill his earliest days didn't come from Marty.

Charles Scorsese wasn't an average moviegoer. Today, there are millions of cineastes—those who grasp an understanding of the cinematic arts. Back in the day everyone went to the movies. They were inexpensive, logistically accessible, and understandable in content. Moviegoing was a weekly ritual for many families. And then there were the Charles

Scorseses—men who loved the movies—men who called movies—pictures. Growing up, Marty Scorsese heard his father say, "That was a great picture!" or, "Let's go see the new John Wayne picture!" During his career Scorsese decided to use the phrase, "A Martin Scorsese Picture" as his signature. Before movies were referred to as films or moving images they were pictures. The picture show—a series of individual pictures in which the action advanced, so projected, the pictures would move.

Classic Hollywood directors, the men who made the movies, were admired by the men who went to the movies seriously, not just to pass the time. They knew the good picture makers: Hawks, Ford, Welles—even if they couldn't invoke the names at will. They knew the stars and the studios. They went to the movies and whatever was playing, they saw it.

Charles Scorsese always loved the pictures. He was an avid moviegoer and enjoyed the world he would never see beyond his self-imposed universe on the Lower East Side. During the thirties and forties, Charles could always afford to go to the movies even if there was no money left for anything else. The movies came first. Charles was an unschooled film scholar. He may have been limited in what he could verbalize about the movies but that didn't matter. Charles found a way for Marty to pass the time and share what the father had loved all along. There was little talk between them. Charles' gesture in taking Marty to the movies, at times daily, at times to two different shows, was an expression of love and caring. Marty suffered loneliness more than most children, but in the movies he was not alone. He was with his father, and they were out West, in urban streets, or in foreign lands—wherever the images dancing on the silver screen took them.

To many baby boomers the movie theater was like a church. The theaters of Marty's time were huge, cathedral-like spaces. The lobbies were decorated for royalty, ornate patterned rugs, and chairs so high a boy couldn't sit and touch ground with his Buster Browns or Thom McCann's. The ushers were dressed like soldiers or members of a royal court. The matrons dressed all in white; often their hair was white as well. They wore white shoes. They were like strict nurses, there to keep order. Large flashlights searched for trouble like light beams at night in a prison yard. The theater was dark, cool, and comforting. The sweet odor of hot, buttered, popcorn floated in the air. The ceilings and walls were decorated. A child could watch the stars or look at the ancient statues along the walls.

In those days a picture show had two features—an A movie and a shorter B movie, the kind that would inspire Marty and his generation, as well as a cartoon, newsreel, coming attractions, and short subjects. The show ran for hours. Although a time schedule was posted, most audiences arrived when they arrived, usually in the middle of a movie. They would watch it from that point to the end, see the rest of the attractions, and then see what they had missed of the film. Attendees considered the show continuous and cyclical; you came in, stayed, and left. People entered and exited on their own clocks.

Sitting in a movie hall chair, Marty was safe. The air was relatively controlled. He didn't have to exert himself, only stimulate his imagination and mind. Charles was always there. The movies watched in a theater were a shared experience. Everyone was witnessing what the movie had to communicate with image and sound.

The first image Martin Scorsese remembers is a trailer for a Roy Rogers film. The color process was Trucolor developed by Republic Studios. The process featured an impressive and vivid flesh tone that was very faithful to green and brown—bringing forth the background in the Westerns, their specialty. Trucolor was not equally true to other colors in the palette, but Republic's representation of the West caught Marty's eye. The shot Marty remembers depicted Roy Rogers jumping from a tree to a horse. This may have caught his imagination because of the romanticized view the boy had of his backyard tree. Charles saw that his boy was animated by the coming attraction and asked Marty if he knew who Trigger was. Marty was too young to know Roy's trusty steed was named Trigger; he raised his thumb and extended his index finger, imitating the firing of a gun, an image Scorsese would replicate during the climax of *Taxi Driver* when Travis Bickle raises his bloody fingers to his temple and fires his "gun." Charles explained that Trigger was Roy's horse and promised they would see the movie in its entirety the following week. For Scorsese the thrill of anticipation was the most memorable part of the experience. If these images were in the film, boy, what else could there be!

His older brother Frank took him to the pictures. On occasion Catherine brought Martin to the movies. In 1946 when Marty was four, he asked his mother to take him to King Vidor's Western epic *Duel in the Sun*. The film was condemned by the church. Once the church made its decision, the decree was printed in the church newspaper to warn all good Catholics to stay away. The movie contained sin. If Catholics disobeyed, they would be committing a sin that would count against their soul. Many Catholics went to see the condemned film anyway. *Duel in the Sun*—nicknamed "Lust in the Dust" had a sexy poster image of handsome Gregory Peck and a sultry Jennifer Jones.

Marty let the movie affect his senses and emotions. Dimitri Tiomkin's orchestral score made Marty feel he was watching a horror movie and he became frightened. At the end two people were so in love that they had to kill each other. Marty couldn't look up at the screen; the picture entered the forbidden zone of real emotion beyond religion or societal law. The sensitive boy understood the feelings projected on the screen and it overwhelmed him. Catherine, in textbook Italian-American mother tradition, saw Marty averting his eyes and yelled, "Look at it; you took me here to see it, now watch it!"

Marty couldn't get enough of the movies. There were only so many films playing in his vicinity and Charles made certain Marty saw every one. Although they didn't know it, Charles and Marty were what collectors call "completists." Some filmgoers and collectors are particular and specific about what they see or collect, but, from the earliest age, the archivist and historical champion of the cinema was alive in Marty Scorsese. He watched everything and paid serious attention to all of it, soaking in film history.

In 1948 when Marty was six years old, the Scorsese household was among the first families on their block to own a television set. When it arrived Marty was playing in the backyard, probably deep in an imagined narrative inspired by the many Westerns he had seen. Daydreaming about movies was not an escape from reality, but a way of dealing with it. Images and stories were always forming in his mind stimulating his budding artistic instincts.

Marty heard his cousin Peter shout gleefully that the screen was bigger than the whole house! Marty ran in and saw a sixteen-inch, black-and-white RCA Victor television. A sign of an embryonic filmmaker is their response to a screen, or, in this case, a television tube. The image is only as big or small as the images imply—not their actual measurement. Those fascinated by moving images respond to a forty-foot screen or a television monitor, a virtual postage stamp compared to a motion picture theater screen. They are brought into the picture by what goes on within the frame. They can enter it regardless of size; it is visual storytelling. Now Marty had a new way to see movies. Early television programming licensed and ran as many films they could get their hands on. Marty had everything to fill his world; the physical limitations dropped far back in his mind; as long he went to the movies, watched television, and played in his backyard, he was living a life fuller than he could imagine—asthma or no asthma.

Marty learned to enjoy when things were going well. Italian-Americans lived with a black cloud of doom, knowing anything could happen at any time. This was reflected at family gatherings—first everyone was laughing and then they were angry, maybe fighting. But, as quickly as it started, it could end, now everyone laughing, hugging. You couldn't plan or anticipate those moments—it was part of the culture.

Marty Scorsese could not predict or be prepared for how his life would change in an instant. He was around six or seven. Catherine and Charles announced to their sons they were moving out of Corona. Inquiries and requests for answers didn't provide the reason that Marty's pastoral world was about to end. His father had "business problems" and they had to move. Charles and Catherine never explained the reason for this drastic step. They had moved out of Little Italy to raise their children in a kinder and gentler environment; now the boys were sentenced to live on the same block, Elizabeth Street, where Charles and Catherine had been raised. "Business problems" rolled around in Marty's head. What did his father do? Why couldn't it be explained? The answer was never revealed; the adult Martin Scorsese still doesn't know. Not knowing makes it seem as if something terrible happened to force Charles to leave—but understanding the old-school Sicilian code of silence, Marty knew that it was serious to Charles, his pride, and his reputation.

There would be no grassy backyard, no tree, no friendly homes, and no neighbors. There would be concrete, tenements, asphalt, constant noise, and potential danger. But there would be movie theaters, a television, and a bedroom window.

4

Little Italy: *Inferno*

Martin moved abruptly to his grandparents' four-room apartment at 241 Elizabeth Street in Little Italy. He was there for almost six months until Charles and Catherine found a place for the family to be reunited. Marty was assaulted by culture shock. If he looked out the window he could see children playing with garbage pails.

Charles and Catherine were both born on Elizabeth Street. For Marty it had been a place to visit his grandparents—that far-off magical place where children are welcome and treated specially. The surroundings didn't matter much; once inside, children were front and center, pampered, and adored as special visitors.

Now that same apartment was a holding area until a new Scorsese family residence could be found. For Charles and Catherine their dream of getting out of Little Italy to a kindlier, gentler place was not sustained. As if some sort of Sicilian destiny was in control, they now found themselves exactly where they started, met, and married. Frank and Marty were now assigned the same fate. Catherine and Charles had no choice. Elizabeth Street was never a chosen home to Charles and Catherine; they tried to venture out on their own to the country, free of the capos, codes, and danger, but they knew all the rules of the turf. Charles reestablished himself, maintaining as much pride as possible. The Italian-American community of Little Italy covered a ten-block area. Elizabeth Street was primarily populated with Sicilians, and like the Scorseses, those of Sicilian ancestry. As far as the citizens of Little Italy were concerned it wasn't the United States' government, politicians, or police they answered to. "We felt we were right in our own ways," Scorsese observed. The construct was a series of villages, just like in old Sicily, run by the padrones and the capos—an insular society where the citizenry answered only to those within their turf—an infrastructure as complex and effective as any mankind has devised.

Marty was old enough to understand that there were tough guys, whom he later recognized as wiseguys, all around him. The outside world called them Organized Crime, the Cosa Nostra, and the Mafia. Those names weren't spoken in Little Italy. The wiseguys did the actual dirty work—stealing goods, illegal gambling, and demanding protection money from local businesses. The wiseguys and their overlords managed the neighborhood and kept peace by their own law. Many bought clothes off the rack and goods that "fell off a truck." Most resolved problems through "local enforcement" and were "d&d" (deaf and dumb) to the authorities. No one in Little Italy ever saw anything. People fell off buildings, stores were vandalized, and bodies were found. "I don't know nothing." "No, I didn't see anything." No, I didn't hear anything." They were shown pictures of men they couldn't identify because those men were both respected and feared. If you kept your nose clean everything was fine.

Like an alternate universe, everyone in Little Italy dressed differently than the rest of Manhattan; they drove oversized or out-of-date model cars not seen elsewhere in New York. You could identify Little Italians by their lack of casual wear; blue jeans didn't exist, men and boys wore ties, not for an occasion but for around the apartment, to work, school, street business, or for an idle or purposeful walk. Frank Sinatra was the best-dressed man in their world; Frankie didn't assimilate to the Brooks Brothers look, he was always decked out and accessorized with Italian Bling-Bling, pinky ring, tie clip, and cuff links. Big shots in Little Italy didn't walk, they drove everywhere, and their sedans were a status symbol while doing business. The wiseguy double-parked as a badge of honor, the most *connected* had a spotter, usually an aspiring kid who was handsomely tipped for developing a watchful eye. Italian-Americans were most always right, they dressed correctly—everyone else didn't have style, and drove the wrong cars—not enough understood the significance of the year-round use of the color black. If you wore black or your wheels were black or jet blue, you were taken seriously. The way one dressed and drove established their *rep*, someone to be feared and respected, most often in that order.

The streets were dirty physically and spiritually. Men staked out their turf. Someone was always looking and waiting. Charles taught both of his sons the *omerta*, the Sicilian code of silence. Always be wary, keep an eye out—when asked, you saw nothing and said nothing. Marty especially took the watching and listening lesson to heart. He became an observer of human behavior and a historian of street life.

Frank took his father's words literally. The boys slept with the windows open in the late spring and summer. Many nights, violence would erupt on Elizabeth Street, or the surrounding blocks. The sounds broke all silence and sleep. Frank would wake, walk to the window, pull down the shade to dull the noise, and make sure no one thought he was looking, as the wiseguys did their business. The next day there would be no questions asked. A whistleblower was a fool—a dead man. *Omerta* meant if you opened your mouth about anything you had seen or heard—you would be silenced—for good. Frank was an obedient older brother. His father told him to keep his brother Marty close and watch over him, and that's what he did.

Marty Scorsese's world narrowed when he moved to Elizabeth Street. His universe shrank. Now he had only fear and trepidation about the danger of the streets. Marty's natural-born sense of observation, heightened and sharpened by his limited physical activities, worked overtime when he was outside; he took it all in—not as fantasy, but as reality.

Going to the movies increased to obsessional levels. The window of his Elizabeth Street apartment was a frame where he watched a living Italian neorealist film. What Marty saw outside his window was a movie as real as an Andy Warhol long-form epic, with all the expressive action of a John Ford Western, as brutal as a Warner Brothers gangster movie, as defined and vivid as the New York cinema of Kazan, Lumet, and Cassavetes, and as splendid as a biblical epic or ancient Roman gladiator opera.

5

In My Room

Martin Scorsese's view from his room onto the world of the street was so limited that the height and width of the open window became the aspect ratio for the films he would make, even before he knew he was going to be a filmmaker. Scorsese's visual insights—watching movies in a movie theater, looking at motion pictures on a sixteen-inch television screen, and peering out of the window in his room—all merged. It was vision, images, observations, and how they made him feel that guided him. At first he wanted to be a painter. He spent hours drawing. The act of sketching was a way of expressing the creative ideas formulated by his intense exposure to the movies. He read newspaper comic strips and storybooks and began to imagine narratives cross-fading with every movie he had seen. He copied comics, a sequential storytelling art, which became a seminal step in his development as a filmmaker. From ages eight to thirteen, Marty created movies by putting comic book drawings behind a piece of cardboard on which he cut out a screen, transforming the drawings into shots that were put together in his imagination.

Marty was cognizant that movies came in different sizes and formats. He drew in simulated 1:33.1—the traditional aspect ratio for most of the Hollywood films he had watched—and in Cinemascope, a long and narrow movie canvas. Marty's life at this stage, as he has repeatedly stated, was movies and religion—so it was no surprise he was enamored with Biblical epics in widescreen and expressive color. He was especially attracted to United Artists and their relationship with Hecht and Lancaster Productions—to Marty, the name was personal and represented a point of view and a voice.

The first Martin Scorsese Picture was never filmed, but was planned in detail, then drawn and painted in watercolor in the style of traditional

Sicilian puppet shows that featured ancient knights fighting for the pride and glory of their nation. The cast included his favorites of the day, combined in the tradition of a studio extravaganza: Jack Palance, Rita Moreno, Richard Boone, Jeff Morrow, Hans Conreid, and Anthony Quinn. Marty's credit was not the common "produced and directed by" but instead "Directed and Produced by Martin Scorsese."

Of course, included was "And a Cast of Ten-Thousands." The drawings, filled with pageantry and violent imagery, depicted soldiers in symmetry marching through a brick archway in Cinemascope format. There is an unusual sense of dark, light, and image size. Marty didn't consciously understand he was drawing the language of film: closeups, camera movement, and progressive visuals, but the vision of a filmmaker inhabited him. Bernardo Bertolucci, one of Scorsese's most sacred heroes, claims he saw camera movements as a child—so did Scorsese—he saw whole movies and put them on paper. At age ten Marty sat down and drew storyboards for a movie he dreamed of making—the story concerned the life of Jesus.

Of all the films Martin Scorsese viewed as a child none made a greater impact on his vision of cinema and personal approach to filmmaking than the Powell/Pressberger production of *The Red Shoes* released in 1948. *The Red Shoes* dramatically captures the intersection of life and art. It is set in a ballet company led by Boris Lermontov (Anton Walbrook), an impresario who is both genius and controlling dictator. Lermontov becomes professionally and personally obsessed with his protégé Victoria Page (Moira Shearer) who falls in love with Julian Craster (Marius Goring), the composer of "The Red Shoes"—the ballet that launches Page to stardom.

The form and content of *The Red Shoes* is filled with aesthetic properties that Scorsese embraced as a philosophy of film. *The Red Shoes* is a backstage drama, a genre dear to Scorsese's heart. The genre serves as entrée into the inner lives of artists.

Many directors revise the list of films that influence them, but Martin Scorsese's inspirations are so crystal clear that they are constantly reflected and referenced in his own work, in his film history and restoration projects, in interviews, talks, and on endless Scorsese "best" lists. Every time his core-value films are mentioned, they remain in their initial context—the experience of a young boy learning about cinema, the world, and his artistic passions. In DVD commentaries and interviews, such as on the Criterion release of Jean Renoir's *The River*, Scorsese is teaching film history, but in a totally subjective voice. Scorsese is in awe of Renoir's artistry, but Marty Scorsese, the youngster, is the center of the discussion—how the film made him feel and his sense of discovery as he watched it with his father.

In 2005, Scorsese was asked by the Philips Company to compose a list of the greatest color films as a sophisticated marketing ploy for their new ambient light plasma television—for Scorsese, another blessed chance to talk about movies—the movies that most influenced his understanding of the cinema—the lists are English language films: *Barry Lyndon*, *Duel in the Sun*, *Invaders from Mars* (1953), *Leave Her to Heaven*, *Moby Dick*, *Phantom of the Opera*, *The Red Shoes*, *The Searchers*, *Singin' in the Rain*, and *Vertigo*; and international films: *Contempt*, *Cries and Whispers*, *Gate of Hell*, *In the Mood for Love*, *The Last Emperor*, *Red Desert*, *The River*, *Fellini Satyricon*, *Senso*, and *Shadows of Forgotten Ancestors*.

Martin Scorsese is a cinematic encyclopedia, a film historian, and a scholar, but his judgment and taste reflect a highly emotional and particularized reaction to films. They form a Rosetta Stone to an understanding of Scorsese and his choices. His interpretations of these canonical Scorsese films reveal his inner core.

Scorsese is not an adult who lives in the past, but one who remains in touch with the power of his inaugural film experiences and the indelible impact they have had on his work as an artist. The impetus and its result is the first challenge to understanding how a film has affected Scorsese; finding the references as they are filtered through a cinematic and sociological prism is second; and recognizing the original talent and creation that the combination produces is the final step. This metamorphosis has eluded many, who stop conveniently where their own limitations cause them to cease exploration. With Scorsese, the more you know, the more you'll search and the more you'll understand. Scorsese is a translucent filmmaker who, like all great artists, transfers and translates creative inputs into a concrete form, utilizing the tools of camera, sound, design, music, narrative structure, and the intense and trusting relationships he cultivates with actors.

The portrait of the artist's life in *The Red Shoes* made a lasting impression on Scorsese, as a man married five times and as a filmmaker who often visits the theme of the impossibility of two artists balancing their creative and personal lives. Lermontov creates a family within his company who live in an insular world. Lermontov lives in a world where everything is dance, and everything he does concerns his work. No contemporary filmmaker lives the life of the cinema more fully than Martin Scorsese. He makes movies, teaches, writes, lectures, and participates fervently in the preservation and archiving of film. Like Lermontov, Scorsese's life is his art, but happiness in romantic companionship is a desire often out of his reach. Scorsese has explored this theme of the romantic attraction of artists in *Alice Doesn't Live Here Anymore, New York, New York, Life Lessons, The Last Waltz*, and *The Aviator*.

Boris Lermontov is in total creative and business control of the dance company. To Scorsese he is an embodiment of auteur film director, an overseer who controls every aspect of a production and puts his personal stamp on a film through cinematic style and the content of the narrative. Lermontov is surrounded by his subordinate collaborators who function for the purpose of making his vision a reality. Throughout his career Scorsese would grow more and more like Lermontov, a filmmaker accessible to the public under his own generous rules, but in total seclusion during the making of a film. While on the set Scorsese is constantly protected by his loyal staff, making it difficult for anyone else to approach him directly. In the tradition of both the Hollywood studio system and Sicilian unwritten law, one must go through a hierarchal structure to get word to him. While filming, Scorsese talks freely to the actors and his director of photography, production designer, and other key collaborators, but to few others. He is protected as he was as a sickly boy from the dangers of asthma, protected as an artiste from those who may distract him, and protected from the outside world to preserve the kingdom of his cinema world. Like a man of respect, Scorsese is friendly, generous, secretive, and filled with rage and passion. He has created an environment where he can control access, involvement, privacy, and the adoration he has earned.

Powell and Pressberger based *Lermontov* on legendary producer Alexander Korda, and the resemblance is potent. There is also a bit of the dance genius Diaglev in *Lermontov*. What links *Lermontov* securely to an auteur director is Anton Walbrook's uncanny resemblance to the personification of the dictatorial film director—Josef von Sternberg. Von Sternberg's relationship with his muse Marlene Dietrich is mirrored in Lermontov's obsession with Victoria Page. Although Scorsese has no actress with whom he is solely associated, his relationships with Harvey Keitel and Robert DeNiro have a similar thrust. He has never tried to control the lives of these actors, but Keitel has been a Scorsese on-screen surrogate in *Who's That Knocking at My Door*, and *Mean Streets*, and DeNiro has played out the director's rage and passion in *Raging Bull, Taxi Driver*, and *GoodFellas*, as well as supplying emotional and psychological satisfaction by playing characters Scorsese has fantasized about—those who can physically act on their desires.

To Michael Powell and to his student of film, the young Martin Scorsese, who has watched *The Red Shoes* over and over again, this film about dance and a ballet company has a subtext. Just as *Taxi Driver* is not about the life of a cabbie, *Raging Bull* is not principally about boxing, and *The Aviator* is about more than aviation or even Howard Hughes—the dance company in *The Red Shoes* is a metaphor for a family of filmmakers and the process of moviemaking.

As an Italian-American, Scorsese was born with a deep sense of family both of blood and friendship. *The Red Shoes* revealed to him what it took to create a work of art: the people, their struggles, joys, and interactions, the meticulous step-by-step process of connecting the art to the story, the endless practice and dedication. Growing up as an outsider in mainstream America, Scorsese has spent his life and career attracted to the margins. The artistic community of *The Red Shoes* is a society within a society. Art is not a profession but a way of life. It was not a job and then a family—the two were one. This romantic notion, filled with tragedy in *The Red Shoes*, has eluded Scorsese for most of his life. How does the artist balance work and personal life? *The Red Shoes* demonstrates that there is no hope for balance. For the artist, all of life is contained within the art. Those who leave the "family" are no longer artists. Those who stay sacrifice everything for their creative expression through art.

Scorsese also connected with *The Red Shoes* in a visceral aesthetic sense. As promised in the title, the dancer's shoes are red. Although they may be linked historically with Dorothy's red shoes in *The Wizard of Oz*, the shoes serve a different purpose here. Dorothy's shoes are possessed with the power to get her back home. Vicki's shoes possess the ability to dance. When she puts them on she dances with absolute abandon. The specific color red is linked to this ability. To find the right color, the company's art department prepares a long row of shoes in pairs, each in a different shade of red. Lermontov walks down the line; a tracking shot follows him as he looks and finds *the* pair.

Red is a dominant color in *The Red Shoes*. The theatre curtain is red. Vicki Page's hair is red. The color exhibits a sexual power and an artistic passion. Red is a dominant color in the cinema of Martin Scorsese. For him, one of our most Catholic filmmakers, it represents the blood of Jesus Christ, the blood of violence, the crucifixion, the stigmata, and the garish design of Italian life. Although red is one of the colors of the American flag, wearing it represents a "loud" uncultured individual. To the Italian-American the color is also on their homeland flag and to wear red is to show pride, conceit, and defiance.

The Red Shoes and the films Scorsese viewed as a child that captured his imagination are a thruline in every film he has directed. The mature filmmaker of *The Age of Innocence, Gangs of New York, The Aviator,* and *The Departed* continues to be entranced with the images of his adored films. The nature of his artistry is in the way Scorsese personalizes these images in his own vision.

6

The Church

As a child living in Little Italy, Martin Scorsese was exposed to power in two forms—wiseguys and priests. Tough and colorful street guys functioned as the government, law enforcement, protectors, and punishers. Gangsters set the rules, ran the numbers games, sold merchandise off trucks, and kept an *eye* over the local shopkeepers. As with most power figures, wiseguys were revered, reviled, and respected. Their power came from fear. These larger-than-life, outgoing goodfellas who lived by their own rules, would do favors, expect a return, and deal swiftly with anyone who stepped out of line. A warning might suffice, but if necessary, any member of the community could disappear overnight and become landfill or part of the aquatic population. The gangsters answered to higher-ups in the organization but ultimately, the wiseguys respected only one figure, and his *organization* was headquartered in The Vatican.

The Catholic priest, the man with the turnaround collar, the one played on screen by Pat O'Brien, Barry Fitzgerald, and Bing Crosby, was the only mortal man fully respected by the street guy. Scorsese was impressed that the wiseguys tipped their hat and took the time to say hello to a priest who was always addressed as "Father." To the gangster, priests were the ultimate godfathers. Although they broke all of man's laws and many of the Ten Commandments, the street guys attended church every Sunday, gave generously when the basket was passed, and contributed when the church was in need. A priest represented the power of heaven and hell. They operated on a more cosmic level of fear—an eternity of burning in the inferno.

No gangster would use common language with a priest, so there was no cursing around them. When a wiseguy bought an expensive and flashy car, the priest was asked to bless it with holy water. The men were married in the church, their children received the sacraments of baptism, communion, and confirmation, and the wiseguys were given the last rites. They even had their pets blessed by a priest. It was an unbroken rule back in the day that no hit would be carried out on church property.

At eight or nine years of age, Martin Scorsese decided he wanted to be a priest. His reasons were driven primarily by the notion that it was the quickest route to salvation from original and accumulated sins. Marty was born a Roman Catholic. His family, like most Sicilian clans, was respectful but highly suspicious of the church. As with many young men of his era who considered the priesthood, Scorsese enjoyed the promise of being close to God, having a reserved seat in heaven, and living in a society even more confined and regulated than Little Italy. After the end of World War II, as the unease of the Cold War grew, the thought of being cared for by the church and dedicated to the saving of souls was comforting. The boy was attuned to the ritual and pageantry of history. His favorite films were biblical and historical epics. He marveled at religious spectacles, gladiator movies, and stories of ancient cultures. He was also intrigued by films that had garish and saturated color palettes, intense myths, and ceremony. To Scorsese the church fit in with these schemas. The vestments were bright colors, each having significance in the Catholic cycle. The architecture of the old churches was ornate, recalling antiquity. Sunlight exploded the already vivid colors of the stained glass windows. The mass, like a filmmaking project, was a process. Each mass recreated the turning of bread and wine into the body and blood of Christ. There were masses for the dead, masses for celebration, and masses for the saints; and like myriad movie genres, they each offered their own wonders.

Martin Scorsese received his Holy Communion on May 26, 1951. If he followed the path to priesthood, he could be a man of respect, without doing the evil of a wiseguy. The priest was of the highest order, above the street, above the government—the priest answered only to Jesus Christ—who Marty accepted as the Son of God.

Marty attended the Sisters of Charity, the oldest parochial school in New York City, where all the Italian families sent their children to be educated in the Catholic way. The student population was comprised of the sons and daughters of the working class and the offspring of mobsters. Irish nuns taught the children; the Italian priests conducted mass. Marty was told by the nuns that every morning at 10:30 A.M., God came to the altar. Scorsese committed to serve as an altar boy—he would be there when the visitation occurred.

In observance of church law, Marty never ate meat on Friday. He fasted for Lent and was spiritually invigorated every Easter. During Passion

Week he followed the Stations of the Cross, which told the story of Jesus' last days in images. To Marty this was pious storytelling and, akin to scenes in a movie, the story of the passion took on greater significance as he fathomed the connection between the images, the story, and the process of moving from station to station.

During Lent a Catholic is supposed to give up something that bestows the most corporeal satisfaction; some gave up smoking, others a favorite food, or candy. Marty never was able to make the ultimate sacrifice and give up movies for Lent. For Marty film would become a guilty pleasure until he discovered that cinema was his true religion and the movie theater his actual church. So during Lent, Marty continued to devour movies at the local picture show and on television, especially his beloved *Million Dollar Movie*, where he would delight in sin, watching the same movie in repeated viewings during the course of the week.

The old St. Patrick's Cathedral was on a block that was treeless except for a graveyard over two hundred years old. The Irish nuns took little Marty under their tutelage. They taught him about the scriptures. When they saw Marty's fascination as he listened to a visiting missionary, they began grooming him to be one of God's world messengers. Marty was frightened and enticed by the missionary's dramatic narrative of a tour in the Philippines where he exorcised a young boy possessed by devils. The nuns used a slogan analogous to "the few, the proud, the Marines," as they told the boy, "many are called, few are chosen," implying he was one of the holy few. Over the course of his early education missionaries from all over the world came to Marty's classroom to tell stories about their quest to serve Jesus by helping the sick, the poor, and those rejected by society. The content stimulated the sensitive boy's psyche and the mesmerizing stories were a link to his Italian-American culture of oral storytelling. He grew up in the last great era of folklore. His father, uncles, Elizabeth Street locals, the nuns, priests, and these larger-than-life missionaries were part of a tradition that preceded movies, television, and radio—when a speaker could hold a crowd or an individual enrapt.

The nuns taught Marty that the soul, the most sacred component of Catholic life, was at the center of a spiritual battleground—a war between God and the devil with an afterlife in Heaven or Hell in the balance. What the nuns admired most about Scorsese was his gift of acceptance. Marty, unlike many curious and rebellious children, didn't question what he learned. The nuns coveted this—the more Marty learned and accepted about his religion, the more the nuns could teach him without needing to explain what they considered unexplainable—they could prepare him for a life of devotion. The Irish nuns could not know (nor did Marty at the time) that his attraction was more aesthetic than religious—he gravitated toward the pageantry, ritual, ceremony, and theatricality of the mass. He loved to hear the old Italian men and women sing hymns in ancient Latin, although Latin was not a religious school subject in which he excelled. Marty was searching for history, purpose, and expression. Religious statues and icons were Marty's art. Following the rituals of feast days and Catholic festivals filled his personal calendar and absorbed much of his energy and commitment.

Marty's grandmother had a portrait of the sacred heart—an image that represented divine worship of Jesus' heart of flesh—proof of his divinity and love in dying for the redemption of his followers. Of all the iconography associated with Jesus Christ, the sacred heart was among the most consecrated and frightening to children and laymen; the mystery was in the symbolism—the image revealed the human heart not in a scientific, but in a highly expressive manner. Many religious Italian and Italian-American Catholics freely exhibited this image in their home as if it were a family portrait, unaware of the image's impact on those who might not understand or accept its religious meaning. Grandma also had a statue of the Virgin Mary grinding her foot into a snake, a symbol of triumph over the devil. For Marty, these images, although representations of faith, created an obsession for extreme, evocative imagery that he would look for in the films he admired and would become part of the lexicon of his personal films.

Like many Catholic boys, Marty had a crucifix over his bed as a reminder of the sacrifice Jesus made for him. The crucifix was there to watch over him and make the bed a holy place. Most teenage boys felt this concept was violated when sexuality became part of their lives and they experienced massive Catholic guilt. Scorsese was not the first filmmaker driven by a sense of Catholic guilt and conflict; the French auteur critics long understood the impact of Catholicism on the work of Alfred Hitchcock—a major influence on Scorsese and the American New Wave.

Marty was constantly exposed to the poverty of the Lower East Side. The Catholic Worker House, which served the poor and downtrodden, was located on Chrystie Street not far from St. Pat's and only a block from the infamous Bowery.

The Bowery was a street name as well as a sad Mecca for the lost. While Marty was attending school at St. Pat's, Dorothy Day, a Brooklyn-born American Communist and founder of the activist newspaper *The Catholic Worker*, dedicated herself to broken citizens of the Bowery delivering a personal blend of politics and religion as she helped the poor. The boys were confused and repelled by the men they saw in a constant state of inebriation, stumbling along the street in search of cheap wine and urinating in the doorways. They couldn't understand why Dorothy Day was devoted to them. They would ask their priest about her, thinking she must be unbalanced herself—missing the connection to the teachings of Jesus and her adherence to the gospel. This lesson had a powerful effect on Marty, who had great faith but needed to apply it to street life as he understood it. Helping the poor became his mission as a young man on the path to priesthood. Marty was also in search of redemption from the stain of original sin. He studied the Saints who had transcended sin and earthliness in life and became holy. Pre-Vatican II religion was strictly fire and brimstone. Marty was looking for a way to avoid hell. The crucifixion loomed large—one must suffer to be redeemed. He was drawn to the dramatic story of Father Damien, the priest who dedicated himself to the lepers of Molokai, in Hawaii, but it was William Friedkin, another filmmaker of the American New Wave, who would chronicle Father Damien's story in *The Exorcist*.

By the time Marty entered third grade he learned about the transformation of bread and wine into the body and blood of Jesus Christ. The mass was spoken in Latin—the whispered words, "This is my body, this is my blood," signaled the sacred moment when the presence of Jesus Christ entered the church to recreate the miracle first experienced by the apostles during the last supper and repeated over the centuries at Catholic masses all over the world.

As an altar boy at old St. Pat's, Scorsese became deeply imbued in the process of the mass. He often served at the 5:00 A.M., mass and received special training to serve as an altar boy for the Saturday morning funeral masses, known as the Mass for the Dead or Requiem Mass, where respect for the dead engendered thoughts of life, resurrection, afterlife, and the nature of an everlasting soul.

Everything embraced purity—unalloyed gold, 100 percent cotton, and natural beeswax were used. The altar boys burned special coals to create billows of incense clouds, which permeated and purified the entire church. Color, which fascinates Scorsese, the filmmaker, surrounded him. There was gold during feast days, purple during the period of penance, white to represent the Blessed Mother and saints, and his precious red, symbolizing martyrs. He was attracted to the various colors he needed to wear, especially the red robe used for the wedding ceremony. There were textured mosaics, the rows of candles aflame, and the vestments worn by the priests that symbolized their purpose of faith as they performed the ceremonies of life and death. He understood each detail that led to Christ's presence in the form of the Holy Eucharist. Marty studied and practiced the ritual, which he performed over and over producing the same sacred transformational results. During Scorsese's tenure as an altar boy, the host before and after the mass was not a symbol of Christ, but an actual sign of his physical and spiritual presence. The serious boy felt that power during transcendent moments when material objects—the chalice, wine, round wafers of bread on a plate—brought Jesus into the hearts of those receiving communion. When Scorsese discovered filmmakers who sought spiritual enlightenment through their work: Bergman, Dryer, Bresson, Ozu, and others, he came to understand that movies could also be a means of spiritual expression. The movie process had its rituals in the form of film stock, light, camera, sound, editing, music, props, sets, actors, and other details that were constant components of a cinematic experience. His definition of spirituality would go beyond the scriptures into the pain and joy of everyday existence.

As Marty developed a sense of imagery he began to paint religious iconography that reflected his interpretation of spirituality. He painted two eyes, unattached to a face, just watching eyes on his bedroom walls and told his parents that the eyes looked over him while he was sleeping—the power of religious symbols had overtaken him. When it was time to move Marty wanted to take the eyes with him; even though the building was owned by his second cousins he was not allowed to take his "fresco." Later when he got into filmmaking he brought in a photographer and made a print of the artwork that helped keep him from the devil's disciples while he slept.

Marty began to hear the calling to become a priest. This was a momentous decision for any young man and one that Catholic families considered above reproach. Scorsese's parents responded with a Sicilian mix of respect and skepticism. They also harbored a wary Sicilian attitude toward the church's constant interference into the personal lives of its parishioners, but Charles Scorsese tried to be welcoming by claiming there was a priest on his mother's side of the family but "way back," which in Italian-American parlance meant he really didn't know but had heard it with little evidence or proof. Catherine commented on this genealogical issue by arguing with her husband about whether his family even went to church, let alone had a man of God in their midst. The Sicilian culture that produced the Scorsese family took a dim view of men who became priests. They were considered less than men because they did not engage in physical labor and their celibacy denied them the manhood right of procreation and extension of the family name through their sons.

Scorsese's most profound experience as an altar boy was the portion of Passion Week devoted to the final days of Jesus—from Good Friday when the crucifixion took place to the reappearance of Christ on Easter Sunday. The Passion has dominated Catholic culture for centuries. For Scorsese, Passion Week was terrifying, exhilarating, and beautiful. It was the dramatic story of the Stations of the Cross—the sacred narrative and the liturgies, which he found among the most beautiful in the Catholic canon.

Redemption was a personal theme for the young Scorsese. The Catholic state of redemption fascinated him. Priests had insights into the mysteries of redemption to which the congregation was not privy. Redemption penetrated many Scorsese movies: *Mean Streets, Taxi Driver, Raging Bull, The Color of Money, Cape Fear, Bringing Out the Dead*, and *The Aviator*.

In 1953, while in seventh grade, Marty met Father Frank Principe, a priest in his early twenties, who came to Marty's Little Italy parish and spoke to his class. The Catholic citizens of New York were identified and defined by their parish, and Little Italy had a special reputation because of its association with old-world mores and its wiseguy population. Principe was not like the more traditional priests. He listened to classical music, involved the local boys in athletics, and took them to the movies. Principe disliked rock and roll on both moral and musical grounds. He was dedicated to classical art and the integrity of the artist. He exposed the children to Beethoven and Tchaikovsky, while they were listening to Doo Wop, Elvis, and Little Richard. The young priest earned their respect because he lived in and understood the secular world. To Principe motion pictures were a serious art form to be used for a righteous purpose. He encouraged the boys to avoid trifling entertainment and study serious films. His gospel of moviemaking included Fred Zinneman, who directed films with social and moral themes such as *The Search, The Men, The Nun's Story*, and *A Man for All Seasons*.

Father Principe came to Marty's class the day after the Academy Awards ceremony. The priest took the occasion to give a powerful and convincing sermon. He told an impressionable Martin Scorsese and his classmates that statues like the Oscar were false gods representing greed, an obsession with worldly goods, and glorification of the ego. He was preaching right out of the Bible and the Ten Commandments. Principe even compared the look of the Oscar to the idol Moloch in the fable of Samson and Delilah.

Father Principe questioned the boys about their existence and purpose on earth. He talked about the mystery of Christ and called it a truth too deep to understand. An extraordinary priest and man, Father Principe encouraged the boys to question, gently explaining that Christianity was filled with paradoxes that were part of its sacred mystery. He taught them that love, compassion, and beauty were all-important. When Marty made the personal decision to become a priest, he began to engage in further conversations with Father Principe. Without Scorsese realizing it, the priest was really mentoring him on ethics and truths about his yet-to-be acknowledged chosen profession—the cinema.

Principe viewed movies through his own moral prism. In a discussion with Marty of the Hitchcock film, *I Confess*, in which a priest is involved in a murder case, Principe totally rejected the premise that the priest, played by Montgomery Clift, was jilted by a young woman (Anne Baxter). Principe told the boy this man could never have been a priest. When Marty and his classmate, Joe Morale, went to see Frank Sinatra in the musical *Pal Joey*, Principe dismissed the story of a girl-chasing dancer, and dressed down his students by suggesting they would have been better served playing basketball on such a beautiful day.

On the Waterfront, directed by Elia Kazan, is a landmark example of the New York School of filmmaking of which Scorsese would become a contemporary leader. An exposé of union corruption on the East Coast docks, the film set the tone for socially conscious street movies and broke Hollywood conventions that favored artifice over realism. *On the Waterfront* has been a major influence on Scorsese over the decades. Its breakthrough method acting techniques and personal urban poetry would be responsible for birthing *Mean Streets* and the director's quest for a cinema that reflected life as he knew it.

Many filmmakers have been inspired by *On the Waterfront*, but Scorsese's orientation to the film was Biblical as fostered by Father Principe's viewpoint. Principe strongly identified with Karl Malden's portrayal of the longshoremen's priest in the movie. Principe interpreted the film's climax as an allegory for the Passion. As the priest saw it, Malden compels Terry Malloy (Marlon Brando), to stand up after a brutal beating, and walk the walk to Calvary. To Principe the film merged loyalty to Catholic values and the laws of the street.

Principe borrowed a bit from Malden's street priest and Pat O'Brien's sweatshirt padre from *Angels with Dirty Faces* by meeting the boys on their own turf—he played baseball and basketball with them. He would go where his young parishioners hung out—their favorite street corners, the schoolyard, and even neighboring Chinatown restaurants.

Marty attended retreats during his "aspiring priest" period. To the Catholic boys not part of the church's intensive educational approach, the concept of a retreat was looked upon with skepticism and trepidation. A retreat took place over a few days; the boys of the parish would travel to a country setting. According to *A Catholic Dictionary*, they would "pray, meditate and receive instruction in the spiritual life." There was always a great mystery around these ventures, but there seemed to be a code of silence about exactly what went on during a retreat. When Marty arrived back at Elizabeth Street he would not talk about it—not to his friends—not to his parents.

To the average street kid a retreat seemed to be a cross between a religious revival and a homoerotic orgy. The primary purpose of a retreat was to involve boys who were seriously considering the priestly life and remove them from their day-to-day environment for an Old Testament lesson about the dangers of sin.

In September of 1956, when Marty was fourteen, he took the next step to the priesthood by entering Cathedral College, a junior seminary located on New York's Upper West Side. The romantic phase of his aspiration was over as Scorsese quickly faced the discipline required. For those, like Scorsese, who thought they had received a calling the issue became dedication to celibacy. The teenage Marty met a girl, fell head over heels, and suffered the pangs of Catholic guilt that would grow, fester, and ultimately be expressed in his work. He became distracted from his studies and was expelled after his first year. A fuller examination of the behavior that led to Scorsese's expulsion reveals the influence the streets had on him. Traditionally, boys who attended Catholic grade school were so repressed during class hours that their base energies were unleashed outside of the church's confines. Most Catholic children who attended public school and received religious instruction only one afternoon a week and after mass on Sunday, were frisky during school hours and didn't need to act out after the school day. So the Scorsese dossier at the junior seminary included roughhousing, which was a way of life and the essence of survival on Elizabeth Street, and bringing fake guns to school—perhaps a product of his exposure to television and feature film Westerns, gangster movies, and the neighborhood wiseguys who always packed a piece. Discipline was required, but without the nuns orchestrating his every move, Marty had trouble with his studies and began reacting to what he had gotten himself into by declaring his choice of the priesthood. He put in his time daydreaming, most likely about the movies, and was known as a Klass Klown, with poor grades—not the preferred personality profile for the seminary.

Sex, drugs (not quite yet), and rock and roll began invading Marty's psyche; he was becoming obsessed with women's bodies and listening to the rock music that was shaping teen culture.

Marty's commitment to celibacy was doomed from the start. He grew up hearing the neighborhood philosophy on the subject. Little Italy's residents never bought into the piety preached about the vow of celibacy. To the Sicilian mind, a life outside of society and denial that a man needs the flesh and body of a woman was unrealistic; they saw the local priest as a man like any other. It was common knowledge that when a priest had the urge he discreetly took care of it like any other man in the neighborhood— he shacked up. The majority of Italian-Americans had a pagan attitude toward the church; they were respectful, attended mass, but did not accept all the teachings and beliefs strictly on faith. Like the young men of *Mean Streets*, they looked to the street for their moral compass and put the church into perspective as a business and social/political force.

After the junior seminary, Marty began as a student at Cardinal Hayes High School in the Bronx. He still clung to his dream of the priesthood, but soon other distractions consumed him. In addition to his growing obsession with moviegoing and girls, Marty developed rock and roll fever. He constantly listened to contemporary radio and bought the 45s he liked at a record store. When he began making films and wanted to use the music of his teens, he often used his own records on the soundtrack, scratches, and all. This was not a retroperspective or a planned aesthetic trope; those records contained the DNA of his cinematic ideas and became a complex narrative and contrapuntal device.

Scorsese still made plans to join the priesthood intending to go to the Jesuit University at Fordham along with friends of a similar bent and ambition, but when his grades landed him in the lowest quadrant of the class, it ended any possibility of serving the Lord in a traditional manner.

When Marty first decided to follow the priesthood everything he felt and thought was holy. Although surrounded by sin, he was able to attain a state of grace by living within the confines of the church's moral code. Eventually, his faith was tested when everything that brought him pleasure was deemed sinful by the church. He gravitated toward literature that challenged Catholic doctrine such as Graham Greene's *The Heart of the Matter*, in which the main character commits suicide in order to stop his cycle of offending God and to escape the sense of judgment Catholics suffer by living a life that inevitably cannot please God.

During his confessional sessions he not only told the sitting priest of his impure thoughts, but also of the intellectual and emotional struggles that eventually moved his spirituality away from the church. He fell into the status of a lapsed Catholic looking for redemption on the streets in the only reality he could truly accept—not the eternal truths of the teachings, but the truth of life as it was lived—there was no escaping that. Scorsese understood but no longer totally believed in the dogma of the Catholic Church. He found the endless rules unfair and intolerant toward other religions. Scorsese remained connected to the doctrine if not the dogma because of the intense Catholic guilt he endured with every impure thought and remained devoted to redemption, if not in the canonical sense in the eyes of the Lord, but in the eyes of those who truly judged him—those around him in the encapsulated world he was trapped in by birth, until his cinematic journey could take him beyond Elizabeth Street in body and mind.

Marty's haberdashery habits reflected his new attitude. Like many Italian boys Marty wanted a red jacket. Often the color attracted because of its boldness, but for Scorsese it was a complex iconography; religious, temperamental, and personal. He was dissuaded by family and friends. His father told him only pimps wore red and the guys on the corner complained it drew police like flies. New York City gangs of the era wore black leather jackets, tee shirts, and jeans like Marlon Brando in *The Wild One*, but Scorsese's crew wore tailored sharkskin suits.

The film buff in Scorsese continued to bloom. In addition to watching films, he began reading about them. Film literature was sparse when Scorsese was growing up. Marty couldn't afford to buy the first film book he read, so he would visit it at the Tompkins Square Library and take it out, return it when it was due, and repeat the process. He just couldn't get enough information about film history. The book was *A Pictorial History of the Movies* by Deems Taylor, a highly influential cultural figure who was a composer, critic, author, and radio personality. Among his accomplishments, Taylor is best known for his participation and contribution to Walt Disney's landmark music/animation experiment *Fantasia*.

First published in 1943, the year after Scorsese's birth, *A Pictorial History of the Movies* had been updated and reprinted many times. Scorsese first read the edition that covered the year-by-year history of motion pictures until 1949. The book was illustrated with black-and-white stills and the text contained descriptions of films, many that Marty had not yet seen or heard of. The book became a personal journey as Scorsese ultimately described in his documentary about American movies. He would read the text, stare at the pictures, and dream about all the films that were ahead of him.

Every time Marty looked through Taylor's book he fought the urge to take a scissor to a picture. He knew this was a sin beyond a local or federal crime. On a few occasions Marty clipped out a picture he obsessed over. Scorsese's confessed this in a documentary about the American Cinema— a profoundly Catholic act. One can also say that Scorsese attained redemption for this particular sin, since he has devoted his life to sharing and teaching the gospel of film to millions. On the library's hundredth birthday, Scorsese presented the institution with a copy of the book.

Scorsese did manage to save up ten dollars to buy *The Film Till Now* by Paul Rotha, a noted British documentary filmmaker. This classic was first published in 1930, with numerous reprints—its subtitle reads: *A Survey of World Cinema*. *The Film Till Now* sits on the shelf of practically every baby-boom filmmaker or cineaste. For Scorsese, and all who treasure it, the book lays out a lifetime of film watching and is a formidable overview of the medium. With the purchase of this volume, Scorsese shifted decisively from religious devotion to a creative vow to the artistic world of film.

7

The Street

The harsh realities of Little Italy were as vivid to Marty as the Italian neorealist films he admired. Scorsese remembers witnessing a graphic example of Little Italy's brutality while playing one day in a sandbox and hearing the terrifying sound of a baby hitting the concrete after a fall from the roof. There was so much physical conflict on Elizabeth Street that rivalries even existed on opposite ends of the same block. When Marty walked to grade school just one block away, he had to cross into the Bowery where the streets were even meaner. Carrying his tiny briefcase filled with schoolbooks, Marty passed homeless alcoholics slashing each other with cheap wine and whiskey bottles—tearing human eyes from their sockets. The eight-year-old had to navigate around the shards of broken glass. A river of blood filled the street, not the sacred fluid of Marty's religious experience or the Technicolor brand that flowed in DeMille's remake of *The Ten Commandments*, but by-products from the wounds of unwanted rejects of society—men who Scorsese had wanted to save during his missionary period, but later ridiculed along with the neighborhood tribe who considered these men less than human.

Fights were everywhere. Marty and his friend Joey, the inspiration for aspects of both Charlie and Johnny Boy in *Mean Streets*, were constant companions. They traveled everywhere together. They were attracted and repelled by block fights, but managed to protect themselves by ramping down their pace so they would arrive too late for the action.

School was a prime location for fights because it brought together diverse ethnic tribes. The Italian-American and Puerto Rican groups especially clashed. The differences were not only cultural, but also extended to warfare preferences. The Italian-American boys preferred baseball bats or sticks, and used any method to get an opponent on the ground so they could be kicked into submission. The Puerto Rican fighters preferred the stiletto retractable knife, which allowed them to keep all comers at a distance.

Marty Scorsese was a likable boy, small in stature, not threatening or a troublemaker, but a good kid known to be funny. In a culture where men were identified by their first name followed by a nickname, his moniker was Marty Pills. The neighborhood knew he needed medications to control his asthma, and with one word they stereotyped him.

In his teen years, Scorsese fit in with the local street guys. He developed a sophisticated sense of humor, laughed easily, and was very bright. His ever-growing encyclopedic knowledge of film history made him a *professore* respected by the street guys. Wiseguys and toughs were especially attracted to clever kids, finding them amusing and harmless.

In Little Italy there were only two definitions of manhood—either one was a tough guy who meted out physical punishment, or a brave guy who could take whatever was given to him. Marty was diminutive and sickly so he had to take punishment—he earned his stripes and was accepted. So Scorsese was not a victim of bullies. His peers assigned him as the advance man sent on a mission to start trouble by provoking a target. Once accomplished, Marty would step back and let the others apply the muscle.

For citizens of Little Italy the idealized concept of America as a melting pot was rejected outright. Growing up, Scorsese witnessed prejudice, which he forthrightly revealed through on-screen characters especially in his early films. *Mean Streets* courageously manifests the hostility the young Italian-American men share concerning gays, African-Americans, and Jews. Marty recalls that when he was five years old, he saw a man hurled onto the street; his head cracked open and he was bleeding profusely. His brother Frank turned to him and said, "He's only a Jew." This matter-of-fact kind of bigotry would add to the realism of Scorsese's street films. It was brutal but real, put on the screen not for judgment or criticism, but because that's the way it was.

Marty was barely cognizant there was a world outside of Little Italy. Occasionally, he would venture to Times Square, the movie Mecca, to see a movie not playing in the neighborhood. He visited relatives who lived in Staten Island or Queens, but they were communities with similar Italian-American enclaves. Although Marty lived only blocks away from Greenwich Village, he visited the bohemian paradise of social, political, and artistic experimentation just once for a friend's ninth birthday party, before going to college at New York University.

Marty and his friends were so marginalized that they believed only their customs were right and everyone else's were wrong. They were so outside of mainstream society that to them long pointy shirt collars popularized by Billy Eckstein were right and the Brooks Brothers traditionalist collars were wrong. People who drove compact cars were wrong and the large two-door deluxe model Cadillacs, Lincolns, and Buicks were right.

In September 1963 Marty had a seminal experience that profoundly affected his transformation from street kid to creative artist. The violent ending of *Mean Streets*, in which there is a life-and-death confrontation, was triggered by an actual event. Marty and Joey were spending a typical night hanging out and cruising—the ritual of riding around the neighborhood in an intense but aimless state. The young men were in the backseat of a local guy's red convertible and looking cool about it, while a teenage boy rode shotgun in the front passenger seat. For no other reason than destiny, good luck, or karma, Joey and Marty decided to retire for the night; their shift was over so they were dropped off on Elizabeth Street. When the driver pulled out he was blocked by another car challenging the turf. The wiseguy-in-training pulled a gun to show he was a big man. Blocks later and no more than three minutes after Marty and Joey were out of the car, shots rang out from the adjacent car and the teenager was shot in the eye. Sudden violence was an everyday reality for Marty, but this was too close. Those three minutes would define his life and inhabit the characters he created for his signature film.

PART 2

A Portrait of the Artist as a Young Man, 1960–1971

8

The Home without Books

Catherine and Charles wanted Marty to go to college so he could earn good money. In a blue-collar family Marty would be the first to go to university. He was raised in a house without books. Intellectual stimulation came from within Marty. His parents were anxious about their son's professional prospects. Marty told his parents he wanted to be a teacher and applied to New York University (NYU). This satisfied them as a respectable profession that would allow their son to be independent and responsible for a wife and children in the future.

Emotionally Scorsese was dealing with issues he was not sharing openly with his parents. He acted the role of the nice Italian boy and dutiful son, but his mind was absorbed by obsessions about art, devotion, and ambition, fueled by his early experiences in the church and the movie theater.

Formally, he had a long relationship with a local Sicilian girl, who had the approval of his family. His parents assumed it would proceed to marriage and a family. From the moment Marty was aware of the opposite sex, his rules of attraction were in overload. He was cursed with the Madonna-Whore syndrome at a time when a sexual revolution was taking place. This inner turmoil would be a dominant theme in *Who's That Knocking at My Door*.

Marty had a plan to realize his dream of making movies. He enrolled as an English major at NYU and registered for film courses as a minor; his parents were just able to afford the tuition for their son's secret self-created curriculum—for them it was a solid investment in his future. Eventually they discovered his intentions and were surprised, but supported him loyally.

Marty walked to NYU's Washington Square campus from Elizabeth Street in less than fifteen minutes. Every day he traversed the short physical distance from an old-world civilization to a new orbit of culture and experience.

NYU was evolving into a modern campus as new buildings rose to meet the climbing numbers of baby boomers seeking higher education. When Martin began his university experience in 1960, the campus was quiet; the boys sported traditional crew cuts and wore suits, and the girls were collegiate in Madras Plaid and white shirts. The discovery of blond females was the first revelation Marty experienced. He had pined over Monroe and Harlow on the screen, but was never in the presence of a girl with golden locks. In Little Italy he was raised with brown hair, brown-eyed Italian girls, many of whom were either repressed or unapproachable. NYU girls were sweet, friendly, and attracted to exotic Latin types. Marty's libido was unleashed by the same liberating discovery made decades earlier when the Anatolian Greek, Elia Kazan, left his ethnic ghetto and landed on the campus of Williams College in Massachusetts to be surrounded by lovely, sun-touched WASPS.

As a freshman, Scorsese's was registered in The History of Motion Pictures, Television, and Radio. It was a two-credit course, given every Thursday, usually held at 170 Waverly Place, remembered by Scorsese as either a three- or four-hour session. The professor, Haig P. Manoogian, was a force to be reckoned with.

Manoogian had an impressive résumé although he did not have a traditional background in theatrical feature filmmaking. He was a master of fine arts graduate from the celebrated Yale Drama School. During World War II he was an information and education specialist. For the Works Projects Administration he had created productions for the Living Newspaper Company. These potent forms of visual communication presented political and social issues utilizing dramatic forms and documentary evidence as calls to action to inform the public of social problems. His philosophy was that films must have something of import to say and that it must be articulated in expressive cinematic language.

Manoogian was an Associate Professor of Motion Pictures and director of the NYU Summer Motion Picture Workshop, and his dossier was of great value to East Coast students. New York had little feature film activity during the early sixties but was a rich resource of documentaries, industrial filmmaking, and a thriving commercial advertising industry. With Manoogian's deep understanding of film history and dramatic cinematic storytelling, he was able to offer a multilayered education to his students who, under his tutelage, had won national and international awards for short films. During his long tenure at NYU, Haig Manoogian was, at times, the head of the graduate and undergraduate film programs.

There have always been film students who sign up for any course that shows a feature film in its entirety, so they can watch a movie, catch some snooze time, and pick up easy credits. The true believers attend these classes for discovery and to explore new cinematic avenues.

When Scorsese began his first semester there were 200 students in Manoogian's required class. This was a course in motion picture, television, and radio history. It began with an hour and a half lecture, followed by a screening of a film, then by a discussion.

Manoogian didn't actually lecture; he delivered a cinematic homily in Old Testament tradition. As the students sat, Manoogian took the stage. He was a serious looking man with thick, salt and pepper combed-back hair, the consistency of fine wire. His large features and thick-rimmed glasses conveyed the impression of a man on a mission, not interested in whether he was liked, but that he was heard and understood. It's been widely noted that the young Scorsese spoke at a rapid and clipped pace—but the student was no match for Professor Manoogian, who was a combined orator, priest, classicist, propagandist, and truth seeker. In his lecture Manoogian set high aesthetic standards and challenged his students to see the art in movies.

Manoogian's method was to take no prisoners. He threw out any and all nappers. His critical arguments were so detailed and vigorous that only the strong could survive, others left or were uninvited to the blood sport of analyzing movies the Manoogian way. The professor claimed the classroom as his bully pulpit and the administration with their tidy plans and rules be damned. When Manoogian screened Von Stroheim's *Greed* without any musical accompaniment, a student was banished from the class simply for asking, "Why?" Only the strong respected him enough to disagree with conviction. Manoogian believed that all films worth making should be personal. Scorsese was given a B+ for a passionate and intelligent paper on *The Third Man* on the grounds that he challenged the professor who labeled it as only a thriller. Scorsese and Manoogian often clashed about specific films, but the teacher was impressed with the young man's knowledge and conviction, and the student admired the integrity and honor of his teacher. One major point of contention was about the importance of Alfred Hitchcock. To Scorsese, Hitchcock was one of the great masters of cinema language and, although he made thrillers, he was a deeply Catholic and personal filmmaker. Manoogian was just not as enthusiastic. To the professor the cinematic canon was too wide and deep for such intense hero worship.

The decision to explore filmmaking at NYU still wasn't enough to totally banish all thoughts of the priesthood, but when Scorsese met Manoogian, a transference occurred—it was devotion that Scorsese was seeking and he recognized this man as devout as any priest he had ever met, and that the movie theater was a sacred church in which to worship. As Manoogian spoke passionately about the great filmmakers, Scorsese understood he wanted to be a film director. Manoogian espoused the auteur theory, and along with the fervor of his students, totally revised the curriculum to honor American masters such as John Ford and Howard Hawks, Hollywood directors who, through their films, mentored the American New Wave.

In 1966 Manoogian wrote *The Film-Maker's Art*. Billed as a handbook or textbook on filmmaking, *The Film-Maker's Art* is a landmark text, which fused form and content, and technical and aesthetic concerns. As a historical artifact it is filled with a philosophy of filmmaking, which guided and shaped Martin Scorsese. The book is not an easy or "good read," but a polemic on Manoogian's principle that technical skills are worthless to the filmmaker without a personal vision.

Manoogian perceived filmmaking as a Sisyphusean task that required knowledge, physical labor, form, substance, and technology to serve the personal content created by the director. While many professors, critics, and theorists were unable to fathom the breadth of the cinematic medium, often reducing it to an offspring of literature, Manoogian called it the "debtor art" because it borrowed freely from all other arts.

Manoogian understood that film was a flexible medium capable of great range. The essential nature of film lies within action, physicality, and the emotional and intellectual life of the story and characters.

Manoogian was a practical teacher as well as a deep thinker. He taught about the power of the marriage between the visual image and sound. He demanded films reflect the creator's point of view, what later came to be known as the vision of a filmmaker. He analyzed the structure of a film from the shot, to the scene, to the sequence, and to the superstructure that connected to the central theme or subject of a work. He encouraged experimentation within form and structure. Using figures and charts he demonstrated narrative structures and their variations.

Manoogian was greatly influenced by the exploding global cinematic revolution of the late fifties and sixties. He taught his students to understand the construction of Italian neorealist films and English comedies and dramas influencing the world movie stage.

For the professor, writing a script was a personal experience and a disciplined process, a structured course that began with an outline through many drafts until a shooting script was realized. Structure was Manoogian's mantra; he stressed it during the screenplay process, as the film was shot, and during postproduction.

In addition to theoretic instruction Manoogian taught the language of film; continuity, crosscutting, camera blocking, angles, sequencing, matching action, reverse angles, cutaways, the importance of screen direction, and the application of opticals. Manoogian set the standard high with the examples he chose: *High Noon* and *The Seventh Seal*.

Once the script was completed Manoogian stressed the planning of the production; a process that involved perceiving the film about in progress as a visual narrative. He taught his students to search for the meaning in each scene and sequence; then to create the necessary practical and aesthetic plan involving the relationship between the visual and verbal, production design, shot structure, the use of lighting, lenses and filters, and the search for the style without style, the correct cinematic language for the story being told. Manoogian constantly warned against art for art's sake.

Control of a director's point of view involved the preparation of the actors, the timing and movement of a scene, and the values within each narrative moment. After production Manoogian applied the same concept of control to the editing process where the filmmaker found the rhythm of the story and the ultimate structure of the film.

Haig Manoogian was a dedicated and serious film man. He taught his students the Hollywood formula and then encouraged them to seek the antidote; new narrative forms, and a transcendence of technique to produce a personal experience for the viewer.

The future of a film student is determined by the education and the era in which they study. Scorsese had the remarkable opportunity to study with a professor dedicated to the total art and craft of film. While this intense instruction was taking place, the Classical Hollywood Studio System was being reexamined and it was a golden age of international cinema. The film students of the next wave would study during the seventies when Scorsese and the American New Wave reinvented their national cinema by melding the best of the old and the new: the French New Wave, Roger Corman's Poe cycle, the independent cinema of John Cassavetes, the experimentation of Jonas Mekas, Stan Brakhage, Shirley Clarke, Asian, Italian, Swedish, and Czechoslovakian masters, the breakthrough cinema of Jean-Luc Godard, Michelangelo Antonioni, and Francois Truffaut, and innovative works from Latin America. Out of these influences and the rigorous technical and aesthetic training under the tutelage of Haig Manoogian, Scorsese began to formulate a new kind of cinematic vocabulary manifested in camera movement and editorial structure.

Going to as many screenings as possible, Scorsese expanded his cinematic campus to New York City, a haven of repertory cinema in the sixties.

In 1962, Michael Powell's *Peeping Tom* was playing at the Charles Theater located on Avenue B and 12th Street. This infamous cinema landmark was the venue where Jonas Mekas hosted screenings of many experimental films, which he categorized as "Baudelairean Cinema: A world of flowers of evil, of illuminations, of torn and tortured flesh, a poetry which is at once beautiful and terrible, good and evil, delicate and dirty." The Charles Theater was the home of independent films that defied the conventions of Hollywood in content and form.

Scorsese's friends had told him about the scandalous film in which a filmmaker murdered women with his tripod, simultaneously filming the moment of death. Classmate Jim McBride was so altered by the screening of *Peeping Tom* at The Charles that the event inspired his own landmark film, *David Holzman's Diary*. Generally fearless about exposing himself to innovative films, Scorsese was irrationally reluctant to see *Peeping Tom*. Eventually Scorsese caught up with the film on safer turf, and its macabre celebration of the cinema as voyeurism had an irrevocable impact on Scorsese's work in the seventies, in particular, *Taxi Driver*.

Scorsese's second year class was greatly reduced by Manoogian's test of artistic wills. Students took a production course where they made three-minute, 16 mm films, working in small groups. There was a lot of motivation but not much equipment, mainly a 16 mm Arriflex and a Kodak Cine Special, which could be handheld. The students were taught the craft of lighting, lenses, and control of the frame rate to create slow, fast, or stop motion. Due to equipment unavailability, and financial limitations, the senior class made six films in six groups. The student body had to be whittled down to around thirty-six, and even then only six students would be given the opportunity to direct a short film.

Scorsese felt the gravitational pull toward editing from the beginning of his hands-on experience with film. He would spend hours in the NYU editing room, hunched over a Moviola. While working on a project he would lose all sense of time and routine. Catherine made sure Marty ate, often bringing homemade Italian dishes to feed her son, while he worked without regard to the world outside the frame.

In 1961, John Mavros, a young man of Greek heritage at NYU, who later worked as an assistant editor on *Raging Bull*, told Scorsese about the book *The Last Temptation of Christ* by Nikos Kazantzakis. Like many students and artists, the information entered his memory bank, to be recalled when a creative connection was made down the path.

The process of filmmaking at NYU was arduous. Scorsese learned the rules of traditional cinema: the purpose of a master shot, medium shot, closeup, the dolly, tracking, and pan shots. Student scripts had to be approved before production.

Manoogian stressed personal filmmaking; "Film what you know" was his mantra. He allowed only those with an original script to direct a five- or six-minute film. If you were waiting around for someone to hand you a script, Manoogian didn't consider you a director. By his definition, a director was an artist with something to say, not a hired hand. These circumstances created politicking and maneuvering and identified those who could survive a tough industry environment after graduation. There would be six groups, six films, and only six directors, and Martin Scorsese made the grade.

Manoogian's home, one with books, was a second home for Scorsese. He visited his mentor constantly to talk movies and share their devotion to the cinema. His parents loved him unconditionally; Haig Manoogian fed his artistic soul.

9

The Apprentice

In the fifties, sixties, and seventies, budding filmmakers didn't wait for film instruction; they picked up daddy's 8mm film camera used to document domestic life and set about making a movie. Around 1959 Scorsese made his entry into 8mm filmmaking—*Vesuvius VI*, a mini-Roman epic inspired by the popular television series *77 Sunset Strip*, a Warner Brothers production about an L.A. private-eye firm. The show's appeal came from the rat pack cool of the detectives and the parking lot attendant, Kookie, played by Edd Byrnes.

Vesuvius VI is set in Rome. A group of Marty's friends wear sheets to represent togas. The shooting locations range from a Lower East Side rooftop to the basement of a family friend's bakery. The camera was on loan from a pal. Images play out to the soundtrack music, "Does Your Chewing Gum Lose Its Flavor (On the Bedpost Over Night)?" The silly and catchy ditty, released in March 1959, was popular among adolescent boys.

This is the first example of Scorsese experimenting with a visual narrative, mimicking the Roman epics he so enjoyed as a child, in counterpoint to a pop song.

An image of note is the director credit. "Directed by Martin Scorsese" ignites in actual flames—an effect executed on Catherine Scorsese's coffee table, perhaps implying the fall of the Roman Empire or the fires of hell. The damaged coffee table caused some family strife during the production of the opus. Scorsese's childhood friend, Dominic Lo Faro, remembers various screenings of *Vesuvius VI* at which Scorsese experienced the plaguing problem of projecting a film against a tape-recorded soundtrack; the two machines rarely ran in tandem. Scorsese originally recorded lines read by the actors but, when he realized the tape couldn't stay in synch, he brought the troupe to each screening where they read the lines live as the director twisted the knob of a variable speed projector to keep the film running as directed.

Scorsese's first 16 mm film was an NYU project: a nine-minute black-and-white collaboration with Robert Siegel, a fellow student. The title is variously listed in Scorsese literature as: *Inesita, Inestia: The Art of Flamenco*, and *The Art of Flamenco: Inesita*. The class assignment was an exercise to explore the connection between music, film, and dance. Attribution is murky. The film was either codirected or directed by Scorsese or by Siegel. Scorsese seems to remember Siegel as the director. Many sources cite the photography as Scorsese's; one adds prop man to his participation. Theories abound as to the film's position in the Scorsese canon. Its significance may be as a precursor to the method Scorsese used to handle the relationship of music and image in *New York, New York* and *The Last Waltz*. The editing is not clearly attributed, but the assumption is that Scorsese cut the film, which features a female flamenco dancer in segments that deconstruct the music and dance in an experimental and highly cinematic fashion.

During a summer workshop taught by Manoogian at NYU, Scorsese made his first solo 16 mm short, *What's a Nice Girl Like You Doing in a Place Like This?* The title was the first in a series of movie line clichés applied to his early work. As a film student in an academic environment, Scorsese was flooded with influences. For his first film, at least three unrelated antecedents were in play—Scorsese's admiration for the daring cinematic language of the French New Wave, the fiction of Algernon Blackwood, and the short film, *The Critic*, created by Mel Brooks and Ernie Pintoff.

Scorsese began the short two weeks after seeing Federico Fellini's *8 1/2*. The story is about a blocked writer obsessed with a picture of a boat on a lake; eventually the scribe, named Algernon (after Blackwood) but referred to as Harry, disappears into the pictorial image.

The film, *What's a Nice Girl Like You Doing in a Place Like This?* is not a direct adaptation of a Blackwood story but his writing is a jumping off point. The film is a conglomeration of filmic references to the New Wave and New York underground cinema. There are comic notions on the meaning of art, allusions to the history of cinema, and evidence of Scorsese's burgeoning love affair with the moving camera. The short includes animation, montage, jump cuts, associative editing, and freeze frames—an exploration of film grammar in an attempt to discover a new movie language. Scorsese managed to experiment with the medium and also pay homage to its past.

The story of *It's Not Just You Murray!* (Scorsese's second major 16 mm short), is not so much constructed on plot but more a dead-on satiric portrait of a readily identifiable street thug from Little Italy. The bits and pieces Scorsese collected for this film found their place in secondary characters replicated and morphed in *Who's That Knocking at My Door*, *Mean Streets*, *GoodFellas*, *Raging Bull*, and *Casino*.

The character of Murray is a mob wannabee, an underling who is pretty close to the bottom of the Mafioso family tree. Murray is a common thug whose daily activities include numbers running, prostitution, and gambling. These wiseguys lived score to score and presented themselves as a traditional Italian-American character type—*The Big Shot*.

The Big Shot is all about pseudosuperiority. A fresh razor haircut, an imported cigar, flashy clothes, and a big American gas-guzzling car, were prize attributes. The prime trait of the Big Shot is *attitude*. Plenty of attitude. He wore his suit jacket or overcoat draped around his shoulders. His eyes were always focused upward, not to the heavens but *above* the peons.

Scorsese was not interested in a generic satire; *It's Not Just You, Murray!* tells the story of Murray (Ira Rubin) and his rise and fall through the ranks of small-time hoodlums, as he is manipulated by his mentor and idol, Joe (Sam De Fazio), who controls his fate.

Scorsese experiments with the revolutionary filmmaking techniques of the sixties. *Murray* is part cinema vérité, part self-referential, has moments of homage to traditional Hollywood movies, and ends with a tribute to Fellini's *8 1/2*.

Murray is designated as the on-screen director. He can dictate camera placement, what the microphone hears, what is shot, and what is not. Scorsese is playful with this trope and does not adhere strictly to its rules, so he can juxtapose Murray's self-proclaimed stature against the truth of his extreme limitations as a hood.

Scorsese establishes Murray's ability to direct the crew by having him gesture when the camera should pan, directly addressing the lens ala Jean-Luc Godard, and by actually calling cut when he is unhappy with the progress of a "take." Murray tries to alter the truth with whitewashed accounts of his life and goes as far as to physically prohibit the crew from continuing, but what we see is still the truth—Murray tries to cover up by bragging, showing off, and remaining in denial about his friend Joe.

Murray, the Big Shot, begins with a bragging riff about the cost of everything he wears. "See this tie—twenty dollars," increasing the dollar amounts as he graduates from his shoes to his two hundred dollar suit. A cut from his office to the street allows Murray to display his most valuable commodity—a five thousand dollar car. As he offers the audience a ride, Murray realizes he's forgotten to introduce himself.

Behind his desk and next to an American flag, Murray tells us he is rich, influential, and very well liked. This explains the psychology of the Big

Shot. He is extremely insecure. He knows he's not really powerful and charismatic. If he were he would not have to say it all the time.

Murray insists we understand that he would not be living *la dolce vita*, the sweet life, were it not for his friend Joe, who has taken Murray under his wing and offered him the prestige he has always craved.

Business for Murray is making bathtub gin in a jerry-rigged still. The audience can easily predict Murray's downward trajectory. When bootlegging brings the law, Joe lays low and Murray takes the rap. Murray ends up spending time in Ossining, New York—jail time.

Joe becomes the narrator over a montage of Murray taking abuse from the *bulls* and other gangsters. Switching narrators is a clear violation of classical Hollywood rules that Scorsese most brazenly breached in *GoodFellas*.

Joe tells Murray to take the punishment like a man and get revenge when the time is right. Murray is anything but stoic and the payoff is a shot of him confronting himself in the mirror and smashing the image with his hand. It's played for comedy but the themes of self-loathing and self-punishment do not go unnoticed.

Murray takes over as narrator. He is in the hospital. Joe is responsible for Murray's injuries since Murray always takes the fall. As the bedridden Murray is hugged by his Mama (Catherine Scorsese), Scorsese intercuts Joe and the nurse, a willowy blonde—who is Murray's wife-to-be, ogling each other.

The boys go legit by producing a stage musical, *Love Is a Gazelle*, so Scorsese can pay tribute to the thirties' Hollywood musicals like *42nd Street*, complete with a Busby Berkeley rotating multiple-image kaleidoscope shot of a dance number.

Murray sums up the business successes the partnership with Joe has yielded. We see a series of tableaus: Their chain of hotels—a sleazy motel and the street lined with prostitutes; their political achievements—a dead man behind a wheel, the result of a mob hit; their work in the funeral business—a drive-by shooting (Warner Brothers style), and a man falling off the steps of a building, riddled with bullets; and their sports venture—mobsters bribing an athlete. Foreign aid—a man in Arab garb (probably Murray) handing out rifles. Imported products—a full shot of the Lincoln Memorial statuette and a close shot of the chair engraved with "Made in Japan." A grainy faux newsreel depicts Murray at a federal hearing. The scene satirizes the mob hearings of the past with Murray unable to pronounce the word "incriminate" when he invokes the Fifth Amendment. Murray plays solitaire and brags about his empire as Joe and Murray's wife betray him. In a montage of still photos Murray carries on about the three of them as the lovers cavort alongside him. Murray grins at the camera still blind to the truth of his fabricated existence. The stills show Murray's children with their "Uncle Joe." Visually Scorsese reveals the real father by intercutting the faces of the children with the boastfully smiling Joe. Back at his desk the camera is now peering from a side angle. Murray summons Joe to the office while Mama tries to feed her son more spaghetti. Murray tries to confront Joe over this paternity issue and is unable to get privacy, shouting "cut the sound," but the film goes on as Murray breaks out of his big shot character and expresses anger at his partner who is backpeddling defensively. Eventually the sound does cut out. As Joe wins Murray over with sweet talk, Murray's voice-over explains they had only one fight and proceeds to deny and explain away the truth. The silent conversation shows Joe's power over Murray the weakling. The conversation without words continues—we don't need to hear the traditional two-character sequence—cutting back and forth from speaker to reactor tells the whole story without dialogue. What we hear on the soundtrack is Murray's indomitable ability to weave the Big Shot illusion as long as he breathes. Scorsese freeze frames on a closeup of Murray where the truth is etched on his face—no phony smile, no big shot persona—he looks despondent as if he finally accepts who he really is.

The film could have ended here, but Scorsese was puzzled about how to complete it. What follows is a referential homage to the ending of Fellini's *8 1/2*. As in the legendary autobiographical film, we see the characters of Murray's life, joined by men and women in festival costumes, dance in a circle as if they were a circus troupe. Murray, like Fellini's Guido, the film director, played by Marcello Mastroianni, has finally found a way to control his life. He takes on the role of film director as circus master. Murray wears a hat identical to Guido's and uses a bullhorn to direct the ensemble, including his mother (still dressed in funereal black), as they celebrate Murray by obeying his every command.

What may be dismissed as a film student's folly, an adolescent reference to a favorite film, is really a return to the concept of Murray as the director of the short. His many attempts during the film have failed because he was *just* Murray, a man whose life was being filmed. In the conclusion he has taken control over Scorsese's movie and by so doing has resolved his conflicts. He accepts that we are the directors of our own lives; the others are players in our story.

Scorsese's primary objective was to start earning money by working in the industry and *It's Not Just You, Murray!* at first seemed to be the ticket. The film won the Hollywood Screen Producer's Guild award as the best student film of 1964. Scorsese was to receive a six-month internship at

Paramount Studios in Hollywood with a salary of $125 a week. As he was just about to leave for the West Coast, he received a classic studio "Dear John" letter—there had been a change in Paramount's management. As is often the case the new regime was making sweeping changes—the internship was cancelled. Scorsese was frustrated, angry, and depressed.

On screen a young man enters a white, gleaming, bathroom. He proceeds to engage in the everyday, mundane task of shaving his face. He lathers the skin with ivory, puffy shaving cream—then begins to pull a safety razor across his skin removing soapy peaks and stubble. Everything appears to be normal—a daily, bland reality. During the process one of the razor strokes pierces the skin and he begins to bleed. Nonplussed, the young man continues his morning ritual but now each lash of the blade tears into his tender flesh. Soon, the young man's nondescript features are totally lacerated. A daring ear-to-ear swipe of the cutting edge literally slashes his throat. He has cut his own throat.

Martin Scorsese's *The Big Shave* is an unsettling and disturbing short film that from its conception was rich in personal obsessions and the filmmaker's desperation.

The Big Shave has been critically interpreted in many ways, most emanating from context rather than content. The short was made during the height of the Vietnam War. In context *The Big Shave* becomes a comment, allegory, or black comedy about Vietnam. It was shown during the War period, as was Peckinpah's *The Wild Bunch*, a film that became a metaphor for the War. Mainly to justify its existence and shift the emphasis from the personal to the political, Scorsese made artistic statements claiming the film was a Vietnam allegory. At one point he considered inserting actual Vietnam battle footage, which would be undeniable proof of the director's intent, but the idea was dropped and the film merely ends with the words, "Viet '67," and a reference linking the whiteness and purity defiled in the film to Herman Melville. This coda allowed analysts to link the film to Vietnam.

In Mary Pat Kelly's *Martin Scorsese: The First Decade* written with the director's participation, Scorsese put the critiques concerning *The Big Shave* into perspective:

> ...Actually it drew out of my feelings about Vietnam. Consciously it was an angry outcry against the war. But in reality something else was going on inside of me, I think, which really had nothing to do with the war. It was just a very bad period, a very bad period.

At the time Scorsese was sincerely angry about America's Southeast Asian involvement, but it may have been an easy and simple diversion for the deeper meanings of the six-minute film. Scorsese, always an open and honest filmmaker, has acknowledged that the motivation for the shocking demonstration of explicit violence in *The Big Shave* were his explosive inner feelings when he was making the film. Screen violence had always represented a catharsis for him. As much as he honored musicals and broad comedies, the morality and street justice of the Western and the gangster film were most reflective of the life he lived in Little Italy. Like many men of his generation, Scorsese found it difficult to express himself in words, but when his feelings were translated into images he was able to communicate with brutal honesty and with the full intention of presenting the truth as he knew it, pretty or not. He was raised in a coded culture that fenced out all others. He was an outsider in a wasp-oriented world, a member of a misunderstood culture in which one was perceived as a gangster, a Romeo, or a laborer. He was tortured by conflicts presented by his two masters—the church and the cinema. As a boy he could always go to the movies, or draw a movie, or dream a movie. From the outset of his NYU shorts, Martin Scorsese was a filmmaker; if he wasn't making a film, the demons took control. He was self-conscious about his looks, and questioned his masculine identity. He wanted to be a Hollywood filmmaker like John Ford, Howard Hawks, or Vincente Minnelli; he yearned to be an Italian filmmaker like Rossellini, De Sica, Fellini, Passolini, Visconti, and Bertolucci, a man of his own generation. He wanted to reinvent the cinema like the French New Wave and craved the independent spirit of John Cassavetes and Elia Kazan, as well as the artistic freedom of experimentalists Kenneth Anger, Jonas Mekas, and Stan Brakhage. He was an American who lived by an ancient Sicilian code and who adored the sophistication of the British Cinema.

The Big Shave is a perplexing work. Without explanation or the cryptic clue offered by the "Viet '67" in the closing titles, which baffled the audience upon its completion and now, far removed from the personal and political context that holds its secrets, it can be read for what it represents in the scheme of the Scorsese oeuvre.

The true starting point for a filmmaker is the revelation of his or her expressive and thematic nature, full-blown and without qualifications. *The Big Shave* is the first film in which Scorsese allowed his emotional life to become the content of a work. The short film heralded the arrival of the Scorsese who would mature with *Mean Streets, Raging Bull,* and *GoodFellas.*

An autobiographical filmmaker transforms elements from his or her own life into a film narrative. The emphasis for a personal filmmaker is on the expression of emotions and feelings from the inner life as well as the outer.

Depressed, angry, and deeply frustrated, Scorsese found great difficulty with the simple act of shaving in the morning. Violent emotions and the feeling of self-loathing are powerful. Everyday chores become strained when one is in the grip of negative feelings. The mind is constantly balancing the rational with the irrational. Faced with a usually effortless chore, Scorsese began to have lurid fantasies and fears. The razor became a focal point for the physical expression of those emotions. As an artist Scorsese became obsessed with the idea of filming these emotions. By desecrating his flesh through an on-screen substitute, he cathartically experienced those violent emotions and hoped to purge himself at the same time as he cried out to the world. Scorsese was revealing his obsessions with Old Testament values: revenge, redemption, and the ancient rite of purification by blood. These stimuli would fuel one of the most expressive careers of the New Hollywood generation.

The color red, which so dominates *The Big Shave*, held great significance for Scorsese. It was not only a key element in *The Red Shoes*; Michael Powell used the vibrant and highly symbolic color as a psychological, mythic, and metaphoric aesthetic element in film after film. There is even a fade to red at the end of *The Big Shave*, as if the blood of the self-massacre soaks into the grain of the celluloid and fills the entire frame.

In Catholicism red has two principal emblematic relationships. It is associated with the fire and pain of mortal sin and an eternity in Hell, ruled by Satan, the prince of darkness and all evil. Red is also identified with blood, the Passion of Christ, the Crucifixion, and the suffering Jesus endured on earth for the salvation of mankind.

It is also believed that God singles out individuals with noble souls to unite them with the suffering of his son Jesus, so they can enjoin in forgiveness for the sins of others. The stigmata are wounds that bleed openly, corresponding to the feet, hands, side, and brow of the crucified Christ.

A substitute for a baptism of holy water is blood. A baptism of blood is an act of suffering martyrdom for Christian faith or virtue. This supreme act of love must be accompanied by a martyr who has received attrition for his or her sins.

The scriptures are the source of many connections to blood, sin, and redemption, themes Scorsese has obsessed about for his entire career. Before creating images Scorsese read about the tenets of Catholicism and the blood of Jesus:

Matthew 26:   28 (of the New Testament) For this is my blood, which is shed for many for the remission of sins.

1 John 1:   7 But if we walk in the light, as he is in the light, we have fellowship one with another, and the blood of Jesus Christ his Son cleaneth us from all sin.

Eph. 1:   7 In whom we have redemption through his blood, the forgiveness of sins, according to the riches of his grace.

Col. 1:   14 ... We have redemption through his blood, even the forgiveness of sins.

In Sir James Frazer's influential and seminal work *The Golden Bough*, a spiritual and cultural study of primitive cultures, the symbolism and religious presence of blood in ritual practice demonstrates the power, the image, and the purpose of human and animal blood throughout the ages and in diverse cultures. Frazer examines the presence of blood in rainmaking ceremonies and in purification rituals, when it is drunk to acquire the qualities of men, to communicate with a deity, as a medium of inspiration, or is sprinkled onto seed and fields for growth and smeared on the woodwork of a house to guarantee protection from harm.

The six-minute *The Big Shave* is carefully structured in three sections or movements as in a classical piece of music. The three can be interpreted as a reference to the holy trinity of the Father, the Son, and the Holy Ghost. Although Scorsese rebels against traditional structure in his work, his admiration and scholarly understanding of the three-act paradigm, the standard narrative construct during the studio system, influenced the form for *The Big Shave*.

The short is not a traditional narrative, but it is a story, albeit short on plot. In the first part the environment is established as a character. The first shot is taken from the eye level of a bathroom toilet, the white porcelain is clean and shiny, and the tile floor dominates the space of the frame as a way to communicate the playing area and as an ironic note on the sanctity of a room devoted to sanitary collection of human waste. This act is comprised of fourteen shots, which detail the bathroom, a sink, a faucet, and gleaming metal and ceramic fixtures. The only colors in this landscape of white and chrome are the blue of a toothbrush and a red-handled brush—white, blue, red, white, white, white—a deconstructed arrangement of red, white, and blue at a time when the American flag was a potent symbol to define personal positions on the War. In Scorsese's montage it is more a subtle clue, part of a larger scheme rather than a blatant use of the flag's colors in the spirit of Jean-Luc Godard's conscious application of the French colors throughout the devoutly political film *Weekend.*

The montage is a progression that creates the environment. For Scorsese, the student of film, montage could be an Eisensteinian collision of images where each cut added specific resonance to the shot before and the one to follow. In Russian montage one and one never added up to two—images that appeared to stand alone became part of a didactic unity in rapid succession. Hollywood rejected the political power of Russian montage and applied the system as a means of presenting the rapid passage of time during an action—the boxer trains as the calendar pages fall, and images tell the story of preparation for a big fight, and weeks pass by in seconds.

The bathroom section of *The Big Shave* demonstrates that Scorsese understands both schools of montage in sequential storytelling, where each image advances the narrative.

Many commentators have examined the use of space as a statement of confinement. The room is tight and close. This is apparent in the opening moments of the film. In reality, after the equipment and crew were set up in this practical bathroom, there was no real opportunity for Scorsese to move the camera in his signature style. A blessing in disguise, the location informed the correct shooting style, static over fluid. Everything in film is a choice; a set or a larger bathroom would have accommodated other approaches, but, of necessity, on a no-budget film the camera positions were dictated, making a small room in reality even smaller on screen. Because of the space limitations Scorsese made the decision to shoot the bathroom in a series of shots you would see in a commercial, images that could be rearranged during the editing process.

Water, like blood, is a life-supporting fluid. Droplets on the bathroom fixtures, establish that water is available here and foreshadow its purpose in the ritual to be performed.

Of course, there is a mirror on a medicine cabinet, a bathroom standard. Mirrors in films can represent duality and they do in many other Scorsese films. Here the mirror is a way to see the man shave, rather than serving as a reflexive surface for introspection and self-examination, as well as containing symbolic properties for many viewers.

As the score, Scorsese selected the 1937 Bunny Berigan recording of "I Can't Get Started" released on the Victor label, a classic recording inducted in the Grammy Hall of Fame in 1975. Berigan, a trumpet player, is considered by jazz historians to be a crucial link between jazz architect Louis Armstrong and modern masters such as Dizzy Gillespie, Miles Davis, and Wynton Marsalis.

The track begins with suspended chords as Berigan soars high above with an introduction that features flurries of notes covering a wide range of high to low in a masterful combination of short bursts, sustained tones, trills, circular riffs, and a confident lead-in to the melody that ends with a high note that pulsates with a perfectly controlled vibrato. Berigan then lays down the melody with a clean and controlled tone that improvises New Orleans style reaching out to a modern style he was discovering. The orchestra plays a mellow and traditional arrangement of the melody followed by Berigan's vocal, then a solo taking the tune home in which one can hear not only the future of the trumpet but also the foreshadowing of towering rock guitar solos by Eric Clapton, Jeff Beck, and Jimmy Page.

The Ira Gershwin lyrics lament a man who has done it all, traveled the world, negotiated political unrest, and surveyed unexplored land, but is down in the dumps because he's met a woman he can't have and woefully sings that without her, he "can't get started." She is unattainable, a person who cannot be wooed, bought, or courted.

The editing follows the rhythm of the music and is also determined by the number of shots available. Some seem to be held to structure the length of a movement. On occasion Scorsese presents a flurry of images that visualize Bunny Berigan's trumpet trills as tension is built about what is going to happen in this clean, white, setting.

The rhythm of the editing is constant, but not demanding or leading, and with one exception, it moves from shot to shot in order and duration in an instinctual pattern rather than with didactic purpose. The choice of music, not the meaning of the unfolding images, sets the pace. Like a musician, Scorsese responds to the ebb and flow of the composition.

It is crucial to put *The Big Shave* in perspective. When Scorsese made the short he was in a spiritual crisis. Catholic guilt over masturbation and other thoughts eventually delivered him to therapy when the counsel of a priest failed to bring his mind to peace. The reality of his marital and professional inabilities to succeed drove him into a psychological depression, which could only be reconciled through his artistic persona. Martin Scorsese had to make *The Big Shave*. He had no choice. As a filmmaker with the ability to directly express his feelings in stark visual terms, there was little fear he would do physical harm to himself or others, but with a camera and splicer as weapons he was a dangerous man.

In *Mean Streets*, *GoodFellas*, and *Casino*, Scorsese would develop a more complex yet intuitive sense to wed nondiegetic, previously recorded, pop, rock, classical, Neapolitan, jazz, and movie music into an intricate context with narrative sequences. Scorsese's command of the atmospheric, psychological, lyrical, associative, and contrasting impact of sound and image opened up an additional channel of experience and meaning in the synapses of the viewer's receptive capabilities.

Who is the "You" Scorsese can't get started with? The song is a product of his parents' era. Although baby boomers created, celebrated, and consumed their own musical culture in the sixties and seventies, they were raised by a generation that came of age during the twenties, thirties, and forties. They absorbed the music of Glenn Miller, Tommy Dorsey, Hoagy Carmichael, Duke Ellington, and Count Basie and singers Judy Garland, Rosemary Clooney, Frank Sinatra, Perry Como, and Bing Crosby and the American Popular Song Book. This music had a nostalgic reminiscence for the Boomers who heard it during their childhood.

"I Can't Get Started" in its many incarnations was extremely popular and the Berigan recording maintains a classic stature. So the phrase "I Can't Get Started" links the Scorsese representative with The Greatest Generation of World War II. "You" could be his first wife Laraine—an outcry for unconditional support in the face of Scorsese's personal anguish.

Scorsese was still very dependent on his parents and continued to live in the family apartment, so Charles and Catherine Scorsese could be "You."

Scorsese was convinced he couldn't start his career no matter what he tried, so this "You" could be Lady Luck or the former altar boy and potential priest praying to his Lord and Savior, Jesus Christ, for salvation.

Scorsese's difficulty in shaving his own face at this time reveals a fragile mental state. "Getting started" could refer to the fear of taking his own life, as the character does once he has severed major arteries by slitting his throat from ear to ear. In this scenario, "You" can be either the courage or lack of will to continue. Still embracing the hubris of a student filmmaker, Scorsese may have been desperate for attention using the cinematic power to shock for shock's sake.

The Big Shave is pure, unadulterated, Scorsese without the explosive marriage of form and content he would create in later works. He is letting the world know he has the "bad ideas" of Travis Bickle and is capable of releasing a torrent of violent physicality, the result of an emotional, internal eruption. Scorsese proves in *The Big Shave* that he's jammed with personal expression and has the courage to splatter it all over the screen. He is without guile, an honest filmmaker willing to expose his darkest self in a search for redemption.

Scorsese's mentor, John Cassavetes, who encouraged personal expression, screened *The Big Shave*. When the film was shown to Scorsese's students at NYU they were sickened and horrified, deeply worried that their teacher was headed for self-destruction. Cassavetes, who understood and believed that film could be personally cathartic rather than manufactured Hollywoodified artifice, had a different reaction—he laughed out loud for the entire running time of the six-minute short.

10

The Big Kahuna: *Who's That Knocking at My Door*

Martin Scorsese's first feature film, the independently financed and produced *Who's That Knocking at My Door*, is a black-and-white personal film whose main character is an Italian-American from New York's Lower East Side.

The film's title originates from the song, "Who's That Knocking," written by Clyde "Sonny" Johnson and Freddy Jones and recorded by The Genies in 1959. Scorsese's inspiration was the song's questioning first line, "Who's that knocking at my door?" and not the actual title.

This is a Scorsese film title that repeatedly shows up wrong. Punctuation police have taken it upon themselves to retitle the film *Who's That Knocking at My Door?* even though a question mark does not appear in the main title credit.

"Who's That Knocking" is a nondiegetic soundtrack element at the end of the picture played during a montage of religious imagery as the main character, J.R., prays for the sins he has committed. From the outset Scorsese has applied pop music as period, mood, and textual comment. The results he achieves are an early indication of the landmark accomplishments he would make with the application of music in his films. From the first frame of *Who's That Knocking at My Door* we hear an inner-city beat that sounds more like a Spaldeen handball repeatedly being slapped hard against a concrete wall rather than a drum. An Italian woman (portrayed by Marty's mom Catherine), hair up in a bun, and dressed in black, goes through the ritual of making a traditional Italian meat pie for a group of children.

The process of making the meat pie is covered in step-by-step detail, intercut with religious figurines and candles, symbols of faith associated with the Catholic Church that adorn the kitchen. When the pie is placed inside a hot oven, Scorsese dissolves to a single burning candle. The shot has three purposes: it represents the heat of the stove, it is a symbol of a religious blessing given to the food, and it dissolves to the woman calling the children to the table as she takes the pie out of the oven—so the image of the candle also serves as a method of time compression.

The children are served. The cramped room suggests a lower-middle-class existence. Images of the religious statues continue to be intercut and appear to play a central role in the spiritual well-being of the family that lives there.

The time frame of the scene is never identified. The woman's behavior and movements are more ritualistic than realistic. The children do not appear to be Italian-American or necessarily related to this prototypical Italian mother.

The musical accompaniment is now a rhythmic snare drum played on brushes with echoed accents. A disk jockey's hyper voice interrupts the Italian home ritual and acts as a sound bridge to a street scene of young Italian-American men hanging out. Harvey Keitel is introduced as J.R., and he watches as his tribe deals with a kid from outside their turf.

Harvey Keitel was a serious acting student and a court stenographer by day, when he answered a casting call Scorsese ran in the trades. The selection of Keitel launched a lifelong friendship and creative collaboration between director and actor.

Keitel, a former Marine, had done summer stock as an unpaid apprentice and had appeared at the legendary Café La MaMa and other Off-Off Broadway venues.

The common bond between Keitel and Scorsese was not superficial. One from Manhattan and an Italian-American, the other of Jewish heritage and from Brooklyn, Scorsese and Keitel understood each other's intensity and need to express the truth as they saw it. They shared emotional intimacies; both were in desperate struggles and needed to be propelled to another place beyond the bonds of their birth and identities.

As the movie's action continues, the leader of the home tribe immediately takes out a stick and knocks the trespasser down as the others kick and stomp the helpless boy. In urban Italian-American street fighting the only objective is to get your opponent on the ground and defenseless as quickly as possible. It is the feet and not the hands that commit the beating. This sequence is intercut with the main titles. Scorsese builds editorial vitality by intercutting the beating of the off-his-turf gang leader with the stomping of his equally helpless lieutenant, overpowered by the presiding tribe.

J.R., in a full-length black coat and his gang's leader, Joey (Lennard Kuras), dressed in an off-white, full-length trench coat, walk down Elizabeth Street (where the Scorsese family actually resided at the time of the filming) like Sicilian kings. The restless camera now zooms in as they approach The 8th Ward Pleasure Club, part of a system of New York social clubs used as hangouts and private places to plan dreams of power, sex, and crime, while consuming booze and engaging in plenty of illegal gambling.

Harvey Keitel is perfect as J.R. He has the look, the attitude, the street smarts, and the diction of an Italian-American. Keitel understood the code of the tribe—its insular, walled-in morality, and the limited, old-fashioned Sicilian way of seeing the world. Lennard Kuras, an inexperienced performer is not quite up to the role of gang leader, unable to project the necessary charisma and sense of danger typical of this social type. Michael Scala who plays Sally GaGa has the native looks and 'tude with limited, yet convincing, acting ability. Joey explodes and accuses GaGa of stealing. GaGa's lack of command and leadership traps him in the rank of what the Italians call *stùpido*. Joey's physical outburst is a dark trait often seen in Italian-American males. The mood of an event can change suddenly with a burst of anger, and then dissipate just as quickly. This eruptive moment looses some of its power because the obvious fake movie slaps don't hit their mark and the lack of quality sound effects.

Scorsese was still a member of the Little Italy tribal order. At NYU he was steadily able to pursue filmmaking, but on the street he was viewed as one of the tribe. After being exposed to the boiling social, political, and artistic changes whipped up by the zeitgeist of the 1960s, Scorsese was twisted into deep conflict about the morality he conformed to in Little Italy. Scorsese tried to expand his intellectual horizons at NYU by reading Theodore Dreiser and Henry James, but at night he reverted to the insulated, ritualized life that was the only option in Little Italy. It was exactly this conflict between the old and new worlds that motivated Scorsese's first feature film.

A time cut jumps to the social club's bar tended by J.R., as Joey holds court. Another time cut influenced by Scorsese's obsession with the French New Wave, and the bar is now closed—stools are in the classic upturned position as depicted in countless Hollywood Westerns and Warner Bros., gangster films. Joey flings his open hand in disgust as he walks away from J.R. This gesture has been refined over the course of Italian-American cultural history. The right arm (left for lefties) boldly swings out and away allowing the hand to wave dismissively. The head turns in the opposite direction; and facial features are molded in disdain. The gesture can also be combined with a sound produced by pushing air between the lips, "Psssss!" It means many things depending on the situation and is always understood without uttering a word. Translated into language the gesture says, "Get outta here!" "Are you kiddin' ?" "C'mon!" and "You're nuts!"

A profile shot of J.R. represents another signature Italian-American gesture. He looks straight ahead, his eyeline registers that J.R. is looking at Joey, now behind the bar, but J.R.'s eyes are off and distant. His hand is positioned horizontally across his face, the slightly arched index finger crossing the ever-so-slightly puffed up lips at an angle. This is the thinking man, always studying—sometimes about the real time moment, sometimes about events past or future. Every word and deed must be carefully measured by strict standards and the code.

As other young people of their generation grew out their hair, wore jeans, tie-dyed tee-shirts, and moccasins, Scorsese and his paisans held to the tradition of a bygone era. The formal dress code maintained by the young men of *Who's That Knocking at My Door* seemed out of place and without purpose to the outside world, but it was an integral aspect of their existence.

Young Italian-American men standing on a street corner, sitting on a stoop, or milling around in front of a social club decked out in suits and sport coats, crisp white dress shirts with long pointy collars, cufflinks, and shiny black shoes projecting an aura of respect, is an iconic image from the forties through the seventies. They dutifully adhered to a strict schedule for their trims from a neighborhood barber—not even aware of the new unisex salons like Paul Mitchell's in the Village where those who wanted to look like rock stars paid ten times more to be coiffed in Aquarian styles. The tribes who lorded in Manhattan were numero uno. They rarely ventured out of their Lower East Side neighborhood.

Scorsese cuts to what J.R. is thinking about—a girl. Without explanation Scorsese and his editor Thelma Schoonmaker cut back to a front angle on J.R. Now he is deep in thought and looks a little unraveled. A flashback positions The Girl (Zina Bethune) and J.R. on a bench in the waiting room of the Staten Island Ferry.

J.R. summons his courage waiting for the right moment to approach The Girl. The Girl sees him looking at her as she reads a magazine. This uncomfortable dance continues until The Girl breaks the ice by offering the magazine to J.R. He declines, but has been handed the cue he was struggling for. The dark secret about many young Italian-American men is that they are virgins who are inept and uncomfortable around women. They want a girlfriend who can later be their wife and mother to their children. They desire a good girl but are aroused by the bad ones. Their self-confidence is strictly on call for the streets and limited to male bonding. Scorsese and his tribe in Little Italy had little clue about how to approach women other than in an immature manner. They were looking to get laid. This occupied their thoughts and created a false bravado that they were big ladies men, when, in fact, they were intimidated by the opposite sex. Sex for them was lust without commitment or involvement. Women were either good girls who you married or broads you slept with. And then there was Mom, a revered and feared figure in Italian-American culture.

The sexual freedom of the sixties and the subsequent Women's Movement did little to free or enlighten these young men whose destinies had been forged in Sicily generations before they were born.

The Girl belongs to the outside world. She is blond, pretty, intelligent, sophisticated, vivacious, and a WASP. As J.R. remarks that the magazine is not American, he gazes at a picture of Hollywood icon, John Wayne. There is a close cut-in on the Wayne photo. The Western hero wears a black hat and the traditional cowboy scarf. His eyes are hard and staring off.

As a film historian and totally dedicated movie fan, Scorsese constantly references old Hollywood. John Wayne is an idol, a real man, a real American. Respecting John Wayne makes these Italian-Americans equally American.

In the fifties and sixties most Italian-Americans were Democrats. They were "for the people." They were religious, hard-working, middle class, loyal Americans. While their homeland had been on the wrong side during World War II, Italian-Americans bravely served their country in large numbers. Many Hollywood World War II films have a stock heroic Italian-American soldier. The association with World War II and defense of country instilled Italian-Americans of this era with a strong sense of patriotism.

J.R. can't get away from John Wayne and Scorsese can't get away from the film references he cultivated as a film student and cinephile. J.R. tells The Girl the photograph of John Wayne is from the John Ford classic *The Searchers*, a Scorsese favorite and a film with obsessive themes that influenced *Taxi Driver*. J.R. carries on Scorsese's movie-mad tradition by letting The Girl know every film fact he can pull out. J.R., Scorsese's surrogate in *Who's That Knocking at My Door* is also portraying the director's enthusiasm and nonstop mania for talking about movies. J.R. refers to the movie as a "picture," Scorsese's term of choice when labeling his films, as in—A Martin Scorsese Picture.

With his rapid-fire speech pattern, Keitel begins to sound like Scorsese just as an on-screen Mia Farrow picked up Woody Allen's pace and banter. Scorsese's relentless back-and-forth lateral dolly shot is in its infancy here, moving slowly, not quite contributing to the emotional texture of a scene as it would in *Mean Streets*.

The Girl realizes she has seen *The Searchers* but confesses she doesn't like to admit she has seen Westerns. She is taking the ferry for the enjoyment of the ride; J.R. explains he has to pick up a package from his grandmother; perhaps the truth or a cover for gang business.

The relationship between J.R. and The Girl is reflective of Scorsese's encounters with the opposite sex. He had little actual experience with women. His self-image as a sickly boy, a natural shyness, and his slight physical stature were handicaps that did not encourage a healthy connection with girls. He was burdened by the Madonna-Whore syndrome, traceable to religious ideology dating back to the fifteenth century that dominated the mentality of Italian and Greek men who based their image of women on their relationships with their mothers.

Back in the social club J.R. is still deep in thought about The Girl. Returning to the couple, Scorsese shoots the bench as a design element and a metaphor. The wooden structure with the curved top resembles a church pew. As J.R. rises to elaborate on a funny story about a man playing golf during a snowstorm, Scorsese presents a top shot, an overhead angle he would make his signature in *Taxi Driver*. The top shot is also called God's POV by film production insiders. The Girl's smiling face is superimposed over the shot and as a transition to reintroduce the seated two-shot. The camera pulls back, revealing a garbage receptacle with the words For Trash Only in bold black letters, a textural comment on J.R., or a prophecy of how his feelings for The Girl will turn away from her.

J.R. suddenly is hit by a shoe that an angry Joey has thrown because he's lost J.R.'s attention for the last ten minutes. The flashback of J.R. and The Girl is over and J.R. is crudely reminded of where and who he is.

Doo Wop plays in the background—"The Closer You Are" by the Channels. Scorsese is using music to set the mood and create an emotional counterbalance to the story. *Mean Streets*, *GoodFellas*, and *Casino*, would feature a bold presentation of this concept. The music is not just background but an integral aspect of Scorsese's narrative process. A song may define a time or place, the lyrics may comment on the action.

Joey paces behind the bar as he berates his men for owing money to people in the neighborhood. He is wearing a shirt with a Billy Eckstein collar. The extra long points worn by the famed singer and bandleader are Scorsese's favorites. *GoodFellas* features a bold application of the style—most of the Cicero crew wear them. The style was regional Manhattan, not exclusively worn by Italian-Americans in the other boroughs. The style of a tribe identified them and gave them a special cache.

J.R. suggests going to Greenwich Village for a drink. Joey acts insulted since the social club is well stocked; but the underlying reason gets blurted out like a spurt of truth serum. Joey doesn't want to sit with a bunch of *fairies*. He would rather go uptown to see a new *broad*, alluding to a strip-tease establishment. For the Lower East Side guys uptown is anywhere outside of their neighborhood in that direction, so Joey could be talking about Times Square. Joey calls J.R. a jerk-off, a derogatory term that evolves over the course of Scorsese's film career into *jag-off*. We hear the sound of the Staten Island Ferry pulling away at the scene's conclusion. The next shot reveals the sound source and reenters the flashback. Scorsese is searching for new narrative and structural strategies. Rather than continue with the boy/girl story, the story immediately shifts back to the club where the uptown/Village conversation slogs on. Joey ends the argument by announcing he's locking up, a ritual repeated in *Mean Streets*.

Many Italian-Americans employ the argument as a standardized form of communication—as an "I'm right, you're wrong," scenario expressed with fiery passion regardless of subject. The subtext of the argument can reveal deep-seated feelings that eventually culminate with a revelation such as, "I never liked you!" "What have you ever done for me?" or "After all I've done for you!" Or the immortal classics, "You didn't come to my Mother's funeral!" "I never even received a card from you!" Or "I'll never forget that you didn't come to my son's wedding!"

Whether petty or significant, the Italian-American argument is expressed as if life itself was at stake and personal attacks are part and parcel of the exchanges: "You don't know what you are talking about!" or "I can't talk to you about nothing!"

As Joey walks out of the frame and J.R. rises, the image freezes—another French New Wave device used effectively by Francois Truffaut in *The Four Hundred Blows* and *Jules and Jim*. For Scorsese it is a way of getting out of the long scene and to create the metaphor that time stands still for these young men, stuck in the same routine night after night.

There are nude pinups on the walls of The 8th Ward Pleasure Club. They are there for the pleasure of the men and are an indication of the low esteem in which they hold women. It is easier for them to ogle the photographs than to deal with the opposite sex in the flesh. The pictures also embolden their Big-Shot image. In their adolescent fantasies they are super cool and can have any woman they want.

In 1967 Scorsese met filmmaker Michael Wadleigh during a NYU summer workshop run by Haig Manoogian. Students were divided into six groups each having one director. The way to achieve this lofty position was to come in with an original script. Aspiring candidates who announced they wanted to direct but needed a script were told bluntly, "Go home and write it." The project had to be an example of personal expression. Thelma Schoonmaker was a participant in the workshop. She was a political science major at Columbia University. Wadleigh made documentaries in the cinéma vérité style of Jean Rouch and Chris Marker and the Maysles Brothers, who were American proponents of Direct Cinema. Scorsese had worked for the Maysles as a light holder. Scorsese was making a meager living on location with Wadleigh shooting campaign promos for Hubert Humphrey.

Scorsese's attempt at a first feature film was an NYU graduate project. There was no formal department; it was literally Scorsese, Wadleigh, and a handful of NYU students under Manoogian's supervision. Charles Scorsese took out a $6,000 loan for his son's film, but the students were unable to complete the project, which Scorsese has stated was the first student film on the East Coast to be photographed in black-and-white 35mm—the accepted professional Hollywood standard.

Although innovative work was being produced in 16mm that format was relegated to amateur status, since the more affluent purchased 16mm camera to document their home lives. Professional moviemaking at all the major studios on the West Coast was committed to the high technical quality of 35mm film stock.

In 1965 Scorsese was able to get the picture together as a very short sixty-five minute feature entitled *Bring on the Dancing Girls*. A large screening was held for the debut with disastrous results—no one could understand the story or make head or tail of Scorsese's approach.

That year was significant for Scorsese. After graduation he married fellow student Laraine Marie Brennan, a worldly Irish/Jewish girl. The nuptials were a surprise especially for Charles and Catherine. Marty had been in a four-year relationship with a neighborhood Sicilian girl named Phyllis of whom his parents were fond. According to Joey Morale, Scorsese's boyhood pal, a local bully named Chick was so outraged that Scorsese disrespected Phyllis and married out of his tribe that he took out a vendetta, which forced Scorsese to lie low until Joey made Chick an offer he couldn't refuse—to "break off his balls and feed 'em to him for breakfast" if he didn't dissolve the vendetta.

Scorsese's marriage produced a baby girl, Catherine, named after his mother, on December 7, 1965. The next year was difficult. Scorsese stopped attending Catholic mass and stopped going to confession. His marriage to Laraine Marie Brennan was quickly disintegrating and Scorsese was literally on the street looking for any opportunity to earn money as a filmmaker. Scorsese and Mardik Martin, a young Iranian who Scorsese met at film school, began to write, often shivering in Mardik's car during a snow-filled, brutally cold, New York winter. Both were married men unable to work in their cramped apartments because their wives were disillusioned and angry with their husbands.

Out of desperation Mardik Martin developed an idea for a skin flick, *This Film Could Save Your Marriage*. The title was a pseudoeducational ruse that sexploitation producers used to give their films respectability, although the sole purpose was to present naked ladies to lonely guys and the raincoat crowd. The concept was to deliver the wrong marital advice to the audience—a narrative strategy most likely to annoy those who wanted unadulterated tits and ass. The scheme never left the freezing interior of Mardik Martin's car.

When Thelma Schoonmaker had completed a year of graduate work in primitive culture at Columbia University, she responded to a want ad in the *New York Times*, requesting a candidate to be trained as a film editor.

The opportunity turned out to be less than rewarding artistically. The market for foreign films to be programmed on late, late, night television was blossoming because local stations and the networks needed movie fodder to fill out their schedules. The good news was the programmed films included the work of the finest European directors: Federico Fellini, Jean-Luc Godard, Michelangelo Antonioni, and Francois Truffaut. The bad news was the editor's dictate was to cut these dubbed masterpieces so they could fit a 2:00 A.M. to 4:00 A.M. time slot that included an abundance of commercial interruptions. The job was to extract the exact amount of overrun from the film with no consideration for narrative, content, or character development. This editor was a hack who used the film splicer exclusively to cut out footage, not to *edit*.

Schoonmaker did learn the necessary skills including negative cutting. The experience led her to change course and pursue a film editing career. An article about an NYU summer course provided the ingredient of fate that often brings great collaborators together.

Scorsese and Schoonmaker were not part of the same filmmaking team that summer, but Manoogian brought them together asking her to assist Scorsese with negative cutting. When Schoonmaker visited Scorsese he had gone without sleep for days. He was so exhausted that he was sleeping with his eyes open while sitting in a chair. Schoonmaker put on her white gloves and searched for the edited shots in the rolls of negative. She would confer with him if a decision needed to be made about whether to lose film frames from the head or tail of a shot; Scorsese would answer and Schoonmaker would diligently execute the celluloid incisions.

Scorsese has established that the story of J.R. and The Girl is being told in flashback, but he has also structured the narrative as parallel storytelling, a cinematic concept that goes back to D.W.Griffith. The story of J.R. and The Girl is intercut with the story of J.R. and his tribe. Both continue to move forward as they alternate in the timeline.

Locks are locked at The 8th Ward Pleasure Club. As the guys are about to leave, J.R. performs the ritual of methodically buttoning up his full-length coat and putting up the collar just right—gangster style. Joey puts the bar stools up again—is this another night or a continuity mistake? The discontinuity and the appearance of repetition work in Scorsese's favor expressing the tedium and lack of life direction these young men endure. An insert of the front door lock closing brings finality to the club scene. Out in the street they get into Joey's car—a big two-door job.

Night. J.R. and The Girl walk down the steps of the ferry station. J.R. insists The Girl must know something about the movies. Throughout his life and five marriages, Scorsese has struggled with relationships hoping that shared interests would be the answer—but knowing they can represent disaster. The Girl asks J.R. what he does with his time and he can only reply "It depends." In a mock sophistication he says he is in-between professions, the street con's mantra, and that he was in banking, which is close to the truth—number runners work for the bank—but not Chase Manhattan. When she probes too hard about what he does he delivers a one word answer, "Why," giving her the hint to move on.

Joey, J.R., and GaGa are driving uptown and that reignites the argument that began in the club. Joey's attitude is it's his car. J.R. strikes back saying he'd like, just one time, to see Joey get a girl without paying five dollars for her. Joey knows what's wrong with J.R.—It's about that girl. J.R. explodes in anger and Joey throws him out of the car. As J.R. stands staring off on an island divider Joey pulls up and says "Come on"—the cruising continues—and loyalty and friendship remain. J.R. gets into the backseat out of respect—he doesn't deserve shotgun after the venal sin of speaking against the leader. A flashback, push-in profile shot of The Girl reminds us that she has never left J.R.'s mind.

The car and the men are on a lift. As the car rises up all the boys can see are crumbling old walls.

Daytime. The Girl and J.R. are on a rooftop talking about Lee Marvin. J.R. schools The Girl about the Marvin persona and street lectures about the John Ford film, *Who Shot Liberty Valance*? (a film Scorsese is fanatical about). As they walk on the roof amid the mounted antennas, J.R. tells The Girl he used to have a chicken coop, a popular urban hobby. Rooftops were critical to these boys, a place to be above the city and one's troubles. It is impossible to listen to J.R. talk about his pigeon coop and not think of Brando and Eva Marie Saint in Kazan's *On The Waterfront*.

The elevator continues to climb; the boys are pensive. In a room GaGa makes out with a young woman. A time cut brings her to a mirror where she combs her bouffant hairdo. She has lost forty dollars. GaGa promises her they will find it. A flashback to the makeout session reveals that GaGa lifted the money from her bag while she swapped spit. As they discuss the problem it flashes back to her at the mirror then back to behind the bar at The 8th Ward Pleasure Club, as GaGa offers to give her a few dollars so she can get home. She asks for five, which leaves him a profit of thirty-five dollars. He locks up the place and is jump cut to a face-front position to shut off the naked light bulb on a string.

In 1966, Scorsese wrote a forty-page treatment, *Jerusalem, Jerusalem*, in which teenage boys embark on a three-day religious retreat held at a Jesuit residence. Again, the main character is J.R., Scorsese's surrogate. *Jerusalem, Jerusalem, Who's That Knocking at My Door*, and *Mean Streets* (originally titled *Season of the Witch*), would have formed an autobiographically based trilogy about young Italian-American men from the Lower East Side, inspired by Fellini's *I Vitelloni*, and Bernardo Bertolucci's second feature, *Before the Revolution*. These were both movies investigating young Italian men in their insular world, struggling with the larger universe they found incomprehensible.

The unproduced *Jerusalem, Jerusalem* presented a theme that personally affected Scorsese—the great moral struggle between the teachings of the Catholic Church and the temptations of the flesh.

The title *Jerusalem, Jerusalem* was not as frivolous as Scorsese's earlier films. It is taken from the New Testament as Jesus sadly contemplates the city that would betray him; "Jerusalem, Jerusalem, how I would have gathered you to me as a mother hen gathers her chicks."

In the story the neighborhood tribe embarks on a retreat held in a bucolic Jesuit monastery. J.R. participates to retrieve a lost sense of spirituality destroyed by his obsessive habit of masturbation—a self-inflicted act the Church deemed as sinful. Tortured with visions of hell and damnation, J.R. is wracked with guilt.

Sermons from Father McMann, the retreat master, loosely based on Father McNamee from *A Portrait of an Artist as a Young Man* by James Joyce, structure the action. As the priest bonds with the boys by playing basketball with them (as Father Principe did with Scorsese and his classmates), he exploits the occasion to espouse dogma about the pains of hell in graphic detail, in the Church tradition to educate through fear of the inevitable for the sinner and to save them before it is too late.

During the three days of introspective contemplation, J.R. reads books as part of his spiritual penance. His choices reflect his inner conflict—Butler's *Lives of the Saints*, is an eighteenth century work that chronicles the inspirational lives of saints from many nations and experience. *The Screwtape Letters* by C.S. Lewis is a volume of reverse theology that instigates the thought and methods of temptation structured as a series of letters exchanged by two devils. Temptation visits J.R. through the rock and roll he hears in his head and the images of his girlfriend and mother.

Father McMann's sermons have a powerful effect on J.R. who fantasizes about his street life intertwined with the scriptures. For J.R. the wedding feast at Cana is transformed into a marriage celebrated in a tenement building in Little Italy. As Father McMann takes the boys step by step through the Stations of the Cross and preaches about the evils of sex without marriage, J.R. creates his own urban passion, as we see the young man's feverish religious vision.

A youthful street criminal is transposed from the passion figure of Jesus, apprehended by the police, symbolic of the Romans, and then dragged through the streets of New York City as crowds humiliate him. The Empire State building is J.R.'s Calvary. The young man's wounds, like those Jesus suffered, are documented in graphic closeups.

In the end, the retreat leader does little to help J.R. with his spiritual crisis. The priest dismisses the young man's fears. The narrative for *Jerusalem, Jerusalem* was based on Scorsese's youthful experience at a retreat, which concluded with the advice given to J.R. in the script—Scorsese entered into a seven-year process of psychotherapy, convinced his issues went beyond religious training to the moral and psychological complications of everyday life.

Scorsese and Mardik Martin also worked on the script for *Season of the Witch*. The title comes from a song by Donovan, an Aquarian folk/rock poet/singer/songwriter who was believed by his followers to have spiritual and mystical powers. Nine years later *Season of the Witch* would become Scorsese's breakthrough film, *Mean Streets*, in which the Scorsese surrogate, now named Charlie, dreamed of owning a club called *Season of the Witch*.

Donovan's lyrics have long been open to interpretation. Written in first person, the song's protagonist learns there is a world outside his window (a metaphor deeply etched in Scorsese's psyche) and when he looks inside his window, a metaphor for self-examination, he comes to the realization he can be many people with many facets to his personality. For Scorsese and Charlie the club name, *Season of the Witch*, is a bridge between old-world Little Italy and the Aquarian movement of the sixties that was reinventing youth culture. Charlie dreamed of owning his own place, not a gin mill, but a fashionable high-class club. The title *Season of the Witch* is provocative, but Scorsese's intention has less to do with witches and more to do with individual confrontation—who they could be if they escaped the iron bonds of tradition. The repetition of the lines has always attracted listeners. Significant are the two words that precede the phrase, "Must be the season of the witch"—"Oh no." For Scorsese's Italian boys, life was changing whether they were ready or not.

J.R. and The Girl play out a mating rite in front of a mirror. A cross with the figure of a crucified Jesus lords over them from the back wall. This is Charlie's family apartment. The camera follows them into the bedroom where an even larger cross protects the room from evil. The ceramic religious statues watch over J.R. even while he is kissing The Girl. He is on top of her but decidedly off to the side avoiding genital-to-genital contact as they makeout fully clothed. They kiss passionately first in a full shot, then in intimate closeups. The montage is deft, the camera glides over eyes and fingers, moves gently over faces, and the moment is pure and romantic. Then in a full shot J.R. suddenly pulls away from The Girl—she looks on concerned. She probes but J.R. won't divulge why he's suddenly stopped kissing her, simply saying there was no reason. After a long soulful look, The Girl moves toward J.R. and they begin to kiss once again. Another montage captures this rare moment of male/female intimacy in a Scorsese film. J.R. explores her breast first on top of her blouse then moves his hands inside to the flesh. She doesn't resist like the good Italian girls J.R. has experienced. The Girl is giving herself to him. Once again he abruptly pulls away. He tells her he loves her. Then a mirror shot combines the Madonna statues in the foreground and the interrupted couple in the background. J.R explains that if she loves him she will understand, then repeats "Just not now." He explains he loves her as herself. J.R. can't express his real feelings of conflict. The Girl doesn't really understand. They stand and he kisses her in a way that shows polite affection but will not lead any further.

For Scorsese and Mardik Martin the original trilogy was to be religious in nature, a search for a messiah in the Lower East Side. Young men with large ambitions, Scorsese and Martin wanted to create a cinematic epic about Catholic mysticism, a major work like Eisenstein's *Ivan the Terrible*, or the humanist trilogy of the French filmmaker Marcel Pagnol—*Marius, Fanny*, and *Caesar.*

Scorsese began work on his first feature by writing a thirty-page screenplay complete with drawings to visualize the film before he shot it. The characters were composites from Scorsese's neighborhood. Creatively, Scorsese was able to subtly shift the actual reality contained in his narrative to create greater dramatic depth by representing the actions and personality of a whole neighborhood, and a whole ethnic culture, through his small tribe on the screen. Scorsese's primary objective was to make an honest film and to make it real.

The astute young filmmaker and historian instinctively knew that cinema was heading in this direction. Artifice and entertainment had been the mainstay of Hollywood from the twenties, but the sixties inspired change in every avenue of American life. Scorsese discovered a kernel of a new kind of American film, but his story did not immediately come into focus and revisions would take place over a long period of time. Elements were shot and then added until Scorsese was closer to what he hoped to achieve—a film inspired by the French New Wave, Italian neorealism, and John Wayne. Eighty percent of the dialogue was written—the rest would be improvised by the actors while in character.

The script was still not what Scorsese envisioned the film to be. An earlier version of *Who's That Knocking at My Door* was submitted to the New York Film Festival in 1965. Richard Roud, the festival's programmer was familiar with Scorsese because the festival, which programmed short films to precede the features, had selected one of his student films for an earlier NYFF. This time, however, through a letter sent to Haig Manoogian, Roud, also an erudite film critic, succinctly summed up his rejection of Scorsese's first feature. He wrote, "I believe you are living aesthetically beyond your means." The feature was put aside. Scorsese was deep in debt and desperately needed to earn money.

Scorsese still considered himself a student and missed having his mentor's full attention. Manoogian wasn't involved with the writing or production process when he viewed a cut of Scorsese's feature that ran about fifty-eight minutes and realized there were major structural and narrative problems. Manoogian strongly believed in the scenes of the posse hanging out in Little Italy. To the veteran film educator they expressed a rare truth and realism.

Two years after Scorsese had finished at NYU, Manoogian was still thinking about Scorsese's feature. The story didn't work and many of the actors were too amateurish to carry a film. The first version of *Who's That Knocking at My Door*, a film with so many working titles even Scorsese can't remember them all, didn't include scenes that revealed the growing romantic relationship between J.R. and The Girl. Scorsese had attempted to create sequences between J.R. and the unnamed girl without synch sound (MOS). It might have worked for Scorsese's heroes in the French New Wave but at the time he just couldn't pull it off. Proceeding on faith, Manoogian, and Joseph Weill, an NYU student and a lawyer, and the publisher of the *Cahiers du Cinema in English*, raised $37,000 to finance a more complete version.

Scorsese, Weill, and Manoogian carefully examined the early version *I Call First* and pulled out all the scenes that worked—the rest was scrapped. Scorsese began to rewrite. After six months he had a new structure in which J.R. and The Girl were intercut with the posse sequences. The intention of the scenes between J.R. and The Girl was to develop the conflict J.R. experienced in his dual role as crew member and boyfriend. Due to budgetary restrictions they proceeded to shoot the new scenes with an Éclair 16mm camera and that material was blown up and cut into the 35mm scenes from the *Bring on the Dancing Girls* version of the film. Scorsese then hired Zina Bethune, best known for her role as Gail Lucas on *The Nurses*, to replace the first actress who played The Girl. Scorsese convinced Harvey Keitel to come back for reshooting. The struggling actor complied but was not happy about the disruption. To express his rebellion, Keitel continued to get haircuts on his regular schedule and they rarely matched the original footage, a detail that drove Scorsese to distraction.

Michael Wadleigh agreed to shoot the new material. Scorsese shot on weekends when the actors were available and reedited the new material at Wadleigh's production company.

As he continued to revise the film, Scorsese pressed forward and landed a job at CBS where he edited news footage that was shot and cut on celluloid. He never stopped writing and developing new projects, in hopes one would break through.

When Scorsese's NYU crew found out he did not have the funds to complete his feature on 35mm they all offered their services. Mardik Martin proved a valuable commodity on the project. He was the only one in Scorsese's circle who held down a job. Working as a waiter Mardik earned good money, enough that he was actually the only one who owned a car. Martin was put to use as a location scout, he carried heavy film equipment as well.

Scorsese wanted his film to be about the endless hanging out on the street and internal and cultural conflicts of his characters. The real locations included Mott and Houston Streets.

Ray Baretto's classic party disc, "El Watusi" is playing. The immediate assumption is the song is coming from somewhere in the apartment, but it is another phase of Scorsese's musical mosaic. A series of slow pans linked by dissolves reveals the kitchen is filled with the tribe dressed in jackets and ties at a stag party. They drink hard liquor and smoke, now in slow motion, another Scorsese signature that would mature in *Mean Streets* and *Taxi Driver*. A gun is dropped into J.R.'s hand and he fumbles with it clumsily. The phone is constantly being worked. Scorsese is rigorous with the pans, always moving left to right not changing direction—a mainstay rule of the Studio Era, changing direction may confuse the viewer. Scorsese augments the pattern by occasional slow zooming in on a moment. One of the guys points a gun menacingly at the others who mock him by putting up their gun thumb and pointing their forefinger at J.R. as they laugh. The slow motion reveals there is more than humor here; there is the immediacy of fear and violence. J.R.'s movement now from right to left breaks the rigorous pan pattern as the camera diligently follows his change of direction. Scorsese moves the camera as an internal energy force connected to his emotional relationship to the content of a scene.

The other boys point their index finger at him (a Renaissance painting technique to determine the center of action) in an orgy of nonverbal communication. The Italian-American trait of using hand movements for expression is widely misunderstood. These are not random gestures with a folksy charm. The pointing fingers are challenges to the "gunman" who is acting like a big man. A pointed finger can convey emphasis, but here it is to put one on notice. The slow-motion horseplay gets serious when J.R. grabs GaGa and puts the gun to his head. The others duck, partly in feigned fear but also because they know the split-second nature of violence on the Lower East Side.

Now huddled in another room for safety the guys begin to mock the scene but then run out of the room. One of the boys, a nonactor, is caught looking into the lens of the camera. Fourth wall reality is broken for a nanosecond—part of guerilla filmmaking in its pioneer days. The scene goes on much too long; a tradition in early low-budget and exploitation films where action fills in for plot to stretch the film to a legitimate feature film length. Scorsese's images serve the structure of the song. During the commotion a record player is discovered, anointing "El Watusi" as diegetic music.

A series of gunshots explode liquor bottles cueing a montage of stills from *Rio Bravo*. The gun shots continue as the bottles break through a rapid montage of stills from the Hawks film. The full title *Rio Bravo* from the poster is presented. The camera pulls back from full poster "Howard Hawks' *Rio Bravo*," and pans over to J.R. and The Girl as they leave the theater.

The *Rio Bravo* montage has been a time transition from the out of control party to a narrative flashback in which J.R. and The Girl have just seen a favorite film of J.R.'s. The violence and chaos from the party is associated with the film. These Italian-American men love John Wayne and Westerns. In their urban manner they are emulating the Duke. The montage takes the place of film clips, which would have been difficult for the no-budget production to obtain, but the abstraction of fast cut stills and camera movement to direct the viewer's eye captures their perception of the movie as righteous manly behavior. The boy/girl relationship is progressing and J.R. is insinuating The Girl into his cultural world. She is receptive but centered in a different, outside world.

"Shotgun," a raucous lead sax instrumental by Junior Walker and the All Stars, is another rock song that appears to be nondiegetic and serves the dual purpose of complementing the time period and referencing the tribe's love of guns and gunplay. J.R. and The Girl talk as the camera glides backward to follow them. The music is the only soundtrack element—a classic low-budget technique, shooting as many silent scenes as possible to save the expense of synch sound and dubbing.

The Girl tells J.R. she really liked the girl in *Rio Bravo* (played by Angie Dickinson) but J.R. tells her that girl is a *broad* deliberately making a distinction between girls and broads, good girls and bad girls, girls you marry and girls you fool around with.

J.R.'s dissertation is interrupted by a sex fantasy imagined by J.R. This sequence was not in the original script or even in the early version and was inserted when Joseph Brenner, a soft porn distributor trying to go legit insisted on nudity to sell the film. The sequence is artfully lit in a European style at odds with the rest of the film. The silent montage is scored with *The End* by The Doors, later used in the opening sequence of Francis Ford Coppola's *Apocalypse Now*. J.R. is naked on a bed his arms outstretched on the headboard as a pretty young woman walks behind him. The camera is often moving sensuously as J.R. has sex with several different women. The oedipal drama of the song gives the scene a threatening, hallucinatory, yet somehow spiritual aura. There are plenty of naked bodies, breasts, and behinds to satisfy the distributors and the Forty-Second Street audiences. Scorsese pulls it off with his arty film student approach. The sequence comes off more like a foreign film short than an American skin flick. J.R. is indulging and enjoying himself, but Jim Morrison's vocal won't allow the viewer to be totally immersed in the joys of the flesh. The song indicates there is a price to pay for sin. J.R. believes in the double standard; he would like to have his way with *broads* but is looking for a nice girl to marry, the Madonna-Whore syndrome has taken over his id. Three hundred and sixty degree shots are jump cut together as J.R. goes from one woman to another. Now he is dressed in shirt, dark vest, trousers, and a light tie holding a deck of cards. In slow motion he flings the cards at a naked woman on a bed—she reacts as though he is killing her—a sexual climax gesture complicated by film student symbolism.

J.R. continues to explain his broad/virgin theory to The Girl as they walk past a church. As they wait for a cab "Shotgun" is refrained—this time it is directed at The Girl. She watches J.R. as he scans the street for a cab—she is questioning who J.R. really is. She has strong feelings for him but deep down knows his life is not for her.

Joey, J.R., and a country friend of his are in Copake, New York. J.R. and Joey are absurdly out of place. They refuse to relinquish their city identity and make fun of "the country" with wiseass remarks. They have three days to spend in the country. This is a retreat without a priest but the local boy is a spiritual guide for "God's country," a place every self-respecting Hippie had discovered long before *Who's That Knocking at My Door* was shot and released.

The trio hike in the mountains, among the trees, heading toward the top. There is hope for J.R. in the world beyond the streets of Little Italy as there was for the young Scorsese.

J.R. and Joey trail badly as the guide steadily heads to the top. He rattles the cages of the two fishes out of water by casually announcing there are snakes in the vicinity. On foreign soil, J.R. and Joey switch roles as leader and follower. A fast zoom out reveals the boys are surrounded by an alien environment. The trek to the top also reminds cinephiles of Stan Brakhage's epic experimental film *Dog Star Man*, rich with symbolism and myth inherent in man climbing a mountain.

They reach the top of the mountain. J.R.'s friend stands tall in front of the majestic sight. J.R. and Joey sit down from exhaustion. The sun streams into the lens and flares, a technique handed down to Scorsese through the bold experiments of cinematographers Conrad Hall (*In Cold Blood, Butch*

Cassidy and the Sundance Kid) and Laszlo Kovacs (*Targets, Easy Rider*) who defied Hollywood's restrictive cinematographic grammar.

Joey whines. For the silent and contemplative J.R., it is a revelation, a spiritual experience. The magnificent sunset is contrasted with a pan up from buildings to the New York City skyline accompanied by "Don't Ask Me," by The Dubs—a song in which a young man pleads with a girl not to be lonely. The Girl lights a votive candle next to the Madonna statue. She is trying to appeal to J.R.'s world dominated by religious ritual. They discuss J.R.'s country trip. He loved being on the top of the mountain but not the climb. The Girl pauses and contemplates J.R.'s inability to understand the connection between effort, commitment, and achievement. As they sit in the kitchen The Girl tells J.R. she has something to say. He becomes attentive. She looks determined and serious. Scorsese stays on a full two shot and lets his actors do their work. The coverage on the scene is similar to the dialogue scenes Scorsese studied from Old Hollywood: closeup, two-shots from angles that favor one character or another. She tells J.R. a story about an early relationship and there is a flashback to The Girl and her date Harry (Harry Northup) driving on a long, secluded road.

"Don't Ask Me" continues to play. The Girl, now in voice over mode, explains that the radio was loud; the volume increases intimating that the song has transitioned from nondiegetic to diegetic, from present to past. In the flashback the boy crudely approaches The Girl sexually. The voice of "The Dubs" that begs, "Please Don't Ask Me to Be Lonely," directly comments on the serious consequences unfolding in the car. Scorsese wants his audience to fully experience The Girl's emotions. Abruptly, the scene becomes a brutal date rape. J.R.'s startled reaction is intercut with the back story. Scorsese and Schoonmaker deftly transition a flashback (the entire story of J.R. and The Girl) to a flashback within a flashback (the date rape). The attack is explicit. There is no nudity, but the raw, violent male behavior on display, and The Girl's valiant fight to preserve her right to decide, delineate the incident. The intercutting becomes more complex. J.R. is recalling The Girl's ecstatic face when they madeout on the bed in his apartment. J.R. rapidly comes to a judgment against The Girl proscribed by his atavistic and repressive values.

The attacker exits the car as The Girl tumbles out onto the snowy ground; the man continues to stalk her. As the attack progresses, Scorsese staggers several takes of the song so it repeats and echoes out of synch—reinforcing a relationship gone very wrong. The actors go all out. The early stage of the rape looks entirely real, no stage slaps, Bethune is savagely knocked around as she desperately fights for survival. At the table the conversation has stopped, The Girl sits quietly in that terrible moment. The consummation of the rape takes place on the front seat of the car when Harry finally overpowers her. The song stops and her screaming covers the act and J.R.'s distorted interpretation of what he has now learned. The Girl concludes telling J.R. how the experience made her feel alienated and tainted. She is telling J.R. this story because she loves him and wants their relationship to last. Only the truth can free her, but J.R. has shut down emotionally. She tells J.R. for them lovemaking would be the first time but J.R. cannot understand and doesn't believe her sincerity. He repeats the word believe, a key concept in Catholicism where one must not question but believe. The street has taught J.R. to always be wary, untrusting. The sensitive side of J.R. is not in attendance now; he grows angry and yells at her in a condescending voice. The Girl, both disappointed and angry, quickly leaves the apartment. A selective focus profile closeup of J.R. shows The Girl slamming the door shut in the background—the shot is repeated. A freeze-frame of her struggle with Harry serves a dual purpose. It is an image in J.R.'s mind distorted by his street code and is also a reminder to the viewer that this event really happened the way The Girl told the story. We hear a final door slam. In his mind J.R. has turned a good girl into a whore to be dismissed from his life. The door slam is repeated three times, to call attention to its significance. J.R. has lost something he cannot get back. The abstracted black and white graphic image of The Girl closing the door behind is repeated twice. J.R. sees the world as black and white. J.R.'s mind is closed.

Nighttime. J.R., Joey, and GaGa sit down at a bar and order scotch and water—Johnnie Walker, of course, the holy water of Italian-American men. They are already drunk and acting very silly. They grab and touch each other, horsing around with napkins, blowing off steam. GaGa stuffs a napkin into Joey's mouth. J.R. quickly wipes GaGa's face in a mock gesture. Balled-up napkins fly like World War II bombs across the bar. The shot of The Girl and her attacker in the car is repeated. Closeup on J.R. as he throws his head back in laughter. A closeup of the attacker is intercut, followed by his predatory move to The Girl and a jump cut to the tussle between them, then back to the shenanigans of the three men/children. The attack on the snow is editorially fragmented interpreting thoughts trapped in the mind replaying in and out of order. Scorsese constantly reminds the viewer that the story's present is in the bar so these flashbacks are either from the interior point of view of J.R. (although he doesn't seem to be reacting as such) or they are offered as argument for the viewer to judge J.R's. callous treatment of The Girl. In the later scenario, Scorsese is making his value judgment on J.R. (and himself through his on-screen surrogate.) The motor of this montage are freeze-frame images of The Girl screaming synchronized to the yelps in the song now clearly functioning as score for the flashback within flashback, since they appear to fit in her mouth. The song ends, freeze-frame on J.R.—back to the bar as Joey is pulled off his stool and to the ground in a sham symbolic gesture that connects the rape and J.R.'s dismissal of The Girl.

Scorsese has repeatedly explained that he has always storyboarded his films including *Who's That Knocking at My Door* because "paper is cheaper than film," but the significance of this method goes well beyond financial considerations. The method insures control of the visual language and sequential images related to the storytelling. Not every director has, or even desires, total control of the visualization of a film. Many, especially in contemporary Hollywood, leave that area very much to the director of photography and the production designer. Scorsese is the author of his films, collaboration is significant and encouraged. The artistic dialogues are conveyed through Scorsese's drawings and visual ideas that interpret the narrative. Scorsese creates the visual blueprint of a film before it goes into production with storyboards and intricate, detailed notes he makes in the margins of his script. The distinctive cinematic grammar he has cultivated through his extensive knowledge of filmmaking, film history, and his own artistic sensibilities connect to thematic nature, content, and narratives on a film-by-film basis.

Shooting conditions on *Who's That Knocking at My Door* were oppressive. Scorsese and the small cast and crew could only film on weekends, which stretched the shooting schedule over an entire winter. Locations were so confined that after the large and unwieldy 35mm Mitchell BNC camera (the Hollywood camera of choice at the time) and lighting equipment were set into position, there wasn't much space left for the actors to perform. This limitation forced Scorsese to shoot without moving the camera.

The project had no real formal budget, just a small sum of money used for necessities. The locations were not by choice but by ability to gain access: Mardik Martin's hallway, the Scorsese family apartment, a local church, and his grandmother's apartment. This last location was particularly stressful because they could only shoot when Grandma was out of the apartment and they *had* to be finished before she came home. Fight scenes staged on the street were interrupted by the homeless.

While many filmmakers stay seated in their director's chair, Scorsese was up on the balls of his feet pacing back and forth as well as viscerally reacting to the actors and action as he did as a young child engrossed in his movie-going experiences.

To make conditions even more challenging, the film stock was slow, the lenses were slow, and there often wasn't enough light to produce a serviceable image. Scorsese was fired up with the new aesthetic and narrative storytelling structures, but the technology was not yet available to render the new freedom the director craved.

A recent New York City law dictated all street lamps were to be fitted with bulbs that emitted a bright yellow light not kind to film stock exposure. The crew placed light bulbs in doorways of tenement locations to boost the illumination, without the added luminescence images, which were barely discernable through the camera's viewfinder.

For the stag party shoot, Scorsese was able to access a 16mm Éclair camera. The footage was later blown up to 35mm. Speaking in hindsight on the DVD commentary, Scorsese wishes all of *Knocking* could have been filmed by this method—it was the look he was going for. The Éclair was mobile and allowed Scorsese freedom of movement denied by the bulky and sedentary Mitchell BNC.

A party is in progress. GaGa is the host; the guys crack down on him. There is a crucial element missing—the *broads*. Joey in his leadership capacity orders GaGa to get rid of the off-screen people who make up aural presence of the low-rent film party and to go down to the street and get the girls/*broads*. GaGa agrees, but will take no responsibility for what happens when he returns from his mission.

Joey and J.R. are in the dark, illuminated only by the light of the television they stare at to pass the time. The door opens. GaGa returns with Susan and her girlfriend Rosie. Formal introductions are made; the rest of the crew literally appears out of the woodwork at the sight and smell of live, in the flesh fresh *broads*. Susan seems comfortable, Rosie friendly, but hesitant, trying to figure out what is going on. Susie orders a Scotch and ginger ale like a trooper, Rosie dittos after a hesitation, but doesn't say "I'll have the same," rather she repeats Susie word for word.

A live fish is plunked into one of the drinks. J.R. interrogates the girls and learns they are from the Bronx, an alien turf so far from Little Italy it may not even exist to the guys. The girls are not Italian-American—they inquire if the guys are. Susie is given her aquatic drink and begins to scream and laugh when she sees the tiny swimmer in her glass. She is up for a good time. GaGa has clutched onto her arm and won't let go. Rosie is not a "good sport." She is upset while her friend continues to laugh and mingle among the guys who grab onto any of her female parts they can. The soundtrack is chaotic and unfocused like an early John Cassevetes movie, *Shadows* or *Faces*. This scene could be homage to Cassevetes—people being, not acting, raw emotions, and primitive but very human behavior. Scorsese's attempt at cinematic art in early sequences is gone—this is cinéma vérité and the actors and nonactors all thrive on doing improvisation.

Later. The rowdy mood has disappeared by a cut to a dark room. The television dialogue drones on while GaGa and Susie make out. In another part of the apartment Rosie is in lip-lock with one of the guys. J.R., Joey, and Bobby glare at the TV, again, just biding their time. Bobby delivers his critical view on the picture—it stinks. Joey agrees but is distracted and anxious to figure out who is going in to make out with the girls next. J.R. says, "I call first," one of the film's many early titles. The ritual of choosing is decided by Bobby, Joey, and an offscreen tribe member. They stand in a circle to choose it out. J.R. is reluctant because he feels jinxed, he never wins. Destiny arrives and J.R. loses every "choose" assigning him to last. J.R. runs the old riff that he called first and announces that if he isn't first, no one will be first. Abruptly J.R. lets out a clarion call and they all storm the room. Pandemonium breaks out as they grab at both couples. The male smoochers yell with anger; the girls are hysterical and frightened. Susie and Rosie manage to escape. GaGa is furious—his friends think it is just about the funniest thing they've ever seen. J.R. and Joey celebrate their coup. GaGa leaves with the girls in a manufactured air of chivalry. GaGa pleads with Susie and Rosie in the stairwell but they are inconsolable. Then the entire tribe follows in pursuit.

J.R. walks into The Girl's apartment building—he looks tired, pensive, and determined. Scorsese deconstructs the elevator ride with inserts, punctuating the journey with J.R.'s finger pressing the number nine button, and later a slow pan on the floor number panel as the elevator climbs digit by digit until it arrives at nine. J.R. walks to her door in a deliberate and measured manner. In a nod to Scorsese's beloved *Citizen Kane*, the scene is photographed in deep focus to accentuate the distance he must travel. The distance appears longer than reality could allow. The sound of J.R.'s knock is a transition from the hall to inside The Girl's apartment, and she wakes up with the noise. She lets him in—it is very early morning, 6:30 A.M. J.R. announces he is here to see her. The Girl is a little bewildered at first but genuinely glad to see him. J.R. surveys The Girl's apartment. It is the first time he and The Girl are not on J.R.'s turf and he becomes a bit vulnerable admitting he has no clue as to why he is here at this hour. J.R. explains that he and his tribe have been out drinking and links the out-of-control aspect of his behavior at the party to his presence in The Girl's apartment. After utilizing nonlinear structure for the movie's preceding scenes, Scorsese plays out the final result of this relationship in real film time. The Girl makes coffee. J.R. looks around the apartment and examines the differences between how The Girl lives and his own existence. Checking the view, he notices that she doesn't have a television. Wanting to please, The Girl mentions (offscreen) that she has a record player and for him to put on a record if he wishes. J.R. pauses, and with a perverse grin, then tests her once more saying he likes Giuseppe Di Stefano and asking if she has any of that opera singer's records—he knows that just isn't possible. J.R. is again defining their differences. He thumbs through her record collection: *Sinatra, A Man and His Music*, a Stan Getz/Astrid Gilberto album followed by a Dinah Washington disc. Her taste is modern popular jazz, not opera, not Doo-Wop. He tests again, this time asking if she has any Percy Sledge albums, but The Girl doesn't follow R&B, soul. Sledge is most famous for "When a Man Loves a Woman," another textural reference. Next he fiddles through a hardcover edition of F. Scott Fitzgerald's *Tender Is the Night*. J.R. politely refuses an offer of something to eat. The apartment is tastefully spare; a few abstract paintings are on the walls, there is an artful wooden chair, a tall white table lamp, and an open couch bed where The Girl sleeps. She reenters the room; J.R. takes The Girl in his arms and begins to kiss her aggressively. She quickly pulls back—he is hurting her. J.R. apologizes for his earlier actions, specifically his callous reaction to the story of her viscous attack. He waits briefly to see how his apology has registered but then challenges that she doesn't seem pleased to see him. The Girl is sincere and firm. She had been waiting to see if J.R. loved her enough to come back and accept their relationship as it really is. J.R. professes his love for her, they kiss on equal ground, and she holds him tenderly for a long beat. The ice is broken. They both relax and confess how much they have missed each other. Then comes the beginning of the end. J.R. assures her everything is alright and that he *forgives* her. The tender moment is over. He explains that his forgiveness means he is going to marry her anyway. The Girl quickly rises and confronts J.R., understanding totally now that her past really does bother him. This is a young woman of integrity and a strong sense of her values—she refuses to marry J.R. on his terms. A young man with a limited emotional range, J.R. turns angry and bitter at her independence.

He calls her a *broad* and identifies himself as a reasonable average guy. For J.R. it can only be about blame, right and wrong, black and white. J.R. pushes her further away accusing her of making a fool out of him. One of an Italian-American male's worst fears is that they will be played for a fool.

J.R. gets more and more visibly angry calling her "brain," convincing himself that she is deliberately doing this against him. Telling a woman "I love you" is enough for J.R., no questions asked or answered. He attacks her integrity by telling The Girl the problem isn't his—it's hers for calling herself the Virgin Mary. He is losing all sense of logic and decency. J.R. goes for the jugular branding her a whore who no one will want to marry. The Girl stands silent and firm as J.R. ponders his next move; he "sincerely" apologizes for the hurtful remark—trying to take it back as another ploy to get his way. With her back to J.R., The Girl coldly and firmly says, "Go home." There is a dissolve to a reverse angle now on both of their faces and she repeats her final answer. J.R. storms out and slams the door behind him; The Girl slowly walks over to her reading chair and sadly contemplates what has occurred. In the hallway J.R. impatiently rings for the elevator then charges for the stairwell. As he runs down the steps in a fury he trips and falls down, then throws a violent kick yelling "mother," a word with many meanings to him; his revered mother, the mother of god, and the commonly used street curse "motherfucker." At this moment he is in a burst of irrational rage. He smashes a glass at the wall although the prior existence of the object was never established. What was important for Scorsese was the explosion of temper. It is not a healthy or liberating act—anger festers and is stored up until the moment it is unleashed with no warning.

J.R. goes to church. He enters the confessional booth. Two shots, structured by a jump cut, return his tormented memory to the early days of his relationship when he kissed The Girl in his room with the crucifix on the wall. Inside the booth, where another large crucifix watches over him, J.R. awaits the moment of confession. A young priest opens up the panel, which divides them as sinner and an agent of redemption, and J.R. makes the sign of the cross, ready to cleanse his soul and spirit. J.R. and The Girl kiss again in flashback—the priest returns J.R.'s gesture by the ritual of making his sign of the cross to signal the beginning of the holy process. In a close jump cut the boy and The Girl approach each other and kiss passionately, and church bells are ringing in the background. The priest slams shut the panel. J.R. performs his prayers of forgiveness offscreen as the camera zooms into a statue of the Virgin Mary and the child Jesus. As J.R. continues the penance of prayer, he flashes back to The Girl making out in the car, two blurred freeze-frames of the attack in the snow, then the bare breasts of a woman, three shots of hands touching, a swing pan of J.R. and one of the girls in his sex fantasy dream. The face of a religious statue of the Virgin Mary is in a state of extreme sorrow—zoom back to the dead body of Jesus draped across her lap. Cut to a statue hand with the stigmata, a wound on the body of Jesus, his foot bleeding from the crucifixion. Dolly back to J.R. who is kneeling in a pew, a signature shot that will be reprised in *Mean Streets*. A statue holding a plate with two eyes, then a full shot of an enormous crucifix on the church wall follows. "Who's That Knocking" by The Genies blares onto the soundtrack, as a montage of zoom-ins to statues, a dolly past the statue of the dead Jesus in the lap of his mother, and various close, locked off-shots and glide-overs of the statues that sanctify the church as holy, play out. In two shots, one full, the second a closeup, J.R. gently and with great respect kisses the feet of Jesus on a small crucifix hung on a wall. After another series of statues and religious icons Scorsese and Schoonmaker intercut a hand moving up a woman's leg. J.R. enters the confessional booth again to repent for another sin, he kisses the crucifix again, but this is a fever dream fantasy as blood drips down J.R.'s lips—the blood of Christ who suffered for our sins. More images of the stigmata and bleeding parts that will obsessively dominate Scorsese films follow. To purge sin, Scorsese is saying, one must physically suffer as Christ did. In three swift shots, starting full, and ending close, Scorsese and Schoonmaker cut in on the large crucifix that is the centerpiece of the church. The number three arises again. Scorsese has learned this cinematic technique of cutting from far to close without changing the angle—only the focal length—from Alfred Hitchcock's *Shadow of a Doubt*, when it is revealed that Uncle Charlie is really a psychotic killer just waiting for the right moment to strike. More church images, a repeat of the hand groping a female leg, her stocking is violently torn away, and then a recall of the mother figure serving the children her homemade Italian meat pie delicacy. The context has changed, we now believe that one of the boys is J.R. and the woman is his mother. A slow dolly past J.R. contemplating in the pew is segued with the sound of The Girl during the sexual attack as her eyes shift from left to directly into the camera. The sequence ends with a zoom-out from Christ on the cross to the entirety of the holy church, photographed in the old St. Patrick's Cathedral, where the young Scorsese worshipped and struggled with his identity. The song "Who's That Knocking" as written by Johnson and Jones concerns a man who gets involved with two girls, hears a constant knocking on his door, but doesn't know who it is, and seems unwilling to find out. Is it one or both of the girls who have found out about the double-dealing? Is it a boyfriend of one or maybe both of the girls who have learned of the man's existence and are letting their presence be known? For the film Scorsese uses the key phrase to interpret the lyrics as an outcry from J.R. Who is knocking at *his* door? Is it the power the church has over him or the streets that pull him in a totally different moral direction? Is it his relationship with The Girl doomed by J.R. because he cannot break away from Sicilian/Catholic tenets?

A freeze-frame of J.R. and Joey out on the street unfreezes. They leave with the iconic hangout lines, "All right, I'll talk to you tomorrow, okay?" "I'll see you tomorrow, huh," and go their separate ways—it is just the end of another day, to be repeated on the next. The camera pulls back looking down at the street from a high angle as the credits play over "The Plea," sung by The Chantells.

Who's That Knocking at My Door was edited on the Upper East Side on Eighty-Sixth Street. Scorsese was waking later and later each day and pushing to edit into the early morning hours of the next day. His insistence on working longer and longer hours was demanding on his editor, but Schoonmaker realized that Scorsese was in the grips of a passion—he knew where he was going and was relentless in achieving his goal as a personal filmmaker. The loyal editor, who was walking home at the most ungodly hours, aligned herself with the man who would later become a lifetime collaborator.

Joseph Brenner was a distributor of low, low-budget films. His company, Joseph Brenner Associates Inc., was responsible for delivering exploitation films: *Violent Woman, Street Fighter, Cuban Rebel Girls, The Sin Syndicate, Make Me a Woman*, and *Schizo*, to grind houses for the guilty pleasures of insomniacs, the lonely and disenfranchised, who sat in the dark for hours in New York's Times Square.

Brenner had amassed a large collection of World War II footage. Figuring he could get some young-bloods to cobble together a feature film out of the miles of footage boxed in his office, he offered Scorsese and Mardik Martin the opportunity to make a movie out of the material he already owned. The young men spent long days screening the aged material in search of a screen story. Poorly archived, the overwhelming majority of the footage was deteriorated and not usable. After finding a few gems among the muck and mire, Scorsese, hungry to make a feature film, told Brenner he and his buddy could make a motion picture out of some of the more interesting shots they discovered during marathon screenings.

Scorsese and Martin dedicated months scripting and developing a film they called *Aquino Battle*. In this war opus four soldiers return from the battlefield, each with a personal issue, the stuff of drama. *Aquino Battle* was never made; Scorsese and Martin did not receive one red cent for their efforts.

What became *Who's That Knocking at My Door* was not only guerilla filmmaking, but also evolutionary filmmaking. Scorsese had a script he thought was the movie and set out to make it—that turned out not to be the case. When shooting was complete Scorsese plunged right into editing. The result was called *I Call First*, a reference to a line spoken by J.R. during the party scene.

The *I Call First* version of the film featured a more complex narrative but was constructed without any intercutting between J.R.'s life with the tribe and his "other life," the relationship with The Girl. When the film was entered into the 1967 Chicago International Film Festival (not 1969 as erroneously stated in *Scorsese on Scorsese*), Scorsese was broke and was not able to attend but some of the actors and crew did. The founder and artistic director, Michael Kutza, invited the young Scorsese to screen his first feature film, which came in on a final budget of $75,000, for its international premiere.

The film was well received in Chicago. One of the attendees was a young Roger Ebert who liked *I Call First* and put kind words in print. Ebert has always been a champion of independent cinema and his Roman Catholic background gave him an inside perspective on Scorsese's point of view.

Distribution was another story entirely. Scorsese's student short, *It's Not Just You Murray!* was distributed by Don Rugoff and his Cinema V theater chain, but Scorsese scored the feature with previously recorded, copyright-protected, rock and roll records. Scorsese didn't have the rights and Rugoff couldn't move forward. Scorsese went to music man Morris Levy who gave him two or three songs. Others in the music business followed suit, but Scorsese had to take what they gave him, not the songs with which he had constructed the film—a hard lesson in the realities of commercial filmmaking for a guerilla filmmaker who really had no choice. Scorsese needed to use music he had grown up on—that was the personal connection he contributed to the semiautobiographical story.

1969 was a particularly difficult year for Martin Scorsese. He was struggling to get work in the film industry, trying unsuccessfully to get film projects off the ground, such as *Battle Queen* about five World War II veterans who met every year to trade tales of violence and killing. The year was filled with social, political, and personal turmoil. Scorsese experienced the death of his maternal grandfather, Martin Cappa. This loss triggered emotions about an era represented by his first-generation ancestors, a link between the old world in Italy and the rapidly changing one into which Scorsese desperately tried to fit.

After a first feature film that was clearly a personal independent film, Scorsese was hired to direct his second feature, *The Honeymoon Killers*. The budget was $150,000 and the production required a fast and economical approach.

The project was initiated by Warren Steibel, a producer for the popular and long-running political television series *Firing Line*, which featured conservative guru, William F. Buckley. Steibel was friendly with mutual funds guru Leon Levy, who was interested in funding a motion picture as a tax write-off. Steibel discussed the proposition with his live-in companion, composer Leonard Kastle.

Steibel's idea was to make a film based on "The Lonely Hearts" murders, a true crime story from the 1940s. Raymond Fernandez, a con artist gigolo who bilked a string of women out of cash and belongings, crossed paths with Martha Beck, a large-sized woman, whose hard heart and pathological jealousy turned the pair into serial killers who met their maker in the electric chair at Sing Sing in 1951.

To keep the microbudget under control Steibel convinced Kastle to write the screenplay saving what Steibel estimated to be a $10,000 fee required by a Hollywood screenwriter. Kastle had never written a screenplay but his partner encouraged him by reiterating Kastle's accomplishments as a librettist. Thirty-nine at the time, Kastle, who attended Julliard and had spent most of his life as a composer was recognized for his operas, *Deseret* and *Pariah*.

When the script was ready for production locations were secured in upstate New York where Steibel and Kastle had a house in New Lebanon, Columbia County. An open casting call was held. Tony Lo Bianco was just starting out when he auditioned for *The Honeymoon Killers*. Lo Bianco was a former Golden Gloves boxer, with Latino and Italianate good looks. Shirley Stoler was a large and imposing figure, born in Brooklyn and a member of the avant-garde performance groups *La Mama* and *The Living Theater*. Stoler had no film experience but Kastle and Steibel immediately knew they had their Martha Beck.

Warren Steibel had seen Scorsese's *Who's That Knocking at My Door*, and was impressed with the young director's abilities. Kastle arranged a meeting with Scorsese and he was hired to direct *The Honeymoon Killers*, which would have been his sophomore feature.

Steibel and Kastle wanted the film in black-and-white, a combination of a film noir and a documentary style. Scorsese was insisting it should be in color. They came to a compromise and agreed to shoot the film in a tabloid style. For reasons known only to Scorsese he claims he was playing the self-indulgent student role of artist, saying, "A director who really knows what he's doing does it in one take." Scorsese began shooting the film in long takes with no coverage and no retakes. According to

Leonard Kastle, the breaking point came when Scorsese and director of photography Oliver Wood spent hours shooting take after take of a beer can on the ground.

Donald Volkman, an assistant on the film was promoted to director when Scorsese was fired by Steibel and Kastle after one week, just five days of shooting. Volkman who was inexperienced and lacked confidence did not fare much better than Scorsese. He needed constant reinforcement from Kastle, turning to him after every take for approval. With a crisis on their hands, the budget and schedule dwindling, Steibel and Kastle decided that Kastle would take over the directorial chores at the heartfelt suggestion of Lo Bianco and Stoler. Kastle continues to credit director of photography Oliver Wood (*Alphabet City, Mr. Holland's Opus, The Bourne Identity*) as the driving cinematic force behind the film.

Ironically, Kastle who acknowledges he was an amateur, did direct the film mostly in long takes on a suicidal one-to-one shooting ratio. With the correct, specific coverage and plenty of rehearsals, he succeeded in making the film he envisioned.

Disagreement remains concerning Scorsese's contribution to the finished film. He did preproduction with Oliver Wood on *The Honeymoon Killers*, when the visual style would have been established. Scorsese did begin shooting and some of that material is in the film, so Wood and Kastle would have followed the basic stylistic formula that had been established once the decision was made to include Scorsese's footage. Kastle agrees that Scorsese directed the sequence in which Martha, jealous of Ray's involvement with another woman, tries to drown herself. Shirley Stoler is on record that Scorsese created an atmosphere of pure terror for the scene and that the fear, panic, and emotional pain the actress revealed in the scene was real. Stoler also credits Scorsese with the effective B-movie opening where the camera follows her down a hospital hall, in a long choreographed shot, with precise movement, rhythm, and intricate reframing techniques, but Kastle is not willing to concede. The scene has no other precedent in the remainder of the film as directed by Kastle and certainly looks like the Scorsese of *GoodFellas* and *Casino*.

Ironically *The Honeymoon Killers* attained cult success, which would have jump-started Scorsese's career had he found a way to make the film. Not only did it receive good reviews and a rave from Francois Truffaut, who called *The Honeymoon Killers* his favorite American film, but it eventually also made it to the Blockbuster Videos list of the hundred greatest films of all time. Ironically, Leonard Kastle has never been able to get one of his many projects into production. *The Honeymoon Killers* is his only film.

By this time Joseph Brenner decided he wanted to cross over from tawdry exploitation films to the new independent American art film that was gaining popularity with the under-thirties, now the industry's targeted demographic. *Greetings,* featuring Robert DeNiro and directed by Brian De Palma, was released in 1968 and brought in a financial return for investors. It even won the prestigious Golden Bear at the Berlin Film Festival. Robert Downey's *Putney Swope* and John Cassavetes' *Faces* attracted attention in limited theatrical runs and at international film festivals. Scorsese had an independent film with no sex, no nudity. Even independent films have to conform to audience demands, which become a deal breaker for distributors. Scorsese's feature needed a nude scene to qualify for release in a rapidly changing film market.

Scorsese was in Europe with his friend and *It's Not Just You Murray!* cinematographer Richard Coll who was directing commercials. This was Scorsese's very first trip to Europe. He was trying to make a living in films any way he could. His strong family background compelled him to be responsible and send money home.

Scorsese's exposure to Europe became more than just a strategy for finding his way into the film industry; it also gave him direct access to the foreign cinema he so admired but had only seen on his small family television set or in revival theaters like the Thalia and Dan Talbot's New Yorker. The trip took him to Amsterdam, Munich, London, and Paris. Scorsese was an eyewitness to the Paris revolt that began in May 1968, a seminal event in political and cinematic history. Godard was artistically compelled to reference the event in his films and, well over thirty years later, Scorsese's directorial hero, Bernardo Bertolucci, put his impression of that fervent time into his film, *The Dreamers.*

In the midst of the screening of *The Bride Wore Black* and *Marnie,* a massive demonstration broke out. Francois Truffaut made a speech to the crowd. Henri Langois, founder of Cinemateque Francais, who saved priceless French movies from destruction by the Nazis during World War II, who fed and nurtured Truffaut, Godard, Roemer, Renais, Malle, and Chabrol on the history of film and America Cinema had been fired by government forces. Truffaut whipped the gang of cinemaphiles into a frenzy.

The kid from Little Italy barely understood the language let alone the unique state of French political and social thought. Scorsese did know the French were famous for their strikes. He thought the furor was about a taxi strike. As revolution and dissent spread throughout Paris, Scorsese began to understand the enormity of the situation. As the city shut down, Scorsese couldn't get back to New York to shoot the nude scene that would finally allow his first feature film to be distributed.

Scorsese decided to shoot the scene in the sexually liberated city of Amsterdam in the Netherlands. Harvey Keitel was summoned to fly over to act in the scene. Cinematographer Richard Coll was stricken ill, so Scorsese called in Max Fisher, who was an experienced cameraman in television commercials. The sequence was photographed in 35mm black and white and was shot in two days.

The scene was edited on a flatbed editing table using "The End" and also "The Lantern," a track from the Rolling Stone's witchy answer to *Sgt. Pepper's Lonely Hearts Club Band*, appropriately titled *Their Satanic Majesties Request*. Keitel and Scorsese stayed at a friend's house because they had no money between them. When they returned to New York, Scorsese had the cut picture of the nude sequence in one pocket of his raincoat and the soundtrack in another. The material was never declared to customs.

While he was in Amsterdam Scorsese met industry friends who led him to much needed work. Dutch filmmakers Pim de La Parra and Wim Verstappen hired Scorsese to write what they called "tough American dialogue" for their latest project. Scorsese's vast knowledge of the American cinema and vernacular was quickly getting around.

The project was ideal for Scorsese's private obsession with the voyeuristic aspects of the cinema supported by his adoration of Alfred Hitchcock and Michael Powell's *Peeping Tom*. *Obsessions*, as it came to be known, was the story of a medical student who watches a man and woman making love through a hole in the wall of his flat. The girl becomes unconscious after the man gives her an injection. The student breaks into the apartment and finds a second woman, naked and unconscious, in the bathtub. Scorsese continued to develop projects of all forms and subjects to promote self-generating work that would support him financially and assist him in gaining entry into a closed film industry. One of the most ambitious and daunting of these attempts was a proposed documentary on the history of soldiering that he began to formulate after the abrupt and damning firing as director of *The Honeymoon Killers*. This project, like many others, was abandoned when Scorsese conceded it would be impossible to fund. Scorsese was interested in ancient cultures and the remnants of feudalism to which he was exposed in contemporary Little Italy. To Scorsese, the Romans in the religious epics he loved were soldiers—Westerns portrayed army troops, and the gangster and film noir genres taught him that men in organized crime were the soldiers of the families to whom they gave their loyalty.

Scorsese was strapped for cash as he continued to find ways to earn money in films. He worked as a lighting technician for the Maysles Brothers. The experience not only served as a job that helped pay the rent and deal with the debt of student loans, but also the opportunity to observe the two masters of cinéma-vérité filmmaking had a profound influence on Scorsese's later work in documentaries and fiction films. It gave him another cinematic approach to capturing life in a truthful and immediate manner. NYU, his artistic and spiritually creative home, became another resource for financial support. In 1969 through the grace of his mentor Haig Manoogian, Scorsese began teaching as an Assistant Professor. He taught classes in basic 16mm film production, senior film production, and film history. He was already a developing scholar in film history under Manoogian's tutelage and through independent study at incessant screenings of classic and contemporary films on television, at revival houses, museums, Forty-second Street grind houses, and Manhattan movie theaters. His teaching philosophy was grounded in the dogmatic methods of Manoogian, the film director as auteur rigueur of Andrew Sarris and the Cahier du Cinema crowd and in the grammar and aesthetics of both the Classical Hollywood Studio System and the New York independent film scene. The students were required to make three-minute film exercises, which Scorsese supervised.

One of the classes he taught was Film Criticism, traditionally taught by screening international films such as *Wild Strawberries* and *Nights of Calabria*, and assigning the students to read a literary work that complemented the film. The students rebelled against this tradition and their young teacher led the way by celebrating the classical American cinema of Ford, Hawks, and other auteurist idols.

Two of his pupils became accomplished filmmakers, Oliver Stone and Jonathan Kaplan (*Night Call Nurses*, *The Accused*, *Breakdown Palace*, and director and producer on television's *ER*).

Kaplan attended a few early classes and then disappeared from his professor's field of view to go off and make a movie. When Kaplan reemerged late in the semester with a rough cut of his film *Stanley Stanley*, it was so good that Scorsese was tolerant of the excessive absences labeling them "field study." The short was a student film festival prizewinner in 1970 and was screened at the prestigious Robert Flaherty Film Seminar in 1971.

In contrast Oliver Stone was a serious and dedicated student enrolled at NYU under the G.I. Bill after his tour of duty in Vietnam. Stone was experiencing difficulty adjusting to civilian life and discovered filmmaking as an extension of his love of literature and an outlet to communicate his ideas and feelings. "Being able to go to NYU on the G.I. Bill right out of Vietnam and then accidentally running into a teacher like Scorsese in Filmmaking 101, is about as lucky as you can get," Stone told Mary Pat

Kelly. "And not only was he a great teacher, he was inspirational. He loved movies, and that's what he conveyed to us—his love for movies."

Stone had made three or four short films he considered to be "silly exercises." Scorsese told Stone he should make films about something personal, an idea with feeling and emotion connected to the filmmaker.

The result was *Last Year in Vietnam*, an eight-minute film inspired by Stone's feelings of alienation since returning from the war filtered through the filmmaker's attraction to the dark side.

Scorsese, sporting hair still parted on the side but now down to the shoulder and often wearing the Italian-American chic of the times, a waist-length leather jacket with Edwardian lapels and a colorful paisley scarf loosely knotted around his neck, sat with Stone as the film, based on his actual experience, was structured during the editing process. His faith in Oliver Stone's ability to probe his psyche in film may have just been the creative spark that eventually produced *Platoon*, *Born on the Fourth of July*, and *J.F.K.*

Scorsese's students admired his high energy and rapid-fire speech pattern as he talked about a film he watched on television at 3:00 A.M. He could bring any film he discussed to life as a cinematic narrative. The classes respected his insights and constant support delivered with charm, grace, and fervor for the cinema.

In front of a class he was exploding with nervous energy. At times he would hold court with monologues about the history of film delivered with reverence and great humor. He was so mesmerizing that students and other NYU personnel would enter the classroom from the corridors just to hear the young man engage in a glorious rant about his beloved cinema.

While he was teaching film at NYU, The Film Society at Lincoln Center appointed the teacher/filmmaker Artist-In-Residence for local city high schools and put Scorsese in charge of programming the inaugural season of Movies in the Park during the summer of 1970. Portable movie screens were set up in Central Park, Prospect Park, and Riverside Park for a free summer night at movies open to the public. Scorsese saw the events as a way of educating the public by presenting short films that expressed personal visions and experimental cinematic language.

Satisfied that the nude scene now guaranteed a shot at box-office success, Joseph Brenner took the film on for distribution. It was Brenner who changed the title to *Who's That Knocking at My Door*. The film was released in 1970 (after the demise of the sixties), a year in which the film won the Golden Siren award at the Sorrento Festival.

Brenner opened *Who's That Knocking at My Door* after its four-year production journey at the Carnegie Hall Cinema, a theater with an art film, foreign film reputation, located just around the corner from the famed music hall.

The recently formed Motion Picture Association of America (MPAA) led by Jack Valenti gave *Who's That Knocking at My Door* an R rating, which restricted younger audiences from seeing Scorsese's first effort. The frank subject matter about religion, the brutality of the violence were certainly contributing factors, but the clincher was Joseph Brenner's mandate that the film, a serious drama, contain a nude scene for which the MPAA pigeonholed it in a category that included sexploitation.

When *Who's That Knocking at My Door* was released Scorsese showed it to his friend and mentor, John Cassavetes, whose film *Husbands* had just premiered. The maverick independent filmmaker told him he just loved the film; it was honest and truthful—the only standard that meant anything to the rebellious Cassavetes.

Scorsese remains embarrassed by his first feature effort. He was just learning about long-form storytelling, structure, time, and place. Scorsese was tough on himself; as a master student of film history he knew his film did not have the cinematic invention of a young Godard or Bertolucci when he made his masterful *Before the Revolution*. For Scorsese movies were like dreams, ethereal in nature. He thought about what he had accomplished and where he wanted to go—he needed the language—not just words—but the cinematic syntax to express the inner feelings of a personal filmmaker.

As an artifact of film history *Who's That Knocking at My Door* may be crude cinema, but it contains the DNA of a major personal filmmaker looking for his voice and the cinematic language necessary to express himself. Many have identified *Who's That Knocking at My Door* as a sketch for *Mean Streets*, but it really was about a film artist openly beginning to express himself. Scorsese set out to put his heart and soul on the screen. Scorsese's most significant achievement with *Who's That Knocking at My Door* was a debunking of an Italian-American stereotype. Finally a *paisan*, one of their own, put the truth about the culture on the screen.

11

The Sicilian Butcher

Most film directors have a particular aspect of the motion picture process that expresses their cinematic strength. Martin Scorsese is an "editing" director. Others considered "editing" directors are Sergei Eisenstein, Akira Kurosawa, Sam Peckinpah, John Woo, David Lean, Bob Fosse, and Oliver Stone.

To be an "editing" director doesn't mean the director necessarily performs the physical act of editing, actually operating the Moviola, KEM, Steenbeck, and splicer during the film technology era or an Avid, Final Cut Pro, and a mouse in the current landscape of nonlinear, computer editing. Peckinpah, Stone, and Bob Fosse composed their films and shot them with a distinctive dynamic editing structure in mind and took a proactive role during the postproduction process as they collaborated through the hands of the credited editor or editors; Kurosawa and David Lean have been credited with actually editing some of their films.

Martin Scorsese is recognized in both circumstances. His contribution to the art of film editing is undeniable. The artistic relationship between Scorsese and Thelma Schoonmaker is well documented and deserved. On each Scorsese film since *Raging Bull they* edit the film together. Schoonmaker may be operating the tools but both are making every decision. Scorsese understands the postproduction process like an editor. His actual material achievements as an editor have become urban legend among cineastes, critics, theorists, academics, and historians. However, when the record is carefully examined, Scorsese's editing accomplishments have been exaggerated to mythic proportions.

The written documentation on Scorsese's involvement on the Oscar-winning documentary about the Woodstock festival has fueled the impression that he was the major force behind the direction of the landmark film and the principal force behind the editing of the multiimaged film that revolutionized the manner in which music was captured on film.

Maria T. Miliora in *The Scorsese Psyche on Screen: Roots of Themes and Characters in the Films* claims, "Scorsese also co-edited *Woodstock* (1970), an epic film that recorded the historic rock festival." Les Keyser writes, "*Woodstock* eventually won the Academy Award for Best Documentary feature in 1970 for its putative director, Wadleigh, and for its putative assistant directors, Scorsese and Thelma Schoonmaker" (even though the Oscar actually was given to producer Bob Maurice from the Wadleigh-Maurice production company). Keyser continues, "Accurate credits for films have always been a tricky issue, but in the case of *Woodstock* the matter is especially tangled. Schoonmaker was also mentioned as a candidate for an editing Oscar for *Woodstock*, yet most agree that Scorsese played an equal role in editing the literally hundreds of hours of footage shot during the concert." Michael Pye and Lynda Myles in *The Movie Brats: How The Film Generation Took Over Hollywood* state that Scorsese cut *Woodstock* "with his friend Michael Wadleigh." Lawrence S. Friedman in *The Cinema of Martin Scorsese* states Scorsese was the "supervising editor" on *Woodstock*. In *American Film Now: The People, The Power, The Money, The Movies*, James Monaco writes, "In 1969–70, he (Scorsese) worked as assistant director and supervising editor on *Woodstock*, the most successful and still the best of concert music films. Michael Wadleigh (né Wadley) was credited as director, but the real honors go out to Martin Scorsese. The crew came back with an overwhelming amount of footage—more than one hundred hours by some accounts. The real creative job lay in reducing this amorphous mass of raw material to a running time of three hours and giving it shape and pace. *Woodstock* remains one of the most notable models of the craft of editing since the Steenbeck editing table was invented. Its thoughtful and moving use of the split screen (which allowed another hour or two of footage to be squeezed in) has never been equaled."

Over the decades Scorsese has been honest about his participation on the production and postproduction of *Woodstock*. He hasn't overstated his actual participation during the shooting of the concert or in postproduction of the massive project. He has repeatedly stated that his biggest contribution to the editing of *Woodstock* was for the *Country Joe and the Fish* segment. Because of the documentary conditions under which *Woodstock* was filmed, there were instances when the sound was less than industry standard. Vietnam Vet turned antiwar activist/hippie/and West Coast counterculture rock star Country Joe McDonald looked out at the massive audience while they were playing their particular form of psychedelic/blues rock and realized his band was not making much of an impression. He addressed the throngs and yelled, "Give me an F," and a quarter of a million yelled "F" in response. When Joe was finished spelling and had completed his repetitive call, "What's that spell?" With the audience gleefully shouting the four-letter word, the band played what became the national anthem of the Woodstock nation, "The Fixin' to Die Rag," a blistering satire about America's military involvement in Southeast Asia.

When the dailies were screened Wadleigh, Schoonmaker, and Scorsese were immediately aware that these iconic lyrics were not very clear. Scorsese had a suggestion that was used in the film and encouraged millions of viewers over the decades to join in with Country Joe to send an antiwar message to Washington. His suggestion—"follow the bouncing ball."

As Country Joe sang, the lyrics appeared graphically in the lower third of the screen while an animated ball bounced from word to word to keep all the sing-a-longs in synch with the screen.

According to film historian Gene Stavis, "The 'bouncing ball' actually goes back to the silent days when audiences would sing along to live music. After sound it was a natural, everybody used it. There was a famous series actually called the Bouncing Ball series produced by Max Fleischer for Paramount. These were cartoons interspersed with live-action sequences featuring well-known jazz musicians of the day. Sometimes Betty Boop was the star, sometimes a dog named Scrappy. Some of the musicians involved were Cab Calloway, Duke Ellington, and the Mills Brothers."

As a film scholar Scorsese would have been well aware of this convention. Members of Scorsese's generation might recall these bouncing ball sing-alongs run in between double bills, newsreels, and other short subjects at their neighborhood movie house during the 1950s.

Paradigm Films was a New York production company founded in the mid-sixties by Scorsese's classmates Michael Wadleigh and John Binder. Thelma Schoonmaker was working for a documentary producer who hired Paradigm, a nonunion unit for a few of their projects. She then started working for Paradigm as an editor on their productions. Scorsese often worked as an editor on Paradigm projects. Michael Wadleigh was considered more of a leader than a production company boss. Paradigm became an outside contractor for the popular *Merv Griffin* show. The production company was known for its experimental approach to filmmaking, which appealed to the growing under-thirty audience.

At Paradigm Scorsese's approach to postproduction was considered "two-fisted" and he was dubbed "The Sicilian Butcher." Thelma Schoonmaker was the chief editor at Paradigm who worked on or supervised everything that passed through the company. Teletape was a regular client who got them the Merv Griffin assignment. They also produced a series of spots for Ringling Brothers, Barnum, and Bailey Circus.

Scorsese was a regular presence at Paradigm. He would drop by to show the crew films he discovered. His passion and knowledge of cinema was an inspiration for the counterculture businessmen who managed to make a living in filmmaking in New York. They all looked like hippies but were highly professional, very skilled, and progressive filmmakers.

Scorsese arrived at Woodstock with cameraman Ted Churchill carting tons of equipment necessary to pull off the job. For Scorsese the Woodstock Festival was a culture shock. He was wearing a white dress shirt with cuff links consistent with his old-school Italian-American identity.

Michael Wadleigh is the credited director of *Woodstock*. When the film was released he was generally unknown in the national and global film community, but in the New York film scene he was a highly respected documentarian and admired for his abilities with the handheld camera. His only fictional feature credit came in 1981 on the horror film *Wolfen*. Over time, as Scorsese and Thelma Schoonmaker became major film personalities, the negative buzz about Wadleigh's participation on *Woodstock* grew. The assumption was that Scorsese *really* directed the cameras and action during the concert, was a major presence and authority in the editing room, and that Schoonmaker literally edited the film herself and through supervision of the main editing team of Stan Warnow, Jere Huggins, and Yeu-Ben Yee.

In fact Wadleigh was in total control of the project as its director and gave *Woodstock* its vision. His experiments with multiple screen images as applied to a concert film and the forceful direction of camerawork, which dominates many of the musical sequences, have their basis in fact. Scorsese's brilliant use of music throughout his directorial career and Schoonmaker's dynamic editing style could lead the uninformed to believe that the most famous and accomplished director/editor team in film history were the true auteurs of *Woodstock*—but that would be the stuff of urban legend and not historical reality.

Wadleigh brought Scorsese and Schoonmaker onto the project as assistant directors during the three-day event. Along with the cameramen they were hooked into a jury-rigged communication system that, in theory, would allow them to talk to each other. Wadleigh directed his own camera position and gave orders and suggestions to the other cameramen. Just prior to the concert, Wadleigh, Scorsese, and Schoonmaker went through every act slated to perform and utilizing their substantial knowledge about the music of the American Rock renaissance, they came up with a plan on how to approach each act cinematically.

Although there are no written accounts of these plans, Scorsese's immaculate track record in visualizing music and linking lyric and tone to emotion and soul would guarantee impressive results, like those he demonstrated later on *The Last Waltz* for which every shot, lyric, and note of a performance was storyboarded.

Martin Andrews, a technical wizard for Paradigm films, came up with a two-way telex-type system that would allow the cameramen to communicate with assistant directors Scorsese and Schoonmaker. Andrews began with headsets that had microphones attached and an amplifier. With an hour to go before the concert's kickoff, Andrews hammered large nails into a wooden board and hand-secured the cable wires to the metal nails to make electrical connections from the headsets to the amplifier. Just as the first performer, Richie Havens, hit the stage the system came alive allowing Scorsese to talk to the cameramen and cue them to the shots he and Wadleigh had worked out—but factors proved the old adage about "the best laid plans."

Just before the concert began Wadleigh gave final instructions to the cameramen who had been handpicked for their self-reliance and interpretive abilities. He told them to trust their artistic judgment, to shoot what they saw in front of them, and to use the camera as an extension of their mind, body, and soul connections.

This inspiration and gift of personal freedom began from the very first act and continued act after act for the three days. No formulaic or preplanned style was forced; each cameraman reacted to every act as the spirit of the performers moved them.

Scorsese immediately began cuing the cameramen to moments in songs where the preconceived ideas he and Wadleigh discussed were to occur. The roar of the music and the electronic screeches and squeals pouring into the ears of the cameramen caused them to rip their headsets off and charge full ahead to film the music as they felt it coming back to them. Even during a casual viewing of *Woodstock* it is evident that the cameramen were performing along with musicians executing daring angles and handheld camera movements in a music and dance of their own.

"Martin Scorsese and Michael Wadleigh had hoped to be able to direct the many cameramen on the stage through headsets and plan concerted camera moves at some dramatic moment in a song," Thelma

Schoonmaker told Dale Bell, the associate producer of *Woodstock* for his oral history book on the making of the film, "But for some reason the cameramen were getting loud squeals in their headsets, and you see them ripping their headsets off simultaneously, which effectively put an end to any attempts to plan camera moves."

The cuing from Scorsese and Schoonmaker continued on through the concert, information was relayed, but in no shape or form is it fair to say that the startling and fresh results, which were to influence MTV, documentaries, and music on film had been directed by either assistant director. In general Woodstock was a festival where the planning was overtaken by the lifeblood and spirit of those who participated in it, on and in front of the stage—it was a seminal twentieth-century cultural event that celebrated tribal youth and their dream for freedom and peace.

Warner Brothers insisted on getting the film out immediately to cash in on the spirit and immediacy of the times. The first step was to synch up the 350,000 feet of 16-mm film that had been shot at Woodstock, which was comprised of 875 cans of exposed raw stock, a total of 175 hours of film. Normally on a fiction film or most documentaries each camera roll is slated so the editor has a visual and aural reference to put the separate picture and track into dead-on lip synch. None of the *Woodstock* material was slated, each and every roll had to be sunk by eye and ear.

Scorsese took on what became an impossible task, synching the footage of The Grateful Dead. There was not enough light to produce a serviceable image. Brian De Palma visited Paradigm while his friend desperately struggled to find synch points. Scorsese was a big fan of the penultimate West Coast jam band and wanted them in the film. De Palma urged him to give up and eventually Scorsese admitted defeat.

When the dailies were all in sync the first viewing of the material took place in a makeshift screening room at Paradigm. The process took over ten fifteen-hour days to screen every foot of film photographed during the festival. Wadleigh and Schoonmaker watched every frame, taking notes as they closely looked for the film in the ocean of footage. Scorsese and the editing team of Warnow, Yee, and Huggins were always close at hand, but did not screen the entirety of the available material. It was essential for the director and supervising editor because they would be responsible for the look of the film, the longest single optical ever created, an editorial feat that included a constant shifting of images on a potential of three screens, running simultaneously on one strip of film.

After a week and a half of constant screenings of dailies, the editing began. Wadleigh, Schoonmaker, and Scorsese decided which editors would cut a particular act's song. Schoonmaker was the supervising editor on the whole project and took on the job of searching for and editing the documentary sequences that would bring cultural significance to *Woodstock*.

In addition to her nonfiction, nonmusical responsibilities, Thelma Schoonmaker edited the Richie Havens, Joe Cocker, Ten Years After, and Country Joe and the Fish segments. She also worked on several segments containing acts that were eventually dropped from the released version of *Woodstock*. Along with director Wadleigh, Schoonmaker was constantly screening cuts edited by Warnow, Yee, and Huggins, discussing changes and reviewing recuts until each scene was refined to the satisfaction of the supervising editor and the director.

Recollections about *Woodstock*'s postproduction place Scorsese's editorial involvement on two musical performances. Muffie Meyer was assigned to work with Scorsese on the Sha-Na-Na sequence, a perfect choice given Scorsese's encyclopedic knowledge about Doo Wop and A Cappella street repertoire. Scorsese had proven himself in this arena with *Who's That Knocking at My Door*, which made use of the song that inspired the title and other neighborhood corner classics.

The roles of director and editor during the editing of a sequence present a challenge to the historian. Who actually cuts a sequence? Is it the editor who is physically making the cuts and making a considerable number of decisions, or the director who is giving notes, suggestions, inspiration, and may well be the conceptual auteur of the realization of the sequence?

Meyer's discussion with Dale Bell about her experience working with Scorsese clarifies some issues regarding contribution and working method. "My first task was to edit Sha-Na-Na, a fifties' revival group. I had never heard of them before. They wore gold lamé and sideburns— way before *Grease* and *Happy Days*. They were fabulous and very funny. Six cameras 'covered' the stage performances. (The KEM editing machines had three picture heads, so we could watch three of the six on-stage cameras at one time.) I picked three cameras and cut them together, choosing the best angles for any given moment. For example, when one guy was singing the lead, I chose the camera that was on him. Then when two other members of the group did the 'do-wahs' I chose the camera that shot a closeup of them. Then I put up the other three cameras and added in the best angles from those cameras. I showed Marty my cut of the song. He was extremely nice and indicated that it needed a little more work. For the next two days, he sat next to me and made suggestions: 'Try it here . . . what happens if you cut there . . .' In a gentle, collaborative way, he told me exactly where to make each cut. And all of a sudden, one day, I got it! It was a revelation! In a flash, I understood how you could use the rhythm of editing to create a 'build' to create a climax, to create a kind of closure—in short, to create (even in a funny, three-minute, fifties' song) an emotional experience."

Meyer's reportage gets to the heart of the matter. Editing is a collaborative enterprise. Scorsese has proven throughout his career his intense understanding of editing. He thinks like an editor and should always deserve the accolades for those achievements. It may seem a semantic argument but editing is cerebral and theoretical as well as physical, aesthetic, and highly technical. Scorsese is a master nonphysical editor; his hands-on work is not on par with the artistry of Schoonmaker and the many great editors he's worked with over his career.

In her interview with Dale Bell, Thelma Schoonmaker seems to support the concept of Scorsese's hands-off editing accomplishments. "Scorsese, who is a great editor by nature, did some wonderfully witty multiple-image editing with the *Sha-Na-Na* sequence. After he left the film, we didn't change that piece very much at all. It's a wonderful little jewel of a scene." "By nature" implies an intuitive and developed sensibility toward editing as opposed to a direct and practiced one.

There is less clarity from Schoonmaker concerning the editorial highlight of *Woodstock*, the Santana band's performance of the show-stopping "Soul Sacrifice," which features a commanding drum solo by a then nineteen-year-old Michael Shrieve. Continuing her comments about Scorsese's work during the editing of *Woodstock*, Schoonmaker is more the diplomat and loyal Scorsese team member than a contributor to a complete telling of the story behind this landmark musical sequence. "The same was true of the Santana sequence, which Scorsese blocked out before he left. Wonderful. Stan Warnow finished the sequence, but Scorsese had done some significant things first."

Interviews with anonymous sources from within the *Woodstock* cutting room remember the senior staff of the production certainly include Schoonmaker and Wadleigh not being pleased with Scorsese's conception of the Santana sequence, which was more flashy than the documentary approach established by the director and supervising editor. The sequence was then assigned to Stan Warnow whose work is on display in the finished film.

Scorsese left the postproduction of *Woodstock* early on in the process to relocate to Hollywood so he could pursue his directing ambitions. Scorsese did, however, benefit quite a bit from his participation on *Woodstock*. Schoonmaker, personally nominated for an editing Oscar for her work on the film, did not appear to receive a career boost from the project, held back by the archaic rules, which then governed membership in the editor's union. After *Woodstock* her official credits are

Street Scenes—1970, a collective project supervised by Scorsese, and a special thanks on his own music documentary *The Last Waltz* released in 1978. In 1980 Schoonmaker edited *Raging Bull,* thus beginning a steady collaboration now running over twenty-five years. She won her first Academy Award for *Raging Bull.*

Warner's wanted to cash in on the rock doc craze of *Woodstock.* Fred Weintraub, the vice president responsible for securing *Woodstock,* put Warner's behind a French coproduction directed by François Reichenbach, a forty-eight-year-old Parisian documentarian who began making films in the cinéma vérité tradition in 1955. He had a particular attraction for the more curious aspects of life in the United States. The project to which Weintraub committed was *Medicine Ball Caravan.* The concept—Reichenbach and his crew followed a bus filled with a troupe of 154 musicians and assorted hippie types, and their trucks of equipment, on an 8,000-mile United States concert tour to spread peace and love. The *Woodstock* performers were a who's who of contemporary rock and roll and were destined to define the classic rock era of the sixties and seventies. The *Medicine Ball Caravan* participants fell more than slightly short of that stature: Delaney and Bonnie, Alice Cooper, Doug Kershaw, B. B. King, David Peel & The Lower East Side, and Stoneground featuring Sal Valentino of the Beau Brummels of "Laugh, Laugh" fame.

When the tour was completed Reichenbach worked with editor Gérard Patris, whose only other official credit is as codirector on Reichenbach's Arthur Rubenstein film. Fred Talmadge is also credited as an editor; his only other film credit came twenty-seven years later as the twenty-four frame video operator on *American History X.* Trying to make sense of the footage was a challenge. *Medicine Ball Caravan* was shot on three different gauges—8mm, largely considered a home movie format or used by experimental filmmakers and film students, 35mm Techniscope, a wide-screen process created by Technicolor Italia, which had a frame half the normal height that projected as 2.35 through an anamorphic lens, a poor man's wide screen used on *Once Upon a Time in the West* and *American Graffiti,* and plenty of 16mm footage, which had to be blown up to 35mm for theatrical presentation. The result was a nine-hour film that was a structural mess. Weintraub brought Scorsese out to L.A. from New York in January 1971 to get the film into a releasable form. Martin Scorsese is credited as associate producer and not supervising editor or editor. It was Scorsese's first time living in Los Angeles.

The psychological and physiological impact on Scorsese of life in Hollywood did not help matters of coherent editorial expression on Warner's lot on *Medicine Ball Caravan.* He was a young man from New York desperate to work in the film industry, but Scorsese was the product of an alien milieu. For Scorsese, Hollywood meant the studio system, movie stars, legendary directors, and films that were his daydream reality. He moved into a small apartment with Harvey Keitel, also trying to break into the big leagues. Scorsese left New York under the impression the *Medicine Ball Caravan* assignment was a two-week engagement. To make himself feel at home and to assuage his anxieties he purchased a poster of one of his many favorite films—*Two Weeks in Another Town*. For a filmmaker who created motion pictures out of his personal experience and the history of cinema, this simple act was filled with references.

Viewing the rarely seen *Medicine Ball Caravan*, it is readily identifiable as an artifact at the tail end of the sixties—an attempt to keep the Aquarian spirit alive in the politically oppressive and socially bankrupt seventies.

It is fair to compare *Medicine Ball Caravan* to *Woodstock*. It is a rock documentary in the tradition of the genre, which came to maturity with *Monterey Pop, Festival*, and *Woodstock*, in the late sixties and continued into the seventies, with *Gimmie Shelter, Joe Cocker: Mad Dogs and Englishmen, Popcorn, Rainbow Bridge, Fillmore, The Concert for Bangladesh, Ladies and Gentlemen: The Rolling Stones, Wattstax*, and many others in search of the counterculture market.

The cinematographers Gérard Patris (who is also credited as an editor) and Jean-Michel Surel have only films directed by François Reichenbach in their official credits. Both men photographed *Amour de la vie—Arthur Rubinstein*, and Surel was the cinematographer of the documentaries *Mexico-Mexico, Yehudi Menuhin Story*, and *Houston Texas*. Their work on *Medicine Ball Caravan* is cinéma vérité at its most chaotic, shaky, zooming camerawork, lacking in coherent composition and concept. Most of the film looks like it was shot with little planning, prethought or artistically controlled immediacy and vitality, in stark contrast to the stellar camera team on *Woodstock*.

Viewed out of context in a new century, *Medicine Ball Caravan* is barely comprehensible. It does cover a troupe of musicians, hippies, and counterculturalists on a road trip, where they make stops to hold concerts and spread the Aquarian message of peace and love. Unlike *Woodstock*, the public reaction of young people is mixed, and toward the end of the film on a stop at the campus of Antioch College, radical students become downright hostile toward the caravan. The directorial and cinematographic approach is so raw and undisciplined it is difficult to understand the flow of events and the purpose behind the trip beyond the most trivial aspect of spreading the "good news" about the youth revolution. Sequences do not have a logical beginning, middle, or end and there are barely any transitions in the film. We are either on the bus, in the middle of an Aquarian celebration, or watching a music performance. The structure is very forced and applied to the footage by the postproduction process. The multiscreen presentations are weak imitations of the brilliant work in *Woodstock*. The images rarely have an organic interaction and come off haphazardly and as a frivolous attempt to give the kids what they want. This is your father's (or grandfather's) psychedelia.

Scorsese certainly had his hands full with this project, one destined for the dustbin of rock cinema history. Scorsese was unable to bring a sense of a principled journey to this fractured nonfiction road movie and often contributes to the film's lack of cogent communication by crudely manipulating the editing, manipulating the material to form a shape it was never intended to support.

The stay in Los Angeles extended from two weeks to nine months as Scorsese struggled with the editorial structure of *Medicine Ball Caravan*. The prolonged strain wreaked havoc with his chronic asthma. In addition to the stress of the project and the unfamiliar environment, Fred Weintraub, who brought him to the project, left Warner Brothers. Scorsese was constantly in and out of the hospital dealing with breathing problems and respiratory attacks. His unsteady adaptation to an uncomfortable environment contributed considerably to his medical issues. Although he did drive, maneuvering on the streets of New York was not comparable to the freeways of California. Scorsese was petrified of the Los Angeles car culture and would only venture on local streets in his 1965 white Corvette.

Sleeping was a nightly battle. He would wake up in the middle of the night in coughing fits. An oxygen tank was always by his bedside and tissues were strewn all around him. After hours of breathing complications, Scorsese would take his asthma medication, allowing him to fall back to sleep for just long enough to arise cranky and out of sorts. This often caused him to be late to the studio. He was constantly relying on his pocket inhaler, which sped up his speech pattern and caused his expressive movements to become erratic beyond their normal hyper-New York velocity. Regular doses of cortisone to treat his illness combined with his transposed diet from Catherine's homemade Italian cooking to L.A. junk food, caused an unusually rapid weight gain.

As a fish out of water, Scorsese isolated himself in the California environment by finding another sealed society. In New York it was the Italian-American street guys of Little Italy, then the film students at NYU, then the independent film community. In Hollywood Scorsese's tribe away from home became the men who would be the nucleus of the American

New Wave. There were two salons available to them. The members were Francis Ford Coppola, the elder statesman of the film student generation, who had achieved some success with his early films and was now working on *The Godfather*; Paul Schrader and Scorsese, who were trying to scratch their way into the studios; Brian De Palma, who had been creatively removed from his studio feature *Get to Know Your Rabbit*; George Lucas, who was wrestling with Warner Bros., over control of his project *THX 1138*; and Steven Spielberg, who was directing drama television episodes. They gathered at the Coppola house in San Francisco and hung out in his screening room, which was bought with the financial bonanza of *The Godfather*, and watched prints sent over from the Pacific Film Archive. And every Sunday the nascent American New Wave tribe would gather at Fred Weintraub's home.

New Hollywood also established its salon headquarters at a home shared by two of the movement's actresses, Jennifer Salt, who appeared in four Brian De Palma films, *Murder à la Mod*, *The Wedding Party*, *Hi, Mom!* and *Sisters*, John Schlesinger's *Midnight Cowboy*, Robert Altman's *Brewster McCloud*, and *The Revolutionary*, directed by Paul Williams; and Margot Kidder, who also starred in *Sisters*, the horror cult classic *Black Christmas*, and *92 in the Shade* directed by Thomas McGuane, Kidder's husband for a short and tempestuous period. Every weekend Salt, Kidder, De Palma, Spielberg, Susan Sarandon, Paul Schrader, and other "young turks," as they were known at the time, partied and discussed how they were going to take over Hollywood.

PART 3

Break on through to the Other Side, 1972–1975

12

The Roger Corman Post-Graduate University of Sex, Drugs, and Rock and Roll B Movies: *Boxcar Bertha*

Scorsese needed a job to survive. His relocation to the Mecca of movies was not a calculated career move as much as it was a way to follow the next paycheck. Once there, he felt lost and uncertain—but he was in Hollywood.

Scorsese put himself wherever he thought he could find a movie to direct. He went to parties, production offices, and meetings. He saw every movie that was released. At the time, studios and producers, once disdainful of young people trying to penetrate their hallowed gates, were actively courting the *Easy Rider* set.

This was not New York. Scorsese was used to directness—yes, receptive because it would make money, or no, and downright hostile with crude rejections. In Hollywood no one said yes or no. It was always a noncommittal "Let's do lunch," I'll have my people call your people," or "I'll get back to you."

Scorsese had met so many producers and studio suits who never followed up that he developed a polite but skeptical attitude to anyone who called him "baby," and seemed to say yes to a pitch.

Consequently, when his William Morris agent, Herb Schecter, arranged a meeting with Roger Corman, Scorsese attended but expected nothing and continued to make the rounds.

In his cineaste heart Scorsese revered Roger Corman. He had studied Corman films while attending NYU, watching them in grind houses across the city. The man known as the King of the B's was the only Hollywood figure of his time who regularly gave young actors and filmmakers their start. Corman's genius was the pragmatism behind his goodwill toward young, untested, talent. The neophytes got to make a movie and Corman packaged it and sent it off to drive-ins and grind houses. He was pound-for-pound one of the most successful moguls in Hollywood history. Not only did he "never lose a dime," as stated in the title of his 1990 autobiography, he built an empire on movies made by and for young people and devised an exploitation formula that was a perfect box office business model. Corman was irresistible to the movie-mad kids who looked up to him as if he was the owner of a 24/7 all-you-can-eat candy store.

The films independently produced by Roger Corman and American International Pictures (AIP) form the prehistory of the American New Wave of the seventies. Corman was always on the lookout for trends and ways to exploit them in movies shot fast and on the cheap. Corman's unparalleled roster of America's cinema youth includes Jack Nicholson, Peter Bogdanovich, Francis Ford Coppola, Jonathan Demme, Jonathan Kaplan, Ron Howard, and countless other actors, crafts people, and producers.

Scorsese was an admirer of Corman's Poe cycle starring Vincent Price: "Back in 1960, another important stimulus to would-be-filmmakers of my generation was the first of Roger Corman's Edgar Allan Poe films, *The Fall of the House of Usher*, which had a beautiful atmosphere in its use of color and Cinemascope. We loved this blend of English, Gothic, and French *Grand Guignol*, mixed together in an American film."

In the sixties when the youth movement hit full force, Corman was there with a sex, drugs, and rock and roll catalog to fuel and satisfy the supply and demand of the generation raised on Hollywood classics but seeking screen fare their parents would disapprove of—flicks that would celebrate juvenile delinquency, fun in the sun, violent crime, horror, and rock and roll music.

During their sit-down, Corman told Scorsese he had seen and admired *J.R.* (the LA retitle of *Who's That Knocking at My Door* changed without the filmmaker's blessing). He offered Scorsese a sequel to one of Corman's favorite films, *Bloody Mama*, which had been released on March 24, 1970. *Bloody Mama* is the retelling of the story of the notorious Kate "Ma" Barker and her four murderous sons (one of whom is played by Scorsese's soon-to-be male muse, Robert DeNiro), who during the Depression era went on a spree of ultraviolence and debauchery.

On the fourth anniversary of the assassination of President John F. Kennedy, the film *Bonnie and Clyde*, produced by its star Warren Beatty and directed by Arthur Penn, was released and the floodgates trying to contain the under-thirties burst wide open. *Bonnie and Clyde* was a direct commentary on the legacy of violence in the United States and its current incarnation—the Vietnam War.

Corman decided to cash in on the landmark film, which linked a notorious couple of the thirties, Clyde Barrow and Bonnie Parker, with the antiestablishment tenor of the late sixties. *Bonnie and Clyde* resonated in a country torn apart by the War. Corman describes *Bloody Mama*, his first attempt at a Depression/crime/antihero genre, as being about "the power of family, blood ties, clans.... It was about the breakdown of rationality ... a state of pre-civilization when the most important, the only important bond of loyalty is family." Cultists and European critics agreed with Corman, but the under-thirty audience that had become the marketing demographic after *The Graduate* and *Easy Rider* largely ignored the film featuring a middle-aged Shelley Winters in the title role. His follow-up attempt, initially planned as a sequel to *Bloody Mama* based on *Sisters of the Road: The Autobiography of Boxcar Bertha*, would star young, sexy actors, would adhere to the Corman exploitation rules, and be led by a hot new director—Martin Scorsese.

After Corman's pitch, Scorsese asked if the film would feature costumes and guns, when Corman said yes, so did Scorsese. The producer, who was just about to get married, told Scorsese he would send him the script in six months. Scorsese left with the same doubt he'd experienced after other Hollywood offers—he didn't think much would come of his encounter.

Scorsese continued to struggle for survival. He finished *Medicine Ball Caravan*, then John Cassavetes put Scorsese on the payroll for his current film, *Minnie and Moskowitz*, financed by Universal Pictures. Scorsese was given the job of sound editor and paid $500 a week to do very little. Cassavetes knew firsthand the difficulty of making a living in the film business and not only gave Scorsese a temporary cash flow but also a place to stay. Scorsese slept on the set of *Minnie and Moskowitz*.

According to various Scorsese accounts, six or nine months passed and Herb Schecter phoned Cassavetes' office looking for Scorsese. He told the secretary that Scorsese's big break had arrived—he was going to make a movie. In the true anti-Hollywood spirit of her boss, she laughed and hung up. Luckily Schecter persisted and the message eventually got through—a script was in the mail and Scorsese was about to direct his first commercial feature film.

Scorsese was given the script and told he could rewrite it to suit his directorial personality within the Corman rules. He was given a $600,000 budget and a twenty-four-day shooting schedule. Corman told Scorsese he could do anything he wanted as long as nudity, or the prospect of nudity, was included along with violence and explosions every fifteen pages. Corman instructed Scorsese to create a great first and last reel and not worry much about everything in between. The nine-reel film was allotted just three days for the rerecording mix. Corman's theory was that audiences, especially those at drive-ins or in balconies at grade B movie theaters, wanted to know what the story was about, which was in the first reel, then later they would want to know how everything turned out in reel nine.

Set in Arkansas during the Depression, *Boxcar Bertha* begins as Bertha (Barbara Hershey) witnesses the death of her father, killed when a hard-nosed boss pressures him to fly his badly damaged plane to complete a crop-dusting job. Bertha meets union activist Bill Shelley (David Carradine) who is being stalked by the McIvers (Victor Argo, David R. Osterhout), goons hired by the railroad company. After an encounter with Shelley, Bertha meets Rake Brown (Barry Primus), a gambler who joins a gang of robbers on the run including Von Morton played by former NFL star Bernie Casey. The gang steals valuables from Sartoris (John Carradine), a railroad robber baron determined to stop Shelley and his unionizing permanently. The gang is apprehended when Bertha and company attempt to kidnap their tormentor. Shelley and Von Morton are put on a chain gang. Bertha becomes a prostitute. Shelley escapes, is recaptured, and is crucified to a rail car while his devoted lover looks on.

The Sartoris name was borrowed by the screenwriters from William Faulkner who had created the family of aristocratic pre-Civil War slave-holders in his novels. Scorsese contributed the character of Rake Brown to introduce a New York gambling con man to the Southern tale. Rake tries to hide his New York accent, but the fast-talking slickster who has masculinity issues concerning sex and violence is clearly an indirect on-screen Scorsese alter ego. Scorsese also created a cameo for himself with autobiographical overtones. Scorsese's cameo is as a brothel client who asks to spend the night for a few extra dollars because he doesn't like to sleep alone. He is not one of the two clothed brothel customers in a room with a standing naked woman as he has been misidentified by Jim Sangster in *Scorsese* for Virgin Film, by first implying he may be one of the two men, then asking the reader if Scorsese is a painter at the brothel—there is no indication of a painter in either scene. Michael Bliss in *The Word Made Flesh: Catholicism and Conflict in the Films of Martin Scorsese*, goes out further on a limb stating that Scorsese is one of the two men in the room and linking this character's invitation to Bertha and her john as a precedent to Scorsese's notorious cameo in *Taxi Driver*, when he forces Travis Bickle to participate in peeping at his wife during an indiscretion. The careful and objective viewer will clearly recognize Scorsese as the client asking for company to see him through the night, a personal reference to the director with a need for female companionship.

Corman encouraged the political radicalism theme intending to connect with youth unrest of the early seventies. Scorsese, an anti-war advocate, related well to it, but when he was handed the original script containing the crucifixion, he called the opportunity to develop the dramatic religious tropes that obsessed him "a gift from God." To maximize the Catholic metaphor in *Boxcar Bertha*, Bill Shelley was made into a Jesus figure, misunderstood and willing to sacrifice all for his beliefs. The Bible-quoting Sartoris becomes sort of a God-the-Father presence to Bill's God-the-Son persona, and these symbols are heightened, since the characters are played by actors who are actually father and son.

Boxcar Bertha is a disjointed story with a sprinkling of elements mainly required by the Corman method or permitted within very strict confines of the B-Youth Movie. Scorsese entertained his love for the movies with several references. In general, many clichés, such as the black Von Morton playing a harmonica in prison, are just a part of movie genre tradition. In the opening Bertha is wearing her hair in long pigtails in homage to Dorothy in *The Wizard of Oz*. Later, there is another *Oz* reference when Bertha says, "Oh, pay no attention to that man behind the curtain," as she enters her brothel room. When Bertha paces in front of a movie theater after she's just blown into town and is about to be given work by a Madam, she passes posters of *The Wife of General Ling* (1939), edited by David Lean, and *Drums* directed by Zoltan Korda, examples of Scorsese's childhood fondness for British adventure dramas, especially those produced by Alexander Korda, and one of *Desert Guns*, a 1936 Western. A poster of *The Man Who Could Work Miracles* based on the H. G. Wells story, is prominent in several shots as is the producer, Alexander Korda. This poster catches Bertha's eye. The movie title has also been analyzed by critics as a narrative reference to Bill, who, in Bertha's eyes, has conquered the power elite despite overwhelming odds.

Then there is the mysterious tribute to Scorsese's admiration for the films of Michael Powell and Emeric Pressburger. The credits state the character Emeric Pressburger is played by Grahame Pratt and M. Powell by "Chicken" Holleman. There are no characters addressed or identified during the film as Powell and Pressburger. Tracing the actors is also a dead end. Holleman has no other listed credits and Pratt played a small role in *Skyjacked* in the same year as *Boxcar Bertha*. There are no easily available pictures of either actor. It would seem to make sense that the two henchmen who track Bill would be named after The Archers, simply because they are a team, but that is not the case. It's possible that they play unrelated parts. The best guess is they are the two men who watch Bertha put on a beginners-luck gambling exhibition against Rake, early in the film. The real answer to the mystery is less intriguing than Scorsese's directorial motives as a film artist who uses referencing as homage and high narrative cinematic art.

Screen violence entered a new era starting with *Bonnie and Clyde* and continuing with *The Wild Bunch* released in 1969. Both films reflected American immorality toward human life in the Vietnam era, and each had a direct impact on Scorsese's approach to the violent scenes in *Boxcar Bertha*, which range from brawls to shotgun massacres. Although Scorsese did not carry through the use of slow-motion to emphasize the impact and damage caused by gun violence, he did apply the technique and aesthetics of the bloody results achieved in the two earlier films. In *Boxcar Bertha* the shotgun blasts are larger than life, and in a pushing-the-envelope tradition Scorsese had his sound team practically double the decibel level of gunshots and explosions. When someone is shot, it is bloody and ferocious. Scorsese's contribution to the depiction of cinematic bloodshed came out of his Sicilian roots. Violence can come at anytime, from anywhere, and from anyone. It is swift, permanent, destructive, and without thought or remorse, only the expressed sudden rage toward another, with thoughtless and malevolent intent, and the desire to display pure anger. Red is dominant in scenes of violence in *Boxcar Bertha*. Scorsese signals this in the main title. The words *Boxcar Bertha* are presented in a hand-painted, broad-brushstroke typeface designed to look like graffiti on the side of a wall in the hobo spirit of the story—except the color is blood red.

To prepare for *Boxcar Bertha*, Scorsese drew every shot for every scene— some 500 individual drawings. He would avoid a repeat of his disastrous firing from *The Honeymoon Killers*. When Corman came to Scorsese's hotel on location in Arkansas before shooting began at the end of 1971, he asked to see Scorsese's preparation. When Corman realized that Scorsese had detailed the entire film, he stopped going through the storyboards and left promptly, assured Scorsese was ready.

In the week he was there Corman looked at some Arkansas locations, which still resembled the terrain of the Great Depression, did his routine of scowling at the crew to "motivate" them, and mentioned to Scorsese that there wasn't a chase scene in the script. After convincing the director that a chase was a necessary convention, *Bonnie and Clyde* had memorable ones, Scorsese agreed and asked for an extra day and an increase in the budget. Corman flatly refused and the crew figured out a way to make it happen within the original budget and schedule. After the first day of shooting Corman left Arkansas and Julie Corman remained as the line producer.

Scorsese still had a misconception about the shooting of a feature film. When director of photography John Stephens, who had been a camera operator on John Frankenheimer's *Grand Prix* and *Seconds*, and one of the cinematographers of the indie classic *Billy Jack*, realized that Scorsese was shooting in a master shot style with little coverage, he implored the director to get more closeups, short shots, transitional material, and other coverage; Scorsese credits the experience of working with the AIP crew, especially veteran assistant director and assistant producer Paul Rapp, who Corman assigned the official role of executive-in-charge of production, as teaching him how to make a movie.

When the rushes for the first four or five days of shooting were screened at AIP, some of the studio executives immediately requested that Corman fire Scorsese and take over the direction of *Boxcar Bertha* himself. Films are shot out of sequence because of budget and schedule dictates. Scorsese began production with shots of the train that would be edited throughout the story, often as a transition device, to cut away when necessary, and for narrative purposes—the film is called *Boxcar Bertha*, so the train needed to be covered extensively for practical and aesthetic objectives. After watching reel after reel of trains going back and forth, Samuel Z. Arkoff, one of the founding partners of AIP told Corman, "There was nothing but train wheels going around and around, train wheels going this way, train wheels going that way. ... For Chrissakes Roger, what have we got here, a fornicating documentary on trains?"

Actually, Arkoff turned out to be Scorsese's savior. Arkoff's partner James H. Nicholson had recently died, and the executive production staff of AIP was in chaos. Corman was concerned that many of the executives saw his independence and great track record as a threat, and were scheming to discredit the producer. Corman was planning to leave AIP and form his own company after *Boxcar Bertha* and had only stayed on because of Arkoff. Corman was able to settle Arkoff's anxieties and saved Scorsese from becoming a victim of studio politics.

The love scenes between Bertha and Bill Shelley were comfortable for Hershey and Carradine who, at the time, were real-life lovers. The warmth between Hershey and Carradine brought naturalness to the scenes, which were direct and honest in a European manner rather than the more common sexual heat generated in an average exploitation film. Scorsese was able to satisfy Corman's mandate without contribution to further exploitation of their naked bodies by capturing the honesty and fun shared by the actors who claimed the physicality on screen (at least emotionally) was real and not Hollywood artifice.

Although Scorsese states that *Boxcar Bertha* taught him how to shoot coverage and inserts so there would be options and flexibility in the editing room, not all of the inserts were designed in a shot so they could effectively be part of the larger scene. Two inserts of a gun held by Bill in the holdup scene were shot in front of a rust-colored full frame field that looks like a wall. When matched with the full shots the only possibility to explain the background is Bertha's dress, but she is in the background, the dress shade is decidedly different, and her figure would not have filled the frame. Other inserts of train parts and details to give a scene a sense of rhythm are competently done and seem to come out of Scorsese's collective memory of countless Hollywood movies in which the insert was a staple of the production method.

Many Scorsese commentators have ardently attempted to find the cinematic DNA in *Boxcar Bertha* that would emerge in the director's next film *Mean Streets*. Some have exaggerated the use of camera movement, others the depth of the religious subtext, or Scorsese's expression of the French New Wave style that inspired his use of camera in early amateur projects.

Boxcar Bertha is a handsome B-movie with good production values executed by Corman's crew and above average performances; Scorsese's most significant contribution to the exploitation genre. The camera movement is generally tentative and less than expressive as if Scorsese were waiting to unleash his emotional approach to form and content. The short shooting schedule and minibudget prevented such displays of Scorsese's full-blown abilities and, in retrospect, what he is able to achieve is impressive and indicative of a large talent in the making. This is the first of several assignments Scorsese would take throughout his career as a hired hand in order to keep in the game making movies, while working to realize the personal projects that possessed and inspired him.

An examination of the use of camera, staging, performances, and Scorsese's mise-en-scène on *Boxcar Bertha* in Scorsese's first Hollywood film presents a challenge. Scorsese had not yet learned the feature film form. The process of *Who's That Knocking at My Door* was so chaotic that its strengths must fairly be viewed as an example of sheer will and dedication. Scorsese's self-expectations were enormous. In this context *Boxcar Bertha* is a successful graduate project. It looks like a movie, and it demonstrates that the director can capture the atmosphere of a story and bring the characters to life, while offering rich subtext. Scorsese's identification with characters that live on the fringe of society, and his ability to handle volatile human emotion, draw the viewer inside the movie. What the Martin Scorsese who directed *Boxcar Bertha* lacked in technical finesse and narrative refinement, he made up for with the pure joy of making a film.

The compositions run the gamut from assured to attempting the extraordinary, as Scorsese's use of camera begins to become an extension of his nervous system, at turns agitated, expansive, exploratory, and searching. Most impressive are several high-angle shots, which would eventually evolve into the Scorsese signature top shot and movement of the camera not to follow the action, not led by the action, but as a countermovement that reaches into the lyricism or emotional resonance of a shot or scene. One example of the daring visualist Scorsese would become unfolds in a scene where the gang runs through a tunnel, in which a dynamic use of the zoom lens first establishes a compressed series of boxes or frames that enclose the trapped figures, then pulls back to reveal the gang in an infinite Kafkaesque space that is a moral and spiritual one-way street.

After all of the struggle to get his directorial career going, Scorsese spent the best four weeks of the previous eight years of his life directing *Boxcar Bertha*. He continued to be the good student and learned from Paul Rapp how to light a set, shoot all the shots in one direction, and then relight for the next angle. Scorsese was not used to shooting out of continuity. The AIP crew was a tough and seasoned lot; they appreciated Scorsese's sincerity and love for moviemaking and supported him throughout the process. With that cooperation Scorsese was able to improvise within his shooting plan and give the actors the attention necessary to create dimensional characters.

Martin Scorsese screened a rough-cut of *Boxcar Bertha* for John Cassavetes. What the man known as the father of independent filmmaking said to his young charge has become one of the great apocryphal legends in movie-lore. The story is always told from Scorsese's point of view and he tells it just a bit differently each time. In *Scorsese on Scorsese* he said, "I showed *Boxcar Bertha* in a rough-cut of about two hours to John Cassavetes. John took me back to his office, looked at me and said, 'Marty, you've just spent a whole year of your life making a piece of shit. It's a good picture, but you're better than the people who make this kind of movie. Don't get hooked into the exploitation market, just try and do something different.' " He goes on to say that Jay Cocks advised him to go back to making a film like *Who's That Knocking at My Door*, and asked if he had a project he really wanted to do. Scorsese said yes, referring to *Season of the Witch*, the script that would become *Mean Streets*. In a 1987 article by James Truman for *Face*, Scorsese retells the tale: "Do you realize you just spent a year of your life making shit? Any director in Hollywood could have made that, and you're better than them, you have something honest to say," and then advised Scorsese to work on his own scripts, which led to pulling out the *Season of the Witch* draft. In an American Film Institute (AFI) seminar in 1975 Scorsese told the AFI fellows the conversation lasted three hours and at one point Cassavetes said, "Don't do any more exploitation pictures. Do something that you really—do something better." Then Scorsese told Cassavetes about *Season of the Witch* and was given seminal advice, "Rewrite it." In *Martin Scorsese: A Journey*, the director recalls Cassavetes warning him to stay away from exploitation movies saying, "You just spent a year of your life making a piece of shit. You're better than that stuff, you don't do that again." He asked me if I didn't have something I really wanted to do. I told him I had this script called *Season of the Witch*, but that it needed work, rewriting, He said, "So do it." In Andy Dougan's *Martin Scorsese Close Up*, Scorsese recalls this event saying, "After he'd seen it he took me into his office. He stood for a moment and he embraced me. 'You're a good kid,' he said, 'but you just spent a year of your life making a piece of shit. You're better than that stuff. Don't do it again. It's a nice picture for what it is, it's rotation, but you don't want to get hooked doing that stuff. Don't you have something that you want to do for yourself? Don't you really have something that you want to do?' He asked me. And I said I had. 'Get it made,' he said. 'It needs rewrites, I told him. 'So rewrite it,' he said." In an interview with Marshall Fine for *Accidental Genius: How John Cassavetes Invented the Independent Film* published in 2006, Scorsese told the author Cassavetes had said, "You just spent a year of your life making a piece of shit. You shouldn't be making films like that. You should be making a film like *Who's That Knocking*. You got something you want to do? You've gotta do it. It needs to be rewritten? Rewrite the goddam thing."

The significance of this historic meeting between an elder statesman of the New York school and a young man with the potential to become a personal filmmaker is not the way Cassavetes phrased his career-saving counsel; rather, it is the symbolism of an icon of personal cinema taking a raw and very vulnerable, young talent to the woodshed—that is the stuff of movies.

The editing of *Boxcar Bertha* is another issue concerning Scorsese's career as a hands-on editor. Scorsese has stated that he didn't trust anyone to edit his first real shot as a director. Like the majority of film school graduates of the time he certainly executed actual cuts by hand working on a Moviola and later a flatbed editing table. Directors desire to assert as much control over their films as possible.

Buzz Feitsans, best known as producer of *Dillinger, Big Wednesday, Conan the Barbarian, Red Dawn, 1941, Hardcore, Total Recall, First Blood, Rambo: First Blood Part II*, and *Rambo III*, is credited as the editor of *Boxcar Bertha*. Feitsans began at AIP as the assistant film editor of *Thunder Alley*. Next Feitsans was the editorial coordinator on *De Sade. Boxcar Bertha* is Feitsans only credit as an editor.

Scorsese claims that Feitsans was on location but never saw the edited cut of the film and that he edited the film himself, which is reasonable. The editing room is where most AIP newbies began. Feitsans had no established career as an editor and Scorsese had professional experience as a credited editor as well as responsibility for cutting his short films. This raises concerns over who is actually responsible for the released eighty-eight minute version of *Boxcar Bertha*. Scorsese's rough cut is reported to be as long as two or two and a half hours. The final cut was closely supervised by Corman and unidentified editors. Without comparison of the two versions it is impossible to discern editorial ownership. *Boxcar Bertha* is a professionally edited film, but not especially noteworthy for its editing. Scorsese is known as an editing director, his mature films are driven by pulsating and emotive rhythms, so it seems unimportant whether he made a significant contribution to a film with little, if any, examples of what would become known as the Scorsese editorial style of cinematic storytelling. Directors are often reluctant to admit times when they may have had little to do with the final outcome of the editing of their films. In the case of *Boxcar Bertha*, Scorsese's pride and defiance in claiming he was responsible for the editing reflects more on his directorial self-image as an auteur than what was actually accomplished editorially on the film.

Looking at *Boxcar Bertha* in hindsight through forensic analysis, the film has editorial energy because of the compression necessary to take out over a half hour, so it could be released on a double bill. There is no overall apparent editorial structure, individual scenes move effectively, but narrative transitions are awkward and the pace never really settles in to gain the viewer's confidence in a coherent story. Close examination reveals many save edits to solve coverage problems and to generate excitement when action or performance required them. There is a hint of French New Wave influence, but the material is just not there, nor is the inclination to impose it on what essentially is a drive-in movie. In the end, for a short action film, *Boxcar Bertha* has moments when it comes to life through its editing and many that barely can get a rise out of an audience looking for their sex, drugs, and rock and roll straight up.

Those who come to *Boxcar Bertha* well after 1972 are astounded that the film concludes with a crucifixion sixteen years before the release of *The Last Temptation of Christ*. For others who followed Scorsese in real time, the crucifixion of Bill Shelley reflects a serious artist committed to significant themes concerning his Catholic faith in an expressive manner displaying the belief that Christ suffered for our sins. Bill Shelley suffered for his commitment to the rights of the American worker and the common man. The facts point to coincidence and perhaps divine intervention. The crucifixion sequence was in the original script by the Carrington screen-writing team. Corman's selection of Scorsese as director of *Boxcar Bertha* was the producer's interest in young directors of the era who "had leftist, anti-war sympathies from the 1960s." Corman had a poster of the May 1968 Paris riots on the wall of his office. "It told anyone coming to us where we stood and which side of the barricades they had better be working on in Hollywood." For Corman, Scorsese was, "One of those early 'discoveries' who fit right in...a young intensely dedicated filmmaker from NYU's Film School." In 1998 Corman told his unauthorized biographer Beverly Gray, "Marty was as much a New York man as I've ever met in my life," implying Scorsese was a filmmaker of conviction interested in making meaningful films, not another facile Hollywood opportunist on a career track where fame and fortune superceded artistic integrity.

Boxcar Bertha represented a second chance to Scorsese when *Who's That Knocking at My Door* brought him only minor attention and after *The Honeymoon Killers* debacle.

Scorsese put his full efforts into making *Boxcar Bertha* a religious parable. Bill Shelley is a Christ figure, Bertha as his lover and as a prostitute is a Mary Magdalene representation. When the gang takes refuge in a church a scene is staged in front of a mural depicting Jesus, followers, and a female figure who appears to be Mary Magdalene. Sartoris holds his interpretation of the Bible over Bill who represents the teachings of Jesus. Sartoris is a traditionalist who points to the Holy Bible; Shelley returns by fingering his gun, which he states is his Bible—alluding to Scorsese's conflict with the church over how the laws of God are played out in a book versus on the streets—a theme that would animate his return to personal filmmaking on *Mean Streets*. For the sequence Scorsese selected Matthew 6: 19–20:

> Lay not up for yourselves treasures upon earth where moth and rust doth corrupt, and where thieves break through and steal:
>
> But lay up for yourselves treasures in heaven, where neither moth nor rust doth corrupt, and where thieves do not break nor steal.

There is a plentitude of vivid fire imagery in *Boxcar Bertha*, which on the surface is an exploitation element, but these images are particularly evident as Scorsese's representation of the fires of hell.

In planning the sequence in which ten shots depict the physically vicious process of crucifying a human being, Scorsese designed images to imply the force of the spikes as it is driven into the flesh. Just like

Hitchcock's approach to the *Psycho* shower scene, the actual piercing of the flesh is never directly shown; it is implied and heightened by editing.

The sequence begins from behind the wood on which Bill is lashed. Blood squirts from the direction of Shelley's hand, which is in the background. A close-up of the torturer hammering and the fluid sound design connect the images. The result is evident on a close-up of Bill, experiencing excruciating pain. A full frontal view reveals the group of men holding Bill up to the outer side of the train car. A top shot from behind Bill shows the torturer slamming the spikes into his flesh, but the impact is just out of camera range. Bertha is on the ground, watching; she manages to sit up and screams in agony. The McIvers look on with perverse pleasure. A wide shot reveals the men are finished with their evil deed. One of the men nails a playing card above Bill's head, which is a symbol for the letters INRI written over Jesus' head as he lay dying on the cross. In Latin it stands for Iesvs Nazarenvs Rex Ivadeorvm, translated into English as Jesus of Nazareth, the King of the Jews, to mock the savior. There is a zoom into the card and a cut to Bertha suffering. A return to the close shot reveals the card as the Ace of Hearts and zooms back to reveal the entire scene of Bill crucified to the side of a train boxcar. The Ace of Hearts is said to represent spring in Hungarian lore, it is also the season of Easter. The King of Hearts is the depiction of a regal monarch with red hearts, but the Ace of Hearts has no illustration—just a red heart like the sacred heart of Jesus.

Perhaps the most notable impact Scorsese had on the directorial experience of *Boxcar Bertha* happened off camera. One day Hershey asked Scorsese if he had ever read *The Last Temptation of Christ* by Nikos Kazantzakis, a book she first read when she was nineteen years old. He had heard about the book back in 1961 from fellow NYU student John Mavros, but hadn't read it. She gave Scorsese a copy as a gift and implored him to read it. Hershey remembers telling the director that he should make the controversial book about Jesus, the man, into a movie and should cast her as Mary Magdalene. Later he picked up the book and in his words was "enveloped by the beautiful language of it." It was an experience he needed to savor, so he read some and then put it down as Kazantzakis's story began to inhabit his spirit.

Scorsese has often stated with artistic pride that for the crucifixion sequence in *The Last Temptation of Christ* he used many of the same angles selected for Bill's crucifixion in *Boxcar Bertha*. That sequence in *The Last Temptation* is comprised of seventeen shots that demonstrate the dramatic power of a filmmaker at the height of his creative abilities; but in essence it remains loyal to the intent of the earlier film. Scorsese's integrity as a film director is centered in his consistency of vision and commitment to thematic concerns. A filmmaker who can dramatize with the same conviction the visualization of Jesus dying for humanity's sins in an exploitation movie and in a religious epic, has little to prove about his belief in art and spiritual matters.

13

Neorealism American Style: *Mean Streets*

Mean Streets gave Martin Scorsese the attention needed to propel his career as a major filmmaker. *Mean Streets* is a personal film inspired by John Cassavettes' landmark independent film *Shadows* and Italian neorealism. *Mean Streets* was the first American film to present Italian-Americans as they really lived, away from the Hollywooden and public stereotypes as garlic-eating, hot-headed but lovable, passionate people connected either to middle-class trades as barbers, shoemakers, and fruit and vegetable vendors; or as evil but charismatic members of organized crime known as the Mafia. It is a brutally honest film that in the Joycean tradition is so specific about a particular group of people living on a handful of blocks in a neighborhood that it teaches us about the larger world really made up of turf, neighborhoods, and tribal communities that exist within a social structure that has little or no influence on how its people conduct their lives. *Mean Streets* transcends the bounds of its characters and narrative to tell the story of assimilation, defiance, and the search for home—a place that only exists in the heart, mind, and soul of the individual.

Over a black screen *Mean Streets* begins with a voice-over, "You don't make up for your sins in the church—you do it in the streets—you do it at home—the rest is bullshit and you know it."

Charlie Cappa (Harvey Keitel) wakes up suddenly. The connection between Scorsese and Charlie is made immediately. Charles is his father's first name, Cappa his mother's maiden name, so the family is embodied in the film's principal character. Scorsese's voice is Charlie's conscience. Charlie is wearing a white tee shirt with shoulder straps. Back in those days, it was known to Italian-Americans who wore them as a uniform and to civilians who ethnically codified them, as a "guinea tee shirt." Mother taught son to wear an undershirt to bed and under the dress shirt, to protect from sweat, to conceal the body, and to ward off harsh weather. Dad wore his tee shirt beyond the bedroom out of tradition and pride.

Charlie gets up and approaches his wall mirror. A crucifix is on a back wall, to watch over Charlie as he sleeps, illuminated by a slash of noir light. Charlie contemplates not just his face but also his soul.

A series of three cuts, each moving closer to Charlie as he lies back on the bed, then covers his face with his hands, not in prayer but anguish, deconstructs the act of getting back to sleep. To Scorsese three is a magical number, a representation of the holy trinity, and a reference to Hitchcock's editorial technique, used to emphasize the state of recognition. On the cut dividing the first shot from the second, Hal Blaine's four bass drum beats followed by a crack of his snare drum repeated twice to begin the iconic Ronnettes song, "Be My Baby," which becomes the soundtrack of Charlie's inner-struggle and a musical identification with his past. The record is scratched, signifying that Charlie has played this forty-five-single over and over again.

Scorsese breaks the common connections between a song and a motion picture scene by entering the deeper, more intuitive role of music in consciousness. For Scorsese and his generation, this girl-group classic delineates a time when hanging out was a way of life and music was specific documentation of a moment in time: where you were, who you were, and where you wanted to be.

The main title sequence begins with a home movie projector in operation. Scorsese shifts from a third person narrative to a self-referential film trope. First a strip of white leader runs through the projection gate, then a series of home movie images that establish several of the characters as well as the atmosphere, mood, and context of their lives. The title *Mean Streets* pops on in blood red and fades out. The cast and crew are listed all around the frame of the image in a simple typeface reminiscent of the filmed typewriter credits used by many home movie enthusiasts.

Frame by frame inspection reveals that the standard white Kodak 8mm leader with the words *Date: Title* and *Processed by Kodak* in bright red contain textual material. Written in a black "Sharpie" pen, used by both amateur and professional filmmakers, the roll of film is identified as the property of C. Cappa. The title is *"The Season of the Witch"* (the original title of *Mean Streets*)—baptism. Borrowed from the Donovan song and filled with countercultural nuance, the phrase as codified in *Mean Streets* is Charlie's dream of a nightclub of his own, a place that would take him out of his Little Italy physical and spiritual prison. Baptism is not in quotes but follows *"The Season of the Witch"* with a dash as if it is part of a larger entity. The home movie constructed of actual Scorsese family footage and reimagined shots that form a whole focuses on a traditional subgenre of the amateur film amongst Catholics, the event of the holy sacrament of baptism. It is complete with a newborn, a cake, and a festive family gathering in celebration of a child identified as Christopher (after the saint who carried the Christ child, heavy with the weight of the world, across a river and whose name means Christ-bearer, the patron saint of travelers looking over Catholics as they travel by means of transportation, and metaphorically, through this life).

In the context of *Mean Streets* the baptism category represents Scorsese's birth as a moviemaker and a chapter in the career of an autobiographical filmmaker. Each film would be an extension of his dream to make movies that allow self-expression just as Charlie's Season of the Witch club would grant him the freedom to explore the man he wants to be.

For Italian-Americans the sequence is a treasure out of the secret vault of their ethnic experience. These viewers understand the gestures, the mode of dress and ritualistic aspects of the baptism party, and the shared connections in their closed-society neighborhoods. Looking at the sequence as a genre piece, it contains many trademarks: shaky handheld camera work, uneven exposure, subjects either directly addressing the camera, caught being themselves, or in actions required by the unwritten narrative rules of home movies: shaking hands, horsing around, and posing. There are color shifts, abrupt starts and finishes to shots that grow out of the sensibility of the picture-taker who presses, starts, and stops the camera out of his own impression of what should be seen, and when and for how long, without regard for the rules of camera and editing established by professional Hollywood filmmakers.

The home movie sequence is not in the traditional continuous fifty-foot roll form of unedited film; rather it contains many visible splices indicating it has been edited by its maker, Charlie Cappa. So the *Mean Streets* home movie can be categorized as the product of an advanced novice. Although there are differences between Charlie's personality and life and the personality and life of Scorsese, he is the on-screen representation of the director's soul and conscience. So the 8mm film can be interpreted as the precinematic work of a filmmaker. Charlie is interested in going to movies and talking about them with his friends, briefly touched on in *Mean Streets*, but explored in depth by J.R., his earlier incarnation in *Who's*

That Knocking at My Door. Does Charlie grow up to be a film director? How does he finally *get out*? Is it by owning his own club, or is it by becoming a personal filmmaker who makes movies out of his life?

In this scenario Charlie is making a precognitive movie using family equipment and footage, and material in which he is the main character. He has put a favorite song to *score* the movie and has arranged the shots through editing, not intended to create temporal continuity but to create a portrait of his life and environment. This is a cultural artifact that structures his tribal family rituals and captures his friends and family in their ethnic and social habitat, while he explores the aesthetic and physical properties of film and editing.

There are images of Charlie leaning on a car as he *hangs out*, and Michael (to whom the audience will be formally introduced shortly) as he and Charlie upstage each other for camera "face time." Charlie putting his arm around a local, his hand in the pocket of another, while still another laughs as they enter a topless bar. Christopher (in his baptism gown), the hands of his mother caring for her son, then cutting the cake to celebrate his birth, and Teresa (Charlie's clandestine girlfriend), and Charlie eating the cake. The Don of the family, Uncle Giovanni, enters the party (by way of associative editing, but the shot is really of him entering his social club). Johnny Boy, a principal character, is introduced as a member of the party (mysterious, an Italian James Dean/Marlon Brando-black sheep type), Johnny and Charlie together, and Charlie shaking hands with a priest as he performs the iconic, "It's sunny, I'd better put on my shades while I look into the camera and continue shaking hands" shot. After Charlie's encounter with the priest, Scorsese announces in type, "Director . . . Martin Scorsese," not only identifying that the movie is about him but also expressing his self-images as a priest, a gangster, and a filmmaker.

Scorsese as filmmaker is woven into the family/neighborhood scenes by short bursts of abstract imagery; car lights flashing white, and Scorsese's signature red, a swish pan leaving a face or en route to the next image, the process of camera movement, the movement of white punch holes created by the Kodak processing lab, a few frames of white leader, black screen, then white lights racing by, the flash of a red light, and a momentary starburst. One frame of Martin Scorsese and his actor/stand-in Harvey Keitel as Charlie, hidden to all but the frame-by-frame analyst, is an element in a cinematic time capsule, which says, "This movie was directed by Martin Scorsese and this actor is me, I am this movie," and, then, the side of a deteriorated urban building and a seminal shot of a street corner.

The corner is on the Lower East Side. The cross streets are not identified, the building looks like a warehouse. The shot that comes at the end of the first third of the 8mm movie is from a stationary camera, shooting in long shot. Then the grain freezes and the title *Mean Streets* quickly pops on in blood red and quickly fades out—the frozen corner continues to run. The image is urban and also symbolic of life's boundaries, the crossroads that face us every day. These are the mean streets. The red words make it a film title, the background an anthropological artifact—not a movie location. The corner, although without signs of human life, plays like a shot in a structural film by Michael Snow or Ken Jacobs, and defines the narrative strategy of *Mean Streets*. Each shot is the body and blood of Martin Scorsese, whether diegetic or nondiegetic, whether easily read or there to be discovered by a like-spirit or a possessor of hidden knowledge.

In *Mean Streets* Scorsese begins by celebrating the properties of the film itself. The Kodak leader, the visible splices, the join of a hot-splicer that leaves a clean double line, or the frame-wide field of a tape splice pressed down over two cut pieces of film joined for the act of collision, the animated punch holes, the dance of grain and chemical washes, the hand-applied marks of a Sharpie pen for identification and structural indication, and the glaring home movie light revealed in a shot of Johnny Boy, all inform us we are watching a film and exploring the nature of the medium. The scratches and dirt that dance around the frames remind us this film was handmade and watched, it is a living document. *Mean Streets* is self-reflexive when it utilizes the text of other films for its own cinematic strategies, but it is also self-referential by becoming an experimental film during the credit sequences. Scorsese deeply respected the underground, avant-garde, experimental film movement and embraced the philosophy of Stan Brakhage. Every time there is a visible splice it reminds us the film is edited with a handmade collage element on top of the two butt-to-butt strips of photographic images. This was the technique used in the diary films of Jonas Mekas and Andrew Noren, and the found footage constructions of Bruce Conner and Joseph Cornell.

The movie within a movie ends by transitioning to the feast of San Gennaro, the dramatic background of *Mean Streets*, with a shot of the feast lights unlit during the day, Charlie saluting the camera with an espresso at an outdoor cafe, balloons within balloons bobbing in the air as Charlie moves through the daytime feast crowd, then an editorial cheat, which appears to be his continuous journey through the celebration, but now turning to give an offscreen action a dirty look. This is the last time we see Charlie in the home movie, he is not smiling and glad-handing. The edge of anger he flashes will be part of his conflict between right and wrong throughout the movie. Finally, a full overhead shot of the feast at night, with decorative lights linking the New York location to a village in Italy, becomes full frame through an optical blow up.

A concise but evocative montage captures the spirit and culture of the San Gennaro festival. Arches of white lights transform and delineate the streets that are lined with booths featuring Italian delicacies. The crowd is deep and appears to move side to side faster than forward. The music played by a small Italian band featuring staccato horns and the crisp repetitive snap of a snare drum completes the transformation from a New York City neighborhood to a timeless village in Mother Italy.

The main characters are revealed in a series of sequences that encapsulate their personas. A disillusioned hippie shoots heroin in the back of Volpe's bar. A short stocky man with a predisco layered haircut wearing a loud-patterned sport jacket and a deep red shirt quickly enters, intent on relieving his bladder. He explodes with anger and drags the junkie out of the room, past vending machines from the Pixie Company and others that sell sexual aids like "French ticklers" for thirty cents and into the main area of what he calls "My place," a seedy, red light bar. Another man with an overgrown haircut wearing a forties' hat and black leather jacket, and identified as the dealer, is also tossed out of the bar. Facing the camera the owner composes himself after a blast of violence and frustration, which reveals his territorial instincts. This is Tony (David Proval).

Dusk. Under a highway Scorsese exposes how Little Italy street merchandise "falls off a truck." The camera shoots behind two boxy trucks. In between stands a tall dark Italian-American man, dressed in young Don finery, who supervises the exchange from legit to illicit as boxes fly past him. He walks defiantly into the backseat of a long dark car. A buyer is told the score are German lenses. The man, Nicki Aquilino (Nicki "Ack" Aquilino) rejects the product, which is not German but "Jap," a term left over from the forties; he repeats himself in Italian-American tradition for emphasis, to get his point across. These are "Jap" adaptors not lenses. The Don-in-training closes his eyes in self-disgust, he has the looks, the image, and the moves down, but not the street smarts necessary to excel in his chosen profession. This is Michael (Richard Romanus).

A young man approaches a U.S. mailbox on a street corner in broad daylight. He is wearing a genuine Dobbs hat. Back in those days New York men wore hats all the time in public—the Dobb's Fedora or Bogie model defined style and distinction. He puts a package in the mailbox, then briskly walks, and then breaks into a jog uphill. He is wearing a red-on-red striped Italian knit top. His hair has been fashioned from the greasier pompadour worn during the home movie baptism scene into a cross between the classic Prince Valiant style, via the Rolling Stones circa 1965, and looking forward to Johnny Ramone. As he barely makes it to a doorway, the mailbox is blown sky high. The anachronistic, seventies' Rebel-without-a-Cause is identified as Johnny Boy. Actor Robert De Niro was relatively unknown although he had roles in *Greetings*, *Sam's Song*, *The Wedding Party*, *Bloody Mama*, *Hi Mom! Jennifer on my Mind*, *Born to Win*, and *The Gang That Couldn't Shoot Straight*, and garnered attention for his portrayal of a dying farm team baseball player in *Bang the Drum Slowly*. Now, in a scene that runs only twenty-seven seconds, he made the most impressive debut by an actor since Marlon Brando's first screen appearance in the fifties' *The Men*, and James Dean's *East of Eden* in 1955.

Charlie is in a sacred, beautiful, and empty church. He is the best-dressed and best-coiffed of the tribe, wearing a black and white chalk-stripe suit, blue and white striped shirt, and a red tie. The camera starts high, looking down to express his humility in front of the Lord, then booms down to capture his hands folded and eyes upward. In voice-over Scorsese says, "Lord, I'm not worthy to eat your flesh, not worthy to drink your blood." Charlie in lip-synch repeats, "not worthy to drink your blood" in a merging of conscience, mind, and body of director and actor. When Charlie is thinking on his own, the voice-over is spoken by Keitel. To Charlie the church's conception of penance—forgiveness in which a priest hears the sinner's sins and then hands down a sentence of ten Hail Marys and ten Our Fathers, which, when completed, pay the price of sin and ready the resolved parishioner to eat the body and drink the blood of Christ during Holy Communion—doesn't work for him. For Charlie has to deal with his sins in his own way through action and deed, not prayer. The pain of hell is, in his mind, equivalent to "the burn from a lighted match increased a million times." He puts his finger over a holy candle flame as long as he can take it and meditates on the pain of hell—the kind you can touch—but he knows that the spiritual pain in the heart and soul is what he must deal with every day of his life.

The scene shifts to hell-on-earth symbolized by Tony's bar: the red lights, the pagan rites of pleasure, and temptation—it is here that Charlie is a respected street man, a holy man of conscience—a man with one foot in heaven while the other points to hell.

Scorsese combines neorealism with expressionism. A slow-motion dolly shot moves up the bar lined with sailors and locals. The background sounds are also slowed down and in contrast to the laughter and convivial actions of the visuals, the aural emits deep murmurs of subterranean suffering. Rising on top is The Rolling Stones and their 1964 recording of "Tell Me." Mick Jagger pleads to a lost love. In the context of the song's narrative, "You gotta tell me you're coming back to me," is a man promising he will change if his girl would just come back, the immediacy and pain is evident in the increasing nuance with which Jagger emphasizes the word "me."

Here "Tell Me" is about yearning, urgency—a cry for the physical and the spiritual to become one. Charlie Cappa wants his soul cleansed. Charlie is Scorsese, the boy who wanted to be a priest so he could go to heaven, until he discovered the pleasures of sin. The repetitive call, "You've gotta tell me you're coming back to me," is Charlie's on going negotiation with God. Charlie wants redemption but on his own terms, just as Jagger wants his "darling" because he needs her physical and psychic presence.

Charlie enters Tony's bar as a cross between a benevolent Pope, a politician full of false modesty, and a neighborhood Local Hero. As he enters, the room acknowledges his celebrity. He is greeted by Tony, the proprietor, grateful for Charlie's presence, many turn to watch him make a grand entrance, arms up in the air, his hands signaling his humble acceptance of their idolatry. Diane (Jeannie Bell), a light-skinned black topless dancer, is featured performing to the Stones; her soft copper afro, trim body, and elegant beauty radiating from a timeless smile and erotic charm allow her to transcend the ethnic code of exclusion of the bar's turf.

The nudity fits the Roger Corman credo taught to Scorsese. The shots of her body are primarily in isolation, offered as part of the story, and an exploitation ingredient to please the audience. The duration and context make fetishism difficult, the deconstruction of her body explores the mechanics of the dance over eroticism; white go-go boots pumping out the pop rhythm, while a profile shot of her arms serves to establish the art of the dance, conjuring images of a silent film vamp, or an aged one like Gloria Swanson in her memorable exit as Norma Desmond, extending her arms to entrance the viewer.

Charlie works the room by dancing through his fiefdom. As he floats past his adoring constituents, he is patted on the back by George the bouncer (Peter Fain), and approaches Tony in a front row seat admiring the ceremonial rites; many turn to enjoy Charlie's path to his table, where he conducts business and overlords the proceedings of the night— one young woman ecstatically returns his nonverbal communication by dancing with Charlie without leaving her chair. The glide is achieved by placing Charlie on a dolly platform, the camera shooting him from behind, also on the platform. The fixed position of subject to lens allows the viewer to witness Charlie's charisma in a constant forward movement in direct relationship to the action without alternating perspective interruption.

When Charlie reaches the dance floor he ends his heavenly float by stepping off the platform as he approaches the stage. His suit jacket slides off his torso as part of his own striptease as he dances with Diane.

Time and space at Tony's moves from moment to moment—not in linear fashion. Charlie demonstrates how he can keep his finger over the flame of a lighted match, more preparation for the possibility of facing hell. The moment is serious as Jimmy (Lenny Scaletta), a dark-haired, not especially bright, old school fifties type, and a big boy with an overgrown Italian-fro, look on. This is defused by humor so the men don't have to openly share their common fear of death and the Catholic dictates concerning afterlife. On each table is a votive candle, not a traditional restaurant or club variety. Tony's is a mock church for sinners who can't escape the bonds of their Catholic birthright, openly defying church law, but not its heavenly King.

Charlie sits at his table, he doesn't go to people: they come to him. He conducts business. As he watches Diane, now from afar, he contemplates his feelings toward her. Scorsese's Charlie's conscience voice-over acknowledges he knows she is "really good-looking." That is a plain undisputed fact; she is also black. He questions whether there is a difference. He understands there isn't but knows the moral code of his neighborhood would never accept it. It is the first time Charlie faces his true emotions about love. He knows his feelings are real, but his closed society has put it in stone as forbidden. Charlie is a man in conflict, riddled with guilt. Outwardly he looks confident and in *GQ* Italian-style. He is a charter member of The Rat Pack admirers. Michael enters by placing a carton of Marlboros in front of Charlie. Marlboro is not Charlie's brand, but it is more important to get them illicitly at street prices, than to have free choice. Charlie never takes his eyes off Diane, whose presence is maintained by Charlie's precise eye-line match in her direction. Charlie lets Michael know his appreciation by calling him *bubbie*, a Yiddish term of endearment for grandmother. (Sinatra called his closest friends "bubbie" to express affection and to identify a member of the members-only club he hung out with.) For Scorsese, Sinatra has sociological significance but his characters are the separated-from-birth sons not of Frank, Dean, Sammy, Joey, and Peter, but of Moraldo, Alberto, Fausto, Leopoldo, and Richardo, the young men of Fellini's 1953 film, *I Vitelloni*, who yearn to grow beyond their small town. Fellini's autobiographical film about the boundaries of a neighborhood and youthful dreams to break away is the official model for

Mean Streets, long acknowledged by Scorsese as a film that captured him emotionally and cinematically.

Michael is looking for Johnny Boy who owes him money. He leans on Charlie who vouches for his friend, not because he trusts him but out of self-obligation. Johnny Boy is Charlie's penance. If Charlie can convert this misanthrope, he can redeem his own soul. While talking to Michael, the man with the Italian fro has been brewing bad ideas watching Diane. When he sees a couple enter the area at the opposite edge of the frame, he explodes and leaps for the man. Charlie and Michael jump up and get everything swiftly under control. The threat of violence is always present.

Johnny Boy makes his official entrance into the narrative and immediately establishes himself as a hell-raiser. Dressed as a forties' wild man with long coat, Dobbs hat, brim flipped up, shirt, and a loud tie, he is in perpetual motion, always looking for attention and trouble. He is a Klass Klown, a cut-up so outrageous he is recognized as the outsider's outsider.

The simple act of interaction with the checkroom girl becomes a stunt that brings the activities at the bar to a standstill. Johnny is showboating for the two girls with whom he has arrived. He does not check his coat, but his pants, standing in his boxers making sure everyone sees his antics. Johnny puts his trousers back on, grabs one babe on each arm, and proceeds to make the procession down the bar.

As he looks down the bar at the swaggering misfit, Charlie is immediately engaged with his conscience as another Scorsese voice-over tells God he knows he is being tested. Charlie acknowledges his punishment for not playing by the rules and just saying the ten Our Fathers and ten Hail Marys.

The slow motion dolly makes the trip first to enter Charlie's mind as he stands frozen in a moment of truth, drink in hand, totally unable to control the whirlwind just released inside of Tony's. "Jumpin' Jack Flash" by the Stones infuses Johnny Boy's attitude and audacity. The camera first roars up to Charlie riding on the slow but inevitable move to his position at the bar just waiting for his mission to arrive. Then scores the bull-in-the-china-shop that is Johnny Boy, with his twin trophies, bragging, showing off, and shaking up the bar with his kamikaze defiance. The girls play the part in Johnny's game with total acceptance: laughing, swinging their hair, and flaunting their bodies, as they are pulled by Johnny more than sashaying of their own accord. This is a party in progress demanding to bring everyone into the mayhem.

Jagger sings in first person so the pure image and sound relationship becomes Johnny's boast. "Watch it," as his look-at-me behavior explodes into the bar runway, "I was born in a cross-fire hurricane/And I howled at my Ma in the driving rain." Johnny demands to be accepted on his own terms and the words "But it's all right now, in fact it's a gas!/But it's all right I'm Jumpin' Jack Flash/It's a Gas! Gas! Gas!" is his message for everyone to have a ball with him. The perspective shifts from nondiegetic use of source to comment on the proceedings to diegetic background music playing out of the jukebox well under the next scene.

Johnny Boy introduces the two girls to Tony and Charlie at one end of the bar. Without access to the secret code of Italian-Americans this scene barely resonates beyond the obvious. The girls are announced by Johnny as Sarah Klein and Heather Weintraub. Outside of the code there seems to be little difference between them and the other women at the bar.

Both Charlie and Tony are smiling at their first upfront look at the girls. Johnny says, "This is Sarah, Sarah *Klein*," and "Heather, Heather *Weintraub*," signaling to Charlie and Tony that they are Jewish. He met them in The Village at the Cafe Bizarre. Tony lets Johnny and Charlie know he understands by calling the women *"bohemians."* Charlie's grin widens. The subtext to these Italian-American men is that Jewish girls are *fast*. Unlike the Italian and Irish Catholic girls in their sphere of influence who would only have sex after marriage, Jewish girls, they believe, will *put out*, and have sex easily. Part of the Madonna-Whore syndrome, the *fast Jewish girl* mythos satisfies the male's drive for sexual release without deflowering a virgin who must maintain that status to be worthy as a wife and mother.

Johnny shows off in front of Sarah and Heather, immediately ordering drinks for everyone by pulling out a roll of bills. Heather orders a "Tequila," another coded response. Tony doesn't run a *bohemian* establishment, but strictly caters to a Seagram's Seven and J&B clientele. Charlie, concerned about Johnny's debts, especially to Michael, begins to question Johnny who tries to play dumb, but when Charlie is insistent Johnny warns his friend with his best cobra grin that, "You're embarrassing me in front of the girl's *Charl-ie*. Cappa is always the diplomat and excuses his rudeness with a mock formal request to see, "Mr. Civello," in the back room. As they leave Charlie instructs Tony to get the "matta christos" anything they want. This may sound foreign or even romantic to the outsider's ear, but it means, "get the *Christ killers* anything they want."

In the back room Charlie and Johnny Boy have their private talk. Their intimacy is for their eyes only, much the way De Niro and Scorsese developed their own communication style between director and actor. In public it is masked with formalities and repartee. Charlie and Johnny Boy like Scorsese and his real-life friends embraced the comedy and wordplay shared by Bud Abbott and Lou Costello. Their classic routine, "Who's on

First?" in which they use baseball lingo to confuse and taunt each other and appear to be having two different conversations at the same time has been riffed by a generation raised on their feature films and television show.

The scene was based on an improvisation generated by De Niro and developed by Keitel and Scorsese to add to the flow of an interchange that sets out to explain why Johnny Boy hasn't paid Michael, but goes beyond the subject into a stream-of-consciousness patter that reflects how these two very different men share a bond of friendship and understanding. The code applies here as well. Scorsese has often given the Abbott and Costello reference to explain the genesis of the scene, but to the insider it is layered with Italian-American tropes and has less to do with the beloved comedy team than with the specificity of the Italocentric storytelling tradition and the real way Italian-Americans speak—not the Chico Marx, Mr. Bacigalupe, Jerry Colonna, "Mama Mia, That's-a Spicy Meatball," or "The Olive Garden, "When You're Here—You're Family!" or Tony Soprano dialects concocted by the media and perpetuated by Hollywood Italians.

The conference between Charlie and Johnny Boy is a *sit down* to break through the formalities. As they walk past an old jukebox and a large rectangle, covered with a white cloth that looks like an oversized and less than holy altar, Charlie gets right to it by challenging Johnny's actions. "What are you *do-in'!*" Johnny plays dumb, always set your accuser back by playing the innocent. Through all the back-and-forth Charlie keeps it personal, "Michael is on *my* back." Charlie wants to know why Johnny didn't make his payment last Tuesday." Skipping a payment to a loan shark is unethical and dangerous in Little Italy, just the kind of thing that leads to unexplained deaths, and to ignore a Don wannabe like Michael is self-destructive. Johnny Boy knows he didn't make the payment last Tuesday, but he is buying time to gather his story—"Charlie, you don't know . . ." When Johnny plays *stu-nàde* Charlie keeps it real by telling Johnny that Michael is in the bar. As he turns to get Michael to "straighten this out" Johnny apologizes, the Italian-boy ruse to go in another direction. Charlie states street law, "You give your word about something you got to keep it." It was two weeks ago Johnny made the payment so he appeals to Charlie's sympathy—"You don't know what happened to me." Now Johnny is center stage. He goes for broke with his excuse, a story as amusing and entertaining as it is deceitful. Street names fly: Jimmy Sparks, Joey Clams. Charlie tries to follow but thinks that Joey Clams and Joey Scala are two different people, when they clear this distraction up Charlie acknowledges Johnny's verbal gymnastics with an "Aaaaaa." Johnny follows up the call and response with a little "Aaa." Now we are in the middle of the drama. Johnny is playing Bankers and Brokers. There is always an instigator in the story, here it is a "kid" who sounds the alarm that the "Bulls are coming." Johnny's narrative inventions are vivid. He picks up all the money on the table as an excuse to flee; of course he was going to give it back later but plans are foiled when he finds himself in a backyard with no escape route. His description is plain and simple, "It was like a *box*," preceded by "Minga!" (a word that sounds expressive but really is Italian dialect for the four-letter one). Cappa listens intently, waiting for the story to conclude so he can resolve the issue between Johnny and Michael like a true *consigliare*. Johnny goes back into the game to learn it was a false alarm. He reaches for Charlie's street compassion by saying "I wanted to kill this fuckin' kid," punctuating the line with a gesture that looks like he's about to bite his knuckles with an open mouth while a sound— unnnggggagé, not a word—bellows out instead. "I was so crazy!" Johnny knows all Italian boys have a hot spot, a moment when they loose it, not a meltdown but a controlled expression of rage that can come and go like an emotional aria in opera or an explosion of temper in a melodrama. Johnny got back into the game and got on a losing streak. Down four hundred dollars, Frankie Bones, one of Johnny's loan holders, is unrelenting even when Civello pleads, "Frankie, give me a break," but finally concedes by handing over the *escarole* sealed with the phrase, "Okay Frank-ie." Quoting dialogue within a story and entering the scene within the story is a way of getting the listener to empathize. They can see, smell, even *taste* the moment. Johnny loses the deal and needs to insure that Charlie is still with him. "I know you don't want to hear this," Johnny truthfully says, but this is another manipulation followed by, "to make a long story short," when he is actually making a short or off-topic story long to avoid the real issue. Then Johnny goes for understanding. He was depressed, went to Al Kaplan's to buy a shirt and tie; he tries to con Charlie into agreeing that his shirt is "nice," while stroking the new neckwear. Street diplomacy allows a man to tell his side of the story but when he goes too far, he loses the argument and all reliability.

Charlie tells Johnny that it is wrong and irresponsible to shop and spend when you owe somebody money. Johnny owes a lot of people a lot of money, but Charlie focuses on Michael because he is a friend, because Charlie put his own reputation on the line by vouching for Johnny, and because he respects Michael because he fears him. Charlie takes over Johnny's bankroll and sets up a payment schedule. Johnny hasn't learned a thing. He wangles money for "The Chinks" when they take out Sarah and Heather, and for spending money. When he begs for another five, Johnny yanks it from Charlie's hand with a playful vengeance then changes the subject to wanting to bang Heather. They end with an Italian version of an Abbott and Costello routine, trying to determine if Heather was on Johnny's or Charlie's left.

Johnny is back in action, quickly telling the girls everything is fine. Michael enters the frame and positions himself on the far left. He maintains his composure, "How about me John, I don't get a drink," a reference to Johnny's disrespect toward the monetary obligation. Johnny tries to sweet talk Michael by ordering him a drink, but Michael has a very firm grip on Civello's arm—a nonverbal message that Johnny must answer to him. Finally Johnny faces Michael who gives him a coded warning, "I just want you to stay on top of it. I don't want it to get out of control. I'm doing it for you." Johnny appeases him and Michael, practicing to be a man of honor but a man of respect, accepts Johnny not on his word, but because Charlie is signaling from behind that everything is okay, and Michael respects Charlie as a person of integrity. As long as he gets his money everything is fine. When Michael is satisfied his message has been given, he allows Johnny to step out of his self-defined "office space" just off the front of the bar and walks over with Civello to have the drink that Johnny so desperately wanted to buy Michael to avoid the confrontation. Italian-Americans never forget, and are very wary. When they send a message it is expected that it be taken very seriously.

An old-world restaurant supported and decorated with large columns and ornate arches. The magnificent voice of tenor Giuseppe Di Stefano (referenced by J.R. in *Who's That Knocking at My Door*), who shared with Scorsese the desire to become a priest, the struggle of living with asthma, and a pure love of his art, fills the dining room. The walls are red. Red in *Mean Streets* is the equivalent of white in an Inuit environment—there are so many shades that all communicate Scorsese's passion for the color of the blood of Christ and the tomato sauce that is the nectar of his people. Now that Scorsese has been *baptized* as a filmmaker, he is free to move the camera to express his energy, inner emotions, and his anxieties. The general rule about camera movement is that it should serve the scene, but for Scorsese, moving the camera is a way of entering the nervous system of the characters and expressing his own totally connected internal energy. The shot continues, dollies past a waitress, and then rockets over to Charlie who is patiently waiting at a table set with a deep red napkin, calmly attending to his manicure. Changing speeds during a dolly shot will become a Scorsese signature. He and his camera crew work miracles with traditional technology, radically altering rhythms to simulate the restless changes of an anxious, high-energy mind.

The dolly was created for smooth, orchestrated moves with careful transitions, but here it moves boldly at the sudden impulse of a character or the director. A new wave jump cut allows Oscar (Murray Moston) to appear.

Charlie is at the restaurant on business for his Uncle Giovanni, to collect the weekly loan payment from Oscar for his Uncle Giovanni. Oscar, a simple, hardworking man with a white shirt and pulled down, loosened tie, understands the way things run in Little Italy. He respects Giovanni and calls Charlie, "a good boy," but unloads his troubles. His partner, Groppe, has disappeared. Oscar assumes the Italian-American martyr position, "If he doesn't give a damn, why should I kill myself!" Oscar tells Charlie he can't make the week's payment but he won't stick Giovanni—he'll either get his money or the place.

Charlie's moral sense is shaped by the church and the reality of his situation; he has no choice but to work for his uncle who can make his own dreams come true, like owning a restaurant or a club. His religious training taught him about right and wrong, but the streets defined what is *right* and what is *wrong* in the Sicilian codebook.

Documentary moments add to the neorealistic tone of *Mean Streets*; a shot of police officers warily watching the crowd, a seminal New York image of a woman watching the street action from an open window; an urban communication and lookout system.

As Charlie enters the café, which is homebase for Giovanni, a man is watching the street then darts away; who he is and why he leaves is the nature of Little Italy—everyone is working a job or a scam and no one questions why.

Giovanni Cappa (Cesare Danova), impeccably dressed in a tailored, conservative suit, and well-groomed, with a just-out-of-the-barber's-chair haircut and manicured moustache, approaches his nephew cordially, with supreme confidence, and the air of machismo and power. He brings Charlie over to a private area of the store. Giovanni only has to pull someone aside even in a crowded room to let them know he means business. Charlie reports his findings about Oscar. His youthful inexperience shows as he tells Giovanni he doesn't believe Oscar's story, but asks for *consigliare* advice, even though a conflicted part of Charlie wants to *be* his uncle and enjoy respect and power. Giovanni explains that Charlie must be patient with Oscar. Giovanni shows his true motivation, his compassion to the good people of Little Italy gains him respect, but the Don knows that eventually Oscar will go under and the property will be in his domain. Giovanni conveys this by simply saying, "You like restaurants?"

In the tradition of neorealism *Mean Streets* is not plot-driven but structured around the rituals of everyday life. Little Italy is portrayed as a village in Sicily where customs and the lay of the land have their own rules. Two teenage boys, who can be described as "weekend Hippies," long hairs from the burbs, who venture downtown for action, approach a corner where a tribe member is keeping watch and gestures with his head in the direction of Michael and Tony.

The boys, who are from Riverdale, are looking for firecrackers. Michael tries to take full advantage of his prey but his overconfidence as a street ruler again reveals a fool inside an impressive exterior. As he first mocks innocence, like a prostitute waiting for an undercover cop to take his socks off, Tony becomes his able sidekick. The boys are instructed that firecrackers are illegal and to keep away from "the Chinks." When it is announced that forty dollars are at stake, Michael begins the scam, and Tony joins in. We learn that the best firecrackers come from Maryland and that for *forty dollars*, said in an angry and dramatic voice revealing Tony's inability to be a true player, he can provide anything, until the kid adds women to the list of mini-explosives. The boys are taken in Tony's boat mobile, in which Doo Wop blares over the radio to keep time. A red pepper ornament hangs from the rearview mirror, blessing the interior with Italian spirits. They drive to a spot where they are told to get out and wait on the street, until Michael and Tony arrive with the goods. When they begin to exit Michael drops the scam line—cash up front. Money is exchanged. They drive off with the dough except when Michael counts the bills as if it were a big score; he learns that, in fact, *he* was scammed. The boys from Riverdale were smart enough to realize if they were playing on someone else's turf, they should cut their loss to protect the risk factor.

They drive up to the front of Volpe's. Always wary, always expecting the worst, Charlie says, "What's the matter?" as if there was something wrong. It is as common a greeting to this culture as "Hi, how are you?" or "What's up?" When Charlie hears his friends have stiffed a couple of kids, a common and accepted manner of getting spending money, he smiles broadly, and when he learns the take was twenty dollars, he immediately says, "Let's go to the movies."

Times Square before Disney. A block full of double bill, grind house marquees ablaze, proclaiming Tony Curtis in *Suppose They Gave a War and Nobody Came? Borsalino, Rage, And Hope to Die*, and *Rider on the Rain*. These films appearing during the shooting of *Mean Streets* are representative of the kind Scorsese and his friends viewed during their uptown visits; films that would later be declared art by his generation.

A time cut goes to a full screen movie. The color is vivid, the lighting and visual style from the last decades of the Hollywood Studio system. A cowboy slams into another in a full shot, then in a medium shot in which he is biting the leg of his opponent.

To the casual viewer, Michael, Tony, and Charlie are watching a nondescript, generic Western. For Scorsese the scene was meticulously selected for references on several levels. The film is the New American Cinema icon, *The Searchers*, discussed in detail by J.R. in *Who's That Knocking at My Door*, so there is a through-line in Scorsese's incomplete trilogy. We are seeing the admiration he and his friends have for John Wayne. But Scorsese doesn't show the seminal shot of Wayne in the ranch house doorway—these shots are so obscure, only a film buff with an encyclopedic mind could identify it. The two characters fighting, Martin Pawley (Jeffrey Hunter, best-known for playing Jesus in the 1961 production of Nicholas Ray's *King of Kings*), and Charlie McCorry (Ken Curtis—Festus Haggen, a bad-tempered deputy to James Arness's Marshall Dillon on *Gunsmoke*), are beyond recognition in this isolated clip, but it's their character names and behavior that interest Scorsese. When the dirty fighting begins with the leg bite, the only line of dialogue heard is, "Marty that ain't fair." In the context of the scene we learn that the two men are named Martin and Charlie. So a two-shot reference is a tribute to a director, a Hollywood actor, by inference, a motion picture Jesus (Scorsese and Charlie Cappa), the inner life of a small boy who wished he could fight like the best of them, and a film that introduced psychology and pathology to the contemporary American cinema.

Watching a movie in a Times Square theater was an encounter of its own. As the camera stays on Tony, Charlie, and Michael a chorus of voices depict a scenario in which someone is touched and another is called a "fruit," a back in the day slur for gay. Scorsese does one of the voice-overs out of memory because these incidents happened often. The boys find it funny and laugh.

A full shot of downtown city streets reveals that tucked away on a rooftop is a statue of Jesus looking over the metropolis with a spotlight to provide the savior's light. Tony's car drives down a block as Johnny talks about how much he hates the feast of San Gennaro. To him it is an invasion of privacy that doesn't even allow citizens to walk down a street. The eyes of the world are on Little Italy during its run and this is a community that functions in secrecy.

Johnny, Charlie, and Tony arrive at a pool hall run by Joey Catucci, known by his street name Joey Clams (George Memmoli). It is located in the basement, and is dark, populated by men of dubious nature, where pool is a game of bragging rights, the hustle, and gambling. It is a place for Catucci to run numbers, a street activity that draws in everyone with a dream to hit it rich. In the Italian-American community running numbers was the entry level position for anyone looking to get into the rackets. Organized street crime used cash flow from the numbers as a stable income.

Tony, Charlie, and Johnny are there to meet Jimmy (Lenny Scaletta) who has run into a problem getting his win money. He explains to Charlie the winning number 235 was bet on a combination after Jimmy dreamt of his grandfather, giving spiritual significance to the affair. The old man died in the hospital room number 235.

Charlie is there as the diplomat, the arbitrator, and a man who can talk sense and mediate any situation. Tony and Johnny are there for support and as a crew for muscle if needed.

Jimmy, supported by his crew, tells Joey (who wears a red, white, and blue striped shirt over his white polo-style tee shirt) he placed the key bet with Saly, but the big man continues to stiff Jimmy, "Who the fuck is Saly?" Charlie goes into his "We're all friends here" act, which suddenly jars Joey's memory. While Joey pours Scotch to make amends, Johnny takes an attitude about his twenty-five dollar Dobbs hat, and Joey makes fun of the pride in sartorial prices as Scorsese depicted in *It's Not Just You Murray*, by firing back, "These are two dollar sneakers." Johnny is irritated at the volume of the music from the jukebox, and the quality of women there, calling them "skanks." Charlie, concerned about the tension, tells John to keep his mouth shut, but by calling him out in front of Joey the situation worsens. When Johnny calls Joey an "asshole," the tenuous peace that can turn on a dime is broken by Joey who announces, "We're not going to pay!" When asked why, Joey delivers a defining line in *Mean Streets*, "Because this guy is a mook." Jimmy responds with the traditional street retort, "But I didn't say anything." Audience members who consider themselves devotees of street slang were as stymied by the word as the man on the receiving end, "I'm a mook, what's a mook?" None of the crew has ever heard the word; regardless Jimmy takes it as an insult, "You can't call me a mook!"

In a 1997 answer to the question, "What does it mean (really) to call someone a 'mook,'" referring to the *Mean Streets* citation, even Random House's, The Maven's Word of the Day cyber column found the question vexing, citing it as a vague term of insult. The Random House *Historical Dictionary of American Slang* (Volume II) defines it as "an ineffectual, foolish, or contemptible person." Grasping for further explanation, The Maven's gave usage examples such as "What a mook!" or "You mook!" Even an example from the *New York Press*, which refers to mooks as "not only outer-borough types and out-and-out greaseballs, but Wall Streeters, unattractive, and socially useless Eurotrash, advertising executives and Upper East Siders," lacks linguistic precision. Assumed as a variant of the nineteenth-century word "moke," meaning a donkey or mule (used as a slur toward a black person as well as a contemptible person), both moke and mook are of unknown origin. The earliest use of the word mook was by S.J. Perelman in 1930, and decades later in the musical *Hair* with the line, "Mooky-lookin' blond guy."

Scorsese and Mardik Martin get just the results they want out of the now famous insult; no one seems to really understand when the mere mention of it becomes a clarion call to mayhem with a roundhouse punch from Joey to Jimmy's unprotected jaw.

This single punch begins an all-out brawl. The pool tables switch from a game platform to a confined space to pound Charlie into submission. No rules, a few punches are thrown, grabbing, clawing, and full body assaults are in progress. A vérité handheld camera follows Jimmy in desperate retreat knocking over everything in sight, including a rack of pool sticks. Charlie is defenseless and on his back; Johnny stands on top of a table with a hunk of broken pool cue fighting off his enemies like John Wayne in a Western or War movie, encouraging all takers. Johnny is lithe as a dancer choreographing every swing, kick, and turn fighting a 360-degree battle. The handheld shots are as visceral as live television and encompass the scope of the indoor street fight.

Charlie finally is able to get up, suit and tie intact, and breaks up Joey slamming on Tony, as two police officers come on to the scene.

A time cut finds both groups separated and bent over, legs spread, and hands spread as officer Davis (D'Mitch Davis) frisks them. The Little Italy distain for the police they find less honorable is demonstrated when Davis finds a small penknife in Charlie's pocket and carries on about the law until he is given "carfare," a code for graft. Davis is not satisfied with going to *New Jersey* and settles on *Philadelphia*, which becomes the price of running business for Joey Clams. Davis and his partner leave and Joey offers, "The drink we never had before." This time they finish the first part of the ritual without incident, but when Joey gives Jimmy the money another dispute arises over trust, whether Jimmy needs to count the bills or not. This time Joey tries to be the peacemaker and reaches out in friendship to Johnny. Once again, out of nowhere, a volatile change in temperament occurs by Johnny's outburst, "Don't fucking touch me, scumbag." Joey punches Johnny; the crew quickly works over Joey and foils the crew's involvement. As they run up the stairs, Joey gives them the Italian salute, a stiff arm bent at the elbow, supported by a left arm direct cross forming a defiant "L" yelling, "That's for you! Up your ass! You come back here again you'll find out what's going to happen to you! Douche bags."

Back at Volpe's Tony takes the opportunity to disassemble Charlie's belief system by relating a story to Johnny to expose Cappa's moral weakness. On a retreat a priest told Charlie that before marriage a couple pulled their car over to the side giving in to the temptation of sin. Tony indicates that they "made it" by pumping his arm straight fisted in a horizontal position indicating intercourse. Suddenly a Mack truck plows into the couple, killing them instantly. The tale is not for news value but for the fire and brimstone of the Ten Commandments. Three years earlier, at a retreat, a priest told Tony the same story. Charlie becomes agitated as Tony drives home his point: the church is a business, an organization. Charlie counters that he was mad because the priest lied to him. "Why do you let those guys get to you?" Tony asks, partly to help, partly to dominate his friend, proving he is tougher than Charlie, who says, "They're not supposed to be guys!" "That's where you and I differ," Tony states. The conflict between the two friends is the director's conflict as he explores the characters for answers to his own duality in the eternal struggle between the sacred and the profane. A final irony is delivered when Tony says with contempt, "You want to be saved," implying he is more independent and confident of his place in life than Charlie, as the men's bathroom sign is in view in the background. *Mean Streets* is about men: who they are and who they think they are.

A mysterious young man (Robert Carradine) enters. He appears to be wearing his hair combed straight back, old school player style. When the music ends, a drunk, played by Robert's oldest brother (David), announces he has to go to the bathroom. After making it into the john Charlie laments life at Tony's. He tries to project himself out of the grim surroundings by talking about his dream to open "Season of the Witch," a club with class, action, and style. The moment is not about owning a restaurant but about getting out—the traditional theme shared by young people globally.

Tony's timetable for closing is existential, not based on posted hours, "When everybody leaves we close." Charlie is told to look at a picture of himself. It is a large swastika drawn in chalk. The moment is shocking, immediately evoking an anti-Semitic sentiment. Charlie has little reaction retorting, "Close, keep trying," and calls the artist a dumkoff as if he was a German officer. There's no denying a lack of sensitivity toward Jews; the moment also reflects a fascination with the Nazis felt by many males born during and just after the war. The aesthetics of the Third Reich fascinate them but their naiveté, sense of denial, and lack of social responsibility keeps them as uninformed adolescents who don't understand the gravitas of their unwitting attraction.

Closing up is one ritual that occurs every night at Tony's, the last hours usually bring tedium and boredom, the action has gone home for the night, and there's the wait for the last drinkers to finish their last drink, tally up the register, put up the stools—the procedures. After hours is another phase of Tony's. These night creatures aren't ready for bed. Charlie asks if anyone wants a game of cards after the formal closing. When Johnny says, "For how much!" his reckless gambling obsession takes over. Tony attacks Johnny where it hurts, "Scumbag, you can't pay what you owe!" In retaliation, Johnny flicks a lit cigarette at Tony, an aggressive street move that always leads to a fight as it does here. It leads to greater violence in *Taxi Driver* when Sport does the same to Travis Bickle. Charlie again becomes the peacemaker, forcefully pulling Tony and Johnny apart with the words, "We're friends." The undercurrent of unrest, resentment, anger, and violence are never far away. Behind them, on the wall, mini Italian and U.S. flags are intertwined symbolizing the forming of an Italian-American. In just one of the instinctive moves that De Niro creates to define his character, he pulls up his pants, and struts in front of Tony like a toreador, displaying his constant cockiness and ability to taunt over the line of the rules these men understand.

Both friends apologize but postclosing plans still can't be resolved, the two standards, going out for a midnight meal or any kind of card game are vetoed by the moody and obstinate Tony. After appealing to everyone left, including the mysterious young man who passes Charlie on his way to the men's room, it seems there will be no extracurricular action.

The drunk is barely standing leaning alongside the urinal. The young man approaches and from the back we see him looking on at the pathetic sight. As he brings the collar of his coat back, long-flowing brown hair cascades down his shoulders. The viewer immediately is fooled into thinking this is some sort of gay encounter, but without warning the young man pulls out a gun and fires three bullets into the drunk. At this point the uninformed viewer assumes a random murder is taking place. The cultural reference, however, is immediate—this is a hit in progress. Historically, mob hits take place in restaurants, some of the most infamous include the killing of Joey Gallo in Umberto's Clam House on Mulberry Street on April 7, 1972, on his forty-third birthday, the rubout of Carmine Galante after lunch at a Brooklyn restaurant, his signature cigar still clenched between his teeth; and the execution of Paul Castellano at Sparks Steak House in midtown Manhattan by John Gotti. Hits are also carried out in barbershops, cars, pool halls, and dark streets and alleys. The rules only disqualified carrying out a hit in front of a church, and in the presence of the victim's immediate family—the doorstep of a *gomada's* residence however was a popular moral choice.

What is perplexing about the *Mean Streets* hit is that neither hit man nor victim looks Italian or a hybrid, it's as if Scorsese was more attuned to casting the Carradine brothers for their family movie dynasty cache than for realism.

In another narrative turn, like the "beast that wouldn't die" theme of the fifties' horror and sci-fi movies, the violence moves into the main room as the drunk fights his attacker and the tribe scrambles for safety. Eventually a shot in the chest seems to end his life and the commotion plays out both in terror and as gallows humor. Tony takes charge and orders everyone out. George is told to kill all the lights. Outside the drunk manages to exit Volpe's and smashes himself into a parked car. The lights go out; the boys scramble out the back alley. Although Tony compels them to split up they all run in the same direction as a jump cut emphasizes the inept attempt at escape. Finally Charlie and Johnny get a ride with Michael, once again placing the banker and the debtor in the same space.

In the comic spirit of *I Vitelloni* the absurdity and irony of life continues to make the men of *Mean Streets* unpolished young mobsters trying to adhere to the conventions of crime movies where everything goes according to Hoyle. Two gay men, Benton (Robert Wilder) who is quiet, conservative, and respectful and Sammy (Ken Sinclair), who is drunk, outrageous, and uninhibited, ask Michael, whom they appear to know, for a ride.

This comedy of errors is the cause of Sammy openly flirting, Johnny calling them faggots, and Michael tries to do the right thing, "What do you want me to do, leave them in front of Tony's place?" Sammy begins to yell catcalls to all the men on a crowded street in back in the day gay parlance, "Look at that number!" The men on the street all stare at the car, attracting attention that Michael doesn't want. Sinclair's lines, most likely improvised at this point, include "Hey baby, I want to . . . " and a postproduction car horn blurts out the expletive. The recipient of the line gives Sammy a repeated Italian salute and the street breaks out in hostile reaction. His cover blown, Michael pulls over and the men are thrown out of the car. Sammy doesn't go easily saying, "I just got in," then calling them "animals." Sammy recovers quickly, and once on the street, goes into a strut saying to onlookers, "Hey fellas, going my way?"

Charlie and Johnny are on a deserted street in front of a gun shop. A backstory reveals the time Johnny caught a beating from the bulls to protect Charlie who looked after himself by running as soon as the police arrived. Charlie has street smarts and Johnny the loyalty to friendship.

Now the roles are reversed; Charlie can't run from Michael. Charlie has tried to reform Johnny (an impossible task) rather than physically protect him as Johnny had once done for him. Serious talk never lasts long among them. They exchange insults, some in Nazi lingo, "Swinehundt," and make sound effects like their beloved "John Wayne chin sock," long identified by sound designers as the *kerrrrt* placed on a track every time the Duke decked someone, later used in countless films as the definitive albeit unrealistic bare fist punch. The hijinks end abruptly when Johnny thinks he sees Joe Black up the block, another man he owed money to, and hunches down between two parked cars. When Charlie as lookout says he turned a corner, they engage in a garbage can cover duel. Charlie dumps a full garbage can over Johnny winning the battle. Charlie, continuing his novena project, convinces Johnny to come home with him. Charlie explains that his mother is out on Long Island taking care of his sick grandmother. The reminder that they still live with their parents creates a dichotomy between the boys they are and the men they pretend to be.

The inside of Charlie's family apartment is a series of rooms leading to a bedroom. Charlie and Johnny have no problem acting like the place is theirs because having the house to yourself when the folks are gone is another rite of passage. A handheld camera follows Johnny from behind as he treks to the bedroom. It is 6:00 A.M. and they are just getting to sleep. There's no food in the apartment so Johnny suggests going into his aunt's adjacent apartment via the fire escape, the street kid's veranda. There is a large crucifix over the bed. Charlie, as always the voice of reason, warns he'll scare his cousin Teresa. Johnny who has little respect for anybody and anything snaps back, "She can have a seizure and we can watch." Charlie does not find this funny and uses it as an opportunity to preach to Johnny "That's not funny, you going to be a jerk-off all your life? Grow up!" This is the first mention of Teresa in the text of the film. She is unidentified in the home movie title sequence and now the screenplay sets up her physical location and condition for further development. Johnny gets into bed, then Charlie gets out, as the one minute- and twenty-four-second take continues now following Charlie as he walks out of the bedroom and turns to enter the kitchen. Scorsese's varied experiences and influences as a cineaste flow into moments and scenes throughout *Mean Streets*. Here the long, handheld take following the action is reflexive of the Direct Cinema practiced by the Maysles brothers, D.A. Pennebaker, and Richard Leacock. By inhaling so many cinema styles Scorsese is able to apply his lessons learned in a manner that is less homage or a quote and more his own intuitive vision and hyperkinetic personal energy.

There is an envelope in the kitchen marked Charlie; in it are bills that Cappa counts with ease, flipping them over as he would during a numbers deal. His mother left him this spending money, a tradition extended to children who weren't working. Charlie doesn't have a legitimate job and as long as he lives at home his parents feel obliged to support him. Independence in Italian families doesn't come easy and is readily accepted by Charlie who likes to live large. He even takes additional bills beyond his "allowance" from a nearby cookie jar.

The handheld camera follows Charlie to the window as he positions himself to watch Teresa's bedroom window. Scorsese uses the following sequence as a meditation on voyeurism, moviegoing, and sexuality and to introduce the film's only major female character in a manner that clearly places her in second position to the men. Teresa, played by Amy Robinson, is one of the most fully dimensional female characters in the Scorsese oeuvre. It is clear from the creation and construction of this character that Scorsese has insight into young Italian-American women. Teresa is also burdened by the constraints of Sicilian culture and the church. Her epilepsy is an expression of Scorsese's asthma. She is seen as sickly and physically fragile but like the director has a dynamic personality and deals with the struggle to gain independence.

Her introduction is as little more than a female body of desire. Charlie watches as she stands defiantly in front of her open bedroom window and takes off her orange robe and then a conservative pink nightgown to reveal her naked lithe body. In Teresa's mindset the gesture is one of defiance and liberation. With the simple morning routine Teresa is challenging the church's position toward women whose bodies are temples for life-giving, not for display, adulation, pride, or exhibition. It is during the formative years of the modern women's liberation movement and although Teresa is trapped in a chauvinistic world, she is responding to feminism in her own way. Unlike women who embraced the late sixties, "Do you sleep in the nude?" era, Teresa remains conventional but is comfortable and even brazen with her nudity on display and in full view through the window. Does she know that Charlie can and does look at her from his apartment window? Is Teresa defying the establishment's perception of how a good girl should behave? Although the image of Teresa's naked body is clearly presented through a male view it is unlikely a Corman exploitation ploy and more an expression of New Hollywood's attitudes toward sex. In this personal film, Teresa's first nude scene is the point of view of a voyeur suggesting that cinema is a voyeuristic act. Charlie is expressing male urge to see a naked female body without consequence.

Charlie's specific voyeurism is not brazen, but hidden under layers of secrecy. He is watching Teresa through the Venetian blinds on his window, the bars of his fire escape, and then through her window. The horizontal of the blinds and verticals of the fire escape can be seen as a prison cell metaphor in which the confinement is more mental than physical. If this approach to voyeurism seems reminiscent of Alfred Hitchcock's work, the reference and inspiration is completed by cutting closer to Teresa with each step of her undress three times within the same angle, only changing the picture size.

The Classical Hollywood Studio System pushed the envelope in its final decades by revealing enough cleavage to give the illusion of nudity. In this sequence Scorsese lets the camera see the top of Amy Robinson's dark pubic hair as a glimpse of total frontal nudity.

Expanding beyond the Hitchcockian use of three, a fourth shot reveals Teresa putting on her pants, then cutting to a fuller shot position as she puts on a bright yellow shirt. As this sequence ends, Charlie begins to speak in a voice-over. A cut reveals the two of them naked in bed in a hotel room having enjoyed a clandestine "afternoon delight" like Marion Crane and Sam Loomis during the opening scene of *Psycho*. Charlie continues speaking in synch revealing the voice-over as a presound transition. Scorsese makes it clear narratively that this relationship is private, secret, and possibly doomed because it is not accepted by the societal system in which they are both entrenched. Charlie goes from spying on Teresa to disclosing his demons concerning her as he tells about a dream in which they are both naked. There is a large white bed, Teresa is lying on it, and Charlie stands over her. They are just about to make love and he ejaculates in blood, which squirts all over them. He forces a laugh; Teresa doesn't find the story funny. By beginning the account of the dream over the shots of Teresa in the window, Charlie is expressing his guilt over the relationship in biblical terms. An isolated shot of the two with outstretched arms forming half of a crucifix contributes to the Catholic theme concerning the mortal sin of premarital sex.

Teresa looks like the Italian-American girl next door. She has shoulder-length black hair parted in the middle and slightly layered on the sides, the adult version of her Catholic school single-length virginal hairstyle. She is olive-skinned, brown-eyed with full, dark eyebrows, and pleasant ethnic features. Teresa inspires this association in Italian-American male viewers who relate to her as the nice girl who has flashes of an edgy, fiery spirit when out of supervision by the elders. She speaks in standard American English due to the diligence of the nuns who taught her, but with just a hint of street distortion.

The mood of the scene changes quickly when Teresa tries to learn the depth of emotion Charlie feels for her. She openly tells him she loves him; he replies that he doesn't love her. Charlie remains in a conflict that traces back to J.R. in *Who's That Knocking at My Door.* Here the Madonna-Whore syndrome is not in the forefront; Charlie has clearly decided that Teresa is the kind of girl to have sex with and not a relationship that would interfere with his career plans. His answer as to why he can't say, "I love you" is telling and hurtful, "because you're a cunt." When Teresa bolts out of the bed stark naked and angry, he covers up by saying it was a joke, but she knows it means that women occupy a minor role in the life of a player. Teresa stands naked and defiant in front of the hotel's open window. This variation on her display at her bedroom window shows she demands to be taken seriously as she proves she is as ballsy as any man. Charlie's reaction reflects his view of women as the weaker sex, "Go ahead and jump," totally misreading her gesture. As the camera gazes at Teresa in a full shot, Antonioni is evoked—the strength and beauty of Teresa's torso, neck, back, and a mane of Monica Vitti-like hair glorifies the landscape of the body.

A time cut takes the scene into a totally different structure; it becomes a deconstruction of the memorable scene between Jean Paul Belmondo and Jean Seberg during *Breathless* as well as an embrace of the entire French New Wave style. Teresa sits on the bed while Charlie shoots off his finger gun, to the sound effect of a real gunshot, a salute to Warner Brothers' tough-guy crime films and a link to little Marty's early movie theater experience when his dad asked him if he knew the meaning of Trigger.

Jump cut. Teresa stands in front of Charlie who is sitting up in bed, her back is to the camera as he extends his arms out in a crucifixion pose implying that Teresa is threatening his freedom as a man.

Teresa gets dressed to send a message to Charlie that his insensitivity has ended their intimacy for this session. To punish him she tells him not to look at her nudity as he continues to stare and smile in enjoyment. Teresa wants to control how and when Charlie can see her. Rays of light bathe her figure in a spiritual image.

Charlie puts his hands over his eyes; this continues over a medium close-up then to an extreme close-up as he peeks through his now spread out fingers. This shot also reveals Charlie's manicured fingernails, as a man of respect he doesn't dirty his hands with blue-collar work.

Thinking that she is in privacy, Teresa throws back her hair, facing the window. Charlie's male gaze stresses the pleasure he derives from looking at her body. He continues to stare, she puts on her yellow shirt, and so Charlie gets to re-experience this ritual. Charlie's hand turns on his right eye, then opens. Teresa pulls her pants up, now her anger has subsided, and she submits to him, laughing and saying, "I see what you are doing!" In a last effort to hold her own with him, Teresa jumps into bed wearing black panties, her rebellion against the virginal white of her Catholic upbringing. They are playful and kiss; Charlie feigns his reaction as if Teresa's aggression is too much for him, "You wild woman! Get your hands off me!"

As they exit the room and walk down the hallway Charlie has his black coat draped over his sport jacket, a style reserved for big shots, noncelebrities who think they are celebrities, mob wannabes, and those who want to look important and engender respect. To emphasize the mob/church dichotomy Charlie is wearing a dark shirt and a blue-black tie. Charlie has left his personal life with Teresa behind as he closes the door to the hotel room. He's telling her about the killing that occurred at Tony's. Teresa doesn't want this side of Charlie to exist, she sees the two of them happy together and away from Little Italy, but Charlie can't help himself, he's in too deep. Charlie retells the story like it was happening in front of him, "He just keep coming at him like Rasputin," comparing the drunk who wouldn't die to the Russian holy man with mysterious powers used to cause the demise of his enemies. Charlie is so imbued in the mob/church dichotomy he sees everything within that prism. Charlie does show vulnerability with Teresa that he dare not reveal on the street telling her that the kid with the gun was scared, but he and his friends were more frightened than the shooter. Teresa represents all the mob outsiders who cannot accept, understand, or embrace the Cosa Nostra rules—that a man could lose his life because he insulted a made man. Charlie quickly explains that the kid was not very bright but a "climber"—someone who kills a guy who insulted a big man to boost his reputation up the ladder to the inner circle. Charlie switches the conversation to Teresa's cousin, Johnny, telling her about Johnny's plan to break into her mother's house for food; but Teresa isn't protective, she just laughs and says, "Why didn't you let him?" She then turns serious, concerned that Johnny may know about their secret relationship. Charlie makes it clear that he's never told Johnny, their illicit love affair could jeopardize his standing with Giovanni—even death if he was a made man. Teresa, angry that Charlie only cares about himself snipes, "Your reputation is still safe," and let's him know that his macho attitudes are silly. Instantly Teresa reveals her own dark side when she sees an African-American maid in the hall and tells her she can make up their room now. The woman replies she only has two hands and Teresa, sticks the verbal knife in, "Well, use them!" Charlie is embarrassed and apologizes to the woman. Teresa, now as irrational and angry as her male counterpart says, "I hate shit like that." Charlie comments that Teresa has "some mouth" on her, to which she replies, "Kiss me," and he throws a phony punch. This scene blends the noir tough broad character with Teresa's rebellion to break free of sexism and traditional values. Her racism is seen as inappropriate to Charlie who has his own conflicts on race but is embarrassed, not for social or political reasons, but because he is equally conflicted between being the "nice Italian boy" and the tough street guy.

A series of carefully composed static shots are edited in sequence to "animate" the bronze statue surrounded by red and pink flowers in the center of the feast. The minimontage is motored by Eisenstein's theory of collision and works similarly to a montage of stone lions in *The Battleship Potemkin*. Here, Scorsese is demonstrating the living impact religion has made in his community and the power of the church as symbolized by statues and religious objects.

A top shot of the feast crowd emphasizes the density of humanity. During his early viewing experiences, Scorsese saw many top shots in Hollywood movies often utilized either as a gimmick or a way to let the audience know they were watching a film and seeing in a new cinematic way rarely experienced in life.

Busby Berkeley often employed top shots to turn his dancers into a recognizable pattern. Jerry Lewis, who worked with Scorsese in *King of Comedy*, was known to use a nondiegetic camera angle and used a top shot during the climax of his take on Stevenson's *Dr. Jeckyl and Mr. Hyde* in *The Nutty Professor* (1963). During the silent era the top shot was used in German Expressionist and Russian filmmaking. Hitchcock uses the view at a critical moment in *Psycho* when Norman Bates is carrying his "mother" from her room across the hall and down the staircase into the cellar.

Scorsese's application of the top shot directly over the feast crowd also gives the viewer a moment to be above the action as an observer before being placed in the point of view of someone working his way through the sea of people.

Charlie walks through the crowd as a handheld camera on the ground follows him. Because of the documentary approach here, a woman looks at Charlie because he is being filmed but the moment can also be read that she feels he is somebody because his attire and attitude calls attention to itself. A girl looks into the camera, a self-referential moment that brings a heightened reality to the film.

Charlie enters a storefront and meets a man working on the jukebox, to insiders a major organized crime business along with cigarette machines. They exchange pleasantries and Charlie gives a tip to play 463 as a combination, a friendly piece of information for the neighborhood pastime of playing the numbers—an activity in which Charlie is a low-level employee. Passing information is another Little Italy ritual. Charlie is told Giovanni is in the back.

Charlie stands in a doorway and sees men sitting at a booth in the back. Giovanni is talking to the men as Charlie moves past them without a sign of recognition. In the bathroom Charlie listens as the men discuss in Italian the shooting in Tony's bar. The subtitles reveal that the boy shot the man in the bar because he was defending Mario's honor. Mario (Vic Argo) sits on one side; the man defending the boy's actions on the other, as Giovanni listens. There are three cups of espresso with lemon wedges on the table, the beverage of choice for a sit-down. Mario explains there was no insult, and that the drunk man was making a fool of himself, not Mario, and that in his estimation the shooting was unnecessary.

As Charlie, who understands Italian, listens from the bathroom, Giovanni is aware he must make the right moral call here for the two men, the neighborhood, their business, and to mentor his nephew. The man insists his son did the right thing in executing the killing. Giovanni is concerned—there is enough heat in Little Italy to deal with, and makes it clear that no hit order was given, supporting the unwritten rulebook on such matters. Charlie washes his hands and scrutinizes himself in the mirror, again as in the opening, peering past his looks into his soul. As Giovanni taps the hole of the sugar dispenser with his middle finger to contain his emotions, he delivers the boy's sentence to his father. He is to be sent to Miami for six months to a year, then everything will be forgotten and Giovanni will offer to do what he can, satisfying the worried father without being committal. For emphasis Giovanni passes his fingers, holding a handrolled cigar over the sugar dispenser, like a priest consecrating the host saying, "But now get rid of him." Charlie runs his fingers over his eyebrows then down the sides of his face contemplating the two sides of his life. Italian opera covers the next cut to Charlie walking on the beach with Teresa.

This is far from the traditional couple-walking-on-the-sand scene in which a man and a woman discuss their love for each other as the waves break behind them. For city kids like Charlie and Teresa even a local beach represents nature and freedom, at least it does for Teresa. Charlie is not dressed for the occasion, wearing a long-sleeved shirt and sunglasses to keep him incognito, rather than as a way to protect his eyes from the powerful rays. He announces that he hates the sun, ocean, beach, grass, trees, and heat. Charlie is not phobic about nature; he is just not a creature of it. When asked what he does like, he lists spaghetti with clam sauce (without the age-old argument about the white or the red sauce), mountains, about which he makes a Wagnerian gesture with his hands accompanied by a sound effect to define the power and presence they represent, Francis of Assisi, chicken with lemon and garlic, and, of course, John Wayne. He compares the tall buildings of Manhattan to mountains going more for majesty than specificity. He ends the list with, "and I like you," which leads to a kiss.

For Teresa the beach is a place where she can be alone and open to express her dreams. She tells Charlie she is considering taking an apartment and moving out of the family nest. This move is especially difficult for young Italian-Americans who are brought up to believe you live with your family until it is time to marry. The thought of becoming independent from the family for its own sake, being on one's own, is often met with anger and fear that the child is abandoning family and rejecting the rules and mores of their birthright homestead.

This is not the first time Teresa has tried to break free. Charlie says, "Why don't you do it this time," offering his support. Teresa's conflict is linked to the old-fashioned values instilled in her. She is waiting for Charlie to move out and then in with her. Charlie is supportive of Teresa's independence as long as it doesn't affect him. He again tries to explain that he is involved in neighborhood business and cannot leave. Teresa sees through Charlie's posturing; she knows it is fear of being on his own that is holding him back. To show his displeasure Charlie crosses over to the other side of a pole in the sand that divides them. She links Charlie's notions of business with disdain for the lifestyle of Johnny, who she considers "an insane person." Charlie retreats to his inbred rules of unconditional loyalty, "He's your own cousin." Teresa does not share Charlie's blind faith so he explains his position as a contemporary apostle, "Who's going to help him if I don't?" Teresa is the voice of the seventies self-help, telling Charlie, "Help yourself first." Charlie is again deep inside his special brand of spirituality citing St. Francis of Assisi as a man who "had it all down" referring to the Saint's devotion to the care of the poor, and the sick, a life dedicated to helping others. "Saint Francis didn't run numbers," Teresa shoots back, but Charlie, in the spirit of the *omerta*, denies the charge. Charlie is closed-up, cold, playing the role he has been taught, and Teresa who knows this attitude is impenetrable, can only turn away from him for now.

Tony's place. Charlie follows Diane to her dressing table as she prepares for her night's dancing. Charlie looks uncomfortable and out of his element. He tries to put on airs, telling her she is a good performer, but he is visibly nervous and clumsy, knocking items off her dressing table. Diane's confidence and self-absorption has Charlie groping for the right words, at one point saying "Groovy," mimicking the hipster parlance of the day, but sounding like a square trying to fit in. Diane takes off a black Afro-wig she had been putting on her head and replaces it with a copper-colored one, which had attracted Charlie in the beginning because it complemented her blackness rather than attracting attention to it. Niceties fail so Charlie goes in for the hard sell, telling Diane he is going to open up his own place, Season of the Witch, a classy uptown nightclub and restaurant where she would fit in nicely. Diane assumes he wants her as a dancer, but when he says as a hostess, she immediately warms to the idea and to Charlie. Diane, like Charlie and Teresa, also wants to get out of the life to which she is relegated. She agrees to go out for Chinese food with Charlie after work.

As Charlie aproaches their meeting spot in a cab, he orders the driver not to stop but to drive by slowly, as he sees Diane dressed for the occasion, waiting at a corner for him. The fear of actual and psychological consequences are too much—talking to himself, Charlie comes to his senses and abandons the "crazy" notion, abandoning an opportunity to separate himself from his tribe and begin on a road to individuality. The conflict and guilt are just too much and he apologizes to the driver, in his best nice Italian-boy manners, and requests to be dropped off where he was first picked up. "That's all I need is to be caught in the Village with a *melanzana*," he tells himself, just too fearful of what others would say and do if he defied their ancient principles.

As proof of Charlie's quandary he is back in his role in the *family*. A bartender, attired in the traditional red jacket that signifies high-class, takes the coats of Mario and Giovanni as they enter the restaurant. The camera dollies back to reveal Charlie sitting alone at a distant table in his role as seen-but-not-heard observer.

The group of men and Mario and Giovanni hug and pat each other on their backs. Through deft camera movement, a reaction shot of Charlie appears to be rising in the frame as he sits and watches this ceremony of respect, imagining life as a made man.

They are in Oscar's restaurant, an informal clubhouse the men use at their convenience for matters of pleasure and business. Oscar asks permission to speak to Giovanni, but when the Don learns it's about money, he puts it off to a later, private time. Oscar fully understands his place in this old-world universe and asks permission to serve the tripe, a small mysterious fish that lives in total shadow and off the particles of dead animals or plants in the sand. It is a Sicilian delicacy served stewed, in soup, or Olivetana-style prepared with veal and caciocavallo and percorino cheeses. A large bottle of San Pelligrino, sparkling water imported from Italy, is on the table out of custom, a decade before American Yuppies would make it the drink of choice when dining al'Italia.

Giovanni holds court, speaking in Italian and criticizing politicians as "blackmailers" who would starve if forced to live with honor. In English he clearly separates his people from the government by saying, "They are not like us." He boasts superiority over elected officials bragging, "They know where to come when they need us," clearly defining the connection between organized crime and the government. Reminiscing to prove his strength, he tells the men for Charlie's daily lesson that he realized this during World War II when there was a person working for the government taking care of the docks. Charlie, who is more curious than open to learning-by-listening asks what the man did. "He was there" is the defining answer. Then the moral of the story; Giovanni tells his nephew he gave Charlie's father the same information twenty years ago, but he didn't listen. Giving his nephew the chance to get on with the program, he tells Charlie he knows the boy is still in the company of Johnny Boy. Separating himself from the unworthy, Giovanni explains that although Johnny is named after him he is like the still missing Groppe, "half-crazy." Giovanni takes on the role of an understanding mentor with a warning, "Watch yourself. Don't spoil anything. Honorable men go with honorable men." Giovanni has no regard for what he perceives as imperfection. He reminds Charlie that the girl next door to him, implying Johnny's cousin Teresa, is "sick in the head." Charlie tries to explain that the girl has epilepsy, but Giovanni repeats that she is "sick in the head," refusing to accept either science or vulnerability. Proving to Charlie that he is all-seeing and all-knowing, he confides that Teresa's parents came to him for advice over concern that their daughter wants to move out. He is their *compadre*, a godfather in the Catholic and social class sense. "What am I going to tell them? Lock her up?" he says with cold insensitivity but states his responsibility to take an interest, assigning Charlie to keep an eye open but not to get involved. Charlie's mind is swirling with confusion and fear, but he continues to play the role of the dutiful charge.

Class over, Mario suggests Charlie take a look around the restaurant, a code that Giovanni and Mario want to be alone to talk business. Charlie doesn't get it and tells the men he's been in and out and around the place maybe fifty times. Giovanni is decisive as usual, a master of the indirect/direct message. "Maybe you missed something. You should get to know the place." Either Charlie is dense, distracted, or consumed with conflict, but he gets it and leaves the table as Giovanni does what Italians in America do when they want to conduct a private conversation, *talk in Italian*.

In the kitchen Charlie turns to a high flame on the commercial stove and puts his hand over it, again symbolically experiencing the fire of hell. As Charlie's conscience, Scorsese in voice-over says, "Fine," as Cappa accepts his destiny to become what he fears and craves most—to be a *man of respect* like his uncle.

Charlie is getting dressed in his apartment. "The Shoop Shoop" song ("It's in his kiss") performed by Betty Everett is on the soundtrack as score. The lyrics concern a young woman in a dialogue about whether her man really loves her, concluding that it isn't his eyes, face, or charm, but in his kiss. Charlie is preparing to talk to Teresa and to take his uncle's not-so-subtle warning to heart, so the song reflects Teresa's concerns over Charlie's conflict between love and business.

Charlie contacts Teresa through the urban communication system of their open window, gesturing to meet him downstairs. When they meet in the back alley Charlie tells her he can't make their next date. Clotheslines are filled with drying garments, a timeless city image. When she suggests Friday he tells her he can't see her for a while. Teresa explodes with emotion; it's not what she wants to hear, causing Charlie to spew with anger, "You're fucking things up for me. You and Johnny are ruining things for me." When a neighbor complains of the noise, Charlie apologizes profusely, slipping quickly into polite-boy mode.

Back inside the stairwell Charlie becomes so frustrated that he can't control Teresa or his life that he threatens to slap her. Calming down he explains that he has to stay away from her and Johnny so he can get his restaurant—the key to happiness. He assures Teresa that Giovanni doesn't know about their clandestine affair or Johnny's out-of-control debts. Charlie tries to convince Teresa and himself that Johnny is just a kid in need of help but his motives are more connected to Cappa's guarantee to an afterlife in Heaven by way of redemption through helping Johnny. Charlie confesses he doesn't want to stop seeing Teresa, she kisses him and finds the answer to "The Shoop Shoop" song. She does love him, but he can't say it until he gets The Season of the Witch; then everything will resolve. This is a dangerous moment for Charlie. He has now extended his loyalty to divergent paths, Teresa, Giovanni, Michael, and Johnny; still trying to be the nice guy who appeases everyone.

Charlie enters the storefront club, is greeted by Mario, and goes to his uncle's table. "Where have you been? Do you know the news about

Groppe?" As Giovanni tells the story in voice-over Scorsese goes to a flashback in which Groppe visits his mother who is watching television. Wearing his Guinea tee shirt he says "I'm sorry" to her. Then he leaves the room, goes into another room, puts a gun into his mouth and fires, signified by a white flash, which covers the frame. "How do you like that?" Giovanni concludes, "Half crazy at least"; another coded message to stay away from Johnny and Teresa, and the restaurant could now be Charlie's. Michael enters the room signaling Charlie. Giovanni who has no tolerance for rudeness says, "Doesn't he see that we are talking?" Charlie quickly signals back for Michael to wait outside.

Charlie goes from one crisis to another. Michael has lost all patience with Johnny. The scene is shot from across the street on a long lens looking like FBI surveillance, as Charlie is learning he can no longer control anything in his life. He has the customary toothpick in his mouth, a habit that is the tradition of wiseguys and urban Italian-Americans alike. He convinces Michael that the three of them, implying Tony, can get together at a party that evening and knock some sense into Johnny. Michael agrees but makes it clear he doesn't like being taken advantage of or being embarrassed in front of Giovanni. Charlie keeps his nice guy composure and says, "I appreciate it," knowing he has just one more chance to prevent disaster. Charlie walks away with a bit of the cock in his walk. He has been playing the role of complier for so long, he is losing touch with the reality that he can be fallible—nice guy or not.

A sign on Volpe's announces that Tony's place is closed for a private party. Charlie makes his entrance and orders J&B and soda. In a long practiced ritual that mocks and embraces his Catholic training, Charlie places his "consecrated" fingers over the shot glass as the bartender pours the J&B then soda over Cappa's fingers into the glass, as if he was a priest preparing wine to transform into the blood of Christ during the holiest portion of a mass. Charlie cants, "I come to create order, and may God be with you." Tony and Charlie enter a biblical exchange, "Let me ask you something, 'Art thou the king of the Jews?' " (quoted from Mark 15:2 when Pontius Pilate interrogates Jesus), "Does thou say this for thy self or have others take on to me? Am I a Jew? My kingdom is not of this world."

Charlie is the spokesman for the official ceremony of the party. He dedicates their gift by proudly stating that Jerry (Harry Northup) served in Vietnam and is the recipient of the Silver Star for heroism in combat. Bridging their conservative principles with the pop culture of movies he says, "In the immortal words of John Garfield, 'Get them in the eyes, right in the eyes,' " and hands Jerry a properly folded American flag, which is unfurled in a match cut that resolves in a three-fourths top shot. As everyone claps, "drinks for everyone" is announced.

In a montage the party carries on with abandon; a young woman lights her cigarette from a votive candle; George flips his flashlight in slo-mo; Charlie shoots shot glasses down the bar with a pool stick; George throws ice at Charlie, who retaliates by grabbing the seltzer gun; Michael blows slo-mo smoke rings.

In a long, uninterrupted take, Charlie, now drunk on his feet, moves through the party, kissing girls as he stumbles among the partygoers. He is no longer in control but still acknowledged as "the man" of Tony's place, still the center of attention. Charlie becomes sick and lies down now in a drunken coma. Scorsese applied the same technique as used for Charlie's entrance into Tony's at the film's beginning, so Charlie and the lens maintain the same distance apart as he moves. This time the camera is directed at Charlie and facing him, shooting in a tight close-up with a wide-angle lens. The lens application distorts Charlie's face; the movement captures his drunken gait, both giving the viewer an experiential perspective of his state of mind. His collapse is even captured via this reverse POV as the camera turns sideways with the drunken Cappa. The use of a wide-angle lens attached to an actor was accomplished by James Wong Howe for *Seconds*, in which the technique elicited the paranoia of the main character. Scorsese again, a human encyclopedia of moving images, uses that landmark grammar for his own devices.

The nonsensical Doo Wop of "Rubber Biscuit" by the Chips and the old school hard drinking are contrasted with the partying habits of pot-smoking hippies of the time, even though it is not in the text of the film, it was a subtext for viewers back in 1973. In a time cut Michael wakes up Charlie to inform him Johnny Boy has not shown up. Charlie offers twenty dollars to buy John another hour, but Michael is insulted saying that he wouldn't pay the interest for two hours. For the first time Charlie understands the gravity of the situation. With the vig (a gambling term for interest owed) Johnny owes Michael three thousand dollars. Doing the math Charlie is surprised and angered that Michael would charge a neighborhood guy "1800 vig." For Michael this is business, for Charlie it is a struggle to save a soul in order to save his. Finally they agree to lower it to two thousand. Michael now is crossing the line and gives an ultimatum swearing to God that if Johnny is trying to make a jerk out of him he will break his legs. This is the heart of the matter. More than the money Michael's reputation is at stake. Italian-Americans in all walks of life fear and deeply resent a perception that they are being made the fool. The taut discussion ends with Charlie and Michael agreeing that they disagree. "Do we understand each other? Michael states, "I heard you," replies Charlie as Michael leaves. Charlie's says, "Amen I say to thee I will not commit until I must pay the last penny," as he follows Michael who returns to the party. Charlie's biblical quotation seems to be put together in his own words from a combination of Matthew 5. 26, "Verily I say unto thee, Thou shalt not be no means come out thence, till thou has paid the uttermost farthing," and Matthew 5.27, "Ye have heart that it was said by them of old time. Thou shalt not commit adultery." It's unlikely that Scorsese didn't know the exact words—more probable that he and Mardik Martin wrote Charlie's dialogue to present Cappa's own looser version of the Gospel according to St. Charles.

Johnny Ace sings "Pledging my Love" on the jukebox, a song in which a man sings of his eternal love for a woman and asks for hers in return. Jerry is drunk and possibly suffering from posttraumatic stress before America came to grips with this syndrome. As he watches his girlfriend slow-dance with another man he goes berserk, attacking the woman as his friends try to calm him. The commotion moves to the jukebox, which interrupts the ballad actually and symbolically, with skips, scratches, and jumps. Charlie takes the girl into another room and Tony closes the door. As the action continues outside Charlie looks at the girl and they dance cheek-to-cheek. It seems like Charlie may be betraying his friend Jerry, but then she falls asleep and he puts her down to rest.

A knock on the door leads to Teresa who is at the bar waiting to tell Charlie that Johnny is on the roof with a gun. Charlie runs out into the street and ducks into a cramped doorway with other neighborhood guys as Johnny fires away on the roof. Not giving up on his ticket to redemption, Charlie calls up to Johnny who announces, "I'm going to shoot the lights out on the Empire State Building." Another shot sends Charlie back to the doorway and now the guys are *busting his chops* by feigning that they won't let him back in. The scene begins to look like a crime B-movie. Charlie yells, "What ya got?" Johnny like a James Cagney or Humphrey Bogart character replies, "A .38!" Like a movie hero Charlie runs into the front of the next building to get Johnny off the roof.

Johnny is in his element, half-crazed, with no respect for anything or anybody. Wearing a three-quarter length black jacket, not a biker model, but the styled sport jacket one, Civello shoots out of the window of an apartment across the way. Charlie takes Johnny by surprise smacking him on the head to temporarily break the cycle. They stoop down to talk. Johnny rationalizes his psychotic behavior as a way of waking up a dead neighborhood and expresses an irrational hatred "with a vengeance."

Johnny is not finished yet; he lights an explosive and tells Charlie he's going to wake up the neighborhood with a *Back to Bataan* referring to the 1945 World War II movie starring John Wayne. Charlie is unable to stop Johnny, who handles the firework with deft and teasing manipulation.

As it goes off, the boys run along the rooftop to conga drum master Ray Baretto's "Ritmo Sabroso." Although it is a Latin instrumental, the thematic rhythmic tension and bouncing riff, when combined with Scorsese's image, transforms *Mean Streets* into an Italian movie. First introduced as score, the music later becomes source for a party across the way.

Charlie and Johnny enter the cemetery at the old Saint Patrick's Cathedral where the director served as altar boy. The two men enter into a discussion concerning the crisis at hand as they walk among the tombstones. A familiar and comfortable place to both, they simultaneously pull out handkerchiefs to place on flatstones so they can sit without soiling their slacks. Charlie is angry with John because he hasn't showed up at the job that was "arranged" for him, but Johnny feels unloading crates from a truck is beneath him. The animosity builds as Johnny tells Charlie that he doesn't work, implying why should he. Italian-Americans are hypersensitive about class distinction within the ranks; go too far and the other man will say, "You think you're better than me."

Johnny is always ready to up the ante. When Charlie tells him he got the debt down to two thousand, Johnny quickly and without much enthusiasm thanks Charlie for all he's done, but Civello knows he is not in the clear yet. "Don't get mad," he tells his unofficial sponsor, but wants Charlie to talk to Giovanni. Johnny has no limits in his wont to survive at any cost. Charlie is taken aback but smart enough to say no, knowing what the consequences would be for him. "That's what I get for being involved," Charlie says out loud playing the role of the Italian-American martyr. He switches to being Johnny's angel again and tells Johnny to meet Michael on payday, "So he doesn't think you're trying to make a jerk-off out of him." Charlie understands the seriousness of pushing Michael too far but Johnny just yes's Charlie to death.

"Ritmo Sabroso" builds in strength in its last nondiegetic moments then switches to diegetic as the scene cuts to a POV of the boys responding to the sound of a glass breaking, and a fight in progress. Through the windows of an upper-floor apartment a group of young people dance to Barretto, and others try to get out of the way of a swirling fight that sends a few partygoers through the open window and out onto the fire escape. Seeing into and out of windows has special meaning for the urban dwellers, as their "window" onto the world.

Charlie looks up at the violent party and seems to reflect on his life; seeing his own behavior from afar strikes him emotionally. Can he ever escape the life or even the situation he is now in?

Charlie then looks at Johnny lying asleep on a tombstone, both arms extended out behind his head in another of Scorsese's signature crucifixion references using men, as Jesus was a man at the time of his death, to represent persecution of the misunderstood.

The woman's scream references the picnic scene in *Citizen Kane* where a woman's scream reflects the emotional violence Kane has inflicted on Susan Alexander. In both cases the chilling yell is offscreen and a subtext for the scene at hand. The last scream is followed by a car horn blast as the next scene begins.

Charlie meets Michael and his boy Shorty (Scorsese) in front of Volpe's. The conversation is tense, the bonds of friendship breaking down. Michael is no longer polite about meeting with Johnny for his money. Charlie stands up to him saying, "Don't threaten me," in Little Italyeze, "Don't treten me."

Michael has given up niceties. He follows Teresa and stops her in the stairwell of her apartment. He wants to make sure everyone connected to Johnny knows he's looking for him. When he grabs at the insolent Teresa, her groceries fall to the ground. Although she says please, she sends Michael her message by saying, "Give me my fucking eggplant." Michael is offended by her "mouth" and when she is out of sight gives Teresa the under the chin fingers gesture that has many meanings, here something like "up yours."

The Italian feast band plays in the street. An extreme long shot shows the arches of light that line the streets. Its simple beauty in the night sky transforms the urban area into a Sicilian village. The shot holds longer than expected then cuts back even further to isolate Little Italy from larger contemporary society. This shot is also held longer than expected to make the point that Little Italy is a far-off place, culturally, from the rest of the city. It also isolates the characters cutoff in a place with its own rules, customs, and consequences.

Teresa and Charlie are in an apartment, both tense about Johnny. Charlie is anguished over Johnny's disappearance as the showdown with Michael draws closer. Teresa is frustrated not knowing what is going on and at Charlie's inability to share information with her. The voice of an opera singer entertaining the feasting crowd begins a dramatic aria.

Johnny is stomping down a Greenwich Village street. When a long-haired young man comes in his path, Civello viciously punches him to the ground and, when he has him down, kicks him as passersby stop to watch the brutal act. As Johnny turns to leave he makes several false starts and attempts to go back and continue. His anger at his situation and un-controlled self-destructive emotions are driving his fury.

A handheld camera struggles to keep up, following behind Johnny as he runs through the night streets. An instrumental section of the feast per-formance scores the moment. Then a singer continues.

In the apartment Teresa is talking to Charlie about getting out via her own apartment. She is in search of independence, but tells him he could eventually move in (her true dream is to live with Charlie so they can start their lives again, away from Little Italy). Charlie explodes with anger. He has been humoring her about the apartment and expresses anger about her "bastard cousin." He is fed up hearing about her; all he cares about is his situation. When he tells her to leave him out of her plans she becomes quiet and depressed, and slowly sits down on the bed.

In the street, the faithful watch the Italian singer perform. A montage contrasts those who are enraptured by the performance; others just sit there, as they do every year. A large cross, dotted with lights, is contrasted with a turning gambling wheel.

Johnny reaches the neighborhood and runs into an apartment building. Up on the roof he makes his way from building to building. He stops to proclaim he is on top of the world, looking like he's James Cagney playing Cody Jarrett in *White Heat*. As he throws his arms up in triumph and turns to a nonexistent cheering throng, he foreshadows his role as Jake LaMotta in *Raging Bull*, another lost man who in Scorsese's view deserves redemp-tion. Johnny demonstrates his superiority then turns and gives the world (that is, Little Italy), the Italian stiff-arm salute.

Charlie apologizes to Teresa, trying to get her to see that he and Johnny are not playing a game but are locked in a serious situation. Johnny has climbed down the fire escape and is now watching them with his charismatic smirk, from outside their window. When he knocks, they are startled, and the two men drop their roles of savior and the saved. Charlie is angry that Johnny has not shown up to deal responsibly with Michael. Charlie is not in control of his temper and pushes at Johnny as he walks into the kitchen. Civello is containing his feelings and gets a perverse smile on his face. In the kitchen he asks in a mock innocent, but hostile tone, if the couple has made plans to get married. Charlie decodes the message instantly that Johnny is threatening him with the secret that could destroy everything he's worked for. Johnny finally exposes his hurt for being treated poorly. He tells Charlie that he's not smart but stupid, a *strunze*. His resentment pours out, "I'm so stupid you have to look out for me." Johnny is a master button pusher, knowing everyone's sore point, called *busting chops* or *busting balls* in street terms, it is effective in getting to an opponent. "Charlie likes everybody, everybody likes Charlie—a fuckin' politician." Charlie warns Johnny not to say anything about his relationship with Teresa giving Civello the feeling that he finally has power over Charlie. As Johnny leaves the apartment he gives a long list of people he wouldn't tell leaving the best for last—Giovanni. Charlie and Teresa rush out to the hall. Charlie is furious—Johnny continues to taunt that he wouldn't even tell Giovanni—meaning he will. Then there is that terrible pause and transition most Italian-Americans have experienced when a relationship has gone sour and hurting someone is all-important. Johnny becomes very relaxed, as one does when about to deal the final blow. He tells Charlie he was always curious about something concerning Teresa. "What happens when she comes? Does she have a fit?" Charlie is out of control and lunges at Johnny, who repeats the offensive line, engineered to destroy all trust and respect. Charlie continues to attack Johnny, which triggers his anger and reveals how he really feels about Charlie as a "dirty-two faced," who has betrayed him and refuses to get him out of his dire straights by calling on Giovanni. When Johnny moves to leave and says he will tell Giovanni Charlie's secret, the two attack each other. Teresa finds herself in the middle of a devastating brawl between her cousin and the man she loves. The emotional upheaval is too much, triggering an epileptic attack. As Teresa writhes on the ground gasping and choking, Charlie is helpless, and Johnny is cruel, refusing to help because, "She's your fucking girl." An Italian woman (Catherine Scorsese) comes out and tends to the young woman, and the men run out of the building.

Scorsese has carried identification with Charlie over to include Teresa. Both have illnesses that, at the time, were considered highly psychosomatic, misunderstood as a sign of weakness, helpless figures who could never be tough or strong.

Time cut to Charlie slamming Johnny up against a store security gate. The two have an Italian reconciliation. Apparently, Charlie has just told Johnny about all he has done for him, "What do you mean what you did for me—you didn't do anything for me you fuckin' bastard." Johnny is crying, more hurt than angry now, and Charlie has gained control over his self-selected charge, "Don't show up tonight, we'll see what happens to you." Johnny only has eight dollars on him to give to Michael, so Charlie gives him twenty-two to make it an even thirty, which leaves him eleven dollars for the weekend and money for "chinks" later after the sit-down. Charlie still thinks he can broker the situation. Johnny is reluctant to take the money but Charlie proves his superiority by saying, "Take it, I'm doing it for you." No longer cocky, Johnny pleads with Charlie to talk to Giovanni, but Cappa knows not to step over that line.

The feast performance continues as Charlie and Johnny enter Volpe's to learn from Tony that they are over an hour late. Michael has left but he'll be back.

Charlie orders a shot, which he lights with a match to Tony's chagrin. The pressure of the moment brings out the perversity in Charlie, who, like Johnny, also thinks he is invincible. A young man and a woman at the far end of the bar seem to be having a miscommunication and he goes to the men's room. In the strongest and most blatant example of the anti-Semitism Scorsese has observed in his people, Charlie inquires about the girl. "Jewish," Tony says implying she is of loose morals. When Charlie questions her nationality, Tony says, "She's here every night with a different guy, you know how *they* are."

Charlie turns on the charm, telling the woman (Lois Walden), "Ever since that first day when I saw you playing volleyball with the nuns I couldn't help myself. When the man returns Charlie becomes aggressive, grabbing her and challenging the man to, "Take her away from me—physically." Tony and Johnny intervene on Charlie's behalf. He spews, "You Jew Bastard!"; they are thrown out. The woman has forgotten her coat and Charlie flings it at her calling her "Joyce" and saying "Maybe we'll meet at Bingo some night," with the same racist intent as the more obvious slur.

The Italian singer builds up drama (musically) as Michael enters, as if he owns the place. Shorty is right behind him. Johnny is smirking behind the bar, next to Tony who is eating out of a small bowl. Charlie stands in front of them and Michael joins him. Michael, barely containing his rage beneath his Don wannabe façade, tells Johnny that he was kept waiting for over an hour. Charlie, still the broker of peace, explains that Johnny has around thirty dollars for him. When it is handed over Michael sees it is only a single ten-dollar bill. Still maintaining the order of the street, he defers to Charlie (because of his connection to Giovanni) and says he will accept the money out of respect for Charlie, even though Johnny continues to push up against the situation by telling Michael he bought a few round of drinks with the rest of the paltry sum, in lieu of a two-thousand-dollar debt. Michael needs to save face in order to accept the insulting amount, so he rolls it up into a tight ball, then suddenly with intent to humiliate, throws it quickly at Civello. Johnny, as before with Charlie in the stairwell when he used Teresa to get back at his friend, becomes calm, a broad, cocky smile on his face. With the deliberate movement of a master stage performer, he picks up the bill, opens it out with fingers outstretched on each side telling Michael, "You're too good for this ten dollars, you're too good for it? It's a good ten dollars." Pronouncing the last word as doll-isss, Johnny won't humble himself, but continues to attack. Then in the most stunning moment in the film, one that led to DeNiro becoming an instant sensation, with his dénouement, which starts by stating that Johnny has borrowed from everyone in the neighborhood and never paid anyone back. Tony won't even give him credit anymore, "I borrow money from you because you're the only jerk-off around here that I can borrow money from without paying back, right, right, because that's what you are—that's what I think of you—a jerk-off." He pulls out a lighter and begins to set fire to the bill. "And I'll tell you something else Mikey. I fuck you right where you breathe because I don't give two shits about you or nobody else." Michael can no longer contain himself as he leaps over the bar to get at Johnny. Suddenly Johnny goes even further pulling out a gun from behind the bar and pointing it at Michael, "C'mon, c'mon, c'mon, c'mon, c'mon fuck-face! Motherfucker! Big shot! D.D. Disappointed Dunsky." Michael and Shorty leave knowing Johnny doesn't have what it takes to use the weapon.

Tony grabs the gun out of Johnny's hand; ironically it is empty. Charlie, still with his wits about him, knows this is time for extreme measures. He gets Tony to lend them his car. Tony tells them not to drive around, to lay low, go to a movie, the movie theater as a place to be alone in a crowd, to survive, to escape from the real world just outside. Johnny tells Charlie, "You got what you wanted," making it clear that he knows Charlie is using him for redemption and that Cappa is playing out the scenario so he can be the hero to himself and in God's eyes.

As Charlie starts the car, the radio starts playing "Mickey's Monkey" performed by The Miracles, which sends Johnny, cigarette dangling from his lips, into a dance mode inspired by the song about, "A cat named Mickey came out of town/ He's been spreading this new dance all around." Johnny's interpretation of Mickey's dance is inspired with moves that recall Jackie Gleason, the Italian street-walk, and every teen dance of the sixties rolled up into a magical moment, as in a Bertolucci film where everything stops for a dance sequence, which appears to be self-contained, but is truly another way of expressing the inner and physical life of a character. Johnny really has no idea what trouble he is in, nor does he care. Johnny Boy is a combination of self-destructiveness, childish innocence, and an irresponsible party boy with a pathological streak that is often disguised by his charismatic ability to attract and amuse people. His antisocial behavior propels him regardless of the situation or consequences. Scorsese makes a comment on Johnny by ending the song on the line, "Monkey see, Monkey do." Johnny thinks he can do what he sees others do. Wielding the gun at Michael may have been in his hard drive through observation on the street or from watching crime movies, but everything a person does in life has repercussions. Charlie is still there to protect him, but Johnny always has another line or stunt up his sleeve.

For the second time in *Mean Streets* Scorsese cuts to another movie for homage. This time the circumstances are very different. Charlie and Johnny Boy are not celebrating a score but are using the occasion to pass the time and lie low. Scorsese places his mentor Roger Corman's *The Tomb of Ligeria* on the screen. The gesture is an acknowledgment of the debt Scorsese feels toward Corman. He salutes the Poe cycle and the film Scorsese and his clan considered the best in the series. In nine shots Verden Fell (Vincent Price) confronts the spirit of his dead wife (Elizabeth Shepherd) as his castle goes up in flames. There are many narrative reasons Scorsese has chosen this scene beyond the gothic poetics that entranced him. Fell is obsessed with his dead wife, and Johnny Boy and Charlie are obsessed with absolving their sins. These two men are juxtaposed with two people symbolically burning in hell. Getting out of their present situation is critical but secondary to preservation of their soiled souls.

Out in the theater lobby, Charlie calls Teresa. Seeing another organic opportunity to pay homage to the movies, the posters in the background are carefully chosen. In the "now playing" section Scorsese doesn't show a poster for what is playing, *The Tomb of Ligeria*, because he's already covered that, rather a double bill of Corman films, *Last Woman on Earth*, screenplay by Robert Towne, and *X: The Man with the X-Ray Eyes*. Coming attraction posters pay tribute to two other major influences—John Boorman's *Point Blank*, a film that redefined screen violence and Cassavetes' *Husbands*, a particularly significant choice considering there may not have been a *Mean Streets* without Cassavetes' inspiration and direct influence.

Charlie apologizes to Teresa who probes about what is really going on. Charlie asks for some money to take Johnny to Greenwood Lake until he can make a couple of calls to resolve the crisis.

Teresa refuses to be left out of the situation and a time cut places her in-between Charlie and Johnny driving out of Little Italy. Charlie drives with a crazed determination to show he is as much his own person as Johnny. Civello tries sincerely to convince Charlie one last time that the only way out is to talk to Giovanni, finally admitting that he is totally dependent on Cappa. But Charlie says no, it's going to be his way. Charlie must follow the rules of the street and pay for his sins his own way. The situation has left Cappa off his game. He quickly gets lost in Brooklyn, talks to himself, telling God that he's "trying," mouths the lyrics to an Italian song that is either in his head or possibly on the radio that Johnny has just turned on. Charlie has given up on his two friends; he's tired of Teresa's outbursts and tired of Johnny's lack of responsibility, but rather than try to control them, he mocks and chastises them as he drives into oblivion.

Legendary radio personality B. Mitchell Reed is credited in *Mean Streets* as (disc jockey) but he is never seen in the film. When Johnny turns up the radio, Reed is heard saying, "Right you are," as "Steppin' Out," by John May all and the Blues Breakers begins (not *Hideway* as listed in the credits although Eric Clapton plays lead guitar on both tracks).

"Steppin' Out" is an effective accompaniment to the *Mean Streets* climax. The instrumental is driven by the electrified and electrifying energy of Clapton's lead guitar. The title implies the concept of going out on the town, also, because Clapton was such a virtuoso playing for blues legend bandleader, John Mayall; Clapton was stepping out to be featured here. Charlie is not out for a joyride, but on a suicide mission that has him moving into the spotlight with an uncharacteristic devil-may-care attitude that surprises Teresa and Johnny, who are laughing at him as he gets lost deeper into Brooklyn and doesn't really seem to care. Charlie is so beyond his element in the volatile situation with Michael and as a getaway driver that he has lost his inhibitions as the well-placed sound edits in the instrumental amp up the pace.

To rock music fans familiar with music beyond the top forty and fans of what is now known as classic rock, the Clapton solo is an inside treat—grooving on the spectacular technical and emotional display as Clapton increases the tempo of the solo, bending notes and producing perfect phrasing. Just as the song is about to explode with blues power, the trio in the car and the viewer are in for a rude but inevitable awakening.

A car is tailing close behind, and the three believe it is just a road pest. The car speeds around with precision alongside them, facing the passenger side where Johnny curses them out from his shotgun window position. It is Michael who is driving. Shorty is in the backseat with the gun. Michael gives him the command, "Now's the time," and Shorty fires into the car hitting Johnny in the neck and wounding Teresa and Charlie, who begins to lose control of the car.

Now Clapton's guitar is wailing, musically hammering on a riff that becomes the score for the out-of-control car heading for oblivion along with the orgiastic guitar solo. Johnny, bleeding from the neck and trying to get out of the swiftly moving car, looks like a Jesus figure covered in blood and experiencing excruciating pain. Charlie is bleeding from the arm and crashes into another car, runs over garbage, into a fire hydrant, and finally into a building to end their car journey and the Clapton solo, which immediately and abruptly ceases, as water shoots up into the heavens from the plug. Only the sound of water can be heard as the shot holds, a poetic urban image. The upward stream reminds city dwellers and movie fans of Hollywood/New York crime films, with kids playing in the street on a hot summer afternoon, but here the water symbolizes the flow of blood inside the car and the force of nature, which brought on this inevitable moment. Michael and Shorty look on, the music and singing from the feast returns; Teresa's bloody hand pushes through the shattered windshield. A group of singers take the stage to for the song's finale. Michael peels out and away from the scene. Johnny is walking along a brick wall holding his neck, blood pouring out, his hand trying to stop or contain the bleeding. *Mean Streets* goes into its final moments, a progression of events that signal life goes on, yet acknowledges the violent rules of the streets. Tony is in the bar's bathroom; Giovanni sits in his living room watching television. Charlie, out of the car, holds his bloody arm and falls to his knees as if in prayer. In beautiful and brutal black-and-white, Glenn Ford (as Sergeant Dave Bannion), pulls his wife Katie (Marlon Brando's sister Jocelyn) out of his car after a bomb left for him by a crime syndicate explodes in Fritz Lang's *The Big Heat.* The police arrive on the scene, and the singing continues. Diane is sitting in a coffee shop as if still waiting for Charlie who will never show up. He will live and continue to be entrapped by the confines of his culture. Charlie is helped into an ambulance, Teresa's hand is dislodged from the windshield and she is taken out of the ruined car by firemen. The song ends; it is the end of the feast. A final top shot shows the stages—the people in the street, the end of another year, and another feast will come next year. A shot of the New York skyline links this American New Wave crime noir with its predecessors from Hollywood's B-past, while an electric piano from the feast plays, "There's No Place Like Home." Michael and Shorty sit in the car on a street contemplating and accepting what they had to do. As a woman closes her window and pulls down the shade, a voice-over from the feast wishes everyone, "good night, good luck, and god bless you." The last action of the film signifies that the people of Little Italy mind their own business, once the shades are down they shut out the business of the street. What they see but never talk about, never admit they have seen anything, and that's what keeps them alive; it is survival to say you don't know.

Over the decades since the release of *Mean Streets* there has been endless speculation concerning what happens to Charlie, Teresa, and Johnny Boy. Scorsese is not a moralist but an observer. He has shown what happens when people in a closed society make certain choices. Charlie will survive and he may get out as Scorsese did; the same is true for Teresa. Whether she and Charlie have a future is doubtful. Johnny Boy may bleed-out, or he may have another one of his nine lives left, but his kind doesn't change in this world, his destiny will then be just up ahead the next time he goes too far.

14

Hollywood! *Alice Doesn't Live Here Anymore*

After an apprenticeship with Roger Corman and the realization of a personal film, Scorsese was positioned to make commercial Hollywood genre films. It was still early in the era of the American New Wave; directors were finding their way through and around the system.

Although Scorsese has the heart, temperament, and proven results of a New York film artist, he believed in Hollywood as a business, a moviemaking method, and a systematic approach to storytelling. What attracted Scorsese the most were stalwart filmmakers like Ford, Hawks, Wellman, and Walsh who made a commitment to direct one film for the studio and then one for themselves.

The one for the studio might be a star vehicle or a prized literary property. Auteurists like Scorsese believe that even when these pantheon directors were working as hired hands they still managed to put in stylistic and narrative touches that reflected particular personal themes. A personal film would be a handpicked literary project or an original script that suited their emotional and psychological sensibilities.

Boxcar Bertha was Scorsese's apprentice feature film as a professional; *Alice Doesn't Live Here Anymore* became his first professional assignment as a director for hire. Directors were no longer on staff at studios, so Scorsese had to make sound decisions about the films he took on assignment. To survive a director must work, but if the work goes too far astray from their vision and style in form and content, they die a little and eventually become anonymous, hacks, or unemployable. Throughout his career Scorsese has functioned as a director for hire: *The Color of Money, New York Stories, The Aviator, The Departed*, and such projects as *After Hours, Cape Fear*, and *Bringing Out the Dead* were designed to keep him going until he could direct a movie he really wanted to make. In spite of these assignments, Scorsese has always been a personal filmmaker. Every project either has intrinsic personal connections or Scorsese finds a way through his knowledge of film history and ability to understand and deconstruct genres (much in the way Stanley Kubrick and Robert Altman did) to make every film a Martin Scorsese picture.

Because of this, Martin Scorsese's filmography is split between films that are totally personal in theme and style and others to which Scorsese applies his aesthetic and storytelling abilities to both make the film his own and accomplish the task for which he was hired.

Scorsese confronted this challenge on *Alice Doesn't Live Here Anymore*, and it is a perfect vehicle to study how he adapts to the task at hand and contributes within its superstructure. *Alice* is an example of Scorsese's pattern on hired-hand films; Scorsese is a filmmaker who cannot avoid or reject his cinematic personality and anatomy. He has no choice.

Alice Doesn't Live Here Anymore was a vanity project for Ellen Burstyn. Burstyn, who was forty-two when the film was released, quickly established herself as an actress of the American New Wave with notable performances in Paul Mazursky's Felliniesque *Alex in Wonderland*, Peter Bogdanovich's *The Last Picture Show*, and opposite Jack Nicholson and Bruce Dern in Bob Rafelson's *The King of Marvin Gardens*. With her work completed on William Friedkin's *The Exorcist*, and production of another Mazursky film, *Harry and Tonto*, she met with Warner's studio head John Calley, before the Warner Brothers release of *The Exorcist* and he invited her to do another film for the studio.

Burstyn's agent sent her a copy of *Alice Doesn't Live Here Anymore*, an original screenplay by Robert Getchell, his first effort. The story of Alice Hyatt, a woman propelled into supporting her young son when her husband is suddenly killed in a traffic accident, was a touchstone transition from the Hollywood woman's picture as defined by *Mildred Pierce, Magnificent Obsession, Imitation of Life, Flamingo Road, A Stolen Life*, and *The Blue Veil*. The genre, popular from the thirties through the fifties, portrayed liberated female protagonists who defied social mores that imprisoned them and often punished them for venturing too far in their freedom journey.

Burstyn found herself in the same situation as many American women at the dawning of the seventies. She was divorced, was raising her young son, and was in a constant struggle to break out of the conventional roles in which women had been cast. The Women's Movement not only created a feminist sensibility and inspired activism toward sexism in the workplace, government, and social institutions, but also had a life-changing impact on the everyday lives of women who openly began dealing with changes in their actions and attitudes toward family, home, sex, and personal and professional expression.

The actress who had been radicalized by the writings of Betty Friedan and Gloria Steinem found that the women in her sphere were all searching to redefine their roles in society. Getchell's screenplay provided the ideal platform to explore these feelings and ideas and make an impact on the portrayal of women in American movies. The New American Cinema was white, male, and although influenced by the seismic changes of the sixties, generally perpetuated the old guard attitudes toward women, both in life and on the screen.

Calley offered the director chair to Burstyn but she turned it down to concentrate fully on her performance. It was clear to her that the film needed to break clear of the old Hollywood approach and she said she wanted someone "new, young, and exciting." Repeating these qualifications to Francis Coppola, he recommended Burstyn screen *Mean Streets*, which was beginning to attract buzz.

During a meeting Burstyn found Scorsese to be "highly charged," "wound-up," and "nervous." She told Scorsese that she greatly admired *Mean Streets* but that film was about men and her project was about women. When she asked Scorsese if he knew anything about women he answered with characteristic honesty and enthusiasm, "Nothing, but I'd like to learn." Confident in her own abilities and in Scorsese's artistry and willingness, he got the job.

Scorsese's strategy called upon his natural skills as a filmmaker, his knowledge of film history, and his innate common sense honed from years of surviving in Little Italy on little more than his wits and abilities. The deficit he faced in preparing to direct *Alice Doesn't Live Here Anymore* was sizable. This was the story of a woman who loses her husband and sets out to transform her life, raise her son, and become the person she wants to be. The screenplay is rich in human warmth and humor, but is about female constraints in a male-dominated world. Scorsese was raised in a chauvinistic environment with traditional gender roles, and was also emotionally shut off by the Madonna-Whore syndrome prevalent in his culture. Understanding his limitations the first step was to surround himself with strong, capable women in the cast and crew. His girlfriend Sandra Weintraub encouraged him to take the project and was given the position of associate producer. Sandy had been involved with pre- and postproduction on *Mean Streets*, in addition to her role as a "Christ killer." As the daughter of a Hollywood producer, Sandy grew up around movies and was a quick study.

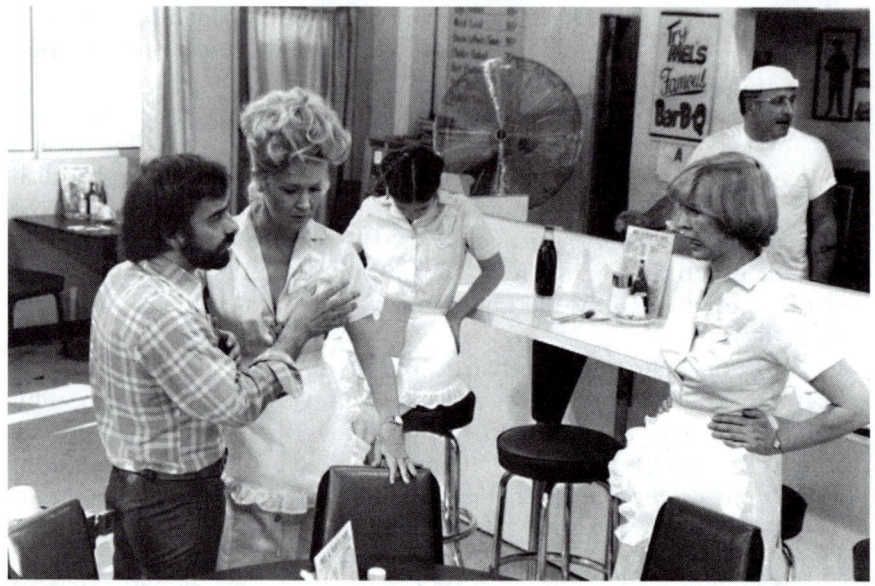

Scorsese, Diane Ladd, Valerie Curtin, Ellen Burstyn, and Vic Tayback on the set of *Alice Doesn't Live Here Anymore*, as the director takes on feminist themes. *Courtesy Photofest.*

Audrey Mass was a writer who in 1959 began adapting classic American works into television movies: *Our Town, The Philadelphia Story, The Heiress,* and *Harvey.* After becoming a producer on *Alice* Mass went on to produce *A Moon for the Misbegotten* and *Eleanor and Franklin* for television, before her untimely death in 1975 at the age of thirty-eight. Marcia Lucas was an accomplished film editor of films directed by her husband and fellow New Waver, George Lucas.

Toby Carr Rafelson, at the time the wife of New Waver Bob Rafelson, was a successful production designer of *Five Easy Pieces, The King of Marvin Gardens,* and Jonathan Demme's *Caged Heat.*

Hairstylist Lola "Skip" McNalley began her illustrious career with *Alice* and Mel Brooks' *Blazing Saddles,* both released in 1974.

Scorsese trusted all the women in his inner circle to contribute to the feminine spirit of the film and to counsel him on matters concerning the story and the characters that were beyond him. This created a working environment of mutual respect where everyone collaborated freely. Scorsese clearly set the tone inspiring everyone with his artistic generosity in a situation where he was truly a fish out of water. On location in Arizona, Scorsese wore a cowboy hat much of the time, but was clueless about life outside of New York City. By leaving matters of gender and geography to others, he was building the thematic nature of *Alice Doesn't Live Here Anymore* as a Martin Scorsese personal picture.

Prior to directing the film Scorsese did his homework by studying the Hollywood woman's picture, especially the work of Michael Curtiz and Curtis Bernhardt. Scorsese was correct in classifying *Alice* as a woman's film and knew that he could deconstruct the classic form into a story of a contemporary woman in a seventies' context. This would still encase *Alice* in a male tradition, but Scorsese knew that any attempts by him to create a feminist style would fail. At the time of production there were very few female directors working (this movement would begin to grow at the end of the seventies and into the eighties). Scorsese also knew he didn't possess the knowledge and experience of Bergman, Antonioni, Cukor, Bresson, and Dreyer who captured the feminine mystique in their work.

Another strategy would be to channel Elia Kazan, who had so successfully directed women in honest and three-dimensional portraits, but it was his cinematic father, John Cassavetes, on whom Scorsese relied the most. Cassavetes was a master of directing actors in search of screen truth. Along with his wife and muse, Gena Rowlands, Cassavetes had put on screen some of the most electrifying and truthful portrayals of women. So Scorsese planned to use the tested approaches of Kazan and Cassavetes, encouraging improvisation and intensive development of characters. The visual style was a much bigger challenge. So Scorsese depended on what he knew best, the documentary Direct Cinema style in nonfiction films and the way it was employed by Cassavetes with a roving handheld camera without pretense of preconceived genre conventions in lighting, composition, design, and blocking.

Sprinkled throughout the film Scorsese planned shots that reflected his attraction to gothic camera angles and movements, references to films he felt were appropriate to this story, and the high-energy use of cinematic dynamics that were pure Scorsese. The mix would get him there but not in any conventional hired-hand manner—the results were a hybrid Scorsese arrived at in almost every assignment that wasn't a pure personal project.

What *Alice Doesn't Live Here Anymore* lacks is considerable and reflects the shortcomings of a personal filmmaker trying to tell someone else's story. The eclectic conglomeration of visual styles and approach to the material result in a film without an aesthetic center. There is no overarching consistency in the use of camera and directorial concept, as a thruline connecting scenes, rather, each scene, and sometimes shot units within scenes, has its own objective; often counter to the text of the film or performances.

Toby Rafelson does a fine job using color, texture, architecture, and patterns to reflect Alice's female sensibility, but the camera approach necessary to contribute to a consistent visual style as part of the film's trinity of director, director of photography, and production designer is rarely on the same page—it follows Scorsese's artistic agendas.

Unlike the first generation of Hollywood directors or revisionists such as Sam Peckinpah and Walter Hill, Scorsese had almost no understanding or feel for the Western states. The locations and vistas are recognized as the West, but seem inaccessible to the filmmaker who failed to encapsulate their essence.

Although the acting is genuine and truthful, some of Scorsese's casting contributions don't communicate the look, feel, and sound of Arizona folk. Harry Northup, a sleazy local bartender doesn't have the regional dialect down (an issue widespread among the secondary characters), Murray Moston fares better as Jacobs, the bar owner who hires Alice to sing, but is less authentic than Kris Kristofferson who had the life experience to guide him, and Harvey Keitel who embodies the character, Ben Eberhardt, a charmer who seduces Alice before revealing his psychotic anger. The background extras throughout the film, especially in Mel and Ruby's café, are too diverse to be believable as locals in the seventies.

Because Scorsese is a stylist rather than a workingman director who works invisibly inside the story, he manages to impose his distinctive vision and directorial character throughout *Alice Doesn't Live Here Anymore*.

The traditional Warner Brothers shield logo, which had been retired, is brought back as *Alice* begins in the classic Hollywood format of 1: 33. The titles are rendered in the typeface associated with a woman's picture as Alice Faye sings, "You'll Never Know," from the 1943 film *Hello Frisco, Hello*. Young Alice is on a homestead designed and photographed in a deeply saturated and art-directed set reminiscent of *Gone with the Wind* and *The Wizard of Oz*. A caption identifies the place as "Monterey, California." Scorsese directs with the sweep of a Minnelli musical, with lavish crane shots. After establishing a nostalgic recreation of a thirties or forties Hollywood production, Scorsese turns it into a parody by introducing the sassy, dirty mouth of Alice, which will collide with the snappy one-liners and clever repartee of the characters throughout the film, as little Alice says, "I can sing better than Faye," and the phrase, "Blow it out their ass!" The deep orange and yellow tones of a Technicolor palette are an ironic context for this seemingly classic farm girl. The opening is eye-catching, stylish, and surprising, as Scorsese shifts to a caption propelling the story to New Mexico twenty-seven years later. A series of vistas establish the terrain, but Scorsese is an Eastern city boy who approaches the environment as a tourist, quickly speeding through the area saying, "Hey, look at that, look at this." On the soundtrack is the glam rock, pre-punk, "All the Way from Memphis" by Mott the Hoople, to establish the rebellious teenage nature of Alice's obnoxious son, Tommy (Alfred Lutter), and the changing attitudes of the seventies. Scorsese does not achieve the contrapuntal narrative richness in the relationship between music and film. *Mean Streets* succeeded in creating a contributing narrative in the use of music for its lyric content to comment on the characters and story and to evoke mood, presence, and emotional attachment by combining the context of song and scene.

The death of Alice's husband, Donald (Billy Green Bush), while driving his Coca Cola multiwheeler gives Scorsese two opportunities for stylistic invention. When Alice gets the phone call with the tragic news, Scorsese cuts three times, each time moving closer to Alice's face, again adapting the grammar from Hitchcock. The technique creates a greater emotional reaction through cinematic dynamics than merely allowing the actor to provide the impact. Combined with Burstyn's facial transformation, the visceral effect of the editing, and the increase in shot size is a physical experience for the audience.

The accident is captured in a full sweeping shot. The crimson blood flows freely achieving a graphic image that looks like Hollywood without the Hays code, a Roger Corman moment of required violence. Scorsese achieves an expressionistic realism that would become his signature on many films containing screen violence. He moves the camera on a dolly, sometimes zooming at the same time. The camera movements are expressive, and as in *Mean Streets*, are not an organic relationship between subject and camera, but are directly connected to Scorsese's emotional wiring. At times when he is not executing a specific designed-in-advance shot, Scorsese moves the camera the way his body responds to life, instinctually—an observer's physical connection with his environment and circumstances. There are moments of perfect synergy, but others send out signals that cannot be interpreted narratively by the viewer because they are Scorsese's internal reactions to the joy of making movies and trying to connect to content. These moments are often on journeys of their own, resulting in a film student's quest to find the film while in the process of experimenting in the act of pure film.

Scorsese combines music of the great American Song Book for Alice and T. Rex, Leon Russell, and Elton John to represent the rapidly changing times of her son's generation. Alice's music relates to Hollywood's past and to her perception of a club singer tapping into a time when music reflected traditional themes and the singer and audience could experience loneliness, joy, heartbreak, and the search for love. Scorsese extends his commitment to a tapestry of music that helps define the characters with Kris Kristofferson's performance of the Hank Williams classic, "I'm So Lonesome, I Could Cry," which echoes America's country music history. Scorsese's distinctive musical gifts are present in *Alice*, but it is his encyclopedic understanding of music history working here—not his deep emotional connection to the project.

Scorsese has little feel for the automobile on the open road and relies on traditional approaches and new technology, which made filming while driving easier and offered more cinematic options. Scorsese's relationship to the car is in crowded city streets, cruising out of boredom, something to do, or out of necessity even writing in a car, because there was no place to go. He is a director of closed, not open, spaces so the scenes with Alice and her son in the car rarely achieve the scope and sense of adventure to support the story.

Scorsese handles the repartee between Alice and her son with a deft ear learned from studying the great screwball comedies, the razor wit of Preston Sturges, and fast-talking tradition of the thirties movies. The rapid speech pattern of the director's Italian-American, New York roots, and his movie savvy, combine to give confidence to these scenes. The writing, performance, and direction are tied to Hollywood's past. Scorsese's unsophisticated ability to enter the feminine psyche produces a warm, sensitive film, but upon close scrutiny, not a very revolutionary one. *Alice Doesn't Live Here Anymore* was an important film in attempting to present a female point of view as women began their journey toward liberation. Scorsese provides artistry, but not specific aesthetic answers, to telling a woman's story in a unique cinematic language.

15

My Voyage through Hell: *Taxi Driver*

Taxi Driver is a landmark film in its ability to synthesize the dark mindset of the American white male during the early seventies. Scorsese achieved this by tapping into his deep feelings of anger, resentment, anxiety, profound loneliness, repressed violence, and the disintegration of the moral and physical state of America.

The idealism of the sixties generation and the euphoria of sex, drugs, and rock and roll, which bewitched them, caused a temporary state of denial that America had been founded on puritanical principles and defended by the military-industrial complex. Along with the Aquarian dreams of peace and love there was a rising level of irrational violence in the cities and states of the United States.

Historically, the assassination of President John F. Kennedy is cited as the beginning of America's descent into chaos and brutality. The events of November 22, 1963, obliterated the hope embodied in a young leader. The murders of Martin Luther King, Robert Kennedy, and Malcolm X opened the floodgates to the proposition that anyone could be eliminated, and violence was a solution that begat more violence.

Many events emblematic of a breakdown in societal and psychic order predate the genesis of *Taxi Driver*. In August 1966, Charles Whitman, a young man who on the surface appeared to be an all-American boy, climbed up the University of Texas tower with an old Marine footlocker, which contained a radio, three gallons of water, gasoline, a notebook and pen, a compass, a hatchet and hammer, food, two knives, a flashlight and batteries, a .35 caliber Remington rifle, a 6mm Remington rifle with a scope, a .357 Magnum Smith & Wesson revolver, a 9mm Luger pistol, a Galesi-Brescia pistol, a .30 caliber M-1 carbine, and a 12-gauge shotgun, as well as additional guns and ammunition.

Without logic or reason, Whitman opened fire on the campus and killed fourteen people, injuring dozens, in a little over ninety minutes when he was shot dead by Austin police officers. Whitman's deadly rampage forced the American male to accept that he could be capable of such a horrendous act against society.

During the late sixties while Vietnam raged and mass riots destroyed lives, property, and civility, and large portions of the population expanded their minds with LSD and marijuana, a confluence of forces was at work. The Woodstock Music and Arts Fair held for three days in August 1969 in Bethel, New York, was the largest-ever gathering of people for the express purposes of communal experience, music, and love in modern times. It became a microcosm of what society could be: peaceful, tribal, cooperative, and self-generating.

This all ended on December 6, when the Rolling Stones appeared at the Altamont Speedway for a free concert that was to send off the historic year of 1969 with another seminal gathering. The event was the antithesis of Woodstock; violence erupted with the stabbing of a gun-wielding concertgoer by a member of the Hell's Angels on security detail.

With twenty-five days left to the decade, the sixties ended. As the grim reality of the death of hope took hold, the once-optimistic mainstream population entered a deep depression and plunged into a personal nightmare of "bad ideas": violence against those who threaten, crime against society and the state, an abusive attitude toward women, and a steady cocktail of hard drugs and drinking. The Caucasian American male was at the center of this disillusionment.

During the turn of the sixties/seventies decade a succession of movements and national episodes surrounded white men who began to believe they were powerless. Their feelings were a result of being exposed to unfamiliar experiences and a no-rules, drop-in, and turn-on and tune-out way of thinking. In reality very little substantive change had occurred in the psyche of the American male. Chauvinism was rampart during the sixties. Young men related to women with little difference than the ways of their fathers. Many found themselves threatened by homosexuality. With their macho sensibilities they were afraid homosexuality would lead to the destruction of their masculinity.

The Women's Movement, Gay Liberation, Black Power, the human potential movement of Werner Ernhardt's EST, L. Ron Hubbard's Scientology, the Primal Scream, Rolfing, and other life-altering movements all drew Americans into ideological groups from which white males felt alienated.

Radical politics challenged the government and educational institutions. The Students for a Democratic Society (SDS), morphed into the Weather Underground, who advocated and utilized violence as a means to their end. The peace movement marched by the hundreds of thousands. Richard Nixon, a loser in 1960, invented personal reinvention, with The New Nixon, a repackaging and marketing scheme that included a secret plan to end the Vietnam War, a promise to put down campus revolt, and the establishment of "The Silent Majority," to return control to mainstream America and away from the counterculture.

Tom Wolfe declared the seventies "The Me Decade." Therapy became a way of dealing not only with personal issues but also to stave off what R.D. Lang saw as a national nervous breakdown. Psychotropic drugs were primitive. Before Prozac, Zoloft, and Paxil, Valium, a tranquilizing muscle relaxant, was widely prescribed then abused for treatment of psychological ailments.

Vietnam raged on, expanded into Cambodia, and tore America apart. Everyone was either for or against the war. "America Love it or Leave it," or burn your draft card, or defect to Canada. When four students at Ohio's Kent State University were shot dead by National Guardsmen, America moved dangerously toward fascism.

Watergate further eroded moral fiber, and corruption of governmental officials led to distrust and the collapse of the infrastructure of American cities. New York was in a downward spiral: massive unemployment, a rise in the murder rate, and violent crime.

When the Vietnam War finally ended in 1975, peace with honor was just a slogan and the fall of Saigon evidenced that American blood was shed to fight the communist threat, but had resolved nothing in Southeast Asia. Soldiers returned from Vietnam in disgrace and were treated as murderers by the general public. Veterans struggled to adjust in the posttrauma, and committed suicide, or exploded into violence in large numbers.

The teenage runaway and homeless populations grew. What began as "porno chic," with couples going to adult theaters to see *Deep Throat* and *Behind the Green Door* on neighborhood screens that had been subdivided into multiplexes became an industry, which spawned XXX shops that featured hardcore film loops projected into booths fed by quarters, sex toys, and explicit magazines. Prostitution blighted urban cities.

Exploitation and horror movies entered a new era of splatter, where blood was spilled by the gallon and sex and violence was a potent cocktail. Black Sabbath, fronted by Ozzie Osbourne and Alice Cooper, brought Satanism to youth culture.

"God is Dead" bumper stickers revealed an America devoid of spirituality. Through all of this, the white male Americans, raised during post-World War II idealism and radicalized by the sixties, experienced feelings of dread, acute loneliness, and boiled over with anger, depression, and hopelessness.

The seventies transformed the cities into an urban nightmare and the disintegration of the quality of life and self. The intensity of physical abuse brought on by drugs and selfish, not communal, pleasures, left most young American white males with little to believe in, spiritually void and without a path to recovery in near sight, just extremes they hoped would eradicate or cleanse their confused, restless, lonely, and angry hearts and minds.

The central triad of *Taxi Driver*—screenwriter Paul Schrader, director Martin Scorsese, and actor Robert DeNiro—were three such white males who were experiencing profound loneliness and an uncontrolled desire to express this cinematically, or risk entering into the further reaches of behavior they were surrounded by.

Paul Schrader was the creator of the project, who was able to put on paper what he and his brethren were experiencing. After a strict Calvinist upbringing that did not allow him to see a film until he was eighteen and caused a spiritual frisson within, Paul Schrader first attended Calvin College, then broke out of his repressive upbringing and studied at Columbia, UCLA graduate school, and as an American Film Institute fellow. He published film criticism in the *L.A. Free Press* and was one of the Paulettes, young film critics who were in the Pauline Kael critical camp rather than the Andrew Sarris group with which Scorsese was more at home. He wrote his first screenplay, *The Yazuka*, with his brother Leonard and received a record sum of $350,000.

When Schrader began writing *Taxi Driver* in the early seventies, his life was at a low, he was living out of his car, and his sanity and well-being were threatened.

Taxi Driver is a consistent vision. Scorsese, working with Paul Schrader's screenplay, DeNiro's inhabitation of Travis Bickle, the music of Bernard Hermann, and the cinematography of Michael Chapman, formed a collaboration of artisans who supplied the director with the tools and palette to create a cohesive movie. New York City had fallen from grace and on hard fiscal and moral times. Scorsese created, shot by shot, a personal film that defines a period when the American white male was disenfranchised and desperate. No rational reading of *Taxi Driver* can examine the film for its Italian-American cultural traits. In *Taxi Driver* Scorsese went deeper, past the examination of his ethnicity in *Mean Streets*, to the core of what was really confronting him in post-sixties America. Born out of fact and realism, *Taxi Driver* can be seen as a psychiatric X-ray of Scorsese, as a baby boomer lost and traveling through a living hell. It also is a fable, a visualization of what Scorsese and many males of his generation felt; the bad ideas that weren't physically expressed, but psychically experienced inside the mind and soul. The story in *Taxi Driver* is powerful and contains the horrible truth about loneliness, anger, and primal instincts. Scorsese's visual interpretation is devastating and brutally honest, and continues to be a dark-side document of a point in time in which the present can be traced back.

Martin Scorsese and Robert DeNiro, one of the most successful actor/director collaborations in film history, sit on the set of *Taxi Driver*. *Courtesy Photofest*.

PART 4

In Excess, 1976–1978

16

Disaster Movies: *New York, New York*

When the American New Wavers began to rack up box office bucks and critical acclaim they acquired power—the kind they had fought against like kids with their noses up against a candy store window. They were given blank checks for projects so excessive that could only be traced back to Griffith's *Intolerance*.

To a man, each major American New Wave director had a box office disaster of major proportions. Heavily funded and hyped films grew out of control and beyond the interest and patience of the new mainstream viewer, largely those under thirty.

Coppola's *Apocalypse Now* nearly bankrupted his personal fortune acquired from the *Godfathers* and drove him right to the edge of madness, grappling with the meaning of the Vietnam War. Spielberg, who seemed to have the Midas touch and a pulse on American taste or new entertainment forms that embraced the old Hollywood tradition, also stumbled. He made World War II and the possible attack of California by the Japanese into the first *Saturday Night Live* feature film, *1941*. It took his blockbuster buddy George Lucas until 1986 to launch his disaster movie, when Lucasfilm Ltd. brought the underground comic book, *Howard the Duck*, to the screen. William Friedkin decided to remake Clouzot's *Wages of Fear* into a megabudget, epic, action movie retitled *Sorcerer*.

Brian De Palma coasted, never hitting the box office as big as his colleagues, but his 1990 adaptation of *The Bonfire of the Vanities* is a contender in the disaster sweepstakes. The two cineastes, whose works echoed the Hollywood masters but with polar opposite results, Scorsese and Bogdanovich, both decided their vanity projects would be musicals. Peter Bogdanovich's was first and in his fashion played it conservatively and more for nostalgia than personal expression with *At Long Last Love.*

However, no one wanted to hear Burt Reynolds and Cybill Shepherd sing or watch them dance. *Heaven's Gate*, directed by Michael Cimino and *One from the Heart* directed by Coppola would mark an end to the ascendancy of the American New Wave and to the director-as-superstar era. Film is an art and a business. The masses accepted the blockbuster mentality begun by Spielberg and Lucas with *Jaws* and *Star Wars* that would defeat the American art film and remain the status quo in U.S. filmmaking.

Scorsese survived the seventies even though he fell prey to its decadence and indulgences. Scorsese is a filmmaker who stayed true to his cinematic principles, while working primarily within a system designed to devour personal artists.

New York, New York began before production on *Taxi Driver*, when Scorsese read in *the Hollywood Reporter* that Robert Chartoff and Irwin Winkler had bought the rights to a screenplay by Earl MacRauch, which was a revisionist musical about the conventions and form of the popular American genre. There was no director attached at this point.

Taxi Driver intervened and when completed DeNiro went on to Bernardo Bertolucci's epic, *1900*. Scorsese continued to develop *New York, New York*. *Taxi Driver* won the Golden Palm at Cannes, which elevated all the egos involved. The win made Scorsese an important American film director with clout. The status made him bankable but also vulnerable to the disaster movie syndrome, which had already hit Coppola (until *Apocalypse Now* was recognized as an American masterwork more than a decade after it was released) and Bogdanovich.

Scorsese loved American musicals, especially those directed by Vincente Minnelli, the expressionist master who revolutionized the genre by telling the story through narrative songs, a choreographed, moving camera, a rich application of color, and plenty of subtext to what had been a boy-meets-girl, boy-loses-girl, and boy-finds-girl narrative convention.

Scorsese wanted to contrast the Minnelli mise-en-scene designed to interpret the music via a fluid and expressive camera, especially the Hollywood crane shot with the acting approach of his other-side-of-the-coin movie heroes John Cassavetes and Elia Kazan, who forged movies out of characters, performance, human feelings, and deep-seated emotions.

For Scorsese this was not a trope but how he approached his art. As his second marriage was coming apart, he sought to explore, in a cinematic environment, a potent staple of the musical: How do creative people in love survive emotionally? Although he would draw from a number of sources, the George Cukor version of *A Star Is Born* would be the armature of the story.

Liza Minnelli, then a very bankable star and representative of the new musical as the star of Bob Fosse's *Cabaret*, would play Francine Evans, a character heavily based on her mother Judy Garland and her seminal role as Esther Blodgett in *A Star Is Born*. If Scorsese was taking on the artistic persona of Liza's father, Vincente Minnelli, he was also remaking her into the physical image of her mother, while carrying on an affair with his star. Both Minnelli and Scorsese were married, he to Julia Cameron who was involved in *New York, New York*, rewriting the script with Earl Mac Rauch, Minnelli to producer/director Jack Haley Jr. Robert DeNiro took over for Harvey Keitel in representing Scorsese's inner life on screen. In *Mean Streets* Keitel, as Charlie Cappa, reflected Scorsese's conflict between the spiritual and the hedonistic, salvation or sin. In *New York, New York*, DeNiro's Jimmy Doyle would resonate about Scorsese's insistence on doing his art his way. Doyle embraces the new and experimental, Evans, the traditional; but the ultimate failure of *New York, New York* was centered in the confusion Doyle expressed about what he really wanted to do with his work. Scorsese makes it clear what Doyle doesn't want, which is to play commercial, mainstream music, but is unclear about what he does want as a musician. Once committed to the project, Scorsese treated the Earl Mac Rauch script as little more than a stepping-off point. Scorsese is an intuitive filmmaker with an enormous cinematic archive both in his head and physically at his disposal. As Scorsese began to make decisions that would lead to the finalized story, deep-rooted themes and emotional connections drove his choices. With the highest regard for story, accuracy, and realism, Scorsese set out to make much more than a postmodern musical. The research involved in creating a period film is enormous, and Scorsese embraced this process while obsessions influenced the musical's narrative, which was Scorsese's purpose in making *New York, New York*.

Analyzing Scorsese's motives as well as his results requires an understanding that is part film history, part human science. Scorsese deeply loved the musicals he watched as a child. As a native New Yorker he always understood Hollywood musicals portrayed not the authentic New York City of his life, but a mythical city where the curbs were high, the streets clean (as captured on film with the magical properties of the camera crane that took the viewer high above, swinging through, or floating above the streets), and recreated on a California soundstage.

The directive of Hollywood production design was its own form of realism augmented with the romantic nature of movies and suited to the perceptions of a national and worldwide audience. To a Midwesterner or European, the New York as depicted in a classical Hollywood movie communicated realism as they imagined it. To Scorsese, who lived fully alive in his city, it was an aesthetic. Not a postmodern idea but his reality as a boy of the forties—he knew they were sets and loved the expressionistic visions. While others believed the stories, songs, and dances were the reality of a musical, Scorsese intuited personal stories into the simple narratives. He especially adored the Warner Brothers' musicals for their energy and the ones created by the Arthur Freed unit at MGM for their lush visuals and subcontextual narratives. Admiring *The Bicycle Thief* and Italian neorealism taught him there were rarely happy endings. Hollywood's commitment to the happy ending became part of the American Dream mythology and box office success. George Lucas, whose wife Marcia was one of *New York, New York's* film editors, told his Waver colleague the film could make an additional ten million at the box office with a happy ending. Scorsese politely listened, but as always, went his own way. The subtext of the *New York, New York* story concerns Scorsese, a film director, and his writer wife, Julia Cameron. Scorsese was using the film as an experiment to find out if two creative people in love could cohabit in harmony. Using the *A Star Is Born* paradigm of performers rather than behind-the-scenes filmmakers, Scorsese could explore his personal reality in a subterranean fashion. He understood the characters could have been painters, composers, writers, mix or match; it was a way of working out the question: Could Martin Scorsese ever find happiness in marriage? The conflict between work and home life wrecked his first marriage, and then with Cameron because she was an artist and collaborator. Scorsese seemed to know the answer all the while and it would take two additional marriages to understand the complexities of shared loyalty. *New York, New York* was a lab test with controlled criteria that would prove the impossibility of marriage and art. The narrative was about popular music as identified with Judy Garland, Frank Sinatra, and the American Songbook in opposition to the new jazz of Miles Davis, John Coltrane, and Charlie Parker. This symbolizes Scorsese's struggle with the old and the new. As a filmmaker he respected the traditional and the vanguard and at the time he struggled with where his artistic voice was headed, not accepting that it was the merging of direct life experiences and the whole family of cinema that was synthesized into a Martin Scorsese Picture. Jimmy Doyle talks about new music and plays with friends who are examples of hard bop, but Doyle's own saxophone playing does not truly fit into this category. Doyle is a rebel who wants to go his own way. Because Scorsese was in conflict with his direction as a filmmaker, it burdens the Jimmy Doyle character. Rather than just playing what he wanted to play, it sounds more like a conglomeration of lots of notes and a searching, but not particularly modernist sound. To be true to the narrative drive of the film,

Doyle should have found himself as Scorsese ultimately did—as a fusion artist.

It was sound and vision that captured Scorsese's artistic imagination to make *New York, New York*. The image was a sepia photograph of his uncles in World War II uniforms with their feet planted on the bumper of an old Morton automobile that was the impetus for Scorsese ruminations about the end of the war and what life was like. His parents had 78 rpm recordings of Django Reinhardt, Stephan Grappelli, and the Hot Club of France performing "Deed I Do" and "Love Letter." The music brought Scorsese back to his early life in the forties, and the stories his parents, aunts, and uncles told him. Along with the image he began to create the relationship between story and music that would drive the musical. Scorsese even shot an image of a Hot Club of France record playing, which connected his family to the Doyle/Evans marriage.

Several Hollywood musicals and films about romantic relationships with performers influenced the narrative, look, and sound of *New York, New York. I Love Melvin*, and *The Man I Love*, a Raoul Walsh film noir with music, and *Road House* directed by Jean Negulesco with Richard Widmark, Cornel Wilde, and Ida Lupino, concerning a torch singer and a love triangle entwined with noir passion and impending doom. The Technicolor process had stimulated Scorsese since he first witnessed the saturated and, at times, lurid colors applied to interpret strong emotions, fervent passions, and a world that looked the way the emotional life of the viewer perceived it.

Vincente Minnelli's 1953 musical, *The Band Wagon*, provided narrative stimulation with its story of a wildly creative stage director and his attempts to bring high art to a troupe with a "Let's put on a show! attitude. *My Dream is Yours* (1949) directed by Michael Curtiz starred Doris Day who confessed the story of a radio singer and her romance with an egocrazed crooner she replaced mirrored her own life in show business. The film's Martha Gibson character was one of several models for Francine Evans.

The Wavers had created their own production teams; craftspeople who were also looking to refine the narrative and visual style of movies. For his director of photography Scorsese selected Laszlo Kovacs, who already had an impressive resume—*Targets, The Last Movie, Easy Rider, That Cold Day in the Park, Five Easy Pieces, Alex in Wonderland, What's Up Doc?, The King of Marvin Gardens, Paper Moon, Shampoo*—and was one of the only new-generation cameramen to have shot a musical, Bogdanovich's *At Long Last Love*, which like *New York, New York* attempted to capture the old Hollywood version of the genre rather than the contemporary school of

West Side Story, Cabaret, Godspell, Jesus Christ Superstar, Head, A Hard Day's Night, Sweet Charity, or *Help!*

There were few alliances with the American New Wave directors and Hollywood's old guard. Although they had grown up admiring the visual style of the classic films, these directors were looking to create a new aesthetic sensibility. The generation gap was also a factor. Many of the older craftsmen resented the new blood and many of the new directors didn't trust the over-thirty professionals. Archaic Union rules made it difficult for the New Hollywood directors to work in the manner to which they were accustomed as students or independents.

As with any movement there was a rebellious attitude toward the old way of working. It took two cineastes of the Wave, Bogdanovich and Scorsese, to embrace old Hollywood in their new approaches to filmmaking. Bogdanovich chose Robert Surtees (*Thirty Seconds over Tokyo, The Bad and the Beautiful, Ben Hur*), a studio veteran, to shoot *The Last Picture Show*. For *New York, New York* Scorsese needed a production designer who could design and produce the elaborate sets, especially one attempting to recontextualize the genre. Scorsese wanted to take the concept of artifice and make it even more artificial and to the edge of believability. He envisioned the sets to be, at times, an example of Hollywood realism, at times expressionistic, and at other times bordering on the surreal and postmodern. To accomplish this Scorsese needed a master of the traditional form who would understand his grand experiment. He chose Boris Leven who would go on to collaborate with Scorsese until his death in 1986. Leven, born in Russia in 1908, began working as an art director in Hollywood in 1938 on *Alexander's Ragtime Band*. Other musicals in his illustrious career include: *Just Around the Corner* (starring Shirley Temple), *Second Chorus, Hello Frisco, Hello, Doll Face, The Shocking Miss Pilgrim, I Wonder Who's Kissing Her Now, West Side Story, The Sound of Music,* and *Star!* In addition to comedies, dramas, horror films, and science fiction genre pictures, Leven was associated with high profile classics such as *Giant, Anatomy of a Murder,* and *The Sand Pebbles*. Even with all this experience it was Leven's work in film noir that gave him the ideal credentials to design *New York, New York,* which would introduce narrative elements of a dark film contrasted with the extravagance and grandeur of a classical musical. Leven's work on noirs, which includes: *Criss Cross, Quicksand, House by the River, Destination Murder, Once a Thief, Woman on the Run, The Second Woman, The Prowler,* and *Sudden Fear* gave him the full ability to merge and contrast the two forms at will.

Legendary Hollywood hairdresser Sidney Guilaroff, who began his career in pictures in 1938, had created hairstyles for Norma Shearer, Joan

Crawford, Vivian Leigh (in *Gone with the Wind*), Margaret Sullavan, Ann Southern, Jeanette MacDonald, Rosalind Russell, Claire Trevor, Donna Reed, Lucille Ball, Kathryn Grayson, Ava Gardner, Debbie Reynolds, Natalie Wood, Shirley MacLaine, Elizabeth Taylor, Mia Farrow, Jane Fonda, and Judy Garland. Guilaroff, in addition to his long experience and mastery, was another personal connection built into the production of *New York, New York*. He had worked with Judy Garland, tending to her braids in *The Wizard of Oz* and, critically for Scorsese and Liza Minnelli, was Garland's hairdresser on *A Star is Born*. Throughout the film Guilaroff works his magic to transform Francine Evans from a young WAC at a USO party on VJ Day on August 15, 1945, to her movie debut in *Happy Endings*, a film-within-a-film in *New York, New York*, where she becomes the image of her mother. Guilaroff actually plays Francine's hairdresser in a cameo as a salute to him, Garland, and the grand era of Hollywood glamour.

Scorsese and Kovacs originally proceeded to shoot *New York, New York* in the standard Hollywood ratio of 1:33:1 and did so for the first week of shooting, rather than in the Panavision 2:35:1, which was anamorphic widescreen. Returning to the old format caused too many technical issues and limitations, so they compromised and shot the film in 1:66:1, which was a reduced widescreen that made it easier to compose shots in the old tradition.

Scorsese did intensive research into Technicolor process. No three-strip Technicolor cameras were available so Eastman Kodak stock was exposed during production and later printed on Technicolor to capture the color of classic musicals. Scorsese studied the look produced by various studios and screened *Cover Girl*, *Gilda*, *Jolson Sings Again*, *Meet Me in Saint Louis*, *The Bandwagon*, *The Man I Love*, *Blue Skies*, *My Dream is Yours*, and the Warner Brothers' production of *A Star is Born*. His creative team found they had to achieve some of the color effects through painting sets and objects, even the color of makeup used on the cast. Ideas for shots came from myriad musicals Scorsese studied.

The first six to eight days of production on *New York, New York* were devoted to the opening scene in which Jimmy Doyle meets Francine Evans at a big USO party in celebration of VJ Day. The festival is merry and gets rowdy. In true Scorsese form, fights break out without a signal and end just as abruptly; the violence is out of place in a musical but is in a partying spirit, not like the unleashed rage portrayed in *Who's That Knocking at My Door*, *Mean Streets*, or *Taxi Driver*. Jimmy is on the make with a vengeance. Others make a quick connection and dance and drink with the available ladies, but Jimmy has an edge almost as intense as Travis Bickle, but with charm and style. In his loud Hawaiian shirt he physically sticks out and his aggressive come-on lines sound more like stalking than openers for a date or a dance. He is looking to get laid he says and all the others have the same motivation, but Jimmy has a going-nowhere-fast attitude that recalls the manic energy of a John Cassevetes film like *Husbands* more than a Fred and Ginger picture. After several failures he zeros in on Francine Evans, a cute brunette dressed in her WAC uniform. The encounter, with Doyle pursuing and Evans saying no with every possible inflection and intention, lasted so long it ran a full hour in first cut. DeNiro and Scorsese decided they wanted to take the characters as far as possible, way beyond genre conventions of the musical into the obsessive behavior of a noir. The variation is striking. Francine is not a femme fatale, and there is no logical reason for Jimmy to be doom-laden or propelled into a manic state, not in the plot. As his character develops the inner issues of his life as an artist and quest for what he calls a Major Chord, the announced theme of *New York, New York*—that moment when a man has his music, money, and the girl of his dreams—becomes the impetus for his outlandish, often boorish, behavior. The only official category in which to place Jimmy is antihero; he is strident, stubborn, abusive, antisocial, immature, and prone to fits of anger when he can't get his way. At his best Doyle is a master manipulator, but he always goes too far, which leads to failure and greater frustration.

DeNiro is playing Scorsese in spirit so some of the verbal and physical aspects of the film relate to ethnicity. The hot-blooded temperament, the extremes of elation, despair, and anger, and the impending sense of physical violence or verbal abuse codify *New York, New York* as a Martin Scorsese Picture and as a film as personal as *Mean Streets*, albeit in a disguised context to be decoded by the viewer.

The pick-up scene becomes a battle of wits, stamina, and personal character, more than just: Will they date? Will he score? It is the connection of two people—opposites that attract. Both Francine and Jimmy become symbols for the two Americas—the popular acceptance of assimilation and the rebellion of the outsider. Right from the get-go Scorsese throws down the gauntlet. The scene is so long, emotionally grueling and relentless, it seems to attempt either to exhaust, exhilarate, or alienate the audience.

Scorsese and DeNiro had decided at the outset there would be a lot of improvisation during the film, which is established in this sequence. Rehearsals produced new dialogue and action. Take after take during the shooting produced new avenues to stretch the tension and plausibility of the scene. DeNiro and Scorsese were comfortable and experienced in working in a New York tradition endorsed by the Actor's Studio, practitioners of The Method, and directors Kazan and Cassavetes. The process of improvisation has long been misunderstood as actors making up their lines and actions while the camera rolls. Although some improvisation can occur during a well-written and well-rehearsed scene, the benefits come from exploring the characters and a scene during a rehearsal period.

Earl MacRauch did many rewrites of his original screenplay, then he worked with Julia Cameron and developed Scorsese's personal story and character ideas until MacRauch could go no further. Scorsese brought in Mardik Martin to incorporate changes by working with the actors and with notes from Scorsese and DeNiro.

Liza Minnelli had never improvised before and came from a theatrical, showbiz, and traditional Hollywood background. She was excited and open to the process. Minnelli brought honesty, integrity, energy, and fire to her role, but she took her direction from Scorsese and DeNiro, who after privately consulting with Scorsese, would lead them in a new direction with an improvisational idea. Her introduction to this new way of working involved an hour exploring the scene where Doyle tries to pick up Francine and she resists. This prompted Minnelli to discover at least twenty-seven different ways to say the word "No." Scorsese was highly skilled at directing each of his actors in the way necessary for their talent and approach, but his relationship with DeNiro continued to be private and very special. Their collaboration is closest to the manner in which Brando and Kazan worked on stage and in film, but is unprecedented in the total emersion both men put into the entire creation of a project.

The personal themes that drove the improvisations and changes in the story and characters were expressions of issues then current in Scorsese and DeNiro's lives. True to his nature, DeNiro didn't speak openly about them, but Scorsese used the opportunity to make *New York, New York* as a forum to investigate marriage and his struggle to be an independent artist working within a commercial system. Scorsese uses Jimmy Doyle to make that point about fierce independence, but by using Doyle as a spokesman, Scorsese seems to validate the reckless, arrogant behavior in Doyle's character. Scorsese wanted to confront his circumstances that found him in a bad marriage, a destructive affair, and his increasing use of cocaine. *New York, New York* would bring everything to a head, Scorsese's lifestyle, his conflicts concerning the kind of films he should make, and his acknowledgement that he was headed for a fall that would require redemption.

Scorsese had always designed his films shot by shot. Although he well understood the classical technique of covering a scene with a master shot, medium and close-ups with sufficient angles and cutaways, he looked at each shot as a piece of editing structure that communicated mood, emotion, character, action, and story. In studying Vincente Minnelli's visual style, Scorsese intuited that the Hollywood master would track with the camera at one angle in one direction for twelve bars, then track in another direction for twelve bars, and continued the pattern until it formed a style that connected the music to the image in a poetic dance-like relationship, which enriched the viewers' perception of song, dance, and narrative.

Even weeks of rehearsal, improvisation, and script revision weren't enough to transform *New York, New York* into a personal film or a revisionist musical with a story and characters that mirrored interpersonal struggles to which audiences could relate. Nor could it present a narrative of how America evolved over the postwar years into a prosperous society in which the culture wars between populist and vanguard art played out. Leven and his art department had to move forward and built the massive sets to keep the film on schedule. When the unit was shooting on one set another was being constructed. During that time Scorsese, DeNiro, and Minnelli were taking the story in directions that sometimes went beyond the physical location that was next up, requiring reshoots and rewrites to explain the new material. This continued for twenty weeks. Scenes went on well past their capacity to maintain the story. The music, which was a prime focus at the outset, began to get lost as Scorsese and company took after the character journey fueled by improvisation, expansion, and autobiographical concerns, and a search for little gems in a scene rather than the scope of the music and what it said about a changing America. The end of the big band era, the rise of popular music, and the development of cool jazz remains in the film, but little of the context is there. The original intention of the script was to show through the music America's changing attitudes. When Scorsese got caught up in the interpersonal aspects, from his past and present between his wife and his star, *New York, New York*, became a big budget personal movie that was near impossible for the general public to enjoy and decode. It is unlikely that many viewers back in the forties and fifties were cognizant of the subtext in popular movies. These underlying feelings were clear to Scorsese, but when he tried to go further into autobiography, subtext, and self-referential tropes, he lost control of the film as a mainstream vehicle.

In the end *New York, New York* had doubled its original budget and came in at a whopping twelve million dollars. The original fourteen-week shooting schedule dragged on to twenty-two weeks with extensive revisions, countless improvisations, and searches for new narrative and thematic directions. Scorsese found it difficult to balance the artifice of the

Scorsese on set directing the noir musical epic *New York, New York. Courtesy Photofest.*

genre with the truth of the story and characters. As one aspect expanded one way, the other would follow, but he never found the template that would allow reality to fit neatly into the visual world of a dream America in which the scenes played. More often they were played over the visuals, which became more exaggerated in architecture, color, and size as production proceeded.

Scorsese was still not able to reunite with Thelma Schoonmaker who was not yet a member of the editors union. The editing team for *New York, New York* included Marcia Lucas, who edited *Alice Doesn't Live Here Anymore* and *Taxi Driver* for Scorsese, and Tom Rolf (*Jacob's Ladder, Heat, The Horse Whisperer*), who had also worked on *Taxi Driver*. Scorsese also brought on another old Hollywood hand, Irving Lerner, in postproduction. Lerner, the director of *Murder by Contract, City of Fear*, and *The Royal Hunt for the Sun*, was also an editor (*Executive Action, Steppenwolf*). Lerner died on Christmas day of 1976 at age sixty-seven, before postproduction was complete. Out of respect for the passing away of a collaborator and to praise a filmmaker who made an indelible influence on him, Scorsese dedicated *New York, New York* to Lerner's memory.

The editing of *New York, New York* was a massive undertaking. The team worked in shifts day and night, with Scorsese going from room to room revising and desperately trying to get the film down to a reasonable running time. The first cut of *New York, New York* ran almost four and a half hours. Practically every four days there was a new cut, which was screened for student groups, a process Scorsese found very painful because the film was so different in style and content from *Taxi Driver*, which had made him a brave hero who revealed life as it was. Reshoots were necessary to cover and blend the massive cuts that had occurred since the full version was created. The film was 163 minutes when Scorsese screened it for friends and supporters. This version contained the *Happy Endings* production number, a movie within *New York, New York*, which had cost $350,000 to produce and ten days to shoot. Scorsese was strongly counseled that, although it was a bravado sequence encapsulating the show biz theme of the rise of a star from nobody to icon, it literally stopped the thrust of the principal story of the relationship. Scorsese, exhausted, in poor health from his asthma and excessive drug use, could no longer see the film he wanted to make. He cut two-thirds of the *Happy Endings* sequence two weeks before locking the picture in the editing room. The film opened at the Ziegfeld Theater in New York and the Cinerama Dome in Los Angeles at 153 minutes to largely negative reviews and no more than respectable business, not sufficient for the mammoth cost. After the international success of *Taxi Driver*, Scorsese's follow-up project was clearly pronounced a failure by critics, the industry, and the movie-going public. Scorsese had hoped that stopping the movie for *Happy Endings* would work in the same manner as the ten-minute film-within-a-film in Cukor's *A Star is Born*, but *New York, New York* was too long, and the editing process too chaotic for Scorsese to maintain objectivity. At one point Scorsese withdrew from the editing process for three weeks; he needed to think about where the film was headed.

Happy Endings is Scorsese's pure valentine to the American Musical, as it contains the star-is-born elements and a cornucopia of genre conventions. It also functions, within the larger context of *New York, New York*, as a criticism of the lack of realism and becomes a defense of Jimmy's disdain for commerciality, while still embracing Francine's love for show business dreams. This duality defines Scorsese's attitude toward his work as a filmmaker in Hollywood. It's not a love-hate relationship; Scorsese's love for American cinema is pure. The demons lie in the way the system forces the artist to become what he calls a "smuggler"—getting personal themes into a commercial project or causes alienation prompting a maverick to go it alone, as Cassavetes did.

In 1981, *New York, New York* was re-released in a restored two-hour and forty-three minute version that included the entire twelve-minute *Happy Endings*, seen to rave reviews and enthusiastic box office. The further distance from the Hollywood musical era allowed the viewer to better understand Scorsese's revisionist motives and accept the film as an early postmodern cinematic work.

Scorsese was still using the au currant "A Martin Scorsese Film" phrase and still identifying himself with the color red as often as possible, so *New York, New York*, begins with the color of blood, sex, passion, and Catholicism. A heavily saturated skyline rises to show the *rise* of the city and the titles change to pink and blue as an overture plays, opening the film in grand Hollywood style, only to be immediately radicalized by the manic, truthful, a deeply emotional acting style, which clashes with tradition and demands the viewer to read this musical in a new way beyond the most expressive genre film of the past.

New York, New York begins and ends with the image of Jimmy Doyle's shoes. At first they are the brown and white wingtips of the hipster and relate to the line in Francine's lyrics to the song she cowrites with her husband, "New York, New York," penned by Liza Minnelli's favorite tunesmiths, John Kander and Fred Ebb, "These vagabond shoes are longing to stray / And make a brand new start of it, New York, New York," reflecting the restless mood of Doyle at the opening of the story. At the conclusion Doyle is wearing black leather shoes to prove he has established himself even if there is still a road to go—this links up with the lyrics, which conclude the song, "If I can make it there, I'll make it anywhere / It's up to you, New York, New York."

Scorsese's extensive use of the crane shot throughout *New York, New York* was a staple of camera technique in musicals to enhance the scope and grandeur of music and dance. Although most staff directors of the era used the crane, it is the high art of the crane shot as displayed by Busby Berkeley and Vincente Minnelli that most influenced Scorsese. In addition to the sweeping choreography associated with Minnelli and the high angle forward and backward moves of Berkeley, Scorsese brings his own manic energy to the crane sharpened by his incisive dolly work, giving *New York, New York* both a classical and New Wave excitement in the use of the moving camera.

To identify our (anti) hero, a red neon arrow, part of the art direction, points to Jimmy Doyle. Doyle's loud Hawaiian shirt seems more in place in Spielberg's career disaster *1941*, which takes place at the beginning of the war and in California; it is a character choice that makes Jimmy more Hollywood than New York (even though there are images of the Empire State Building as part of the design), another contrast to his explosive Italian-American based behavior, which puts the autobiographical aspects inside the story, another layer of postmodern context in this period film, which reflects the seventies as much as the forties.

In a melancholy and reflective moment during Doyle's pursuit of Francine, he looks from above down on a sailor and young woman who dance in a spotlight on the street. The moment is designed to show Jimmy's longing for a relationship; it also is a specific reference to a scene in *On the Town* and, in another self-referential reference within a reference, the woman is played by Liza Minnelli in a blond wig.

Scorsese even goes to fine art references relying on Edward Hopper's cinematic depiction of light and space for several images. In a green hotel room where Doyle is conducting an on-the-road affair with the girl singer who replaces Francine, there is a copy of DaVinci's "Mona Lisa" on the wall, bringing a piece of Italian culture to the film, and the image of the elusive woman in the manner in which women seem to mystify Scorsese in life and his work. A bar mural is done up in the magical realism style of Henri Rousseau, who depicted animal/jungle scenes with a surrealistic vision that made nature seem strangely human. The mural works as décor and as a metaphor for the animal instincts displayed by the characters.

Scorsese also references contemporary music by casting Bruce Springsteen's saxophonist, Clarence Clemons, as a trumpet-playing bandleader reminiscent of Miles Davis.

Francine's deep red lipstick is accurate for the period but another opportunity to dominate many of the images with the color of his obsessions of hot tempers more than sexual temperature. The Liza Minnelli, Judy Garland mother/daughter connection is ever-present in *New York, New York*. Garland represented the American popular music Francine symbolized. Garland and Minnelli both had difficulties being married to creative people, the central theme of the film. Garland's affiliation with *A Star is Born* gives *New York, New York* a narrative veracity beyond its own story. By paralleling Francine's life with Garland's own and that of her iconic Esther Blodgett character, Scorsese deconstructs a Hollywood star, and her role; all part of the musical genre and seventies collision. This is heightened by Liza's own seventies struggles with career, finding a show business niche in a poststudio environment, and her own battles with substance abuse. The context was fertile when the film was released and audiences were aware of life imitating art as the public held their breath as to whether Liza would eventually fall prey to the tragedies of her mother's life. All of this was more than viewers at the time could process. At one point Liza was using the same dressing room once used by her mother. When Vincente visited the set he broke down in tears at the image of how much his daughter looked like his former wife. For Scorsese this was explosive material. He was directing Judy Garland's daughter in a musical inspired by his admiration for the work of her father, he became smitten with Liza and was involved in yet another relationship between two creative people that would end unhappily. The fervor of Scorsese's obsession with Liza Minnelli is evident in a long take of Francine contemplating her feelings toward Doyle, while gazing into a mirror and an extreme closeup of her soulful and searching eyes fills the entire scene as she looks through the camera or into Scorsese's eyes.

As Jimmy tries to make his mark as a musician, club owners find his music disruptive to the business at hand—giving the public what they want. He is saved from perennial unemployment or the purgatory of after-hour clubs when it is suggested Francine be headlined as the top billing. It is a time where girl singers, not highflying saxophone players ruled the day. Jimmy, who sees himself as an artist who does what he wants when he wants to, is forced to work in the Frankie Harte band where he must be part of an ensemble. When Harte, played by Georgie Auld, a Canadian musician who taught DeNiro to play a plausible tenor sax and was infused into Doyle's character when actor and director learned of Auld's dark side on the road, decides to pack it in Jimmy takes over the band. The traditional big band era is coming to a close, but Jimmy tries to take the Harte band even further, while struggling with the rise of Francine's star and life on the road with music he finds beneath him.

The Doyle/Evans marriage seems doomed from the start, a sign that Scorsese's quest to learn if two creative people can find happiness is stacked against the odds because of the director's own issues with failed marriages. The proposal and wedding scene, which unfolds on a snowy evening in front of a Justice of the Peace's quaint home, is so filled with Jimmy's manic behavior it goes beyond the cutesy romance convention into an episode in which Jimmy breaks a window because of his persistence in having his own way. When Francine has doubts because Jimmy never formally proposed, Doyle barrages her and even threatens suicide by lying under the back tires of the cab that drove them there. The combustible energy of anger, absurdity, and classic comedy from the preacher and his wife give the scene a disturbing edge and inevitability to a failed marital union.

Doyle comes off like a loudmouth person and artist, his anger never gains the audience's sympathies as DeNiro and Scorsese would achieve in *Raging Bull*, so *New York, New York* often plays out like an expensive therapy session. Jimmy also confronts fatherhood, selecting career over the nurturing of a child, an issue Scorsese also confronted.

The ending of *New York, New York* was hard-fought; dozens were written, considered, and rejected. Ultimately Scorsese decided to dissect the Hollywood happy ending concept by having Doyle come to the screening of Francine's movie debut *Happy Endings*. They meet after a long separation at a party in Francine's honor where she salutes the two of them with a show-stopping rendition of the song "New York, New York"; they make a date to have dinner, a possible chance for *New York, New York* to end happily ever after, but independently both Jimmy and Francine decide not to show up and turn away to live separately as artists. This ending was unsatisfying for a general audience but remained true to the reality of the story and the autobiographical threads that created it. Scorsese's marriage to Julia Cameron ended and both continued successful careers.

DeNiro's performance is the driving force behind *New York, New York*, but also the energy that takes the film off course into personal subtextual journeys. The actor threw himself into the role with his usual dedication. He actually learned how to play the saxophone so he would look believable even when dubbed by his teacher, Georgie Auld. Months of research in clubs and talking to musicians gave DeNiro key background information. DeNiro even went as far as to sit in with the Buddy Rich Orchestra on tour. His private process into character and story with Scorsese delved deeply into the personal lives of the two men. DeNiro was also having marital problems at the time with Dianne Abbott, who as a Harlem nightclub singer, rather ineptly disguised she was pregnant with their child. DeNiro was attempting to play Jimmy Doyle, the emotional life of his director, his own artistic and personal demons, and drive the improvisational nature of the film. It is a tour de force performance, but leaves many viewers angry with the character who seems to have few redeeming qualities. Although playing a character with an Irish-American name, DeNiro interjects the hair-trigger Italian-American temperament into Jimmy. In the most mundane or happy circumstances the viewer is never sure when he will explode in rage. Francine and those around Jimmy are wary, and DeNiro succeeds in evoking these reactions in the viewer, making *New York, New York*, a provocative but sometimes unpleasant and edgy experience, especially when deluded with the expectation that the genre is to entertain and delight.

Scorsese was so despondent over the critical and box office failure of *New York, New York* that he seriously considered moving to Italy to make documentaries for the rest of his career. This despondency was a sign of how much Scorsese put into each of his films and the demands he put upon himself to make films his own way. If that was not possible in Hollywood (a struggle in which Scorsese continues to fight the good fight), he would find another way.

PART 5

Redemption, 1979–1989

"I'm Not an Animal": *Raging Bull*

The seventies took its toll on the generation of baby boomers. Vietnam, cocaine, spiritual disillusionment, Watergate, divorce, gender confusion, the degeneration of the white male, and excess left many confused, lost, and deplete of spirit.

Martin Scorsese lay in a hospital bed. His doctors watched and waited, concerned that at any point an embolism could form and explode within his brain. Excessive use of cocaine was the immediate diagnosis but the state of Scorsese's health in the mind/body continuum was more complex and beyond the help of an internist, psychiatrist, or priest.

Scorsese was in a place beyond a spiritual crisis, or what is termed by a layman as a nervous breakdown. He was in a state of collapse. His body, wracked by asthma since childhood, was further pummeled by lack of sleep, consumed by overwork, and physical and mental exhaustion. His belief system was attacked on every front. Marriages and relationships collapsed. The nature of movies was changing. The blockbuster not only threatened the health and well-being of his beloved American cinema but also his own ability to make movies. Like others in the American New Wave he fell prey to ego and hubris, taking on projects like *New York, New York*, fueled by obsession, power and not personal fulfillment, and misguided ambition. Even in Hollywood the demons of his childhood festered by the streets of Little Italy stalked him. Regardless of genre his movies became a battlefield of emotions and the search for answers that could not be found through the process of moviemaking. *Taxi Driver* and *New York, New York* took on the bad ideas, violence, hatred (self and directed), the impossibility of relationships, the fruitless escape from loneliness and the relentless oppression of being an outsider. Getting the demons on film was his life force, but when they were over the compulsions continued to plague him. He had been a street priest, a cinematic gangster, and lived vicariously the lives of his old Hollywood heroes; but as the decade left time for one more film, Martin Scorsese lay in a hospital bed waiting for his head to explode.

Robert DeNiro traveled his own journey through the seventies but managed to stay one step ahead of the negative forces that had Scorsese enthralled. DeNiro's ability to inhabit his characters and his dedication to the discipline of his craft kept him on his feet when his friend, director, and collaborator had fallen. DeNiro visited Scorsese out of loyalty, male bonding, and because his own psyche fed from Scorsese's artistic pursuits.

Scorsese had spent so many years saying and thinking, "I have no choice," he was at the point where he had to decide whether to save himself or submit to the furies that landed him in the hospital bed.

DeNiro was on a long campaign to play Jake La Motta in an adaptation of the middleweight champion's autobiography, *Raging Bull*. Unlike Scorsese, DeNiro has always been private and deeply secretive about his reasons for playing the characters he chose to get inside of. The notion of learning how to box and the research was inviting. DeNiro, who met and spent time getting to know La Motta, found him a complex man whose profession, life, and essence were intertwined. DeNiro had to understand the heart of darkness ahead, but for him it was the acting process that gave him physical and psychic satisfaction. Scorsese found little peace in the results of his process, one that demanded he find himself in his subject.

DeNiro sent Scorsese the La Motta book hoping it would immediately spark their next project together. Scorsese found some interest but rationalized that he was not interested in sports and actually disliked the art of boxing. Although he had been exposed to it through his father and uncles and the Friday night televised bouts and had even watched matches on the movie screen in between double bills, he couldn't commit to the project.

DeNiro was unrelenting. Scorsese continued to remain uncommitted. Subconsciously he was avoiding taking on a project that would get to the heart of his own dilemma. Scorsese had strayed far from his core beliefs and family tradition, which may have eventually been the cause of his physical and moral collapse. The cocaine delivered what could be the final blow, but it was all of these factors and none of them. Martin Scorsese was suffering from a disease with only one cure. *Mean Streets*, *Taxi Driver*, and *New York, New York* had been variations on his own life, with Martin Scorsese imbedded in all of the major characters. It was self-hatred that was destroying Martin Scorsese and it would take a long, painful look into the life of another for him to understand himself. *Raging Bull* ranks among the greatest of boxing movies but it is not *about* boxing.

After working on a script for the film, researching, developing ideas, and considering all the possibilities, Robert DeNiro came to the conclusion that only he and Scorsese could make *Raging Bull*. On a particular visit to his friend at the end of the summer, he told Marty they could make this film. Scorsese made an active choice this time that he had no choice; he was not obsessed with the project of turning middleweight boxer Jake La Motta's life into a film. He was making a deliberate conscious decision to commit, fully knowing in his present state of mind that when people saw what he put up on the screen (a man filled with anger, hatred, and self-destruction) that he would never make a movie in America again. Scorsese accepted he would make his final personal film, then move to Italy and make documentaries about the lives of saints. Martin Scorsese decided to save his own life and he would make a movie to do it.

Giocobbe La Motta was born in the Bronx, New York, on July 10, 1921. As a boy, Jake (as he anglicized his Italian first name) fought all comers in the street. Encouraged by his father, Jake beat all before him and the change thrown by the crowd went toward paying the rent. Trouble landed La Motta in reform school and after he finished his time he became a professional prizefighter at nineteen known as The Bronx Bull, and the name stuck with him due to his autobiography and the Scorsese movie, *The Raging Bull*. La Motta's career record of eighty-three wins, thirty by knockout, nineteen losses, and four draws made him a legend among fight enthusiasts as a man who took unrelenting punishment and punched as if his life depended on it. La Motta was not a stylist or a dancing master like his chief rival, Sugar Ray Robinson, but a man who fought like an animal. La Motta did not advance the *art* of boxing, he personified the brutality of the sport in which two men met in a ring to punch each other until, within the framework of the sport, one was considered victorious.

In 1970 La Motta published his autobiography, *Raging Bull: My Story*, cowritten by his friend Peter Savage and writer Joseph Carter. The book covers in depth and with graphic detail La Motta's childhood (in which he was physically abused by his father), through his professional career, and beyond. In language as blunt as his writing style, La Motta made no attempt to spin his life but to honestly portray it with the tabloid intensity of a *Daily News* headline and a Weegee photograph.

Robert DeNiro first read La Motta's autobiography while he was overseas working with Scorsese's cinema hero Bernardo Bertolucci on the

On location for *Raging Bull* Scorsese directs Robert DeNiro in makeup and costume as Jake LaMotta. *Courtesy Photofest.*

director's mad communist epic, *1900*, the European counterpart to the excessive personal "disaster" movies made by the American New Wave. Scorsese was directing *Alice Doesn't Live Here Anymore* at the time. Both agreed the book was not well written, but liked the real-life character of Jake as portrayed in the autobiography.

During the production of *New York, New York* DeNiro continued to promote the La Motta project, but as Scorsese moved from his epic musical to his epic rock movie, *The Last Waltz*, he was decidedly turning away from the prospect. He told DeNiro he didn't understand sports and couldn't commit to a film about a boxer.

DeNiro continued to develop the project. He brought on Scorsese's NYU pal and *Mean Streets* collaborator, Mardik Martin, who spent six months researching La Motta, talking to everyone and anyone who ever knew him. He watched every boxing movie available. Martin sat down with La Motta himself, cowriter and Jake pal Peter Savage, as well as Jake's brother, Joey.

Kubrick and Arthur C. Clarke collaborated on a novel loosely based on a Clarke short story then adapted the novel for the screenplay used to create *2001: A Space Odyssey*. Mardik Martin, in an equally daring experiment, decided the writer would turn the autobiography into a loosely adapted play, while also creating a screenplay, and having the play performed while making the movie. Martin had never written a play before. He did complete the first act. The project known under the working title, *Prizefighter*, was never completed and DeNiro continued to press forward.

Scorsese was still hovering in purgatory concerning the project. Paul Schrader was brought in to do a revision. Schrader felt there were significant elements missing from the Martin draft. After conducting his own research Schrader decided La Motta's brother Joey, also a fighter who gave up his career in the ring to manage Jake's, was central to the story. Schrader began to take the story away from La Motta's reality and explore the classical drama inherent in the relationship between brothers. Peter Savage's relationship with the real Jake became a rich vein of material when transferred to the character of Joey. The script was becoming more an original creation than an adaptation concerning real people.

Scorsese became excited by the Schrader revision but DeNiro did not like an infamous three-page monologue Schrader had written for Jake, taking place at the lowest point of his life when in a Florida prison, locked up for statutory rape. Pent-up with anger, Jake, in this never performed or photographed scene, tries in frustration to masturbate by fantasizing about all his old girlfriends. The demons won't allow him to climax so he tries again and again with a new sexual thought, until he finally concludes that it is his hands that are at fault, the weapons of destruction used to fight and express his obsessive compulsions, and he smashes them against the stone wall.

DeNiro, Scorsese, and Schrader met at the Sherry Netherland hotel. After going over the story and their notes Schrader told them they had to find their own way just as Jake did it his way—they would have to do it their way.

In September of 1978 Scorsese was hospitalized for ten to twelve days. He survived the threat to his brain being imploded by an embolism. The crisis that Scorsese faced was the bigger life issue of who he had become and where was he headed. When DeNiro visited and told Scorsese they could do this film, the director understood that the film could be the way back to the personal films he wanted to make and that he could confront his real self. Scorsese still didn't know much about boxing or even care for the sport, but the story was evolving in a direction that would allow him to once again put himself under a microscope. This time it wasn't based on the actions of his real life but on the thoughts, feelings, and emotions he had been struggling with throughout the decade. Because his motive was to make the film to save himself, he was convinced it would be the formal end of his career and accepted (in the tradition of the dedicated priest) that he would carry on his film mission making documentaries about the lives of saints.

DeNiro and Scorsese left for the island of St. Martin to write the script they wanted to make. DeNiro slowly nursed Scorsese back to health as they spent endless sessions reworking the ideas present in the Martin and Schrader scripts and selecting the aspects of La Motta and Savage's life that fit into their personal scenario for a boxing movie.

Producers Bob Chartoff and Irwin Winkler who had produced *Rocky*, the most successful boxing movie to date, which captured box office, awards, and the love of the public for the club fighter who wouldn't give up, the underdog who became champion of the world, were interested in doing another boxing movie, the anti-*Rocky*, *Raging Bull*. Winkler first learned of the project when he and Chartoff were producing *New York, New York*. Winkler saw that DeNiro carried a book with him everywhere he went. At first the introverted person who was an extroverted actor kept the title from the producer but eventually Winkler found out it was La Motta's biography. The producers were more interested in doing another film with Scorsese and DeNiro than making another boxing movie that wasn't part of what would become the solid platinum franchise of *Rocky*. Under most conditions it would have been impossible to sell such a downer of a story as the blockbuster era took shape. *Raging Bull* was full of violence, familial abuse, excessive language, and the black soul of mankind; but the producers had *Rocky* as their trump card. United Artists was so bent on continuing to be a part of the *Rocky* saga they committed with no questions asked and had little to no involvement or gave any interference to the filmmakers. They read the script and were appalled by the characters and their actions, but considered it the price to pay to cash in again with *Rocky* sequels to come.

A series of issues led to the critical artistic decision to shoot *Raging Bull* in black-and-white. Scorsese had shot tests of DeNiro boxing and Michael Powell remarked the red color of the trunks and gloves were the wrong shade. A number of boxing films were in production, *Rocky II, The Main Event*, a remake of *The Champ*, and *Matilda*, and were all in color, Scorsese wanted to go another way. Scorsese was becoming concerned that Kodak printing stocks were fading at an alarming rate, including *Taxi Driver*; if he made *Raging Bull* in color he could avoid this film history catastrophe. The issue of film preservation became apparent to Scorsese during this time. In retrospect, Scorsese's total commitment to saving films grew out of this experience more than the single issue of saving one of his new films from fading to the death of magenta. There were many films that inspired Scorsese throughout his life and specifically for the creation of *Raging Bull*. *On The Waterfront*, photographed in magnificent, real, gritty, but poetic black-and-white by Boris Kaufman, brother of Dziga Vertov and directed by Scorsese's separated-from-birth cinema father, Elia Kazan.

Black-and-white movies never became a trend in the post-sixties era of American filmmaking. In that forty-year period there is only a small list, which includes *The Last Picture Show, Raging Bull, Manhattan, Broadway Danny Rose, Zelig, Stranger than Paradise, Down by Law, Schindler's List, Pi, Under the Cherry Moon, The Blair Witch Project, The Man Who Wasn't There, Eraserhead, Kafka, She's Gotta Have It, Ed Wood, Paper Moon, Dead Man, Rumble Fish, Chan Is Missing, Clerks*, and *Good Night and Good Luck*.

Raging Bull was among the first wave to make a brave return to black-and-white. The many that followed did so for a variety of reasons: budget, subject, realism, and historical association. *Raging Bull* is unthinkable in color, for a variety of reasons: the blood, the vivid reality of La Motta's life heightened by the expression of color, the near impossibility of capturing a period in color when only films like *Godfather II, Barry Lyndon*, and a handful of others have truly found the cinematic time machine to transport the viewer there.

What truly defines Martin Scorsese as a personal filmmaker are the instinctual properties his films have to delve into the private world of his emotions and feelings. Scorsese is also a giving and honest filmmaker. He never withholds concerning his films. All his reasons and analysis concerning his decision to shoot *Raging Bull* in black-and-white are truthful, nothing is withheld. Personal filmmakers work so deep within that they themselves cannot always be in touch with critical decisions that define their work.

To the cineaste black-and-white is a truly realistic medium, which works on the viewer in ways that color cannot. Color is subjective; when the color palette is well chosen for a film it connotes realism and also works to create mood and has a psychological effect on how the viewer comprehends and receives the story and influence their reaction to the characters. Black-and-white is associated with classic moviemaking. For cineastes such as Scorsese, who also is an admirer of expressive use of color in films, black-and-white is cinema. Black-and-white links *Raging Bull* with the great boxing movies of the past, *Body and Soul*, *The Harder They Fall*, *Requiem for a Heavyweight*, *Somebody Up There Likes Me*, and *City for Conquest*. Black-and-white also is a connection to the forties, when Scorsese grew up, to black-and-white television boxing matches, to the movies he saw as a child in theaters, to the films, and to black-and-white or color that he saw and absorbed through his television. Scorsese's world was largely black and white while growing up, a world he lived in to protect himself from harm because of his asthma, a world that was not for escape but for him to find his true love, over religion, over family, and over self-love; it was the black-and-white world of filmmaking that captured his heart and imagination and for a movie, one he thought would be his last, a cinematic voyage into the darkest, purest regions of his soul; it would have to be black-and-white to get to that truth.

Scorsese did his research watching movies and going to two fights. For the first he was way up in the bleachers but noticed in between rounds, when the corner man wiped down the body of his fighter (with a large sponge from a pail of water), that the liquid quickly turned to blood. The image made a deep impact on Scorsese. He was there superficially to learn more about boxing, DeNiro, Jake La Motta as advisor, and others who would tend to the fight choreography and other pugilistic matters would take care of the accuracy. Scorsese was looking for the psychological and spiritual that would take him personally into the film. At the second visit Scorsese was up close. Again it was the brutality of the sport that captured his attention. He was not so much interested in the logistics, technique, the sport, or the art of boxing, but wanting to understand why people put themselves through so much physical punishment. His study would eventually lead him to understand why he put himself through so much mental anguish throughout the decades and how to get to the other side of acceptance. That night he looked at the ropes and saw blood dripping, an image that transcends the violence of boxing into the essence of precious blood and why it is spilled. The image, one of the strongest in the film, is religious, a metaphor from the blood Jesus spilt, and a deeper metaphor about what makes us human and why we risk peace within for what we do with and to ourselves.

DeNiro's preparation was intense; he boxed constantly under the tutelage of La Motta. He went beyond an actor trying to look authentic. La Motta felt DeNiro reached the status of a decent middleweight and could take on professional contenders. DeNiro, who unlike Scorsese keeps his secrets to himself and expresses them through the characters he plays, continued to talk to his director privately. He was not playing the real Jake La Motta; he was playing a man so filled with anger, hate, paranoia, and destruction that he appeared to be without compassion for the well-being of everyone around him. The Jake La Motta in *Raging Bull* as created by Mardik Martin, Paul Schrader, Robert DeNiro, and Martin Scorsese was a character who destroyed everything around him until the only person left to confront after all the challengers, the broken relationships, was himself. DeNiro became this character. His performance is remarkable because it is a fusion of his own inner feelings, and Scorsese's, as well as the other writers, while still being loyal to the spirit of Jake La Motta. DeNiro had been a vessel for Scorsese's issues, but in films that had some autobiographical thread as in *Mean Streets* and *New York, New York. Taxi Driver* was the first attempt to transcend the trappings of Scorsese's life to investigate the inner man. The thin line between autobiography of the psyche and the reality of the main character was held by an anthropological perspective of what the early seventies wreaked on the white male. *Raging Bull* had no line. It could not be about boxing, when compared to the scope of the genre, and it was not a traditional biopic. Boxing was a metaphor and for DeNiro he had to embody the physicality of a fighter with the stained soul of a man disintegrating by self-hatred. DeNiro accomplishes this by playing the dramatic scenes without sentimentality but with raw emotions that demonstrate the character's ferocious nature. In the ring the actor is convinces that he is not fighting to win but to prove something to himself—that he could take endless physical punishment because he deserved it for what he has done in his life and who he had become.

Much has been said and written about DeNiro's tremendous weight gain to play the later scenes in Jake's life. This feat goes beyond an actor's stunt, the definition of good acting, or the limits of realism. DeNiro had absorbed so much negativity from all the sources that went into his character and the story that he had to experience the disgust, the lack of respect, and the hopelessness the character reached at this point. DeNiro had gone so far that his doctors and Scorsese felt it necessary to cut back on the shooting schedule so the actor could be brought back to a healthy state. The mind-body connection was tested during *Raging Bull* as DeNiro found himself gasping for air and getting close to the realization that ends *Raging Bull*—that La Motta wasn't an animal but a man and it was time to stop if he wanted to live. DeNiro never judged the real La Motta and saw good in him that others did not. That may have saved the actor from going over his own bout with sanity because the burden of expressing the destructive forces in others even for artistic purposes is dangerous.

When the narrative structure, the characters, and the subtext of the story was completed, the final script was handed over to the producers and had no author's names, only the initials M.S., R.D. The credits in the film as released state that the screenplay was written by Mardik Martin and Paul Schrader. Neither director nor actor took credit but the script that was shot was shaped by Scorsese and DeNiro to their story as well as Jake La Motta's. Jake's autobiography was systematically stripped of all the back-story of his youth, and the reasons La Motta became the man he became. *Raging Bull* was the story of self-destruction followed by the enlightenment.

After the screenplay was completed Scorsese planned the visualization of *Raging Bull* shot by shot, drawing each frame in his own hand. Each fight would have a different visual style that reflected Jake's emotional state. The dramatic scenes would be stripped of the expressionist fury employed in the fights. They would be approached in the tradition of the great American drama embraced by Elia Kazan, honest realism that depicted the truth of a character's actions. For Kazan and the Actor's Studio tradition he came from the motivation for a character and the subtext was everything. Guided by Stanislavsky, this kind of dramatic work delved into the psychology of a character and charted every word, gesture, and move. It was an intellectual and instinctual method. Scorsese (who had been raised on the kitchen sink realism and the great era of American drama) turned the method inside out. The motivation, actions, and emotions of the characters all resided within him. Scorsese, the great observer who put his world of Little Italy on film, also understood that his motivation for making films, though complex, had to do with self-expression, filtered through the experiences and influences he handpicked for each film.

The opening shot of *Raging Bull* is a single, locked-off full take of La Motta in the ring with his fight robe. He is warming up, throwing punches,

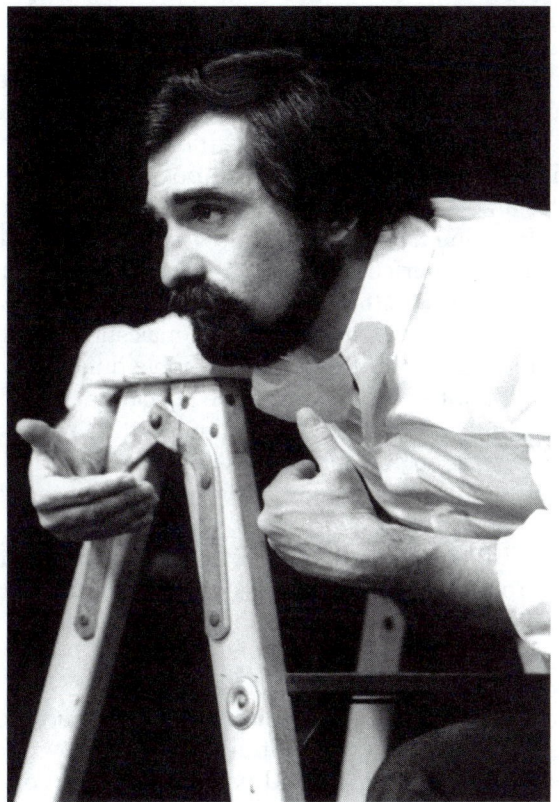

Scorsese expresses his emotional direction through hand gestures during the shooting of *Raging Bull. Courtesy Photofest.*

and taking steps. There is no one else in the ring. Behind him through a thick cloud of smoke men sit and watch, flashbulbs go off from various spots in the crowd, whose presence can be more felt than seen. The title *Raging Bull* is in bright red, now long established as Scorsese's color that defines temperament, religion, emotion, and omnipresent violence.

Simply the shot defines the character. Here is Jake La Motta, the raging bull. La Motta moves instinctually from within and with intent. His raging temperament will not be explained in the film but demonstrated. La Motta, like Scorsese, survives as an outsider within a confined space. Traditionally the camera shoots boxing in genre films from outside the ropes. Scorsese does so in this shot and with a rare exception not in the fight scenes to come. Tradition is to keep the audience safely outside the ring. The fight scenes in *Raging Bull* stay inside the ring because the point of view of the images and sound are emanating from inside Jake's head. Tradition shows the ropes, which define the ring, but without emphasizing the fact that it is the ropes that delineate the world of the boxer. This is accomplished with angle, lighting, and composition. Using the same tools Scorsese creates an opening shot that puts the bull in the ring. The thick horizontal lines confine La Motta and show him not trying to get out but to stay in. The shot is a perfect one-shot movie. It is not directly tied to the narrative but defines La Motta. The Italian opera that scores the opening speaks to La Motta's Italian heritage: proud, majestic, lyrical, and strong. La Motta is inside the ring but defiant as a noble outsider who performs his rage dance without acknowledging the spectators. He is not there to prove that he is a man of integrity as he defines it. A man who won't go down for a dive, or for lacking ability. He will take any and all punishment and deliver blows out of the furies that drive his every thought. It means little that he was abused as a child, or was raised in a tenement, or was a troubled youth. This stunning opening shot transcends boxing: it is a man destined to confront his deadliest opponent—the essence of his soul.

The opening shot introduces us to the character and soul of Jake La Motta, but *Raging Bull* formally begins in New York City, 1964, at his one-man show named "An Evening with Jake La Motta." Jake is backstage rehearsing a poem about boxing in which he makes humorous allusions to Shakespeare and his career. Jake's transition to his own form of show business bookends the film. In a bold narrative move Scorsese first let's the viewer see the older, flabbier Jake, who has found his salvation in a new platform for him to rage. Instead of a boxing ring his act will be on a proscenium stage, expressing himself in words not physical violence. The audience is challenged throughout the film to understand how Jake seeks and accomplishes his redemption. For Scorsese (who created the film to express his own hope to change his self-destructive life) the redemption is subtle, just the simple epiphany that a man can get so tired of destroying himself and others in the process that one day he simply stops. This opening scene doesn't explain the nuances; there are more clues to come in the course of the film. The moment of epiphany is clear and intensely dramatic but the redemption revealed in the last scene of *Raging Bull* eludes many viewers; but for Scorsese it allowed him to continue with his life and work.

The backstory of Jake La Motta begins in 1941 in the throes of a fight with Jimmy Reeves. La Motta, referred to by the announcer as The Bronx Bull, is undefeated but is well behind on points. La Motta is taking his punishment, allowing Reeves to pummel him with hard blows. Jake's corner is livid at him. His brother Joey (Joe Pesci) calls Reeves a *Muleyan*, the Italian slang for eggplant and a racial slur delivered by Italian-Americans. Violence breaks out in the ring suddenly without warning—then silence as the round is about to begin. La Motta is now reenergized, stalking Reeves in a half crouch, then knocks him down with a combination. Jake is so down on points he needs a knockout to win. Reeves gets up before the count. La Motta standing and raging with emotion knocks Reeves down again with a series of punches. Up again, Reeves is bombarded by an unrelenting series of punches by Jake who has unleashed all his fury. Reeves is saved by the bell for the third knockdown and is carried to his corner. The decision is up to the judges. La Motta struts around the ring with his leopard robe, always associated by image or sound with animals. Joey yells, "You waited too long." The relationship between the brothers is clearly defined as Jake orders, "Put my robe on right!" Reeves wins the decision, and La Motta loses his first fight. The crowd erupts—a chair flies into the ring. A woman is thrown to the ground and stomped on by the unruly mob. The organist is signaled to play the "Star Spangled Banner." Bodies fly through the air as the riot continues. Black humor and ironic contrast is used to show the absurdity of the violence. It is immediately established that La Motta fights for his own reasons, his methods more a test of his own will than the opponent. How much punishment can he take? For how long and still fight back to win? Here in the viewer's first look La Motta goes too far, his punishment, a soil on his perfect record analogous to the original sin on his soul.

The Bronx, 1941. Joey walks down the street with Salvy (Frank Vincent) discussing the loss to Reeves. Salvy tells Joey if Jake had been with Tommy, a mob boss, this wouldn't have happened. Jake is an independent. He refused to be associated with the mob and to give them a share of his money. An analogy could be made between an independent filmmaker and working for a studio. Scorsese admires Jake's determination to do everything his way but is examining here the price paid for personal expression.

In his apartment Jake confronts his wife, who doesn't take him or his boxing seriously. When Jake says everyone knows he's the boss, he is really talking to himself. His confidence relies on the acceptance of others. He demands respect but can only bully the woman. They get into an explosive argument because she has overcooked his steak. When Jake realizes she is getting the upper hand by piling the food on, his fury is unleashed on her. It is not the steak that is the issue although he keeps repeating it is—it is respect that Jake wants. By leaving out La Motta's background we see only the result, an angry, restless man who makes the lives of everyone around him miserable because he can't come to terms with himself.

Joey, as brother and manager, is middleman. Salvy tells Joey he's the only one Jake will listen too. Joey walks in during another La Motta bout, a domestic one. They are still arguing over the food. Jake repeats, "I got no choice," here not meaning his is driven by destiny but that he is trapped in a marriage with a woman who won't serve his needs. Jake manhandles her and she runs off to her bedroom. Neighbors complain. Jake gets into another battle with a voice from below that calls him an animal. Joey tries to tell his brother he can't eat and drink like an animal and put up with a wife he calls "this *brasciole*," an Italian stuffed steak dish, but used here as derogatory slang. Joey tries to appeal to Jake who confesses what is really bothering him—his hands. Jake knows he'll never be able to fight Joe Louis. To Jake he is being denied a chance to fight the best. Joey explains Jake is a middleweight, Louis a heavyweight, but Jake has no perspective. He wants to do what he wants to do and is frustrated by all around him; he perceives they are stopping him from greatness. Scorsese intellectually explored the difficulty of a marriage between creative couples, but this impulse comes from earlier and deeper wounds when Scorsese was trying to break into movies and lacked the support he desired from his first wife. Scorsese didn't act out as Jake but the psychic damage is transformed here into a man tormented by a dream to be champion and is the sole source of his success and failure. Jake is the dark part of Scorsese's soul, never expressed outwardly but emotions that led to destructive behavior and to expression of art that made him shine as a filmmaker. The two led to dire consequences for Scorsese's personal life and his health. As an example, Jake would show him the way.

Jake makes one of his destructive transitions, which are controlled by his inner demons. He hounds Joey to hit him in the face. Joey tries to resist but Jake's neurosis has stamina. Jake wants to prove to himself via Joey that he can take punishment. Jake is relentless until his cuts open and blood flows on his face. "What are you trying to prove?" Joey asks. Jake, now satisfied, smiles and pinches his brother. Jake has lost communication with the outside world. His wife looks through the curtains of the bedroom and walks away, a symbolic image that needs no analysis.

As Joey and Jake spar in the gym, Salvy and his men come to visit. Salvy assumed Joey talked to Jake who immediately recognizes the mobbed up guys. As they sit and watch Jake work out, La Motta makes his brother pay a price, warning Joey never to bring them up to the gym again. To teach Joey a lesson and to send a message of his independence, Jake throws his full power into demolishing Joey. Salvy gets the message and leaves, sending two messages. To Joey he says he'll see him tomorrow, which means as Tommy's messenger he won't stop trying to get Jake to join the syndicate; to Jake he says, "Watch you don't hurt yourself," letting La Motta know they're on to him and to stop hurting his brother and his own chances of ever becoming middleweight champion by signing with Tommy. Jake struts across the ring while Salvy goes up to an old timer and assures him if anyone bothers him to let Salvy know; the mob code of protection to the community that Scorsese observed regularly while growing up. Jake has proved his point but he continues to repeat the mob wants to take his money and for Joey never to bring them to his training again, but this time it leaves an opening for Joey, now furious at his brother and punches away, ending the session by throwing his gloves at Jake.

Raging Bull is as much about the brother-to-brother relationship as it is about Jake's spiritual journey. This element of the script was introduced by Paul Schrader, whose brother was also a screenwriter. The Jake/Joey relationship was heavily based on Jake's relationship, not with his brother Joey, but with friend Peter Savage. The least known aspect about Martin Scorsese's personal life is the relationship between Marty and his older brother Frank. As adults they have lived private and separate lives: Marty the internationally known film director, and Frank, who carried on his father's profession as a presser and moved to Staten Island where an enclave of Scorsese's family resides. The brother relationships of two films loom large over *Raging Bull*. Thomas Gomez and John Garfield in *Force of Evil* and Marlon Brando and Rod Steiger in *On the Waterfront*, both films deal with the concept of a brother taking care of the other, the former the younger for the older, the later, the older for the younger. Both deal with betrayal. *Raging Bull* focuses on the roles brothers play in life, the principle of taking care and looking out for each other. Somewhere hidden within *Raging Bull* are insights into the relationship of an older brother who took close care of a younger sickly brother. No conclusions can be drawn, but Scorsese's deep-rooted need to explore his life, often in a coded manner only deciphered with a key, a remark, or a statement from the director, or a fact base. No publicly exists for Frank and Marty, and it is fitting that Scorsese, a man so open and honest with his life, should keep at least one secret, one relationship private.

At a public pool Jake sees Joey, Salvy, and the crew with an extraordinarily beautiful teenage girl, Vickie (Cathy Moriarty). Jake is fascinated with her and asks countless questions about her to Joey. Jake is a man of many questions and regardless of the answers he knows what he knows before he asks. He interrogates those closest to them as a way of feeding his single-mindedness and his florid paranoia. When Joey curses Jake admonishes him, one of many contradictions in a man like Travis Bickle (in *Taxi Driver*) filled with clashing moral views. Jake finds no remorse for the victims of his punches and abuse but doesn't want anyone cursing around him. It also is a ploy to get Joey to tell him what he wants to know about Vickie and to link Joey with his mob friends: to keep his brother close and under his thumb. Joey tells Jake not to keep challenging him and that he always tells Jake the truth. This code of honor is never accepted by Jake's unrelenting paranoia and lack of trust due to his own low opinion of himself, hidden by his outward bravado. Jake watches as Salvy and one of his men talk "business"; he ridicules them to Joey telling his brother they make sure the girl can hear that they are big men. Jake is an outsider, a man who refuses to be part of even a closed society, to close himself off in the ring where his true expression is unleashed. In the most erotic moments in all of Scorsese's work Vickie sits at the edge of the pool, a forties' beauty with long blond flowing hair, full lips, and a womanly figure. In slow motion she slowly pumps her legs through the water as Jake through these POV (point of view) shots obsesses over her.

The brothers get ready to go out, which starts another verbal attack between Jake and his wife. Again the whole building reacts. Joey sides with his brother and feeds Jake's neurosis saying, "How much abuse you want to take?" The end of the marriage is dramatized by the wife throwing Jake's things out of the window, in defiance.

Jake and Joey go to the St. Clare's Church Annual Summer Dance, shot on location at a dance hall his parents used to attend and the same that Scorsese and DeNiro went to as young men. During these dances Scorsese reports there were always fights between Italian-Americans and Italians who were fresh off the boat from Italy. This is alluded to in a few lines and part of a fight in progress, but not played for the specificity and more for the constant violence in Italian-American communities. But understanding the cause and effect, Scorsese's seemingly unannounced violence in this and other films is rarely a shock for the Italian-American viewer who understands the dynamics of high temperature personalities and the flashpoints, and many seem to explode out of thin air. The dramatics of this life are based on action/reaction. When the wife asks, "Are you going out?" Jake immediately is hot under the collar because he sees himself as above questioning (he can do whatever he wants) and replies, "What are you, a cop?" and the fireworks begin. At the dance Joey's friend Beans holds a table for the brothers and greets them by saying he has trouble with some greaseballs downstairs. There is a class distinction between the Italian-Americans and native-born Italians. Hot one second, a comedian the next, Beans greets a priest who is making the rounds by asking the pastor if he wants to get laid. The hostility and crude emotions are instantly transferred but the anger lies in wait. Joey, in the spirit of the poolroom sequence in *Mean Streets*, asks the priest to bless the table as a way of narrowing the line between the church and the street. In a series of slow motion POVs intercut with a transfixed Jake, Vickie is spotted and the fetishization of the young woman continues. Jake is hypnotized by her beauty. The slow motion is his brain obsessing over her. As Salvy and the boys join the ladies at the table Jake is up pacing after them. He can't possibly think he can approach Vickie now but watches them go down the steps, past the inter-Italia fight in progress, past Beans in a flagrant argument with several men, while others tend to their wounds and out the door where to the bass, drums, and whistling of "Big Noise from Winnetka," watches Vickie drive away with the gangster. When they are gone, Bones throws several undesirables out and Jake comes to life, putting his hands on one and throwing him out as an instinctual physical act along with the verbal mimicking of his side saying, "Go back where you came from," without any understanding of what is occurring. Jake does take sides here out of tribal response because of Bones. He is practically as unconscious as Travis when he was around Betsy (in *Taxi Driver*).

Jake's persistence over Vickie takes place offscreen. When Jake first saw Vickie Joey told him she was off limits, he was married and she was a girl you had to spend time with. In-between scenes the first wife is out of the picture and Joey realizes he has no choice but to do his brother's calling. Joey talks to Vickie at the fence surrounding the public pool and sets up a meeting with Jake. The first contact between Jake and Vickie is awkward, crude, and even silly as Jake shakes her finger through the fence. Scorsese easily handles scenes through barriers, a part of his upbringing on the streets, always looking through windows, fences, and other city boundaries, which defined everyone's existence. The symbolism is apparent but natural, more urban than a noir indicator.

Jake and Vickie go for a ride in his car—he is crude; he tells her to move over so he can put his arm around her.

Jake brings Vickie to his father's house where he lived after his first marriage. For Scorsese these narrative details are unimportant but how Jake sees his world is all-important. He brings the girl in and they sit at a small table. Sexual tension is high. Vickie is a good girl but a smart one who has been around men since her early maturity. Jake gets her one chair closer and then to sit on his lap. He bluntly tells Vickie he bought the building for his father, watching her reaction closely. When she asks, "From fighting?"

he says, "What else?" but has gotten the answer he wants, this woman, unlike his first wife, respects him. A tour through the apartment is awkward, religious pictures hang on the wall. His sole purpose is to get her into the bedroom. They sit on the edge of the bed, he holds her around the waist, but she tries to avoid his advances. They stand in front of a posed picture of the two brothers in a mock fight. Jake begins to commit his feelings, tells Vickie how beautiful she is and kisses her gently; she responds demurely like a young girl, mature in figure but pure in her lack of experience with men. The love story is honest, evokes the lack of finesse most young men experience, they know what they want but not how to get it. Jake tries to be aggressive but remains careful and respectful, remembering Joey told him this was a girl you had to spend time with. This is another variation on the Madonna-Whore syndrome but Jake is willing to court Vickie not by traditional rules but by his own, rough around the edges but displaying a yearning for purity and decency he's never experienced.

The La Motta/Sugar Ray Robinson fight in 1943 comes after the undefeated Robinson defeated Jake in their first fight. Inside the ring the two diverse styles are delineated. Robinson: fast, dancing, and a clean puncher; Jake: stalking, and punching with his full body weight. The abstract sounds of animal's noises and other primal sounds begin to enter Jakes head as well as subjective shots of the act of boxing through a fighter's eyes, the camera swirling by the ceiling lights. Robinson is hit so hard he flies out of the ring, and is frozen in the light of a press photoflash. Sugar Ray has never been knocked down before. Jake paces like a lion, pent up and ready to strike for the kill. He pummels Ray some more, the signature bell rings over back, and a microphone drops down. La Motta wins by unanimous decision. It is La Motta's moment: The announcer crowns him as a great fighter who should have a shot at the championship belt.

Vickie comes out of the bathroom and into the bedroom of Jake's apartment, wearing a white negligee. He calls her but she says she can't touch him before a fight. Boxers long held the belief that sexual activity drained them of their ferocity and withholding the impulse built up aggression they could harness to demolish their opponent. Jake took his concept of receiving punishment to the fullest degree. He holds Vickie and in infantile talk has her kiss the boo boos on his face. Then leaning back he has her take off his pants. When she reminds him she promised not to get him excited he gives her a deep soul kiss, orders her to take off her panties as he watches, and continues to gaze as she kisses her way down his body over bruises and further toward his erogenous zone. When she gets to the point of no return and he is experiencing pleasure he stops her abruptly telling her he has a fight coming up, then goes into the bathroom, framed by sacred heart holy pictures, and pours a pitcher of ice water over his lower half putting out the "fire." Vickie comes from behind and they kiss, he begins to caress her body but then pushes her away. As the scene of Vickie at the pool was one of Scorsese's most erotic tapping into the heated male fantasy of fetishizing a woman's body, this is the most directly sexual. The content is arousal without release so the tension building in Jake is transferred to the viewer, as is Vickie's pleasure in serving his instincts. His explicit teasing is pleasurable for her because it builds up control and release for her as his partner. She is empowered for the moment and enjoys the desire it creates in Jake. For Jake the pleasure is in denial and discipline. He subjects his body and mind to punishment because he knows he has done a lot of bad things in his life. Fighting is his profession but also his reason for existence. Adoration of Vickie and the physical pleasure he derived from the relationship have an adverse side, jealousy, mistrust, and the obsession with watching over her every move. Jake systematically destroys himself and attempts to do so with every opponent. He is not there to win or lose but to live or annihilate. By combining and confusing pleasure and pain La Motta heightens his emotional responses to both, which become the same.

The La Motta/Robinson fight, 1943. Their third fight takes place inside a circle of hell in Jake's mind. They fight with smoke and heat surrounding them, the punches artless and brutal. Many of the images are through waves of intense heat, wavering visibility. The fight is a unanimous decision for Robinson.

In Jake's dressing room Joey smashes a stool against a wall. Jake soaks his swollen hands as the anger is transferred over to the more emotional stable brother. Joey rationalizes the loss due to Robinson going into the Army next week. Jake doesn't understand what he has to do having hit Sugar Ray with everything he had. In a moment of self-reflection Jake responds, "I've done a lot of bad things Joey, maybe it's coming back to me." Jake is not convincing, expressing the truth as he understands it; he is being punished for a lifetime of sin through action and thought. To Joey Jake was robbed, strictly the dirty deeds of the fight game; but Jake stares into the mirror and watches his hand move into the ice. He has entrusted Joey to take Vickie home but never seems to have trust in anyone.

In a montage, Jake's boxing career flourishes from January 14, 1944, to March 14, 1947, and his personal life blooms through his courtship with Vickie, his marriage, his honeymoon, Joey's marriage, Jake carrying Vickie over the threshold of their first home, family life for the brothers, children being raised, family barbecues, and good times with growing families.

Scored with opera, the black-and-white images of the boxing matches using still images, stop frame, show the ferocity of Jake's power in the ring, the majesty of his wins, his arms up in the air, and transforming him into a champion. The color home movies show domestic bliss; Jake, tamed by Vickie, enjoys the fun of her company and showing off her beauty. The civil ceremony of Jake and Vickie's wedding is later contrasted with the formal rooftop football wedding of Joey and Lenore (Teresa Saldana). The images are color-faded, scratched, frames missing to create a poetic grace of the late forties. In their specificity they tell the story of the greatest generation and a lifestyle of home, family, and the building of domestic bliss. The sequence is filled with information but its thrust is the rise of Jake La Motta, a time when the demons let him be, only to come back in full force when success as a boxer was at his feet and a domestic life of happiness was threatened by his growing disrespect for his body, mind, and spirit.

Pelham Parkway, Bronx, New York, 1947. The fairytale career of a constant winner and a content family man begins to deteriorate. Vickie, Joey, Lenore, and their children are in the kitchen as Jake storms in as if he was entering the ring. He attacks his brother over career strategy. Jake is gaining weight. Joey explains his plans to get Jake a title shot. The Big Idea, which is summed up in the street corner philosophy, "If you win you win, if you lose you still win." Jake is distracted and works on Vickie to bring him coffee, going from a gentle voice to, "HOW LONG DO I HAVE TO WAIT! in under ten seconds. When Joey has finished berating Jake for all the weight he's gained, which is worrying him, Vickie tries to help by supporting Joey's plan to fight Tony Janiro. In her reasoning she makes the mistake of saying that Janiro is "good-looking," which sends Jake into a verbal attack. Vickie is wise to her husband's ways and stops when he dismisses her out of the room. Jake continues to rant about Vickie's two words that have inflamed his jealousy and fury. When Lenore says a word to defend her sister-in-law, Joey attacks her and sends his wife out of the room. When the brothers are alone Joey convinces Jake to go to a training camp to lose the weight without distractions; but Jake is obsessed about Vickie, ordering Joey to keep an eye on her while he is away. At Joey's suggestion Jake goes into the living room and makes up with Vickie.

The Copacabana. Jake is introduced as a contender for the heavyweight crown. Joey is with another woman. Vickie gets up to go to the powder room and runs into Salvy who invites her over to their table where Tommy Como (Nicholas Colasanto) and the old gang are. Jake watches this from afar and becomes sullen. Salvy comes over and Jake gives him his fingers rather than his hand. The handshake is a critical social component in Italian-American culture, the sign of friendship and acceptance. Anything less than a full contact and a hearty shake is an insult, a message more articulate and cutting than any words. Jake fires off dirty looks at Tommy, and Salvy receives the message; he is gentlemanly, inviting Joey for a drink and jibing at Jake to rib him a little to break the tension. Jake becomes deeply sullen. When Salvy leaves Joey remarks favorably about the suit Salvy is wearing by blow-spitting over the table in disrespect. Vickie comes over to pay her respects to Tommy. Jake is staring, his mind devising plots and bad thoughts out of his own limitations and emotional shortcomings. His POV is depicted in slow motion so a polite kiss on the cheek to Tommy and the other looks lewd and conspiratorial. When Vickie comes back to the table Jake is relentless in questioning her and insists she is interested in them. Jake's grim disposition has made the others uncomfortable. Joey goes over to Tommy's table as an obligation. Tommy has his arm around Jake who keeps his eyes mainly on the table out of disdain for the underlings around the table. He shakes the hand of Tommy's main man, another old-timer played by Charles Scorsese, but when he has to shake hands with one of Salvy's men he runs his hand through the pomade in his hair to send him a message. Salvy feeds Jake's growing paranoia about Janiro by saying he's good-looking and all the girls like him. Jake tries to be respectful toward Tommy but his hatred for the gang is palpable. Jake tells Tommy he can bet everything on him because he's going to destroy Janiro. Tommy asks if it's something personal and Jake manages to make a joke about the hatred toward the other fighter by saying, "He's a nice kid, a pretty kid too, I mean I don't know I got a problem I don't know whether I should fuck him or fight him," which pleases Tommy, but Jake openly turns on Salvy as the wise guy tries to make conversation insulting him in front of his crew. Salvy knows he must suck it in and Jake enjoys his independence from the mob.

Vickie is asleep. A large crucifix from Scorsese's parent's bedroom hangs over the bed. Jake walks in, now consumed with jealousy over Janiro, and tries to get the now half-sleeping woman to admit she thinks about other men and can't stop asking her why she said Janiro was good-looking. Jake is close to becoming a champion but can't accept his good fortune. He is eating to punish his body; he's making those around him miserable about Janiro's looks because of his lack of self-love. The mental torment he has brought on himself is breaking down his psyche.

During the Janiro fight Jake doesn't fight the young handsome fighter but bashes his face in literally, destroying the man's looks in front of the crowd. The hatred and pure anger has become an energy force. Jake struts around the ring after winning; he has proven his point, one only real to himself. Vickie looks worried, watching her husband self-destruct through the win. Tommy is impressed. Jake further relieves the destructive forces within him.

Now that he has conquered the threat in his mind to his wife's love, Jake can address the business at hand. He jogs in place in a steam room; the steam, like the smoke in the ring, is a constant reminder that Jake is residing in a personal hell.

Joey is at the Copa bar talking to admirers of Jake, who are impressed by his savagery toward Janiro. Joey sees Vickie enter with Salvy and his crew. Joey is distracted, goes right to the table, and takes Vickie aside. Vickie tells Joey she loves Jake but he no longer attends to her and she's tired of taking orders. Vickie now knows that Jake will never be a champion because too many people hate him. She understands the fight game and knows he can't win without Tommy, but is too stubborn and too proud and too consumed within himself. The theme of Jake doing things his own way is representative of the personal filmmaker going his own way. Scorsese's profile and personality couldn't be more polar opposite than his main character but Jake projects the feelings of the artist alone, fighting everyone, especially oneself. The outsiders know they have to go it alone but take constant punishment to their psyches by self-questioning, and disliking themselves for being different. Jake is a visualization of those dark feelings.

Vickie comes back to the table and Joey's Italian temper takes over. He turns against Salvy and gets Vickie to leave. Joey expresses his own violence by breaking a drinking glass with a swing of his hand. Salvy explains the meeting is innocent. Joey becomes like his brother, believing something is happening when nothing is happening. Without warning he breaks a glass over Salvy's face and rages as if he were Jake. La Motta's negativity is now destroying his brother. Joey cannot be stopped. He waits for Salvy outside and beats him with a metal pole on a base used to hold the velvet ropes. He kicks the much larger man on the ground and then slams his head with a cab door as Salvy tries to get to safety. The opera begins again and bridges to the Debonair Social Club. The same theme becomes relentlessly tragic. A series of shots capture the culture of the interior: expresso simmering, men playing cards, the cups all around as Tommy conducts a sit-down with Tommy and Salvy, a part of the Italian justice culture of the capos established in *Mean Streets*. The two friends shake hands. Salvy is asked to leave so Tommy can talk to Joey. Tommy explains that Jake is making the boss look bad, and that he can't *deliver* a kid from his own neighborhood. Tommy tells Joey in no uncertain terms that Jake won't get a shot at the title without *us*.

Joey meets Jake at the pool. Water has significance in *Raging Bull*. It is a sign from the heavens, which was the setting for Jake's first vision of Vickie; it bathes his body covered in bruises; now the heavens are open and it is raining incessantly at the pool. Jake is brooding over the time he met Vickie in the sunshine and now the gods are against him. He is convinced she is unfaithful to him. He is not even interested in what Joey has to say about his meeting with Tommy. To Joey it's Vickie who is ruining his life; his denial is too deep yet to see his brother's faults, to accept who Jake really is. Joey tells Jake he'll get a shot at the title but first he has to throw a fight to build up the purse and make money for the boys.

Jake's downfall comes when he agrees to take the fall but refuses to wholeheartedly accept that he must subsist to the mobsters. He's told by the commissioner that the word is out about the setup. Jake lies. All bets are off on La Motta, all the money is on his opponent Billy Fox, a second-rate fighter. The fix is in. Jake's performance is a disaster. He hits Fox so hard he almost knocks him out at the outset of the fight. He throws punches in the air and then stands there and let's Fox punch him until the referee stops the fight in the fourth round of a technical knockout. The crowd jeers and boos, Jakes walks out of the arena. His will is so strong that he couldn't submit to the forces trying to control him. He had to prove to the syndicate that they could make their money but couldn't win his soul; but by taking the step and agreeing to the fix, Jake has lost any sense of self left; the total disintegration is complete. Jake has lost his moral and physical center.

Back in his dressing room Jake is crying inconsolably. He cries and repeats, "What did I do?" It is a moment in which he is truly in touch with his feelings knowing that he has lost his integrity against the mob. He has given in but there is a price to pay, because he couldn't unconditionally sell out: everyone knows the fight was a dive. As he continues to sob like a helpless baby, a *Daily News* tabloid headline announces, "Board Suspends La Motta."

Jake's moment of contrition is fleeting. He rages into his apartment with Joey behind him. He is back to the Italian-American position of the oppressed and crucified. Everything is being done *to* him. What do they want from me? They wanted me to take a dive and I took a dive. Jake still thinks that he can have it his way. He refuses to accept that he agreed to take a dive, which means taking a fall on the canvas when hit. "What did they want me to do, to go down? I don't go down for nobody." For Jake to be knocked to the canvas for real or by design is tied to his pride, his integrity—his persona. He continues to think he can have it his way, take a dive his way, get a shot at the championship his way on his own, but this time the commissioner has intervened. The purse is withheld pending an investigation. Now Jake is concerned how that will make him look, not that his clownish behavior in the ring has hurt him, but the investigation. He tells Joey it's going to make him look like the *mamaluke* of the year. Joey has not given up on Jake. Although he doesn't agree with his brother's behavior he understands him and hopes that he can save his brother the way Charlie Cappa thought he could save Johnny Boy Civello in *Mean Streets.* Joey tells Jake that Tommy will give him another shot at the championship. Again an offhand remark sets Jake off. When Joey says that as long as Tommy is around he'll help them, Jake with his true neurosis of obsession starts asking question after question, convinced there is something wrong with Tommy. The scene is played lightly, almost a comic relief, but it is a sure sign that Jake is continuing down the same path of self-destruction, nothing can get in the way of that. Nothing Jake is aware of as yet.

Two years go by—it is 1949 and Jake gets his shot. He and his entourage are in a hotel, waiting. The fight against Marcel Cerdan is in an outdoor area and it is raining. Jake is always raging but fighting is a form of release as well as restoring his well of anger. He paces around the room waiting for anyone to give him an opening. Joey asks him if he wants anything to eat and Jake snaps back. Joey decides to order Jake a steak that Jake can chew and spit out the meat so he maintains his weight. He continues to watch everyone. Joey suggests Vickie has a cheeseburger and fries rather than a piece of cake and Jake sees this mundane action as a threat to his domination over his wife. When she finally agrees to Joey, Jake must make it seem like it has his okay. Jake isolates himself in the bedroom until he is told Tommy is up to see him. Tommy is there as a kingmaker, just wanting to make sure everything is alright; it maintains his power and respect. Joey tells him how important it is to Jake but Jake, always wary, puts on a phony act to Tommy. Just as Tommy is about to leave, Vickie gets up to say goodbye. Jake's paranoia kicks in full throttle. In POV we see his jealousy toward Joey and Tommy (both growing threats to his marriage) in his mind. When Tommy leaves, Jake begins the relentless questions and in frustration slaps Vickie. Joey tries to intervene, as loved ones do, but Jake unleashes his anger. As he plunges deeper into his self-hatred and distrust of those who love and support him, he is unaware of his actions, over which he has little to no control. Jake has sunk deeper into being a miserable human being; his only worth is the potential heavyweight crown. Whatever redeeming values he had have been eaten up by his seething anger and inability to trust others.

Jake's moment to become champion has arrived. It is not without a price. He takes his final warm up by punching into a chest protector worn by Joey. The punches are as lethal as Jake can throw. He does not understand nuance; there is only one way, his way. Jake La Motta is driven by a single-mindedness that goes beyond winning or losing a fight. He is not a rebel without a cause. His spiritual force is a heat-seeking missile that can only destroy. Jake is a kamikaze artist. He can only do what obsesses him and cannot see the consequences. With each scene Scorsese takes him further into this abyss. The long walk to the ring is a single gliding Steadicam shot scored to Italian opera. There is a moment after Jake and his entourage enter the stadium to wild applause, and the camera passes over the face of a pretty forties' woman clapping, as the men and the camera make the turn into the ring area, and as the music swells, the Steadicam operator steps onto a platform that brings the view into epic proportions. Jake enters the ring: this is his moment. The shot is magnificent: the essence of cinematic depiction of time, place, and emotion but the *moment* when the camera passes the girl whose face can be seen in a million photo albums of the Greatest Generation and the camera rises to Jake's moment in time is high art. It is a moment that represents why we go to the movies and again proves that motion pictures are about moments in time, images, and emotions, a connection between the eye, the ear, the audience, and the screen that reaches the status of the spiritual.

The fight is swift, tough, but not excessive. Jake is unrelenting in boxing Cerdan until his corner throws in the towel. Jake La Motta has achieved all his dreams. He is Middleweight champion of the world. He had the championship belt around his waist. His arms rise in proof that he is the champ. Joe Louis comes to congratulate him. Flashbulbs explode in his face; Jake is a star, but he is also now in the limelight, a place he is unprepared to handle. Earlier, as Jake waited for the referee to determine the outcome of the fight, the sound of a continual rolling dull fire filled his head, the raging has not gone away. One of the keys to the film and its connection to Scorsese is the simple, tabloid, but eloquent title. It represents that Scorsese has acknowledged at this point in his life that he can only rage, but his body and conscience have given him a warning, which Jake never received and would only ignore if given. *Raging Bull* is Scorsese's *It's A Wonderful Life*. This is what his life will be if he doesn't reexamine and readjust his priorities, but like Capra, Scorsese will save Jake so that the answer to continuing his own existence will be clear to him. Scorsese totally believed no one would let him make movies when he finally revealed what he had been working toward, putting his essence on the screen with a truth so brutally honest that there would be nothing left to say. What Scorsese didn't realize was that like *Taxi Driver*, *Raging Bull* was what many needed to see and hear, the soul of a man ungarnished by Hollywood conventions and happy endings. Even though La Motta and Scorsese both thought, "They had no choice," it was one they had to find, which is the definition of self-truth, to understand oneself, and then to accept.

Now that Jake has achieved his goals, as Scorsese had with his career, would he be satisfied or was there still something else, something intangible, unless he allowed himself to *see* it.

Jake's home in Pelham Parkway—1950. Scorseses moves ahead in the continuum of Jake's life to the significant moments that plot his spiritual fall. Joey sits on the couch as Jake tries to fix the television. For a generation of baby boomers and their parents this is an archetypical fifties' scene. The television is broken and the father, regardless of skills, simply by way of gender role, has to fix it. The scene is always the same. The man of the house is behind the set fiddling but cannot see the results. A second person, most often a son, the little man of the house (but in this case Joey) must watch and give information as to whether there is or is not a picture, whether it's better or worse, if the horizontal or vertical has stopped rolling. The communication system is primitive, "That's something...oh, you lost it...how's that...worse...hold that...that's it...how's... now you have nothing." Here the scene is a deceptive device as a text to show Jake in suburban life but the subtext explodes quickly. Vickie comes in. Jake is sullen and immediately asks where she's been, she answers to the effect of a regular day. The camera pans to observe her go upstairs and then back to the living room. Jake is raging again. He starts by berating Joey for kissing Vickie on the mouth. Jake is slovenly, back up over fighting weight again, eating a hero sandwich, while continuing to work on the TV. Joey is losing patience with Jake. As La Motta comes in front to see what Joey says looks like something on the set, his brother jibes him that he can't see the screen with his stomach in the way. Jake is remote, angry, and drinks beer as Joey tries to humiliate him into stopping all the eating and getting back into shape for a title defense in one month. Jake has taken this in but his mind is back to his obsessions, asking Joey what happened to him and Salvy at the Copa. Jake gets him to tell him the story, which Joey quickly resolves but Jake pursues. "It had nothing to do with me? Who did it have something to do with? Vickie?" Joey tries to put it to rest but Jake repeats that he heard things. Joey thinks Jake is *starting* because he's worried about the fight, which may or may not be true because Jake is beyond reasoning. "Did Salvy fuck Vickie?" Joey knows this road and asks Jake to stop. Jake returns to the promise

Joey made to look after Vickie while he was in training. The conversation seems to be circular when Jake asks again why he gave Salvy a beating but this is Jake's demon, to keep asking, keep pushing, to get the answers he wants, not the truth but answers that prove he is worthless and without self-respect. Joey tries to use their brotherly bond but Jake refuses to trust anyone when it comes to Vickie. He forces Joey to repeat the story. The TV continues to flicker as nothing more than a prop in La Motta's grand scheme. He tells Joey he must respect his answer but if he finds out anything he will kill somebody. Joey jumps to his feet in fury. He gives Jake a list of people he could go kill himself, saying, "Kill me," all to make the point that Jake is killing himself with self-abuse. Jake physically steps in closer and psychically steps further into his desperate state. He now is convinced that it meant something when Joey said, "Kill me," linking in his psychotic state to Salvy, Vickie, Tommy—everyone in his paranoid fantasy. Joey tries to get his brother to see that his jealousy over Vickie has brought him to this destructive state. Then Jake utters the most infamous dialogue in *Raging Bull*, "Did you fuck my wife? Did you fuck my wife?" The words are ugly but their true meaning is devastating. Jake has lost touch with reality. Throughout the film he has been all but intolerable as a human being but there was always a dividing line between sanity and madness. Much of the balance was in the love and trust of the brothers, which Jake has now, in his loss of control, given up. Joey has tolerated enough; he will not allow himself to participate in Jake's madness. He leaves, giving some tough brotherly advice. As he goes out the door the camera pans back to Jake standing in the room. It looks like he is making a decision but it is another level of control leaving his damaged sanity. He firmly walks up the stairs.

Vickie is making up their bed. Jake walks over to her and again asks where she had been. He starts interrogating her holding on to her ponytail. Then like with Joey, he goes into that dark place, now asking her about what happened at the Copa. He gets a firm grip on her hair and begins to slap her and accuse her of adultery with Joey. She locks herself in the bathroom and Jake breaks it down. As he beats her he quickly shifts from "Did you?" to "Why did you do it?" entering a psychotic break. As Vickie fights back with her anger over his abuse, telling him in a mocking scream what he wants to hear, Jake is beyond sarcasm or reason. He leaves the house. Vickie follows him and he throws her onto the street.

Inside Joey's house dinner is under way. Joey is distracted with his son's bad habit of putting his hands on his food, now developing a more nasty edge from the exposure to Jake. Jake enters and attacks Joey repeating,

"You fucked my wife." Vickie enters and the women try to stop Jake as the mayhem spills into the living room. The furies in Jake's head are loose, no longer contained in his head. The sound and the brutality of the familial violence is raw as the viewer has a total channel into Jake's last bit of control, which has left him with no place to go. He storms out.

Night. Jake's TV continues to roll, a simple but powerful metaphor for the state of his life. Vickie quietly enters, walks up to the bedroom, and begins to pack. Jake is not raging but a steady low pulse beat expresses that it is there at times, florid at times—just there. The Scorsese crucifix above the bed is a sign of the times, Catholic tradition to protect us while we sleep, and reflects the director's religious culture as well as the contrast in the film's context that unholy things can happen and be said in this room. But Jake is now repentant, talking quietly, begging Vickie to stay. He confesses he is a "bum" but he needs her and the kids. It is a moment of contrition and honesty. They look into each other's eyes then fall into a deep and sincere embrace. Jake is not easily dismissed nor is he not able to express true feelings of love.

Jake is back in the ring defending his Middleweight crown. It is nearing the end of the fifteenth and final round. Jake has let his guard down and is taking ungodly punishment. In an instant he begins to punch relentlessly until he knocks out his challenger and retains his championship belt with thirteen seconds to go, the significance of the unlucky number is just there and not editorialized by the ring announcer. When La Motta stopped taking punches and begins assailing them, we're told he was "playing possum." Jake's behavior is unquestionably destructive but clear only to him or a force still out of his control. La Motta is taking punishment. Is it because he deserves it? Is he trying to prove how much he can take? Is it like allowing Vickie to arouse him and then at the last moment pouring ice water on his flaming member? It is not a boxing strategy but an expression of who Jake La Motta is. Scorsese doesn't provide the answers, only the behavior, just as he was looking at his own behavior and presenting La Motta's destructive path in order to learn how the fighter eventually saved himself. In a larger sense La Motta is still "playing possum," not taking charge of his life, continuing in cycles to annihilate his world.

Dressed in street clothes and walking through the basement of the arena with Vickie, his wife taking advantage of his win and his current state of contrition toward her to call Joey and apologize. He is impassive but gives her a dime to make the call for him. He holds the phone to his ear, Joey answers but is silent. Joey thinks its Salvy, or someone, because he hears breathing. Joey rudely tells off the silent caller. Jake has his way; he did what Vicky asked, he went through the motion as he did when asked to take a fall, and again brazenly defies a call for sense and acceptance.

Jake is back in the ring, in his corner. He is wiped down with a sponge but this time the liquid is blood flowing onto his body and it is rubbed in by his corner. His handler, a priestly looking man, waves his fingers over Jake in a symbolic recreation of the Last Rights.

The POV shifts to the live television broadcast of the fight for the middleweight championship with challenger Sugar Ray Robinson. The audio is from the broadcast, later revealed as coming from Joey's television, as he watches his brother's final boxing demise as he sits next to his wife. Now Scorsese allows the number thirteen to dramatize Jake's situation, all through the words of the actual fight announcer taken from the archives: the voice, the delivery, and words are pure poetry. "Round number thirteen, the hard luck number, there's the buzzer, and I think you know both the boys." *Raging Bull* is also about boxing but not the romance or tragedy. Scorsese creates the atmosphere and lifeblood of the sport so well, he puts the viewer right there in that world, a single line defines what fans have learned over a lifetime about boxing—its not a sport but an expression of life. Not ups and downs but a continuum of heartache, false hope, attention, and then oblivion. The fight has been "rousing" but now Jake will go to his form of Calvary. As he is assaulted, "crucified" by Robinson, he stands his ground, blood splattering over his body and from his head. A Christ-like figure, his knees buckle, blood sprays on those who view, and Vickie as a "Mary" or "Mary Magdalene" figure, bows her head at the spectacle. Jake has lost but tells Ray, "You never got me down," repeatedly. Jake has allowed himself to be crucified, but there are no Romans, no Pontius Pilate. Jake is not a martyr but a man who self-destructed in front of the public and those who loved him. He truly believes he deserves the punishment but remains proud he is still his own man.

As the announcer wraps up, and the decision announced that Sugar Ray is the new Middleweight champion, Scorsese moves into the single most powerful Catholic image in his body of work. The frame is filled with a length of the ring's rope—it is bleeding with the blood of Jake La Motta.

Without transition or explanation the next scene takes place in 1956 in Miami. The shock of the new Jake (and the actor who plays him) has gained so much weight that he is unrecognizable. The internal self-loathing has now violated the temple of La Motta's body. He tells an interviewer he's through with boxing and has everything: a nice home, a wife, and three children. Jake is entering the next phase of his spiritual journey.

Jake's new hell on earth is not a ring but a nightclub: smokey, sleazy, and vulgar. Jake is now a comedian, a further extension of the humiliation he endured as a boxer where he was a clown but the consequences were physically deadly. Now telling bad dirty jokes he is demeaning what is left of his soul. For Scorsese this aspect of La Motta as an entertainer is the perfect completion of the metaphor of La Motta as an independent artist who goes his own way, linking him further to the director as artist, who demands to make movies his own way. No longer a clown in a ring, La Motta is now the Fool. He insults honored guests. Jake's morality is crumbling. He allows two underaged girls to drink at his bar, asking them to convince him, a code for a deep, sexual kiss on the mouth. Jake is reigning in his own personal hell. He is not angry but still raging, against society but mainly himself, challenging both to stop him.

Jake is in a backroom performing the ultimate bar trick. He has stacked up five champagne glasses in a tower, each base inside the other. As three B-girls and another man watch, Jake pours champagne into the top glass, as it fills to overflow, the next glass is filled and so on until all five are filled without spilling a drop. The trick is to pour at a steady, even rate to cause the right overflow so a natural sparkling wine fall is created. The scene is illuminated by a shaft of light filled with smoke, which in *Raging Bull* is always heat, the fire of hell. "Lonely Nights" by The Hearts is playing. The context of the scene is that Jake is told Vickie is waiting for him, but he ignores her plea. The song is a young woman pleading for her man to come back and end her lonely nights. The connection between song and scene are obvious: Vickie is telling Jake she needs him, but there is further significance when Scorsese makes a song choice. Jake is beyond lonely, he is lost. At first he appears to be engaged in an important event, like nothing else matters. A wider shot reveals to his audience that Jake has embraced the low life and has become one with them, wasting time, and his life, as he accepts a new culture of bar girls, and pointless accomplishments, all to fill a void he cannot address. The scene begins with great seriousness, like the bar culture in *Mean Streets* that defined the lives of the Italian-American men who existed outside but *lived* in the bar. The onlookers watch with great awe. This is the height of culture for the unwashed. The song is relentless, the lyrics full of yearning and emotional pain. Jake finishes his feat and for just a second seems as accomplished as winning a championship belt, but then as when he succeeded in the ring, the moment turns to debauchery. Jake clowns like he's going to knock over the glasses in a mock drama to his currently impotent ability to express physical violence.

As the song fades, Jake walks to the parking lot. It is early morning and Vickie waits in her car. She finally has the courage to leave him. His attempts to get her back this time are useless and he seems resigned, as if he expected and deserves this.

Shirtless, with his pants undone, and his enormous fleshy body exposed, Jake is woken up by men from the DA's office. Jake is told the girl he allowed to drink at his bar is fourteen and she was accusing him of having introduced her to men and was taken downtown.

Jake makes an unannounced early morning visit to Vickie to get his championship belt to get money for his bail. He decides it's the jewels in the belt that will bring the money but it is really an excuse for him to use physicality to do things his own way. As he pounds the belt with a hammer, Vickie screams for him to stop so he doesn't wake up the children. He continues to swing at the belt until dishes on the other side of the wall fall and break from an open shelf. Jake reverts to his old husband behavior, blaming Vickie for not putting the dishes away properly; he no longer has power over her and is told to leave.

A jeweler tells Jake that the belt was where the value was, not in the jewels. On the phone he tells an unidentified person he can't raise the bail money.

Jake tries to fight off two officials who are putting him in a cell in the Dade County Stockcade. After a long defiant struggle in which Jake uses all his strength and verbal bile to fight back, he is alone in a small, dark, dingy cell. This is where he has been heading for. This is his moment of reckoning with himself.

In a quiet but agitated contemplation Jake faces himself for the first time. There is no one there to blame, no one to rage against. He stands and puts himself up against the concrete wall and begins to slam his head into large bricks, then throws steady lefts and rights barehanded not punching at but trying to punch through his physical and mental prison. He speeds up the blows screaming "Why" repeatedly, then again smashes his head, trying to get the answer by physically breaking through. The viewer is witness to a primal scream, the final confrontation with what has driven Jake. He becomes frenetic, pounding, flailing, at the wall, and at himself, his screams are full of heartbreak and futility. Symbolically, Jake has finally been knocked down. He sits on the cot crying, "I'm not an animal." When the line was spoken by John Hurt (as John Merrick, the Elephant Man in the David Lynch adaptation of the Bernard Pomerance play), it was not a confession or self-admission, but a man shunned by society proclaiming his humanity to those who can't understand. He has always been human. La Motta begins by asking why people call him an animal. Even his wife has called him an animal but his own nickname, The Raging Bull, supports this. For Scorsese Jake is an animal in a religious sense, simple holy and close to God. His religiosity has taught him not to judge but to feel and love. The scene is a complex set of emotions for the viewer who is forced to confront forgiveness for Jake. Jake tells himself it's so stupid, referring to the incident that got him in jail, allowing a minor to associate in his bar, but his words have deeper significance. He tells himself he's not that bad; he's not that guy, finally willing to admit to himself he had chosen to play a role that almost destroyed him. This is not a traditional Hollywood movie. There will be no happy ending or turning around of Jake. As the film moves into its final section, Jake's redemption becomes complex because for Scorsese redemption is not simple, not prayers, it's doing penance on the street in your own way as he stated in *Mean Streets*, and it's a transcendental state from hurting yourself and others to just living. Scorsese learned that spiritual transformation comes from art that transforms the artist.

Next Jake is in New York City. It is 1958 and he is working as a comedian and host at a strip club, a dive. The audience is indignant and rude. Jake is still his own man, not taking any lip or guff; but the rage is gone. He is no longer in hell but in purgatory, serving out his time. When a heckler says, "Funny Man," Jake replies, "That's why I'm here." The stripper comes out; she is over-the-hill, from a time long ago, a parody of her former self, like Jake.

Jake leaves the club with the stripper. As a cab pulls up for them, he sees, across the street, his brother Joey. Jake and Joey have been estranged for many years. From Jake's POV the sight of Joey is another opportunity toward rehabilitation of his spirit. The shot is in just enough of a slow motion speed to communicate Jake's emotional reaction as fate gives him another chance. Joey walks out of the store and Jake follows him into a parking garage. Jake begs his brother to turn and look at him. He stops him at the car. The reconciliation that later occurs is awkward and one-sided as Jake asks Joey for forgiveness. Joey resists giving in to the hugs and kisses. There is a brief moment of tenderness, which Joey ends by saying, "You don't want to do this here." He tells Jake he'll call him to get together in a couple of days. Once in the car, Jake asks for confirmation, all rancor is gone from his voice, and Joey sounds sincere about calling Jake.

The last scene of *Raging Bull* returns to the beginning of the film. The scenes inside the dressing room of the Barbizon Plaza can be absorbed as bookends, what's in between them is the story of how Jake La Motta reached this point in his life. The opening portrays him about to go on and the ending is the final preparation for his onstage performance. There is very little information in the first scene. The place: New York City; the year: 1964. A sign heralding, "An Evening with Jake La Motta," and then,

"Tonight 8: 30." Jake is near a barren dressing room, a naked light bulb, a small table, a mirror, and a wall payphone. He is rehearsing a humorous poem explaining that he needs a stage to rage but not to fight but to recite. The ending is Jake's redemption and a continuum for the rest of his life.

The sign now reveals the evening will feature the work of Paddy Chayefsky, Rod Serling, Shakespeare, Budd Schulberg, and Tennesse Williams. A montage depicts an existential deconstruction of the dressing room, the naked light bulb, the light switch, and the tops of several liquor bottles, an off composition of the phone and phone numbers hastily scribbled in pencil on the wall, a series of empty clothing hangers, and Jake's jacket in the background. Jake has been going over his introduction to his presentation of the cab scene in *On The Waterfront*. Instantly, the read on the scene is dazzling and multifaceted. Scorsese and DeNiro realized and many critics have since pointed out that the context of this scene concerns Robert DeNiro, playing Jake La Motta, doing a monologue spoken by Marlon Brando who played boxer Terry Malloy. What is perplexing and brilliant about DeNiro and Scorsese's choice is the scene is played as if an actor (DeNiro or La Motta in his new evolution as entertainer) is strictly running the lines, saying the words without interpretation or emotion. As we hear one of the most famous speeches in American film, we are reminded of that great film *On the Waterfront*, the connection between Brando and DeNiro, Scorsese and Kazan, is made; the younger men have inherited the mantle. *Raging Bull* is now playing as the great American Movie in a postmodern time tunnel. The mirror reflects Jake watching himself and it is the process of reflection that becomes the theme of *Raging Bull*; Jake reflecting on his life, Scorsese, and DeNiro on their own, the American movie stripped of all conventions, all the ones Scorsese's mentor, John Cassavetes, shredded through his devastating journey into real life. Jake understands Malloy; he understands the pain brothers can cause each other. As La Motta moves to the conclusion of the monologue, to the truth of *On The Waterfront* when Brando says, "It was you Charley," La Motta knows he has blamed and accused everyone in his life for his own downfalls. He knows he was a contender and a champion and that he "could have been somebody," but Jake has reached his redemption. It may be impossible even upon repeated viewings to understand why Scorsese sees this as redemption. The first time Jake says, "It was you *Charley*," and the second and final time, "It was *you* Charley." There is no meaning here, which is not to say one can't be found, but Scorsese in interviews and in print has said that Jake's redemption is that he finally decides at this moment to stop. Just to stop, nothing more or less—to stop hurting everyone around him. That's not to conclude he has conquered his self-hatred or forgiven himself for what he has done and will live a life to counter the negativity he embodied. When Scorsese finished *Raging Bull* he was relieved to have gotten out this brave and courageous notion and put it on film. Scorsese could not be sure the process of making the film exorcised his own demons.

A stagehand comes down to check on Jake. It is Martin Scorsese. The conversation is played as if it were chitchat, but in a self-referential context their exchange plays like a director talking to an actor who has become the character he is playing:

Scorsese:	How you doing, Jake?
Jake:	Everything all right?
Scorsese:	Yeah.
Jake:	Ready?
Scorsese:	You got about five minutes.
Jake:	Okay.
Scorsese:	Need anything?
Jake:	Nah.
Scorsese:	*You sure?*
Jake:	(pause) *I'm sure.*

Jake talks to himself as if he were about to go out into a boxing ring. He repeats a phrase over and over; they are the final words of *Raging Bull*—"I'm the boss." Jake is still doing it his way, the only way he knows how.

Raging Bull can be played over and over again as if it is a continuous work like *Finnegan's Wake* or Samuel R. Delany's *Dhalgren*. The movie doesn't begin or end in midsentence, but it is circular in that it takes place in that dressing room where in an alternate universe Jake La Motta is performing his one-man show every night as proof to himself that he didn't really have to change, he just had to stop.

Raging Bull was a landmark in Martin Scorsese's career. He had been heading for it ever since he began making films. Post *Raging Bull*, Scorsese would take up other concerns but never again question his existence. He will find himself in many characters to pursue life issues but after *Raging Bull* he began to realize that he did have a choice. He could be a personal filmmaker in Hollywood. When Scorsese as the stagehand asked Jake if he needed anything it was also a question to himself, answered by his screen persona. Scorsese was sure he could make the movies he wanted to make the way he wanted, his own version of one for the studios, one for himself; but the personal stamp on all of them would be indelible.

Raging Bull is dedicated to Haig Manoogian. Scorsese was reunited with his mentor when he was on the NYU campus in May of 1980 to screen his documentary *American Boy*, a profile of Steven Prince who played the gunrunner in *Taxi Driver*. At the time Scorsese was completing postproduction of *Raging Bull*. Manoogian never got to see Scorsese's masterpiece. He died on May 26, 1980.

18

The Double: *The King of Comedy*

Raging Bull changed Scorsese's life. His masterpiece received worldwide critical acclaim and he experienced a heightened sense of celebrity. He had instant name and face recognition, which made it more difficult for him to walk the streets freely as he had done all his life. He was associated with mob movies and violence. The assassination attempt on President Ronald Reagan in 1981 was traced to the shooter, John Hinkley's obsession with young Jodie Foster in *Taxi Driver*.

Celebrities have always needed protection from fans, but the celebrity-stalking era that had its prehistory in the murder of John Lennon by an obsessed and deranged fan in 1980 did not become a societal epidemic until Rebecca Shaeffer, the twenty-one-year-old star of television's *Sister Sam*, was stalked and murdered outside her West Hollywood home on July 18, 1989. During the year of the release of *The King of Comedy*, actress Teresa Saldana was brutally attacked and near death when a fan obsessed with her appearance in Scorsese's *Raging Bull*, as Lenore La Motta, was deluded into the fantasy that she was an angel who had to be killed to send her back to heaven.

Scorsese was beginning to feel isolated because of fame, and as his third marriage began to unravel, he was experiencing loneliness even as he was revered by cineastes, movie fans, the industry, academia, and as a hometown hero. At the end of 1979 Scorsese moved back to New York after almost ten years in Hollywood. He moved into a Lower Manhattan apartment, barely furnished. The television burned 24/7. Each morning he would check the TV Guide for the movies of the day. It was a time of Bressonian seclusion and introspection. The industry had changed and Scorsese contemplated how he fit in.

For his next film Scorsese reread *The King of Comedy*, an original screen-play by Paul D. Zimmerman that had been brought to him by the author and DeNiro almost ten years earlier. The story was inspired by a 1970 David Susskind show featuring autograph hounds who Zimmerman per-ceived as predators and assassins, who coveted a celebrity signature as kidnappers or serial killers related to their victims; the power of owning another person. Zimmerman was also inspired by an *Esquire* article con-cerning a man who kept a diary that contained a detailed assessment of every Johnny Carson *Tonight Show* broadcast. Scorsese was familiar with the writer who was the film critic for *Newsweek*, where he also covered the movie scene; he had interviewed the director in the past. Around 1974, when Scorsese first read the script he had little interest in the nature of celebrity and although it held a challenging role for DeNiro, he passed on it because he was unable to see a personal connection in it. What was lying within the script for *The King of Comedy* was a character who represented the frustration of being on the outside of show business. A man whose outrageous actions had little to do with Scorsese's behavior and all to do with how he felt at the time—a man looking in from the outside and des-perately wanting to be a part of show business. Scorsese's ambition was not fame, which is why the early reading of Zimmerman's script didn't *speak* to him.

After winning the Oscar for Best Actor in *Raging Bull*, DeNiro was reen-ergized by playing Rupert Pupkin, an autograph-hound geek who had visions of grandeur. He believed he could become a great and successful comedian through his obsession with a late night talk show star, clearly modeled on Johnny Carson. Now Scorsese saw the opportunity to ex-plore his feelings concerning the obsession for fame and the isolation of celebrity. Reading it a decade later, Scorsese had the revelation that he was both characters—Rupert Pupkin the artist with unrelenting drive to make it at any cost—a man so self-involved he could only press forward regardless of rejection and the reality of his situation. And Scorsese now related to and understood the Jerry Langford character—the public man who craved for privacy, who needed protection from the outside world to function as an outward, gregarious, and witty host, while in reality he was a somber man who suffered for his art and needed solace from the throngs who all wanted something he couldn't afford to give and continue his craft. Through his own public and private lives Scorsese was aware of the cost of celebrity. He was beyond the stage of anonymous moviemak-ing. Scorsese, ever the gentleman, now had to develop a public persona, the double that performers create, an image the public can associate with. While sitting behind the *Tonight Show* desk, Johnny Carson was there for the public, they had him every night unconditionally; but Carson, a shy and a ferociously private man, guarded every moment, each action away from his late night spotlight. He was a professional and the public loved Johnny. They insisted they knew Johnny, but they only knew the half of the man who came into their living rooms via television. Living as a double, the celebrity craves the attention necessary to maintain success, but the private person also needs to be able to slip back into his own life when the job is done.

Scorsese and DeNiro came together to make *The King of Comedy* in a pattern similar to a dance they danced on *Raging Bull*. DeNiro was undaunted after Scorsese passed on the project and promoted it throughout Hollywood, while Zimmerman continued to rewrite the script, which Scorsese first found superficial, not more than a one-note joke. In 1978 DeNiro was in talks with producer Arnon Milchan for a film about Moshe Dayan and he showed him the Zimmerman script. He received an investor's commitment for ten to fifteen million dollars. DeNiro arranged for Michael Cimino to direct but the *The Deer Hunter* director was about to embark on an earlier personal project that was green-lighted by United Artists—*Heaven's Gate*. After Scorsese and DeNiro completed *Raging Bull*, Scorsese, now deeply involved in his devotion to focus the world's attention on film preservation, went on a whirlwind tour to present his case with the zeal of a missionary. When he returned Scorsese was in a state of physical collapse; again the loyal DeNiro visited him at his bedside and convinced his director that *The King of Comedy* was a film they could do. Director and actor went on a retreat, this time to the less exotic Long Island where they made the project their own. Scorsese had once discussed creating a comedy with *Time Magazine* writer, friend, and collaborator, Jay Cocks, about the pain and fear endured by Borscht Belt comedians. Now, brainstorming with DeNiro he saw how *The King of Comedy* could use the profession of the standup comedian as they had with taxi-driving and boxing. The metaphors were familiar Scorsese territory: violence, psychosis, and salvation. Zimmerman was pleased with the result; the script was now tougher and darker, a scene added, but still within his original intentions. Like Schrader and Martik before him on *Raging Bull*, the screenwriter got full credit for the script. Scorsese and DeNiro were not interested in the ego-domination of credit mongering that had long embattled screenwriters. As a personal filmmaker regardless of the project, Scorsese needed a way into the material. As much as he admired the romantic notion of being a director for hire like his Golden Age heroes, Scorsese could not make a movie if it did not personally connect to his life issues, desires, or thematic obsessions. For Scorsese and DeNiro *The*

King of Comedy narrative was a paradigm to reexamine their early creative ambitions. Scorsese now clearly saw both the persistent Pupkin and the reflective Langford within himself.

Circumstances made production of the low-budget, short-scheduled film even more difficult. When the project was about to go into production a DGA strike was threatened. If the strike was called, only films four weeks into production could continue; the others would be shut down. A long strike could destroy a project in that situation. Scorsese was not in good health, still recuperating from his encounter with cocaine and the consequences of the drug's interaction with his asthmatic condition. The stressful completion of *Raging Bull*, which brought him the redemption he needed to get his spirit back, had also caused the director to suffer from bouts of coughing so severe they often dropped him to the floor. Scorsese's determination to maintain a high-energy creative life was another facet of his double life. To the public he was a respected American film director. In private he was an Italian-American man dealing with life issues particularly complicated by an old-world tribal upbringing. The passion of filmmaking gained Scorsese acceptance, his unconditional love and commitment to the art of film gave him the respect of a capo among the film community—he was a man of honor. Then there was his physical reality, one he never ever wore on his sleeve. He lived with asthma and valiantly fought against its assault on the life-giving right to breathe.

Arnon Milchan (*Once Upon A Time in America, Brazil, JFK*), the producer of *The King of Comedy*, was an Israeli citizen who parlayed his family's failing fertilizer business into a successful chemical company and then acted as an intermediary between Israel and international defense companies. His activities created great suspicion because he was secretly acting as an arms dealer for his country. *The King of Comedy* was his first film with a major director in a successful and controversial career as a producer. Milchan was a mysterious figure, more a man of intrigue than a "let's do lunch" Hollywood type.

Because of pressures due to the possible work stoppage, Milchan insisted that Scorsese begin production in July 1981, a month before the agreed-upon date and before the director was physically and artistically ready. The decision left DeNiro pressured and the production team in disarray. The twenty-week shoot was grueling on Scorsese, who shot every day from 4 P.M. to 7 P.M., in a three-hour intensive session, a considerable percentage on location in New York, while he used the rest of his time to protect and maintain a level of health that would get him through the film. A sequence filmed in the famed Sardi's restaurant in which Rupert fantasizes that Langford is begging him to sub for his show for a few weeks was shot in one day from 2:30 P.M. to 7 P.M., but then a dramatic slowdown occurred. There were up to five trailers used for the location production and countless hours were spent getting the company from one location to another. Scorsese, a director known for his speed and brisk pace in production, only managed four or five setups a day, a long way from his Roger Corman days. Unlike other Scorsese productions there were no breaks or allowances granted on *The King of Comedy*. The company paid for everything and the conditions were counter to the inner rhythms of the street director who quickly moved from setup to setup, getting what he needed because of his meticulous planning and marvelous rapport with cast and crew. The shoot was agonizing. Scorsese enjoyed all the moments between "action" and "cut," but the process was a strain. Off camera Scorsese was more Langford than Pupkin, desiring the quiet of being in his own head and surrounded by his true love: watching classic movies one after the other.

The story by Zimmerman may be ahead of its time, but the absurdities of Rupert's actions emerge out of a growing American ambition to be famous at any cost. Pupkin's plan to kidnap a talk show host in order to get his big show business break is well within the tradition of black comedy, reflected in the growing insanity of American life and a rebellion against tradition and toward impulsive action.

The project was another Scorsese/DeNiro collaboration, but with DeNiro attempting the challenge of going against type. The consummate, swaggering, and overbearing tough guy with a streak of violence and the cult of personality would be exchanged for a geek nobody took seriously. DeNiro was a method actor who became his characters, while often bringing along a bit of himself and the other selves he portrayed. Rupert would be one of his most curious creations, a character not fully formed, totally believable, and one that successfully transcended the actor.

Early in the creation of the screenplay, Dick Cavett was in mind as Jerry Langford, the dry-witted host who dominated late night. When Scorsese committed to the project he approached Johnny Carson. Surprisingly, someone within the production felt Carson was not well-known outside the United States, but Carson himself derailed the possibility when he explained he could only do each scene in one take and was not comfortable with the filmmaking process after years of live performances and a live or live-on-tape show. Sinatra was also a consideration. Scorsese had always been in awe of the rat pack life-style and the chairman of the board and sidekicks Joey Bishop and Sammy Davis Jr. They all had talk or entertainment shows at one time. The attitude, the clothes, all fascinated Scorsese—they were an extension of the Little Italy/Wise Guy life in which he had grown up. Orson Welles was in the running, and although at the time the greatest living American film director was a regular on many talk shows, he was associated more with film and theater than as a show biz type. A consideration of Dean Martin (on whose popular variety show Welles was a frequent guest) led to the final and best choice.

Jerry Lewis was an international movie star, a stand-up comedy veteran, host of his own variety show, and the annual Muscular Dystrophy telethon. The choice of Lewis surprised the legions who underestimated his complex talent; they tended to laugh off the Frenchman's reverence for a comedian many Americans thought was childish, silly, undisciplined, and erratic. Lewis so understood the character of Jerry Langford from his own life and from his intimates like Jack Parr, Steve Allen, and Johnny Carson that he needed little direction. Scorsese, a longtime fan of Lewis as a performer and as an auteur director, trusted that Jerry Langford would not be Jerry Lewis the celebrity, but an inside look at Jerry Lewis the consummate professional, who worked hard to achieve every vocal inflection, physical action, and nuance to formulate his iconic personality—a traditional clown with a manic, sometimes volatile, sometimes humble, but always highly intelligent persona. Like Chaplin, whom he revered, Lewis was also a double, a man willing to give it all to an audience with the discipline to play the character without injecting himself, but also living a personal life often counter to the lovable character fans adored. Scorsese's casting concept would be to have Lewis, known as a flamboyant actor, underplay his part and have DeNiro, the meticulous method actor, explore the boundaries of his character and chart new and dangerous paths for the comic film. Real talk show figures, *Tonight Show* producer Fred DeCordova, Ed Herlihy, Tony Randall, and Dr. Joyce Brothers would bring believability to the show business aspect of the film. Sandra Bernhardt, at the time an inexperienced actor, but a comic with voracious energy, Scorsese's mother Catherine as Rupert's mom (only presented in voice-over), which Scorsese designed and interpreted as his own mother talking to him about the stark realities of life while he dreamt of becoming a filmmaker, and a variety of experienced and inexperienced performers gave the film the guerilla filmmaking freshness on which he thrived.

Thelma Schoonmaker was now Scorsese's editor on this second collaboration. Old Hollywood master production designer Boris Leven had worked with Scorsese on *New York, New York*, and *The Last Waltz*. Costume designer Richard Bruno began his career at American International Pictures before he costume-designed *Two Lane Blacktop* and *The Hired Hand*. Bruno first worked with Scorsese as the men's costumer on *New York, New York*, then as costume designer on *Raging Bull*.

For director of photography Scorsese turned to Fred Schuler, a German-born cameraman who developed a solid career as a New York camera operator for many prestigious cameramen, including: Adam Holender, Bill Butler, Victor J. Kemper, Michael Chapman (on Scorsese's *Taxi Driver*), Owen Roizman, Gordon Willis, Ralf D. Bode, Sven Nykvist, Vilmos Zsigmond, and as part of *The Last Waltz* camera team, before becoming a director of photography on *Gloria* directed by John Cassavetes. These choices have much to do with the outcome of *The King of Comedy*, but it was Scorsese's principal stylistic decision to lay aside his run-and-gun approach to camera movement for a more disciplined and traditional cinematic approach, which has the greatest impact on the cinematic result. Before beginning a film Scorsese taps into his cranial encyclopedia and looks for films and filmmakers to guide his style choice for the content at hand. The cutting-edge director surprised many by announcing he was going to shoot *The King of Comedy* in the tradition of Edwin S. Porter's 1903 film, *The Life of an American Fireman*, without any close-ups. Porter, one of the forefathers of American cinema, discovered the narrative potential of filmmaking in sequential storytelling, his films are workman-like but no less important than the more artful and inventive D. W. Griffith in forging the Hollywood continuity style of cinematic storytelling. Whether or not Scorsese was saying he was trying to get back to a simpler kind of filmmaking where the camera served the content rather than engage in the earliest form of narrative cinema, it seemed an unlikely choice for *The King of Comedy*, a film that also employs the Cassavetes' street style, the direct and gritty traditions of New York filmmaking, and the artifice of the early sixties' Hollywood movies as it began its demise.

The King of Comedy was shot on location on New York City streets and the backgrounds have the same veracity and atmosphere as *Taxi Driver*, with a notable and unexplainable distinction. For *Taxi Driver* extras were carefully picked for authenticity, and much of the background action is composed of real New Yorkers. *The King of Comedy* relies on the methodology used by Hollywood when filming in New York—the casting of "New York types" as extras who stick out as fish out of water. They appear not only in the set pieces where extras have a line or two or interact with the principal action, but also as passersby who look like they were chosen out of Central Casting, and do obvious gestures like deliberately look at their watches, walk past the camera on cue, and are often stilted in their appearance and presence.

Schuler's cinematography is artless, the compositions and use of light are plain and often with little modeling. Leven's sets, particularly the reception area of *The Jerry Langford Show* offices and Rupert's basement are a homage to show business (including a one-dimensional representation of the Langford show, which makes no attempt at realism), but are created in the grand Hollywood style of the American Musical or the comic book representation of a Frank Tashlin or Jerry Lewis film, in which color, architecture, size, and space are presented as artifice and are used to transport the viewer to a place in their imagination.

After establishing that Rupert daydreams, by intercutting a make-believe conversation he has with Jerry at Sardi's in his basement with a recreation, Scorsese does a variation in a scene when Rupert asks Rita (Diahnne Abbott), a beautiful bartender, to go to dinner with him; it first appears that the cut takes us into Rupert's fantasy, but they are wearing the same outfits and by the conversation it appears that this has occurred. Shortly into their dinner conversation a man walks by, looks at Rita, and then sits at a back table watching the two with a grin. After he watches them for a while, the man begins to make gestures at Rita and poke fun at Rupert before getting up and going into a phone booth without ever appearing again. Rupert is regarded as a geek by the world around him, but this interaction, about which Pupkin is oblivious, has a surreal self-referential quality more associated with director Lewis than Scorsese.

The King of Comedy was a box office disaster. At an estimated cost of twenty million dollars, its return was only a paltry two and a half million. Reviews were negative and the audience stayed away in droves. Viewers could not reconcile their expectations for a new Martin Scorsese Picture with *The King of Comedy*. It was an anomaly. Audiences couldn't relate to it as a comedy, a black satire, a social comment, or as entertainment. As Scorsese's least accessible film, *The King of Comedy* defies entry at every turn. It is not satisfying as a New York film because of the clash between realistic locations and the overchoreographed population of extras and secondary characters. The characters are unlikable but not antiheroes. Rupert is persistent to the point of annoyance more than obsession. Lewis only fleetingly displays what the Jerry fans love (which is the genius of his brave performance). The look and action is vulgar, base, and, at times, the whole production seems inept.

For years following its initial release some predicted *The King of Comedy* would one day be recognized for its brilliance. This has not occurred and seems unlikely. Grappling with *The King of Comedy* in Scorsese's oeuvre is daunting and frustrating. Supporters of *The King of Comedy* are enthralled with Scorsese's prescience about the future of celebrity culture that continues to dominate tabloids, television, and the Internet and insinuates itself into our daily lives. That is an argument for its content, but it still leaves the masses unable to enter an inaccessible film by a director known to draw the audience into his world.

This is Rupert Pupkin's story as he sees his life. Scorsese blurred the lines between reality and Rupert's grip on it. Like a dream, nothing in *The King of Comedy* is totally believable, yet the dreamer, and here, the viewer, has no choice but to experience the story through a single perspective. The film takes place in a New York City we recognize, but there is a consistent strangeness about it. All the action takes place within the frame—all the perceived reality is inside the image. Scorsese never implies there is anything outside. The characters are either outrageously larger-than-life (Rupert, Marsha, and the inconsequential players around them), or dead-on real. Rupert does not see these figures—Langford, a producer's assistant, the producer, a chief of security, and an FBI man in a distorted reality, but his actions are fanciful, delusional, out of control, and manic. The Langford show is presented in a video format the way Rupert would see it on television, but like psychotics who are convinced television personalities are either communicating with them or broadcasting their shows directly for them, in this psychosis the celebrity only lives when the viewer puts on the television. By projecting himself into Langford's universe, Rupert imagines he ultimately debuts on the show. Like the surrealist world of a Buñuel film these moments look real but are always a simplified version of reality, not true experience. Rupert's basement is unattached to the reality of his mother's home. We hear her voice but what we see, a mock set of the Langford show, and especially a giant mural of a laughing audience in a long, gray hallway, cannot be interpreted as real, but only as part of Rupert's imagination.

DeNiro's creation of Rupert is a polar opposite of his usual approach where he inhabits a character to achieve verisimilitude. Pupkin's bad hair day looks like a wig, his clothes often red, white, and blue—a parody of bad couture. DeNiro captures Pupkin's instability by constantly altering his speech pattern—at turns, aggressive, fey, a take on an actor's bad line readings, and as a street-smart New Yorker. Like Walter Mitty Rupert elevates his true stature in life. He is a messenger without a shred of talent who wants to be not just a comedian, but also a King, someone like Langford who is respected and revered. *The King of Comedy* takes place in a lonely basement in New Jersey, where the skyline of New York is reversed. *The King of Comedy* transcends real time and place. Whoever the dreamer, whatever takes place in the film's running time of 109 minutes, may be a few minutes or many hours inside the head of a nameless man who imagines, not lives, his life.

In a remarkable performance, Jerry Lewis plays not only an entertainer but also the double that celebrity has forced on him. Lewis gives a dissertation on what it takes and what it is like to be famous. Throughout Lewis' long career as an entertainer, comedian, movie star, film director, host, and talk show guest, a deeply serious and riotously funny man emerges. Jerry Lewis is more than a celebrity. He is a man with noble humanitarian concerns, with endless curiosity about the film medium and television. He is a perfectionist, an observer of the human condition, and a man of unpredictable candor, anger, and good sense; while he still maintains the inner child he cherishes. Lewis wore clothes from his personal wardrobe and used his own walk as the Langford offstage and his real voice, modulated an octave below his "Jerry Loomis" voice. He is intelligent and sober, a man who has witnessed and experienced deep physical and physic pain; a clown who is a successful businessman, a philosopher, a "jerk," and a consummate professional. Langford talks about how what looks so easy to the public is the result of years of practice. He demonstrates that an entertainer is on and off. The offstage persona is private and he believes the public has no right to that time and space. He is patient because that brings success, but explains the frustration of being surrounded by incompetents and hangers-on. The presence of Jerry Lewis in this Martin Scorsese Picture is pure genius. This directorial decision alone gives *The King of Comedy* a dimension not realized in any other Scorsese film. Lewis appears to be undirected. He is allowed to *be*, not to interpret the role of Jerry Langford. Scorsese also utilizes Lewis as a source to understand celebrity at his strata and even allows Lewis to direct the "television" portions of the show for total authenticity. Lewis, the inventor of video assist, is an incomparable craftsman who knows the methodology of both film and video. His respect for Scorsese is evident by his very participation. Lewis, who has the reputation of a megalomaniac, was disciplined and collaborated when asked. Ironically, and with a self-effacing sense of humor, Scorsese cast himself as the television director of the Langford show, conferring with the guest host Tony Randall, who plays himself. Scorsese's interpretation presents a professional who is affable, but only interested in keeping the show on schedule.

A sequence that captures Langford's loneliness at home is a portal into Scorsese's life at the time. A series of monitors run movies and images, a direct reference to Scorsese's discovery of cinema through watching movies on television—here, Samuel Fuller's *Pickup on South Street*.

By November of 1982 Scorsese and Thelma Schoonmaker were still editing *The King of Comedy*. Fox was unhappy with the results and insisted on reshoots to clarify the story. Although the film opened at the Cannes Film

Festival, the national release was so lackluster that Fox considered pulling it from distribution after only two weeks. Audience disillusionment based on expectations of what a perceived Martin Scorsese Picture would be was blamed for the film's failure.

The King of Comedy also took its toll on the relationship between Scorsese and DeNiro. Scorsese has always pushed DeNiro to explore character, constantly praising his choices, but, in the end, the actor was unhappy with the results and felt Scorsese overpraised and didn't protect him. DeNiro was offered and rejected the role of Jesus for Scorsese's first attempt at mounting *The Last Temptation of Christ*. It would be eight years before one of the most accomplished and daring director/actor collaborations resumed, but the hiatus was without rancor. Scorsese and DeNiro had gone as far as possible in one direction; they would work apart and find new adventures to explore in the next decade.

On October 15, 1982, a memo was sent to Arnon Milchan with a request from Scorsese that he would like to change his credit from the New Hollywood standard—A Martin Scorsese Film—to A Martin Scorsese Picture. Both imply artistic ownership of the work in the "name above the title" and "director as superstar" traditions, but Scorsese was defining himself as a moviemaker from the old school when movies were pictures before they became films. He was also referencing a term of art used by insiders in photography and fine art where a work is a "picture," not a photograph or painting. "Picture" implies Scorsese is a picture-maker, someone who makes one after the other. It was not out of nostalgia or classicism in the manner of Peter Bogdanovich, who used the term in his writing and lectures on movies, nor was it for cultural definition as in Spike Lee's signature "A Spike Lee Joint." A Martin Scorsese Picture was the director's humble yet proud way of letting the audience know who was responsible.

19

K: *After Hours*

The failure of *The King of Comedy* stung Scorsese, but with his usual artistic courage he decided to move onto another personal project. He had an option on the screen rights to *The Last Temptation of Chirst* by Nikos Kazantzakis. In 1977 he had given the novel to Paul Schrader and commissioned a screenplay, which was completed in 1981. At first Scorsese's primary concern was whether the book could be translated into a cinematic form. Schrader then charted every scene in the novel and determined its necessity within the structure he created. Scorsese was convinced the story he wanted to tell could be done and in early 1983 he brought the project to Paramount and the studio agreed to finance the film. Irwin Winkler, who had produced *New York, New York* and *Raging Bull*, agreed to be the producer.

In the fall of 1983 Scorsese met with Eleni Kazantzakis, the widow of the author, and Patrolcios Strauru, a dignitary for the Cypriot government who was the literary executor for Nikos Kazantzakis. Scorsese made his case concerning his admiration and belief in *The Last Temptation of Christ*, and both Mrs. Kazantzakis and Mr. Strauru found the director to be honest and determined. He quickly found that he earned their trust as the only director who could make a film based on the novel with integrity and responsibility to the author, and to the sacred subject that many felt betrayed rather than embraced the true spirit of Christ. Scorsese's long commitment to his belief in the body and spirit of Christ convinced them to give the director full support and assistance. They knew he would need it having lived through the torment Kazantzakis experienced after the publication of the novel, which in his country was considered blasphemous. The book was condemned by the church, and even in death Kazantzakis was vilified. The widow and the executor saw the same bravery and unflinching resolve in Scorsese as in the man who created the literary work.

Although Paramount gave Scorsese the impression they wholeheartedly supported the project, their motives were largely centered around the "event" of Martin Scorsese, the seminary student who became one of America's most daring and respected filmmakers, as director of a movie on the life of Jesus Christ. The number crunchers also thought reviving the religious genre was a safe bet because no one had made a religious theatrical film in quite a while, and, since the "God is Dead" era of the sixties, fervent religious expression was reemerging in the nation's consciousness.

Paramount executive David Kirkpatrick, who was an admirer of the Kazantzakis novel, was assigned to honcho Scorsese's production, by working closely with the director and getting the film made at a price that would insure a return on their investment.

The original budget was fixed at between eleven and twelve million at a time when the average film was coming in at fourteen million. The shooting schedule was set for ninety days.

Scorsese insisted that the project be filmed on location in Israel and in January, during his visit, he included trips to Morocco and Paris during his first pilgrimage to the Holy Land in Jerusalem. For the first time he had a direct and palpable sense of the divinity of Christ. It was a very moving experience that intensified his decision that *The Last Temptation of Christ* must be filmed in the land where the sacred story had unfolded.

At the end of February Scorsese proceeded to Paris to see DeNiro. Based only on their past association on *Mean Streets, Taxi Driver, New York, New York, Raging Bull*, and *The King of Comedy*, it had immediately been assumed by industry insiders (and the public who learned of the project) that Robert DeNiro would portray Christ in Scorsese's Jesus movie. What seemed like a sound assumption about how actor and star collaborated was far from the truth. DeNiro and Scorsese never assumed they would make film after film together. What drew them to a project was a personal connection to the subject and each had his own artistic and personal motivation for all the films they had done together.

DeNiro had little interest in the subject of religion and could not see himself playing a character in robes. He read the script, in the spirit in which its was given to him, as a first offer of respect to the actor, and DeNiro was compelled to turn it down. Contrary to urban legend there was no rancor. Scorsese totally understood and respected that DeNiro wasn't as committed to the project as he was. Unchanged was DeNiro's loyalty to Scorsese, both as a collaborator and as a friend. As the short meeting ended, DeNiro made it clear to Scorsese that if he could not find a suitable actor or one with the necessary courage to take on the role in an era so far removed from the fifties and sixties when the religious and epic films were fashionable and widely accepted, then he would do it whole-heartedly as an act of friendship.

Scorsese began to ponder the many actors who had played Christ in the past: Jeffrey Hunter, Franco Nero, and Max Von Sydow, and examined the many sides of Jesus portrayed in *The Last Temptation of Christ*, which allowed him to explore a wide range of performers. By mid-September of 1983 Scorsese had made his choice—Christopher Walken.

Paramount was unhappy with the choice and asked Scorsese to look further. After looking at footage from the still-in-progress film *Reckless*, Scorsese committed to the unknown twenty-four-year-old actor, Aidan Quinn, and the studio gave their official approval.

When Barbara Hershey read in a trade publication that Scorsese was embarking on the production of *The Last Temptation of Christ* she yelped for joy, knowing that she had played a part in the inspiration, by giving him a copy of the book during the making of *Boxcar Bertha*. As to the casting of Mary Magdalene, neither Scorsese nor Hershey felt it was a fait accompli that she would be given the role. After a series of three months of tests, she won the role. Rightfully, Scorsese was fighting the strong pull Italian-Americans feel about obligations. In this culture one either accepts an obligation to another through love, and earned loyalty, or resents the notion of obligation because of expected reciprocation, debt, or force. To free himself of this ethnic tradition and to protect the actress as well, he created a process that assured him that she was right for the part, and gave Hershey the confidence to support her early attraction.

Once underway, the unraveling of a production is a long and painful event in the life of a film director. Irwin Winkler, a support system for Scorsese on two challenging and difficult films, was compelled to withdraw as producer when the budget of his production of Philip Kaufman's adaptation of Tom Wolfe's *The Right Stuff* began to grow out of control. The same expansion of costs and production requirements were beginning to happen on *The Last Temptation of Christ*, which was scheduled to shoot in Israel. Ultimately, the producer couldn't sacrifice being away from his family and engaging in a marathon commute, so after involvement with the development of screenplay, he left Scorsese's project, which he estimated would need an additional ten shooting days and two million dollars, raising the budget to fourteen million. Producer Jon Avnet, whose *Risky Business* had opened that summer to great reviews and box office, became Scorsese's producer on *The Last Temptation of Christ*.

The eighties were not the fifties concerning religion and politics. The evangelical movement had made a significant impact as a force with sway in many strata that interfaced with the motion picture industry. Paramount began to reconsider their decision to support Scorsese's production of *The Last Temptation of Christ*, concerned as to whether the film could have negative ramifications on the corporate bottom line.

Scorsese and Jay Cocks went to Palm Springs for a retreat to write a first revision of the Paul Schrader screenplay that Paramount had approved. When they were satisfied with the results as part of the script development process, Scorsese dispatched copies to the studio's executives. During a meeting in which the director expected constructive criticism, he encountered a direct change in their reactions toward the screenplay. There was a culture of worry developing and a concern that the narrative was inaccessible and the approach too arty, the mark of box office death to most red-blooded movie executives. Scorsese was advised that his project was moving "from a green light to a blinking yellow." Avoiding the trap of studio-speak, Scorsese told them his intentions were devout and that for him the project was an extension of prayer. He left the meeting feeling that the concerns were within the normal jitters studios commonly express before a project goes in front of the camera, and he proceeded to work on the script and mount the production.

In November of 1983 the tides began to turn against *The Last Temptation of Christ*. As word of the production spread, rumors began to fester and ill will about the project and its director spread among the religious right community. Scorsese, as the director of *Taxi Driver* and *Raging Bull*, was looked upon as an anti-Christian family values member of the entertainment community. Learning from the New Left how effective protest was as a tool for change and influence, a call to action against *The Last Temptation* was sounded. The Evangelical Sisterhood (an organization of Protestant women) published a newsletter distributed to the converted, which called for a direct letter-writing campaign to Gulf + Western (the parent company of Paramount) to protest the making of a motion picture that defiled their Christian beliefs.

The megacorporation began receiving at least five hundred letters a day taking them to task for supporting *The Last Temptation of Christ*. In an unprecedented gesture motivated not by religious belief or conviction, but corporate protection of valuable assets, Paramount decided to hold a theological summit to discuss the issues surrounding the life of Jesus Christ and Scorsese's intended presentation of the holiest of stories.

On November 5, 1983, Father John McKenzie, a noted scripture scholar, Mary Pat Kelly, who had prepared to become a nun and later became a close friend of Scorsese and author of *Martin Scorsese: The First Decade*, John Cobb of Claremont College, a liberal Protestant, Rosemary Radford Ruether, a Catholic feminist and theologian from Garrett Evangelical Theological Seminary in Evanston, and John Elliot, a Lutheran scholar from San Francisco State University, commenced to Paramount Studios. The three-hour seminar took place in the executive dining room over brunch at a round table to create a convivial atmosphere. The president of production, Jeffrey Katzenberg officiated. An audio recording of the dialogue was made to be transcribed and distributed to studio heads Michael Eisner and Barry Diller, as well as Martin Scorsese.

Father McKenzie summed up the frisson between theology and the movies by remarking, "This is a dangerous job. Anything about Jesus is dangerous." The interchange was an overview of Christian thought at the moment. The topics ranged from the political and spiritual message in the words and actions of Jesus, concern that the Lord would be again portrayed as what Father McKenzie defined as "a pious wimp" referring to Hollywood's past record, the justification of sexuality for a present audience, and Kazantzakis's claims of divinity not documented in the scriptures.

The majority opinion of the Paramount brass was positive and gave them renewed motivation to make a film that would encourage intelligent debate about Jesus. But Marvin Davis and Barry Diller of Gulf + Western did not share in the enthusiasm revived by spirited conversation between learned and civil theologians. Diller questioned the intent of a project that was generating a steady stream of negative mail to the office at half a hundred pieces a day.

Meetings investigated sensitive issues raised by the theologians. Scorsese defended his concept that Jesus should be presented in a subjective not complacent manner. The director wanted the viewer to experience Jesus' anger at being forced to forge crosses to be used for crucifixions, and to understand that the miracles in the desert evolved out of the reality of sitting in the desert for forty days. For Scorsese the supreme beauty in the life of Jesus is that on earth he lived and experienced life as a man and after the last temptation, which would be presented realistically, he became divine. The film would not only show the process but also embrace the physical and then spiritual event that took place.

Barry Diller had already mounted a solid defense against making *The Last Temptation of Christ* as a Paramount production. The rising public sentiment against the project drove his decision. Although he had known for six months that the plan was to film in Israel, Diller now invoked it as another problem, concerned that this signaled a runaway production, which would drain U.S. dollars from the film to a foreign entity. Scorsese understood that it was necessary to have great passion in the subject of Jesus to commit to the project, and gave Diller the out he needed. His interest did not equal the possible negative impact the film could have on his company. Scorsese's agent Harry Ufland, in an honest but desperate act, offered Scorsese's services for free and a microschedule of only sixty days. Diller rejected the offer.

Scorsese came to the realization that the project should not be made through the Hollywood system, rather in the spirit of Pasolini's *The Gospel According to Saint Matthew*, a film Scorsese greatly admired and was one of his inspirations for *The Last Temptation of Christ*. Scorsese was no longer trying to convince Paramount to support his movie but commenting on how to get it done: "Shoot it for $3 million or $4 million in Italy somewhere."

Now it began to seem like Paramount *was* still interested. Eisner suggested he could help set up *The Last Temptation of Christ* at another studio without revealing the project was in turnaround, the status akin to cinematic limbo when a studio decides not to make a project and seeks out another studio or production entity to do so.

From Thanksgiving to December 21, Scorsese designed the shots for the film and attended meetings about the production with Eisner, Katzenberg, and others. The revised schedule was for fifty-five days in Israel on a budget that quickly went from $7.8 million to $6 million. The salaries for Scorsese, Aidan Quinn, and Harvey Keitel, who was cast as Judas, were sacrificed. On the final day of this period Scorsese met with Barry Diller who remained unmoved. When asked by Scorsese if there was a figure that would balance Paramount's risk factor, Barry Diller remained silent. *The Last Temptation of Christ* was officially dead as a Paramount production.

Moving forward Ufland engaged in talks with major studios to find a home for *The Last Temptation of Christ*. Bad buzz, negative press, and the turnaround status at Paramount along with a growing condemnation for Scorsese and his perceived decadent and disrespectful treatment of his proposed film on the life of Jesus Christ, left the agent without progress or a glimmer of hope in getting a Hollywood studio to support *The Last Temptation of Christ*.

Without reading the screenplay, Salah Hassanein, the man in charge of the United Artists chain of movie theaters, the second largest in the nation, attacked from the rear by announcing, if made, he would refuse to screen *The Last Temptation of Christ* on any of his screens throughout the United States. Scorsese sent Hassanein a copy of the screenplay and set up a meeting with him. Scorsese appealed that he wanted to make *The*

Last Temptation of Christ to make Jesus accessible to the many who were alienated by organized religion. Hassanein, the son of a Christian mother and Muslim father, assured Scorsese he felt the same as the director about God, but for him this was a personal belief not to be imposed on others. Although sympathetic to Scorsese's passion, Hassanein's decision was rooted, as was Paramount's, in fiscal responsibility to his corporation. He explained that the films *Martin Luther, The Greatest Story Ever Told,* and the *The Life of Brian* caused protest and brought negative publicity and disruption at his movie theaters. Dissention turned violent in 1976 upon the release of *Mohammed: Messenger of God,* when the outraged held hostages in Washington, DC, and bomb threats were made to theaters planning to screen the offending motion picture. It was nothing personal, but the man who controlled the booking of films for hundreds of theaters did not want trouble wrought on his business.

The Last Temptation of Christ had a cast, sets, and costumes but no financial backer or distributor. For a month Scorsese and his team tried everything to get the production mounted. Scorsese maintained the booking of two flights, one to Tel Aviv and the other to New York. When all failed Scorsese assessed his situation and decided that survival depended on making a film, anything to keep working and in the game. Even at a time of desperation and rage toward the systematic destruction of his dream project, Scorsese's principles as a personal filmmaker were unwavering. His relationship with Eisner and Katzenberg at Paramount was still intact. They were happy to present him with scripts straightaway. Scorsese was offered *Beverly Hills Cop,* at the time still a Sylvester Stallone vehicle. The high-concept eighties' comedy bewildered Scorsese. When he was told the project was a fish out of water, the execs had to explain it was about an out-of-town cop who comes to New York. Scorsese couldn't understand why it wasn't the same as *Coogan's Bluff,* directed by Don Siegel and starring Clint Eastwood. *Witness* was framed in the same concept but in Pennsylvania, among the Amish. Scorsese wanted to make a movie, but he just couldn't commit to stories he didn't understand. When his agent told him that was what was available, he took the New York flight to his actual and spiritual home—New York City.

When Scorsese arrived, his lawyer Jay Julien, who played Jerry Langford's lawyer, who had threatened to sue *everyone* in *The King of Comedy,* had a script waiting that was the New York version of a fish out of water. *After Hours* is the story of a midtown Yuppie who becomes imprisoned in the downtown nightlife of pretrendy SoHo through unfolding circumstances beyond his wildest nightmares. The screenplay was written by

Joseph Minion when he was a student of Dusan Makavejev at Columbia University, where he received an A for his accomplishment.

The making of *After Hours* was a rebirth for Scorsese as a filmmaker. The property was owned by Griffin Dunne and Amy Robinson who had played Teresa in *Mean Streets*. The two actors had formed Triple Play Productions to produce an adaptation of Ann Beattie's *Chilly Scenes of Winter* (renamed *Head over Heels*) released in 1979 and directed by independent film pioneer Joan Micklin Silver. In 1983, with the more streamlined company name of Double Play Productions, Robinson and Dunne had their second film released, *Baby It's You*, written and directed by another indie legend, John Sayles.

Scorsese immediately recognized he had an opportunity to be rejuvenated and back on track as filmmaker. He could return to the days of *Taxi Driver* working on the streets of New York with a low budget, concise schedule, and a tight crew, working quickly and without interference. It was a venue to reclaim his roots as a guerilla filmmaker in a time when the film industry was making high concept and blockbuster movies that rejected Scorsese's artistic profile as a personal filmmaker.

After Hours, originally named the more on the nose, *A Night in Soho*, was financed by Fox Classics for $3.5 million and scheduled for a forty-night shoot, and a postproduction period of around four months. Robinson and Dunne secured an independent bank loan based on a studio pickup commitment. It was the nature of the story that not only fit Scorsese's dark sensibilities, gave him another shot at a feature length comedy, but also allowed him to personally act out all the feelings endured by the slash and burn of *The Last Temptation of Christ*, along with the excesses of the seventies, which were detrimental to his creative, physical, and spiritual well-being.

The story was a native New Yorker's wet dream nightmare. The central character Paul Hackett (Griffin Dunne) was a computer programmer in search of a romantic adventure in the seductive but dangerous city. His journey begins when he meets an alluring and mysterious young woman (Rosanna Arquette) through fate in a late night coffee shop rendezvous. The story provided a genre concoction of film noir, black comedy, theater of the absurd, with a bit of mystery, thriller, surrealism, and even neorealism. Scorsese always needed to identify with his principal character and Paul Hackett provided the personality traits and emotional makeup that allowed the director to express another side of himself. Scorsese embodied more than the average American's share of paranoia. His lifetime exploits with women left him bewildered, uneasy, and clueless about the feminine mystique. The years of living in the enclosed society of Little Italy made him wary of the outside world. Although he was raised so close to the bohemia of Greenwich Village, he was uncomfortable with exotic artistic types and bewildered by moral codes outside of his hermetic Catholic and Italian-American cultures.

After Hours allowed Scorsese to observe himself through the camera and rather than identify with his designated character as he did with Charlie Cappa, he found great joy and liberation in laughing at Paul's inability to escape from his downtown nightmare. Griffin Dunne recalls his director desperately trying to control his glee, with hand on mouth to suppress wild bouts of laughter as the cameras turned on Paul's deepening misery.

Scorsese visualization and the final crafting of the screenplay, for which Minion and the director worked together mainly on the last movement of the script, achieves a rare feat in film—a relationship between cinema and the literature of Franz Kafka. Most attempts at cinematic adaptation of Kafka fail because, rather than capture the essence of his prose and perspective in intensely examining the individual and his relationship to society and environment, films such as the Orson Welles' production of *The Trial*, Steven Soderbergh's *Kafka*, Woody Allen's *Shadows and Fog*, and countless others are Kafkaesque; a state which stereotypes the author's intentions rather than sift through to their essence.

Minion's screenplay for *After Hours* portrays Paul Hackett as a scapegoat for a corporate bureaucracy that has reduced him to teaching the mundane task of word processing to workers whose ambitions of greater purpose are confined to the reality of society's limitations. Paul seeks the pleasure of sex but is made to suffer consequences imposed by a heartless system insensitive to his predicament.

Like Franz Kafka the writer, Martin Scorsese, the film director, suffered for his art, perceiving each film as a physical and spiritual struggle to express his innermost feelings. Scorsese's JR, Charlie Cappa, Travis Bickle, Jimmy Doyle, Jake La Motta, and Rupert Pupkin sacrificed earthly pleasures and suffered through personal hells to achieve a sense of illumination and deliverance.

Knowing Scorsese would need a director of photography who could work fast and provide the director with his vision, Robinson and Dunne introduced him to Michael Ballhaus, with whom they had worked on *Baby It's You* and *Reckless*, which Scorsese had screened. Born in Germany in 1935, Ballhaus was in the process of beginning his American career by also shooting *Old Enough* directed by Marisa Silver, the daughter of independent filmmakers Joan and Raphael Silver, and *Heartbreakers*. The cameraman was an ardent admirer of Martin Scorsese, and while in Germany he had dreamed of the opportunity to work with him. When the two men met, Ballhaus was already an accomplished cinematographer with over thirty films to his credit. To international cineastes he was widely respected for his work with Rainer Werner Fassbinder. Their collaboration included some of the most important films of the German New Wave of the seventies. His eleven collaborations with the brilliant and notoriously difficult Fassbinder were testament to his artistic abilities, patience, and resolve. A gentle, friendly, and warm man, and the nephew of the great Max Ophüls, Ballhaus and Scorsese immediately formed an effective and productive working relationship.

Scorsese drew small drawings in the margin of his script detailing the visual structure of as many as five hundred shots he envisioned for *After Hours*. Scorsese's ambitious plans for *After Hours* would require sixteen setups a day to keep on the tight schedule. Because *After Hours* was an independent project the crew could not be union members. Ballhaus had a small crew and, as was his method in Germany, the cinematographer operated on most of the photography. This process was essential in getting the specific and often challenging shots Scorsese asked for accomplished quickly, efficiently, and with the artistic quality both men demanded.

Making a movie back on the streets was a tonic for Scorsese; it renewed his cinematic soul after the long struggle trying to get *The Last Temptation of Christ* into production. He enjoyed filming a character that was trapped in his environment and inside a paranoid nightmare. The black humor of *After Hours* helped him to lighten up on his own issues, many similar to Paul Hackett's. This renewed Scorsese's sense of humor about his plight and reminded him that what he did best was make street movies. *The Last Temptation of Christ* project seemed dead, but Scorsese was not a man to give up easily. It was now time to look for work and rebuild his career.

20

Resurrection: *The Color of Money*

The Color of Money, a vanity project for Paul Newman, is Scorsese's most successful outing as a hired hand. Although he had been around pool halls growing up, he was not an aficionado of the game. *The Color of Money*, the sequel to *The Hustler* (1961), is about matters of the soul, part of the qualifications Scorsese brought to the project.

Over the decades the possibility for a sequel to *The Hustler* remained. In 1984 a real opportunity for a sequel arrived when Walter Tevis reentered Eddie's life with a sequel to the novel—*The Color of Money*. At fifty-nine, Paul Newman began with a screenplay by Tevis that stuck very close to his book. Newman was looking for something more profound. He wanted to take Eddie Felson into a place where he would confront the status of his soul, suffer his sins, and contemplate redemption.

Newman put Darryl Ponicsan on the project. The novelist of *The Last Detail* and *Cinderella Liberty*, he had made both into successful films and also developed a reputation as a screenwriter and adaptor on *Taps*, *Vision Quest*, and *Nuts*. Ponicsan wrote several drafts of *The Color of Money*, but none satisfied the direction and dimension Newman was demanding for the sequel.

Newman set out to sign Tom Cruise for the part of Vincent Lauria, a shooter with a ferocious talent, but a clueless and flakey personality. He was motivated by professional and business reasons and drawn to the many similarities shared by the two actors from different generations. Cruise received national attention with *Risky Business* and had just finished shooting on *Top Gun*, the film that would announce his stardom.

Scorsese directs a young Tom Cruise in the sequel to *The Hustler, The Color of Money. Courtesy Photofest.*

Newman wanted the film to be even less about the subject of pool than *The Hustler*, and more about the subtext. What would Eddie have done after his banishment and where would he be twenty-five years later? It is unlikely that Newman was intimately aware of Scorsese's total body of work. When Newman sent Scorsese a fan letter praising *Raging Bull* and extending an invitation to talk about the new project, he addressed Scorsese as Michael Scorsese, possibly confusing him with Michael Cimino.

At the time Newman approached Scorsese, in the fall of 1984, the director had been in extensive talks with Warren Beatty to direct the actor in *Dick Tracy*, and was developing an adaptation of Nicholas Pileggi's nonfiction book *Wise Guy*. Other potential projects were a Paul Schrader biopic screenplay on George Gershwin and *Winter's Tale*, a fantasy script written by the screenwriter of *Cocoon*, Tom Benedek. Scorsese's longtime agent Harry Ufland transitioned from client representation to producing, so Scorsese did not have an agent at the time. Newman's agent, Michael Ovitz, a Machiavellian master of packaging a movie after acquiring most of Hollywood's A-List actors and directors, set out to make the project happen, working his way through the tangled issues of rights to the material, which involved several studios and the Walter Tevis estate.

Newman and Scorsese agreed to give Ponicsan one more draft, but it lacked the transformational qualities Newman and Scorsese were looking for and the writer was dismissed.

Scorsese turned to Richard Price for the assignment. The two men had come together earlier in the year when Scorsese contracted the novelist to write a remake of the 1950 film, *Night and the City*. Both *The Wanderers* and *Bloodbrothers* had been adapted into movies, but Price, like many serious novelists, took the position of selling the option, taking the money, and not getting involved with the film.

Although Price never was interested in writing screenplays, his dead-on, rapid fire dialogue was cinematic and communicated the internal and outward actions that define characters. Both men were fans of each other's work, and both talked so fast that only a like spirit could comprehend every word and each meaning. Their common bond was New York City and the urban experience. To Scorsese everyone was Italian, to Price everyone was Jewish—they were made for each other.

As Scorsese and Price worked on the screenplay they immediately decided not to take anything from *The Color of Money* novel except the title. Scorsese and Price set out to find the story that would uncover what Eddie had done in the twenty-five years since *the Hustler* and to follow his trajectory. To commit to the film Scorsese needed to make it his own in theme and purpose. Price and Scorsese strongly agreed that Fast Eddie would have to be tougher, meaner, and more corrupt and become everything he had hated. Eddie is too old to change his ways, but when he meets Vincent Lauria, he sees the opportunity to corrupt the kid as Bert Gordon had attempted to do with him.

In February 1985 Price and Scorsese didn't have a plot yet, but they knew that Eddie would have to play pool again. Newman agreed to the idea in principle. In order to commit to the project Price and Scorsese had to write for themselves about themes that compelled them, but after many sessions Scorsese understood that if *The Color of Money* was to work, Scorsese and Price would have to subordinate their needs and serve the requirements of a major movie star. As Scorsese counseled Price, they were like tailors making a three-piece suit for the man.

Price worked hard and fast to please his two masters as well as his own artistic designs and wrote more than one thousand pages of draft script in ten months. Price had at least thirty-six script conferences with Newman; Scorsese clocked in many more meetings with his star.

A film starring Paul Newman and Tom Cruise and directed by Martin Scorsese would seem to have been easy to launch. There was no bidding war; actually the film was a tough sell because it was the eighties, the director-as-superstar era was over, Paul Newman had his hits and misses, and Cruise was not yet a megastar.

Fox was enthusiastic about the project, but when Sherry Lansing, the then president of the studio left, the new regime didn't like the Scorsese/ Price script and stunningly didn't want Newman and Cruise in the lead roles. Columbia also rejected the project after Guy McElwaine left the studio. Ultimately the project found a home at Touchstone, where Michael Eisner and Jeffrey Katzenberg of Disney green-lighted the film. The budget was set at $4.5 million with a fifty-day shooting schedule, which meant it would be a lean and mean production. Scorsese and Newman had to put up one-third of their salaries as collateral. Scorsese had his eye on *The Color of Money* and the legitimacy that a Touchstone/Disney production would bring to this tenuous time in his career.

Scorsese accepted the challenge. He had already had his salary cut to make *After Hours* and in the heart of the director he was paying for his sins of excess on *New York, New York* and the failure to get *The Last Temptation of Christ* into production. Scorsese understood that *The Color of Money* had to be shot quickly, so he insisted again on Michael Ballhaus as his director of photography.

Shooting on *The Color of Money* began in early 1986. By shifting the focus of specificity of detail mainly to the pool games and the ways the inner life of the characters influenced their actions, Scorsese slowly made *The Color of Money* into a Scorsese film within the confines of the studio demands and the realities of Paul Newman as a starring vehicle. To develop the visual style Scorsese decided that the camera would never rest; he would always cut on the heat of action. The pool games were not about process, but energy-driven by the character's motivations: excellence, success, winning at all costs, and a forward thrust that would lead them to Atlantic City, the Mecca of money and the holy grail of making it in America.

To design the shots, which resulted in 393 setups during production, Scorsese locked himself in a room, listened to music, watched movies, ate dinners with stimulating companions, and went through stacks of Post-It notes filled with ideas for shots.

On *The Last Waltz* and *Raging Bull* Scorsese applied the moving camera technique Vincente Minnelli utilized in his musicals and experimented to expand the concept to his own work. Scorsese explains the application intended to express inner rhythms of the story and characters: "First the camera would track in on the band for a few bars of music, for the first cut, with no master shot, which would run for 24 bars. Next the camera would track at one angle for 12 bars, then another for 12, and so on back and forth until this became a style. I applied it to the studio sequences in *The Last Waltz* and to the boxing scenes in *Raging Bull*, where every fifteen or twenty punches there was a different angle with no coverage, and even to the pool games in *The Color of Money*." To Scorsese, shot structure, application of camera, and editing structure was not "style" as interpreted by many critics and theorists, but the very properties a director utilized to make the film.

The film's ending was elusive. Eddie and Vincent would play each other in the final moments of the film, but all agreed there should be no winner. Newman was more of an optimist than Scorsese or Price and the studio demanded a happy ending. The solution would have to reside in Eddie's character transformation.

Scorsese's conception of redemption is that it must be attained by actions and behavior on the streets—not in prayer or a house of worship. Eddie couldn't become a hero, but a realization of what his life should be was the answer. For Scorsese the solution would mine box office gold, but leave his admirers wondering if by compromising, he sold himself out. Of course Scorsese could never sellout in a traditional manner; he was too dedicated, too honest, and too true to his art, so he would find a way to end the film, be true to himself and responsible to his patrons.

For *The Color of Money* Scorsese's own brand of cinematic theology saw Eddie as achieving salvation through mortification. To Scorsese Eddie was another misguided and reluctant saint forced to live out evil impulses. Corrupted by money and a material lifestyle where objects gave him pleasure melded the character to Scorsese's concept of the second commandment. As pointed out by the astute Scorsese scholar Les Keyser, actually it is the first and not the second commandment that states not to worship false gods; the second forbids the creation of graven images.

For *The Color of Money* Scorsese became intimately familiar with the pool-playing sequences in *The Hustler*. The process was similar: Newman knew how to play and executed his own shots. Cruise was also familiar with the game and both men worked with the technical advisor, Mike Siegel, winner of over 105 international pool and pocket billiard tournaments.

Scorsese planned each shot on paper and the pool sequences are breathtaking, but they never quite take on a personal connection between player, stick, and ball. There is little subtext and plenty of pyrotechnics and flash as the balls fly into pockets as choreographed by a whirling dervish. Every game of pool involved shot-making expertise but the art of position, making one shot, and getting the cue ball to the next position to make the next shot is sacrificed in *The Color of Money* to dazzle and impress the viewer with wizardry, as opposed to the methodical precision and mental acuity that is exercised by even the most outgoing and outlandish players.

Scorsese and Ballhaus continued the working relationship they forged on *After Hours*. Ballhaus readily accepted the technical challenge of Scorsese's complex shot structure and was a relentless problem-solver in his mission to give Scorsese what he wanted. When Eddie enters Atlantic City Scorsese designed a shot where the camera would begin forty feet above the room, then swoop down and change direction to find Eddie looking at the rows of pool tables in an architectural structure that resembled a church. Scorsese was extending the metaphor of the movie theater as church to Eddie—who would now see his return to the game as a return to his religion—pool.

With all the camera movement during the pool games, Scorsese decided to employ a static camera when Cruise tells Eddie he dumped the match between the two of them to give Eddie a portion of the money. The moment was critical in revealing Vincent's lack of moral character and in sparking Eddie's self-confidence to get back to doing what he did best—playing pool to win. This use of camera was an ideal platform to reveal Vincent's motives and express Eddie's revelation.

The solution to the ending almost appears to have been found in the editing room rather than crafted through the conception and writing process; it is achieved by two words and a freeze-frame. The game begins by Eddie winning the lag for the break. As he smashes the rack with a sledgehammer stroke he says, "I'm back." So the process of redemption for Eddie is to be back playing the best-playing pool he can play, and the lessons learned through his relationship with Vincent make him the man he always wanted to be. It was not a traditional happy ending, but it made the studio happy and was still a compromise in their eyes. For Scorsese, the personal filmmaker who only answers to himself, the compromise underscored the difference between the films he wanted and needed to make and the ones for which he was hired.

The "I'm back" metaphor of Fast Eddie's character can be applied here to Scorsese. *The Color of Money* was his first box-office success since *Taxi Driver*, over a decade earlier. He proved to the studios and players of the emerging New, New Hollywood that Martin Scorsese was back. The film was only as personal as the system would allow. Scorsese had become in his own words in *A Personal Journey with Martin Scorsese through American Movies*, The Director as Smuggler, a filmmaker working within the system, still able through a commitment to themes that animated them to insert narrative and stylistic elements into a commercial project. As a film in which the director was able to subvert the text and subtext of a genre film, *The Color of Money* was no *Cat People* (1942), *Kiss Me Deadly*, *Bigger than Life*, or *Shock Corridor*. Neither was it a sell out, merely proof that Scorsese had to continue to make movies. He did not live in the era of the Studio B-Movie that allowed directors freedom, because the suits were too busy watching the A movie production to realize personal statements were part of their low-budget filler for an afternoon at the movies, so he tried his best not so much to smuggle but to darken the edges, deepen the emotion, and experiment with the stylistic conventions. It was a way of keeping in the game. A personal filmmaker is just another word for artist and Scorsese was an artist in the most expensive medium there was.

Newman calls *The Color of Money* one of his most creative experiences as an actor. Scorsese encouraged his star to go beyond mannerism and expressions associated with the movie star and to stay deep in the character. In 1985 the Academy, after once again overlooking Newman for his performance in *The Verdict*, losing to Ben Kingsley in *Gandhi*, decided to make amends by giving Newman an Honorary Oscar, " . . . In recognition of his many memorable and compelling screen performances and for his personal integrity and dedication to his craft." Newman finally won the Oscar for best actor. Ironically, he stayed home the night of the 1986 ceremony, concerned that he would jinx his chances (and suffer additional embarrassment if he were to lose again). The award was accepted by his old friend and *Somebody Up There Likes Me* director, Robert Wise, who was handed the award from a very ditsy Bette Davis. Wise, ever the gentleman, rescued the surreal moment with gracious thanks from the actor who didn't win the award for his original portrayal of Eddie Felson in *The Hustler*, or *The Verdict*, or for a number of other outstanding productions. At least Davis and Newman won their Oscars before old age (as demonstrated by Davis that night) and made the event even more embarrassing to the Academy's oversights than was already apparent.

The Color of Money brought Scorsese back into mainstream filmmaking. He was a survivor who refused to give up the hope of making personal projects. It was time after making one for *them* to make one for himself.

21

Passion Play: *The Last Temptation of Christ*

When Scorsese's production of *The Last Temptation of Christ* collapsed at Paramount he went on to direct *After Hours* and *The Color of Money*. His longtime agent Harry Ufland was determined to set the film up anywhere and many possibilities and offers came in.

There was the possibility of a French coproduction stewarded by the Minister of Culture, Jack Lang, but protests grew again—this time from the Catholic equivalent of American Christian fundamentalists. The Archbishop of Paris pressured President Mitterrand about using public monies to undermine the Holy Scriptures.

The locations that had been secured in Israel were lost and a plan to make the film in Egypt for the impossibly low budget of five million dollars was raised and failed.

An associate of Michael Powell appealed to Russia to make the film in Tashkent, the capital of Uzbekistan, and that deal also fell by the wayside.

An attempt to set the film up in Greece failed as well.

Scorsese and his team became aware then they had allowed their option on the Kazantzakis book to drop so Harry Ufland, Jon Avnet, the Paramount producer assigned to the early incarnation of the production, and Scorsese, pooled their money and secured the option.

In 1986 Ufland was in discussions with Hemdale, the production company responsible for *The Terminator*, directed by James Cameron, and Oliver Stone's *Platoon* and like the others, the deal fell through.

While Scorsese was out promoting *The Color of Money* he talked to Paul Newman's agent, Michael Ovitz, the head of the all-powerful at the time CAA (Creative Artists Agency). After a twenty-year relationship Scorsese made the decision to drop Ufland as his agent and to go with Ovitz and

CAA, convinced the über-agent could get *The Last Temptation of Christ* into production and distribution.

Universal became interested and Ovitz met with the new head of the studio, Tom Pollack. They in turn sent the script to Garth Drabinsky the head of Cineplex Odeon, the then biggest theater chain in the United States and Canada, who put up half the money to make the film.

Locations were scouted in Tunisia and Morocco and shooting on *The Last Temptation of Christ* finally commenced on October 12, 1987.

After disappointment and perseverance Scorsese finally receives his opportunity to film Nikos Kazantzakis's *The Last Temptation of Christ*. On location in the Mideast, he directs Barbara Hershey, Willem Dafoe, and Harvey Keitel. *Courtesy Photofest.*

In *The Last Temptation of Christ* Jesus is portrayed as a man. Jesus is confused as to his purpose on earth. He hears the voice of God the Father, but doesn't understand what is expected of him. He begins to acquire a following of men, the apostles who believe he is the messiah they have been waiting for. Jesus is in constant conflict, making crosses for the Romans to crucify his own people, the Jews. He spends a day watching men make love to Mary Magdalene, but when he rejects her lustful approaches, in her mind, he cannot be a real man. After meeting John the Baptist he becomes aggressive and takes on the sin and depravity of the Romans. He is tried by Pilate and crucified on the cross. While he is suffering and dying a slow death the last temptation occurs. His mother Mary and Mary Magdalene pray, but the crowd is there to laugh and taunt the man they see as another false god. In traditional readings of the passion, Christ dies for our sins, is summoned up to heaven, and is resurrected. Kazantzakis and Scorsese believe that their human Jesus continued to struggle with his place at the side of God until the very end.

The transformational ending of the film has been misunderstood and ridiculed by fundamentalists, but it posits the idea that in his last moments Jesus did more than suffer physically; he contemplated what his life would be if he lived it out as a man. The last temptation comes in the form of a child who tells him God doesn't want him to die on the cross. There are a series of scenes that are in Jesus' mind as he lay on the cross dying, which are visualized as he sees them. The earth is a beautiful place; he is married, has children, and dies at home as a man. On his deathbed he is visited by some of the apostles and Judas who tells him the child is the Devil. Near death as a human being in his contemplative mind, he makes the decision to accept his purpose. Scorsese cuts back to Jesus on the cross where he has been all the while and shouts into the heavens, "It has been accomplished," finally resolving his conflict and accepting his place in heaven and toward the earth.

Detractors of *The Last Temptation of Christ* call this controversial conclusion of the film a dream sequence, but Jesus is not dreaming, he is being tempted by the devil and in his mind's eye lives his life as a man to the end. What we see looks like Jesus has given up his role as the messiah, but the return to him on the cross clearly without interpretation, proves what has occurred was his last temptation from the devil—a temptation he rejects.

For many who understand and accept the passion through the teaching of the Bible, countless books, and many Hollywood movies, *The Last Temptation of Christ* is a revelation. It takes the concept that Jesus was sent to earth as a man to a realistic interpretation. The crucifixion sequence is the most explicit and powerful put on film at the time of its release. Mel Gibson's equally controversial *The Passion of the Christ* goes beyond Scorsese in explicitness, but remains loyal to the biblical rendition. The imagery is more like a seventies' slasher film than a religious movie. Scorsese based the crucifixion partly on shots he designed for the ending of *Boxcar Bertha*. They are visceral, brutal, bloody, and human.

The body of the film utilizes a mix and match approach of the gospels to create scenes that depict the passion story. A card at the opening of the film states the film is not loyal to the gospels, but many religious scholars were unable to accept a new interpretation of the timeless story.

Scorsese is relatively restrained in his direction. There are several effective top shots, and camera moves that intensify the action, but little of the expressionism for which he is known best. Dissolves are used to move Jesus and his disciples through time and space in a magical movement.

After Jesus proclaims, "It has been accomplished," Scorsese finalizes the film with an abstract section of pure-colored light that signifies Jesus leaving his body and his spirit entering the kingdom of heaven. The images seem inspired by early color experiments from the thirties and forties anthologized in the DVD sets, *Unseen Cinema: Early American Avant-Garde Film 1894–1941*, and *Avant-Garde: Experimental Cinema of the 1920s and '30s*. A lover and supporter of all movements in film, Scorsese is very familiar with the experimental film scene. This sequence plays as homage as well as a self-referential statement about pure cinema. At moments, sprockets seem to appear as if the film is running out. The impact is intellectual and spiritual.

The score by Peter Gabriel, the solo artist once the front man of Genesis, utilizes Middle-Eastern themes and instruments to create an authentic soundtrack unlike the Hollywood dramatic Western music heard in many biblical epics. The music is visceral and transcendent.

Scorsese has talked about the apostles being a bunch of guys like those in his street films. Although this approach makes them real, it has its setbacks. Many of the actors speak in New York accents. The wonderful actor Harvey Keitel throws the film offbalance with his Brooklyn accent, bright red hair, and beard. His intonation borders on the absurd. He may be emotionally right for the character but the accent destroys much of the verisimilitude when he is on screen. Willem Defoe gives a believable and compelling performance as Jesus, speaking in a standard American English with great fervor and passion. His tortured, emotive face and thin but taut body are the personification of the concept of a human Jesus.

Like many epics, *The Last Temptation of Christ* works best on a large screen. Screening the film on DVD and seeing it projected on a large theater screen are two different experiences. As with *2001: A Space Odyssey*, *The Last Temptation of Christ* is an experiential film in which the viewer enters the time and space of the images without distraction.

Martin Scorsese's cinematic adaptation of Nikos Kazantzakis's The Last Temptation of Christ *opened in New York City at the Ziegfeld Theater, a large show house for event films. Kazantzakis was scorned by believers for his novel first published in 1960. By the mid 1980s Christian and Evangelical groups had become highly organized and retained political power and the attention of the media. They were ready for Scorsese and his film. Fifty-Fourth Street was filled with people. A long line of ticket holders waited for the previous show to break. In the street was a meticulously planned and executed protest. Believers camped out and formed a village of those who had not and would not ever see the film but were there to scold, threaten, embarrass, and intimidate all those waiting to see it. The ticketholders were mainly strangers bonded in their conviction not to be bullied and to make up their own minds by experiencing the work. Three such strangers, a man, and two women who had never met until this moment, began to talk and come together for what seemed like an eternity and biblical in the Old Testament tradition. They waited on the line, which continued to grow as the believers came closer and closer. The three, and others, were spit upon. Lew Wasserman, Chairman of MCA, the parent company of Universal who was distributing the film, was called rabid and vile anti-Semitic names. The Jews, historically blamed for crucifying Jesus, were held responsible for this "blasphemy." The shouters forgot, didn't know, or didn't care that Martin Scorsese was an Italian-American Catholic who as a boy aspired to the priesthood. They called the director a cocaine addict, reducing a great artist to the basest level of humanity. The three strangers grouped together and looked ahead as they were told they would burn in hell if they saw the movie, even if they ever stepped into the Ziegfeld Theater now cursed as a palace of mortal sin. The three were brave and focused their beliefs beyond the mob. Finally the previous show ended and the three along with fellow cinematic journeymen entered the theater away from the fanatical demonstrators. Once in the lobby everyone had their bags checked pre 9/11 because a theater in France had been firebombed. There were bomb threats, and death threats against Scorsese, who now carefully navigated the New York streets with bodyguards. Once seated the three looked at the massive Ziegfeld screen, suddenly armed guards facing the audience stood on either side of the screen. The tension couldn't have been greater but the magic of movies allows the viewer to enter a film, in the dark, the images flickering on and off, our persistence of vision creating the illusion of solid images. As the film began all the worldly distractions fell aside. Most in the audience had seen many of the classic biblical films,* The Greatest Story Ever Told, King of Kings, The Bible, The Ten Commandments *and so many others made during the 1950s and 1960s. This film was like no other. The three sat together brought together by their mutual experience. The crucifixion sequence is the most vivid and realistic ever filmed up to that point. (Later Mel Gibson would go beyond realism to expressionistic cruelty to show how Jesus suffered in* The Passion of the Christ.)

As the ritual of the crucifixion unfolded, the woman sitting in the center of the three began to go into a religious fervor in what looked like a seizure. She began to shake and cry uncontrollably. The man and the woman on either side held her hands firmly and comforted her but they couldn't take their eyes off the screen. The power of the sequence comes from Kazantzakis's and Scorsese's deeply felt conviction that Jesus on earth was a man. This realization brought the sacrifice Jesus made directly to the humanity of the viewer. The woman slowly calmed down; neither she, nor the other two, had ever seen the passion played out with such power and expression but didn't question what caused the woman's transformation. The film ended. They said goodbye and left never to see each other again. The man remembers that the audience was able to exit the theater through a back door and avoid the mob that continued their mission to the next group to see the film. It was a moment of peace. He did not want to discuss the film with those who hadn't seen it, nor anyone until the full impact of Scorsese's film of the passion was absorbed, if it ever was.

22

New York, New York: *New York Stories*

In 1986, Woody Allen approached Scorsese about the notion of an anthology or episodic film in the spirit of *Boccaccio'70, Love in the City, Far from Vietnam*, and *Dead of Night*, which had segments by different directors. Originally Steven Spielberg was part of the project, but he dropped out and Francis Ford Coppola completed the trio.

At the start of 1987, Scorsese commissioned Richard Price to write his segment to be based on a relationship between Fyodor Dostoevsky and Polina Suslova, an admirer of the writer. Scorsese was at a screening with Jeffrey Katzenberg and the executive was so enthused with the idea, it became a Touchstone film. The three very different films are linked by their New York City backdrops. Coppola's *Life without Zoe* generally is considered a failure. Woody Allen's *Oedipus Wrecks* is ranked among his best humorous works. Scorsese's *Life Lessons* is a personal film that contains many of Scorsese's most salient themes. With a running time under an hour, it stands alongside his finest films.

Life Lessons begins with a series of iris shots of paint and painting tools. We are in the studio of Lionel Dobie (Nick Nolte), a famed New York postexpressionist painter. Procol Harum's surrealist classical rock classic, *A Whiter Shade of Pale* plays in the studio and creates a mood that illustrates Lionel's disassociation with his purpose and the work at hand. Lionel is blocked and frustrated as he drinks out of a brandy snifter, stomps on a tube of blue paint, and expresses anger when the buzzer buzzes.

Phillip Fowler (Patrick O'Neal) rides up the lift to check on his client who has an art exhibition in just three weeks. Lionel growls at the elevator cage and we learn that the artist has nothing to show. He is surly to his dealer and sends him back down refusing lunch or a viewing of his work. Scorsese is investigating the life of an artist and the pain of creation.

In slow motion Lionel waits at the airport for his assistant. She is revealed in a slow iris in. The girl, Paulette (Rosanna Arquette), is a young beauty introduced as if she were a young Lillian Gish in a silent film. The slow motion represents the idealized and fetishistic image Lionel has of the girl. The painter always is negative before a show and always is in love or lust with his female assistants. He gives life lessons in return for sex.

Paulette is not happy to see Lionel who failed to listen to his answering machine. She is not coming back to the loft and has a new lover who has broken up with her. Lionel convinces her to go back to the studio where Paulette begins to pack in her tiny room above the loft, which has a torn-out peephole. They discuss the other guy, performance artist Gregory Stark (Steve Buscemi). He convinces her to stay and swears she doesn't have to sleep with him anymore.

Dobie slaps the *Whiter Shade of Pale* cassette into his paint-stained cassette player and stands in front of a large canvas as the camera pans around. Knowing that Paulette is going to stay, he can confront his work. Like many artists, including Scorsese, Lionel needs companionship to be whole as a creative person. In a series of jump cuts he plays basketball, then slams the ball against the wall disturbing Paulette on the phone, and then throws the ball into the hole in the wall of her room. He avoids work at all costs, looks at the painting in progress then up at her room. Giving into temptation, he visits her. She tries to stay on the phone as he desperately makes conversation. An iris-in on her foot weakens him in a reaction shot. He continues a sham interest in her health and welfare.

Lionel finally begins to paint as Cream plays "Politician." The painting sequence featuring the hand and artistry of Chuck Connelly is sensuous and masterful. Dobie is screwed up romantically, but paints in bold colors and strokes with dynamic gestures.

While Paulette is sleeping Lionel enters on a false pretense and wakes her up. He can't stop looking at her feet as the iris focuses our attention to enter Lionel's sexual psyche. Next is a blue-tinted erotic scene in which Lionel caresses her face and body. When it ends he is still standing over her in bed. She asks him if he loves her. The sequence was either Dobie's fantasy or Paulette giving in, but it is seen from the painter's point of view.

He returns to painting but is quickly drawn back to Paulette as he looks up at the "window," now covered with a curtain.

Lionel looks over Paulette's recent work. He tells her she has a nice irony going—but doesn't say what she wants to hear—does she have talent, should she continue to pursue art or give up? Dobie's response is one of Scorsese's primary messages. It doesn't matter what others think; you create art because you have to.

Lionel stomps off to his painting and Paulette cries on the phone, presumably to her mother, about coming home for a while until she can return to school. Lionel is blasting a raucous and very angry live version of Dylan singing "Like a Rolling Stone." Paulette furiously tells Dobie to lower the music—a prelude to one of the finest sequences in all of Scorsese's work.

Shot 1:   Paulette yells for his attention.

Shot 2:   Lionel continues to paint furiously and ignores her. She yells to turn the music down.

Shot 3:   She calls out his name again.

Shot 4:   A close up of Lionel deeply involved in painting.

Shot 5:   She turns in disgust and begins to walk.

Shot 6:   Dolly shot swings around—Paulette's POV watching him paint.

Shot 7:   Paulette is now repositioned behind him watching him paint.

Shot 8:   The camera moves around Lionel as he passionately paints.

Shot 9:   Close-up of Lionel's brush swirling bright color in an aluminum pan.

Shot 10:   Jump cut to another shot of the brush picking up more color.

Shot 11:   The brush paints a white X over a golden field of color.

Shot 12:   The camera swiftly moves from the paint tray to the canvas several times as Lionel applies color flourishes to the canvas, ending with an expressive horizontal red line.

Shot 13:   The camera slowly pushes in on Paulette from a medium shot. She is entranced by watching Dobie make art.

Shot 14:   Close-up of brush painting curved orange lines over a mustard yellow field.

Shot 15:   The camera continues to push into Paulette as she watches Lionel paint.

Shot 16:   The brush works in white lines.

Shot 17:   Further push in on Paulette. Her eyes are wide and dreamy, her chest heaves with emotion.

Shot 18:   Tight close-up of more brush strokes.

Shot 19:   Closer on Paulette. She is smiling warmly and slowly blinks.

Shot 20–23: Three shots on Lionel as he paints.

Shot 24: Full shot of Paulette breathing deeply.

Shot 25: Brush strokes.

Shot 26: Close-up of Paulette.

Shot 27: Brush strokes.

Shot 28: Tight shot on Paulette's face.

Shot 29: Red and white brush strokes.

Shot 30: Pull back behind Lionel as he paints.

Shot 31: Push in on painting—a face emerges through the paint. It looks like an expressionistic miniature portrait of Dobie.

Shot 32: Mustard-colored brush strokes.

Shot 33: Lionel applies red paint to the canvas with his hand.

Shot 34: Push into figurative section of painting.

Shot 35: Close-up on Lionel as he paints.

Shot 36–38: Three shots of brush strokes.

Shot 39: On Lionel's face as he paints.

Shot 40: Push in to painting detail.

Shot 41: Tight close-up of Paulette.

Shot 42: Brush slowly applying a jagged yet lyrical white line to the canvas.

Shot 43: Slow crane back to Lionel working the canvas. Paulette appears from the back in the lower left watching Dobie work. The song concludes.

This key sequence is a love story. Paulette falls back in love with painting and with the artistry of Lionel Dobie. She rekindles the passion she once had for Dobie as an artist and for art. This is not a sex scene but a romance about the nature of art. What is remarkable about the editing by Thelma Schoonmaker is the intercutting between Paulette and the painting. Her expressions change very subtly. When intercut with the painting they are heightened as we enter her emotional space and believe we see even more than is really there. This sequence is a fine example of Scorsese's understanding of shot structure and editing to produce emotion.

Paulette and Lionel look into a mirror as they get ready for a black tie party. Lionel grouses about the party-giver who is more interested in monetary value than their true worth as aesthetic objects.

At the party Lionel holds court with outrageous stories about sex drawings commissioned by the government against the Russians. Paulette is surrounded by men trying to pick her up making small talk about art.

She is rescued by a handsome young man as Lionel eyes them jealously. He watches them dance and charges over to Phillip Fowler to learn his name is Ruben Toro (Jesse Borrego), a young artist with the reputation as a lady-killer. Dobie pulls Paulette out of the room. Out of desperation and envy he tells Paulette everyone is laughing at her because of Toro's reputation. He leaves the room and holds it shut to keep her there while talking to a dealer. While cake is served Lionel sees Toro rush out with Paulette.

Back in his studio Lionel glares up at Paulette's room. He hears noises he perceives as lovemaking, slams in the cassette, and begins to paint to Procol Harum's "Conquistador." A composite shot layers three figures of Dobie with his shirt off tackling different sections of the painting at the same time. He lowers the music but hears nothing coming from the room. Nessun Dorma begins to play. Dobie sits down depressed and melancholic. As the composition climaxes, he rises up, his naked torso and beard smeared with paint and walks closer to the room looking up in pain. Like Travis Bickle in *Taxi Driver* and Newland Archer in *The Age of Innocence*, Lionel suffers from repressed love, a favorite Scorsese theme. The painting is now highly developed. It is a magnificent expressive abstract landscape.

In the morning Toro comes down for coffee. Lionel insults him and begins to paint, laughing at Toro as if to say he is the greater artist, if not the greater lover.

Lionel apologizes to Paulette who turns him down for another night out. She has other plans. She's going to see Gregory Stark perform to prove she doesn't give a damn about him anymore; she is just there to see his work. Lionel tries to convince her not to go with girlfriends but with him, to "walk in with dignity."

Stark performs with beams of moving light on a set that is a train track. The monologue is funny and delights the crowd as Lionel and Paulette look on. She enjoys the show. Lionel just stares down.

At a party after the performance, Lionel encourages Paulette to go over to Stark who is surrounded by sycophants. She does, he's glad to see her, but Paulette is cut off by a partygoer who gets Stark's attention.

She runs out and screams at Lionel while they walk in the rain. He's willing to do anything—even not sleep with her because he loves her. The scene is reminiscent of Scorsese's reaction to his third wife, Isabella Rossellini, when she left him for another man.

Paulette tells Lionel to kiss a policeman on the mouth to prove his love by doing anything for her. He goes over and blows a kiss to the officer, but Paulette is gone.

Lionel comes back to the studio and finds Paulette scantily clad. He accuses her of taunting him and threatens that he could just "take" her. She goes to her room and sits in front of one of her paintings.

Paulette is at a bar with one of her friends (Illeana Douglas). She turns and sees Lionel sitting at a table with Phillip Fowler. Then Gregory Stark enters and comes up to her. Lionel abruptly joins them and tells Stark off. The scene ends with Paulette leaving and Lionel physically attacking Stark—a Scorsese sudden eruption of violence.

Back in her room, Paulette throws her paintings around in a rage and tells Lionel that her brother is coming to take her home. She challenges him again to tell her if he thinks she'll ever be a good artist. All he can say is that she is still young. He tells her she needs to love herself and that he'll quit painting for her. She throws him out of the room.

"Like a Rolling Stone" is on the cassette player again. Lionel is painting as Paulette and her brother come down, ready to leave. He tells her he was married four times (the same as Scorsese at the time) and that she can't tell him about love. After they leave he realizes that women have been "chipping away" at his talent.

The gallery show of Dobie's new works opens. Scorsese and Michael Powell appear in a black and white montage as admirers of Dobie posing for pictures. The screenwriter of *Life Lessons*, Richard Price, makes a cameo as a wannabe artist who tells Lionel his work makes him want to divorce his wife. Camera flashes join *Raging Bull* and later *The Aviator* as comments on how the media assaults celebrities. As Lionel looks at one of his paintings a young woman (Brigitte Bako) comes over to touch him for good luck. She's another aspiring artist. After a montage that reduces her to the body parts that are Lionel's fetishes, he offers her a job as his assistant that includes "life lessons," his code for sleeping with him. *Whiter Shade of Pale* plays again, this time not as source but score. The camera pans the room in wide shot, a final iris in tightens to Lionel and his new assistant.

PART 6

The Eternal Flame, 1990–1998

23

"We Make Street Movies": *GoodFellas*

Martin Scorsese's attraction to, and fascination with, the American gangster and the Hollywood crime film harken back to the dual experience of his Little Italy childhood where the life of the gang foot soldier was an integral part of his world, and the hours spent in a darkened theater or with his nose pressed to the small screen television set watching the classics of the Warner Brothers' gangster cycle. The combination of experiences forged to create *GoodFellas*, one of Scorsese's masterpieces.

On location in Chicago during the production of *The Color of Money* Scorsese read a review of *Wise Guy* by Nicholas Pileggi, the true story of the organized crime foot soldier Henry Hill, who eventually committed the ultimate Mafiosi mortal sin of ratting on his friends by entering the witness protection program and testifying on behalf of the FBI against his former brothers-in-crime.

A New York boy, eleven years senior to Scorsese, Pileggi advanced to the position of reporter for the *Associated Press* in 1956. After running errands and menial tasks at the *AP* offices, he was assigned to cover the New York City Police Headquarters where he got his "graduate studies" in street crime, organized crime, and the inner workings of law enforcement. Gathering information, deep knowledge, and sources during his tenure, Pileggi began writing crime journalism for *New York* magazine in 1968, then later for the upper echelons of *Esquire* and *Life* magazines. Pileggi was into crime reporting much as Scorsese was into film, an artist who didn't judge or moralize but observed without sentimentality and with just a little bit of fascination, which the public felt experiencing the exploits of men who lived outside the law from within their confined and mundane life. To Pileggi, crime figures were like rock stars, men who did what they wanted, when they wanted, and only answered to their own code. The articles made the public as well as men like Pileggi and Scorsese, who watched from the outside, feel the glamour and danger of living on the edge, where a wrong move could land you in prison or the ultimate life sentence—getting *whacked*—the street terminology for a Mafia hit, a man targeted because within a lifestyle with little bounds, he stepped outside the rules of *omerta*.

In 1986, well into his second decade at *New York* magazine, Pileggi wrote *Wise Guy* for which Henry Hill did a *sit down* with the reporter and told him all about the life he lived as a Mafia foot soldier.

Enticed by the review, Scorsese read *Wise Guy* in galleys. He immediately related to Hill and his lifestyle. It was straight out of Scorsese's own experiences in Little Italy, watching these powerful men rising up in his community without signs of legitimate backbreaking work to support their families. Scorsese had grown to understand and respect these men as well as learn a salient street morality. Although men like Hill and those Scorsese observed growing up in Little Italy were degenerate gamblers and vicious murderers, he felt and intuited that Pileggi felt a compassion for them. These men were bigger than life, living large, were funny, charismatic, and part of the fabric of New York society. As Scorsese read *Wise Guy* he came to the revelation he could fictionalize the true story of these street guys without judgment or the kind of *East Side Kids* sentimentality toward their dark actions. He could advance the narrative geography of the crime film as well as the personal movie, because although Martin Scorsese was a law-abiding citizen, he was raised in a neighborhood of Henry Hills. Scorsese always saw himself as a gangster/priest, but the reality is that if he hadn't fallen in love with the cinema, he might have fallen into that life just as easily as he pondered and struggled over in *Mean Streets*.

Scorsese entered into a complex collaborative relationship with Pileggi. Author and director independently selected the scenes they liked from the long literary form of *Wise Guys*, which covered areas of Hill's life not shown in the film. With these selected sections, Scorsese encouraged Pileggi not to follow a traditional narrative structure. As a personal filmmaker who was a student of all forms of cinema, Scorsese reinvented the American gangster form by combining tradition with French New Wave musings on that tradition, filtered through the director's autobiographical input based on memory, and emotional interactions loyal to human behavior and action, not literary, theatrical, or, cinematic conventions.

Scorsese's idea was to start in the middle of the story, then flash back and forth. As Pileggi went off and wrote draft after draft Scorsese cut many of the transitional sequences so the story would go rapidly from point to point over a series of decades. By showing an event and then cutting to the reaction or circumstances rendered, "The exhilaration of the lifestyle carries you along, until they start to have problems and it stops—and then you have to deal with that."

Scorsese's inspiration for handling the plethora of voice-over demanded by the interview material culled into Pileggi's nonfiction book came from the same place as all his ideas, aside from the autobiographical streams: film and television. *Jules and Jim* remains a seminal influence for Scorsese; he screened the opening for Pileggi to show how a still or a freeze frame could be used to stop the motion of images and allow the narrator to speak. Scorsese was a fan of the iconoclastic comedian, Ernie Kovacs, who continually discovered ways to address the camera to impart comedic information. For Scorsese, the narrative devices he was exposed to over fertile years of watching movies and television could be applied to any form of filmmaking. The freeze frame was most notably celebrated in an earlier Truffaut film, his first feature, *The 400 Blows*. The freeze frame at the end of the film, which allows the viewer to watch Antonine Doniel as he runs from his present and looks for a future in a new narrative position where a single image could stimulate the audience to ponder the fate of the main character, but there was no use of voice-over. The combination of voice-over and a frozen image had been put together in an earlier American film—one, clearly screened and studied by Truffaut and Scorsese. In Frank Capra's iconic holiday classic, *It's a Wonderful Life*, a shot of Jimmy Stewart demonstrating the size of a fish with his hands is frozen, while Clarence the angel and his superior discuss their new soul-saving prospect. The power and beauty of a Scorsese film is the empowerment of the history of film in every shot expressing personal content. His ability to find the right grammar for each shot and the structure for each film within a personal framework is what elevates Scorsese above others who crib visual style or create it without respect for story and content.

GoodFellas' audacious use of narration includes several techniques, which enrich the dense narrative, storytelling perspective and point of view. Hill doesn't exclusively talk to the viewer over images but often while dialogue is playing off and woven in with his observations we see and hear the participants and action in question. This combination of the past tense, Hill speaking from hindsight when it all fell apart with the real-time unfolding, sets up a frisson that neither could achieve on their own. Again, Scorsese is pushing the limits of film grammar.

There is an extensive use of previously recorded music in *GoodFellas*. As he began in *Who's That Knocking at My Door* and *Mean Streets*, the songs go beyond setting a mood into a dense narrative connection with the scene that is being scored. Because *GoodFellas* covers a period of decades in Hill's life and the world of crime he was adopted into, the music serves to address and connote the period and to establish a point of view toward the characters. The music is universal and accessible to a wide range of audiences, but Scorsese adapts the context to his own needs. By using songs of the years depicted, he transcends the trendy aspects of the music into a cosmic dissertation of how popular music is altered by the circumstances of lives lived at the time. Scorsese uses lyric as another narrative component, as the multilayered mix of voice-over narration; first Henry, then to the surprise of the viewer from Karen Hill, Henry's wife, and back, synch dialogue from the characters playing out in real time, framed by the flashback third-person commentary and the music pushing in and out of a scene. For Scorsese the soundtrack of *GoodFellas* is a tapestry of memory, exploration, context, and the vivid depiction of a lifestyle.

As advertised, *GoodFellas* begins in the middle, but we won't know that until we reach that part of the story, after the film later begins at the beginning and moves toward the conclusion of the opening scene.

After a series of laterally speeding by credits with drive-by sound effects, the screen goes black and a large dark car speeds through the night on a highway. A card flashes on, "New York, 1970." This is when the story starts but it is not the beginning of Henry's narrative. Inside, Henry Hill (Ray Liotta) drives, Jimmy Conway (Robert DeNiro) sleeps in the shotgun seat, and Tommy De Vito (Joe Pesci) is in the rear when they hear a banging in the backseat of the car. Off-road, the threesome lit in hellfire red by the taillight, Jimmy with a shovel, Tommy with a knife. Henry opens the trunk. Inside a bloody, but still alive Billy Batts (Frank Vincent), is wrapped in a blanket looking as if he was just crucified. Tommy stabs Batts repeatedly, followed by a succession of blasts from Jimmy's gun. Red light bathes over the dead body and on Henry as he voice-overs the line that sets up the film to go into flashback, "As far back as I can remember I always wanted to be a gangster, on the run." Henry slams the hood down. The camera pushes into his face, red as if he was standing in Hell. The first freeze frame of the film is not an opportunity for voice-over but for the introduction that precedes Tony Bennett singing the lyric, "I Know I'd Go from Rags to Riches," bringing in the Main Title and principal above-the-title credits. *GoodFellas* is in blood red, but the rest are white on black and with Scorsese taking the traditional, "Directed By" credit.

From the middle of the movie's narrative, through the voice-over of a mature Hill, the story flashes back to one of Scorsese's most personal scenes. The eye of teenage Henry is in extreme closeup and staring out of the window, a seminal image is related to the young Scorsese, the voyeur using his window on the world to develop his imagination for images, creating movies through the frame, the window or the screen with the same purpose—to capture images and express stories. In the voice-over Henry jumps ahead talking about walking into the cabstand, while we see him watching in anticipation of the excitement provided by the colorful characters that inhabit it. Tony Bennett sets the time frame with the song but the lyrics contribute to the story, as if Henry always knew he would go from the middle-class boring life of his parents to the riches of the GoodFellas who have all the cash, flashy clothes, jewelry, the best women, and the best tables in restaurants—anything their hearts desire. Like Henry, Scorsese watched the wise guys on Elizabeth Street as an observer. He knew who they were and how they ran his neighborhood.

It is now East New York, Brooklyn, in 1955. As Henry talks about why he was so attracted to the gangster lifestyle we are reminded that Henry is watching through the slightly parted blinds in his bedroom. Metaphorically Scorsese is shooting himself as a Little Italy boy, watching, dreaming about the world below. Moments such as this transcend their narrative reality to the level of personal filmmaking. Shiny suits, highly polished large cars. Introduction to the padrone, his lieutenant, and the foot soldiers. Colorful shirts, ties, open collars, and overshirts for the larger waistlines. Paulie (Paul Sorvino), the boss of the district, comes out and his sheer presence stops the horseplay.

Henry's/Marty's view of the nightlife of the wise guy switches to a handheld shot following Henry through the middle-class apartment of his family.

When Henry's mother sends him off to school a pan up of the building gives the impression that's where he is headed, but Henry sneaks back, sees she is back in the house, and runs to the cabstand to work for the gangsters.

"Can We Be Sweethearts," the doo-wop side of the era, plays as young girls watch Henry park the mob vehicles, the lyrics speak of their romantic notions toward the handsome boy with everything, and the teenage fantasy Hill is living.

Bright colors of stolen merchandise with Henry working all day is contrasted with his morose father moving toward his son, having found out he hasn't been in school in months. The father quickly humors the boy then breaks into a male rage over the words, *"In months!"* as he beats the boy with a strap. Henry tells us the man is frustrated and angry that he works hard, is paid little, has another son who is in a wheelchair, and knew what went on at the cabstand. He gives his son a vicious beating to avoid him becoming a bum like the gangsters. There is a long freeze showing the anger and velocity of the strap about to come down again on Henry. The sixteen-second hold allows Henry to explain his attitude learned at the cabstand—everyone has to take a beating sometimes. The words register over the still images, and the emotion of the father as his wife's arm tries to hold him back, have a power unique and concentrated.

The Fellas resolve the problem that also demonstrates rage, but not frustration, just power. Henry points out the mailman to the gangsters, who threaten him never to deliver a letter to the Hill household by putting the federal employee's head in an oven. This freeze frame lasts eleven seconds. The mailman's head is held inside the oven not as a holocaust metaphor, but one that represents hell, burning for the sin of disobeying the rule of law, here meted out by the men who ran the neighborhood and went beyond governmental power to control the citizens.

Paulie's power is explained in voice-over; he never made phone calls or talked to anyone other than one-on-one. We see these events with little pieces of dialogue supporting the narration. This opens up and validates Hill's words. The complexity of the synch sound, dialogue, and lyrical content all running in concert, is highly cinematic, and gives gravitas to the world of the gangsters. A slow motion dolly into Paulie eating a sausage sandwich, while Henry speaks of his power and respect earned through fear, give Sorvino quiet power as an actor developing the dimensions of his character with little but defined effort. The thirteen-second shot is menacing in its simplicity. A man with a napkin tucked into the collar of his shirt slowly eating a sandwich is contrasted with the background of his actions spoken over the slowed-down expressionless stare as he methodically chews his food—a harmless act in contrast to the deadly spoken acts.

Henry's ascent to power in the neighborhood among his teenage peers is captured in two shots. After breaking windows and pouring gasoline on the car of some uncooperative "client," Henry runs away as an explosion is detonated. The freeze is fourteen seconds long. The image is aglow with white-hot yellow and orange flames, as Henry emerges unscathed from the fiery hell. The sound of exploding glass continues, then ceases as a grownup Henry tells us a kid carried Hill's mother's groceries home out of respect. This is followed by Henry dressed like a junior wise guy looking into the camera at what becomes his mother's POV as she, and we, see Henry is now one of them.

Henry meets Jimmy Conway (Robert DeNiro) at a party where everyone is eating from a buffet of Italian delicacies—cold cuts, making sandwiches, and being served drinks by Henry. Jimmy comes in tipping everyone; chitchat is covered with Henry's biographical musings about

Conway and his reputation. After Conway orders a seven and seven he pushes a twenty into Henry's pocket and says, "Keep 'em coming." There is a freeze on his face so we can learn of his early hit man activities, then Scorsese cuts to Jimmy doing what he loves best—to steal. A series of scenes demonstrate how goods "fell off a truck" and landed in the neighborhood. Growing up, Scorsese was aware of how the goods became gimmies to the police and officials and bargain prices to the neighborhood.

While selling cigarettes outside a factory Henry is arrested—an occasion the Good Fellas celebrate as a coming of age for young Henry. It is his Bar Mitzvah, his confirmation. As Paulie says, "Ohhh, you broke your cherry!" Scorsese is documenting a maturation he understands from his exposure to gangsters and priests. A long freeze frame of young Henry surrounded in celebration as a doo-wop version of "Stardust" transitions to Ray Liotta as Henry in his early twenties. The transition is photographed to recall Travis Bickle (in *Taxi Driver*) as he makes his transition into psychosis. The camera slowly pans up his body. Henry is at Idlewild airport stealing loads of goods.

At the Bamboo Lounge, in a beautifully choreographed Steadicam shot, Henry introduces all the crew, many by their nicknames: Fat Andy, Frankie the Wop, Freddie No-Nose, Pete the Killer, Nicky Eyes, and Jimmy Two-Times (who says everything twice).

Repetition is a major element in the dialect of these Italian-American street guys. The constant repetition of, "I got no choice!" "What are you doin'?" and "Don't bust my chops!" takes on a greater meaning as a coded communication between tribal members. A singular phrase repeated several times is an emphasis; the way only a suggestive hand gesture, a physical contact from the hand of the speaker to the listener can. "Do you understand what I am saying to you?" is more than a casual phrase in this lexicon but an emphatic verbal sign from the speaker to the listener of insuring the power of their meaning is registering with the seriousness as intended.

Tommy's pathology is revealed as he holds court, telling jokes to the Fellas. When Henry says, "You're funny," Tommy turns the scene into a deadly serious confrontation, which turns out to be a test. Everyone laughs. The scene turns truly deadly when the owner of the club asks Tommy to pay a check and the gangster breaks a bottle over his head, surprising the audience with true violence.

Henry does Tommy a favor and double dates with a Jewish girl so Tommy can score. Here Scorsese takes the bold move of switching narrators. Karen expresses her feelings at Henry's bad behavior. Karen proves she is also tough by screeching up to the cabstand with her car. Henry is turned on by her display of anger and her willingness to confront.

Henry and Karen go to the Copa, a place out of Scorsese's youth, but here he shows the power and glamour of the lifestyle through a sustained Steadicam shot in which they enter through the kitchen and onto the club floor where a front row table is set up for them. This is the lifestyle Henry and the Good Fellas demand.

Karen becomes imbued in Henry's lifestyle. When a neighbor gets fresh with her she calls Henry who pistol whips the man in the face with a pistol. In voice-over Karen admits the violence and power turns her on.

Karen and Henry get married—the two families merge at the reception. Henry immediately returns to his lifestyle, staying out all night. Karen feels out of place with the wives of his friends but eventually she accepts the life. A still photomontage shows her acceptance of this life and how it mimics straight life, with family outings and events.

June 11, 1970. The pivotal sequence of *GoodFellas* in terms of structure and content takes place in Henry's bar the Suite Lounge. A welcome home party is in progress for Billy Bats (Frank Vincent) who has returned from a prison stint. Bats teases Tommy, telling him to go home and get his shine box. Even though Bats is a made man, Tommy's pathological anger again gets the better of him. Later, as Donovan's spiritual "Atlantis" plays, Tommy returns and brutally assaults Bats, kicking him with Jimmy's assistance, then shooting him in the mouth. They put the body in the trunk of the car and drive to Tommy's mother's house for a late night meal and to get a shovel to bury Bats. Tommy's mother is played by Catherine Scorsese, displaying authentic charm, while periodically looking at her son behind the camera. The next shot in the car with banging coming from the trunk returns *GoodFellas* to the beginning and now moves forward in time. Henry explains the consequences of killing a made family member. Hell is envisioned by the red taillight on Henry's face and a sizzling sound of eternal flames.

Henry begins to stray, spending too much time with his girlfriend as the heat over Bats' disappearance begins to pressure Paulie. Janice is set up by Henry in an overdecorated apartment. At a card game Tommy continues to spin out of control shooting Spider (Michael Imperioli) in the foot because he doesn't bring a drink fast enough. Karen finds out about Henry's girlfriend. At another card game Tommy can't take the ribbing when Spider answers him back and shoots him dead. Karen goes to Janice's house to intimidate her and then wakes up Henry with a gun to his face. Paulie comes to see Henry at Janice's apartment and convinces him to go back to Karen to return to a proper family life.

During a job for Paulie, Henry and Tommy are busted by the feds and along with Paulie go to jail where they live and eat like kings. Henry has developed a drug habit, which he tries to hide from Paulie.

Four years later Henry is released. Paulie tells Henry to stay away from drugs now that he's out. Henry doesn't listen and gets Tommy and Jimmy to go into drug running with him. After a tip from Morrie they set up the Lufthansa heist, the biggest in history. Henry has a new girlfriend set up in an apartment where he houses his drug setup. News of the heist plays over the radio as Henry showers. Jimmy's crew ignores his rule and start spending the money, which puts Jimmy into a tailspin. Stacks (Samuel L. Jackson) leads the Feds to the truck because of his sloppiness and is shot by Tommy. Morrie continues to scream for his money. Jimmy becomes paranoid and systematically executes Morrie and other members of the crew. The majesty of "Layla" supports a montage of all the dead as Henry explains in voice over how bodies were found in months as he and Jimmy continue to work together. Tommy gets the signal to become made. None of them see the truth that Tommy had to pay for killing Bats. When Tommy walks into a room he is shot dead.

The concluding section of *GoodFellas* storms the screen as if it were a paranoid symphony conducted by Henry Hill on coke. Attention to time becomes hypersensitive and is delivered in a panoply of ways infiltrating the narration, dialogue, and the sound lyrics, interwoven in a dense montage of images that get inside Hill's drugged out head. Scorsese, a maestro of repetition that builds to an explosive conclusion uses two constants to anchor the scene—Henry's brother, who is confined to a wheelchair, stirring a large pot of tomato sauce for hours on end and the unremitting presence of a helicopter as the Feds track Henry's every move. Henry is simultaneously Chef du Cuisine for the night's meal, a loaded menu with such vast quantities of food; he is actually planning to fry full chicken cutlets as an appetizer, while planning to execute a major coke deal. Hill is obsessed and consumed by the task, which he tries to control as if his life depended on it—actually he senses his days as a wise guy are numbered but the coke fires his energy, while increasing his inability to reason with reality.

Scorsese deftly handles the drug interactions with Hill's body and mind as a survivor in the white powder avalanche years of the seventies. The food, there's always the food in a Scorsese film, which represents Italian culture and a way of life based on the reverse maxim, "More is less." Scorsese internally understands that Hill can't break these two habits, which have take control over him.

As the brother is constantly reminded to keep stirring the sauce (an old wives' tale that warns the tomatoes will stick and clot), the helicopter is everywhere, as a visual and aural reminder that Henry is being watched. Every time Hill gets into the car the 'copter is there; he drives with his eyes up, top of the windshield, putting himself in vehicular danger. Hill's paranoia is heightened by his reality. Scorsese draws on personal experience and character study to create a state of mind where paranoia is not so much a distortion of reality, but an acknowledgement that every one *is* out to get you.

The thwarting of the helicopter blades is a constant reminder that the law is watching him, but Henry is determined to finish his errands, which include family responsibilities as well as criminal ones.

Scorsese is a contemporary moralist. In the Warner gangster films of the thirties and forties crime did not pay. As a keen observer of wiseguys Scorsese sticks to Hill's autobiography and the rules of the street. Henry is arrested outside his house. Of all the cinematic references and techniques Scorsese utilizes, the French New Wave by far remains the most powerful and bold aspect of the director's cinematic language. Truffaut and Godard taught Scorsese that anything goes in the cinema. During a trial Hill (as a protected witness) brings down all his friends, violating the rule, "never rat on your friends." Liotta concludes by directly addressing the camera and it works because of Scorsese's faith in his characters and in the cinema, which is a temple of images, moments, and codes to draw on. In the end Hill is relocated and is forced to live his life as an average schnook.

After the conclusion of *GoodFellas* proper, Scorsese brings back Tommy, firing his gun at the camera, reenacting the iconic shot in Porter's *The Great Train Robbery*; the homage also celebrates the spirit of the dead wise guy supported by the Johnny Rotten cover of Sinatra's signature, "My Way."

GoodFellas is responsible for *The Sopranos* and a slew of films of the nineties, which are intrigued by rat pack gangster cool. Even Scorsese had planned a Dean Martin film that would enter those years of ultimate cool. Scorsese proves an audience deserves and can follow a complex narrative. Ironically, a film about such base characters and primitive behavior resulted in one of Scorsese's most complex ventures. Within the overall, which begins in the middle, Scorsese presents brilliant set pieces: the "You think I'm funny," scene which exposes Pesci's psychotic nature; the Billy Batts murder, the suddenness and rage without bounds of murder; the killing off of the gangster who disobeyed Jimmy's orders orchestrated to the eleatic "Layla"; The Copa sequence—one uninterrupted shot from the streets through the innards of the restaurant to a front table; and, lastly, the hit on Pesci—a final reminder that crime just doesn't pay—we all get what we deserve.

24

The Old and the New: *Cape Fear*

In 1991 Martin Scorsese directed a remake of J. Lee Thompson's 1962 thriller, *Cape Fear*. Scorsese was a devotee of the 1962 film and had obtained the rights in a swap with Steven Spielberg for *Schindler's List*. The hook for Scorsese was right in the title. It was a chance to explore fear in its darkest and most irrational forms. The film also offered his collaborator, Robert DeNiro, a star turn. An examination of Scorsese's revisionist version compared to J. Lee Thompson's original provides an in-depth study of Scorsese's long list of obligatory filmic criteria and unique work methods, which culminate in transforming this remake into a Martin Scorsese Picture.

1962—The film begins with four descending forceful horn notes, then a duo of violin notes answered by less clarion-sounding horns, equal in their suggestion of impending danger; all continue to descend forming the haunting and frightening musical theme of psychological tension.

Max Cady (Robert Mitchum) crosses the street with decided determination. He is wearing a panama hat, a light leisurely cut jacket and trousers, and is smoking a cigar. Cady unabashedly checks out two young, not particularly assuming-looking, women. He smirks at the hall of justice. A matronly woman drops a book. Cady steps right over it and totally ignores the opportunity to be a gentleman. Cady stops in front of a judge's portrait and turns around with an arrogant dirty look. He addresses an African-American janitor as "Hey daddy." He's looking for Sam Bowden. Crushing the cigar in one hand he enters the courtroom with the brim of his hat tilted down. He watches with disdain as Sam Bowden (Gregory Peck) argues against adjournment of a plaintiff's case. As the handsome, well-spoken Bowden leaves the courtroom, Cady stands up and into the frame with a look of revenge in his eyes. Sam gets into his car. There is a cut to Sam's keys in the ignition as they are snapped up by Cady who snidely reintroduces himself, telling Bowden they met eight years, four months, and thirteen days ago. Cady makes it clear he's back for restitution. As Bowden drives off, Cady lets him know Sam has a pretty wife and a daughter, making a disguised but implicit threat to Bowden's family.

1991—Scorsese deconstructs the original 1962 film. The abstracted sound of a storm is heard over the Universal Logo, which appears to be underwater, immediately setting up the water motif that will dominate the film's climax. Over the fast current of moving water during the title sequence, Scorsese's name and the main title are sliced vertically in a reference to the *Psycho*. A vulture in slow motion is superimposed over the water. The music is the 1962 Bernard Hermann score adapted and rerecorded by Elmer Bernstein. A superimposed drop of water turned blood red is the backdrop for, "Directed by Martin Scorsese." Scorsese's biblical reference to the blood of Jesus speaks here to the impending violence and his Old Testament approach to the 1962 narrative.

A déjà vu feeling of Hitchcock's masterpiece, *Vertigo*, is evoked by the use of music, graphics, color, and an extreme closeup of eyes in a negative polarity first red, then fading into the flowing blood field, then purple to blue, then to a positive black and white, then full naturalistic color, as the camera pulls back to reveal Danielle Bowden (Juliette Lewis) directly addressing the camera in a classroom reminiscing about the Cape Fear river as mystifying but magical. A superimposed field of moving water plays over her monologue.

Max Cady is introduced by a pan down his cinderblock jail cell. A montage of photographs and images includes: a Prussian officer holding a saber; a religious figure, arms outstretched with two large arrows piercing his body forming an internal/external X; a highly decorated American officer; cartoon superheroes; a cutout of General Robert E. Lee, Joseph Stalin; a Bosch-like illustration of the Entrance of Alexander into Babylon; a stack of books, *100 Days to an Impressive Vocabulary*, *The Holy Bible*, *Eat Right and Stay Fit*, *Trial Handbook for Georgia Law*, various volumes on the law, *The Cell Within*, Nietzsche's *The Will to Power*, *Thus Spake Zarathustra*, and Dante's *The Inferno*—then Cady's megamuscled body comes into the frame. As he exercises, a full-size tattoo is revealed with two scales, one for truth holding a Bible and the other labeled Justice holding a dagger. He pushes back his long, slicked-back hair, puts on a shirt, as the prison bars, which have been in the foreground of the camera's view, swing open on this day of his release. This Max Cady is quickly and effectively defined as a fanatical devotee in maintaining the mind and body to possess power, supported by the Bible, the law, and thinkers of man as a superman. As he passes by other cells, prisoners watch in quiet awe and fear. In a matte shot worthy of Hitchcock and Albert Whitlock, ominous clouds move in the sky as Cady walks right into the camera.

The exterior of the Bowden residence is southern gothic: updated, well-appointed, and landscaped. Graciella (Zully Montero), the housekeeper (a character not in the 1962 film), steps out of a car and is greeted by Danni.

Leigh Bowden (Jessica Lange) is a graphic designer working in her home studio trying to explain the elements of a good logo to her daughter, who seems disinterested. A close-up introduces the family dog. Leigh is telling the dog that they must have switched babies on her at the hospital, immediately setting up the mother/daughter relationship in teenage angst flux.

Sam Bowden (Nick Nolte) is introduced coming out of the courthouse with another lawyer Tom Broadbent (Fred Dalton Thompson) (another character not in the original), who thanks Sam for handling his daughter's divorce case.

The screen is filled with a scene from *Problem Child*, which first functions as a homage to Kubrick's *The Shining* as John Ritter pokes his head into a smashed hole in his son's bedroom door screaming, "Here's Daddy." Max is attending the movies. He lights a very round, long cigar with a plastic, headless figure of a woman wearing a skimpy red bikini, which prominently displays equally red nipples on her breasts. DeNiro has taken Mitchum's business with the cigar and ratcheted up the macho symbolism. Cady blows the acrid smoke behind him, laughing unabashedly to annoy the Bowden family just a few rows behind. Sam tries to tell the offending viewer his feelings but Cady, wearing a loud white, blue, and orange short sleeve shirt, ignores him.

The Bowdens leave an ice cream shop as Danielle goads her father, telling him he could have been physical with the "loser" in the theater. Leigh gets her digs in by saying, "You know how to fight dirty, you do that for a living." Sam is told the check has been taken care of. The camera quickly pushes into Sam's face, then cuts to his POV—Cady sitting and watching in a red convertible. Sam's emotional reaction is cinematically portrayed by a constant moving in camera, and three cuts from the same angle showing Cady wide, medium, then in close-up as he continues his deadly stare at the Bowden's as he continues to stoke his stogie.

Sam, clearly shaken, tells the "girls" not to sit at an outdoor table. An intercut shows Cady still staring as another car passes him; Bowden turns to check if Cady is still watching them and his POV reveals the parking spot is now empty.

Sam and Lori Davis (Illeana Douglas), a colleague, a character that has been significantly modified from the original, play racquetball. Their interplay seems to be more than friends as Bowden is playfully physical with Lori in an aggressive manner with implied sexual innuendo. Later Sam tells Lori they have to stop doing what they have been doing, implying he's having an affair, but Lori is confused because she states that "we're not doing anything yet." The conversation reveals that Sam feels guilty and uncomfortable. He is in conflict about his marital responsibilities. In a cut, Sam has a 180-degree change of heart and makes a date to see Lori tomorrow for another racquetball match. Cady appears out of nowhere as we see his hand grab Sam's keys out of the ignition, and the narrative has now arrived at what was the first meeting in the 1962 version.

Cady introduces himself as they play cat and mouse with the keys. Sam remembers Cady from Atlanta in 1977. Cady has been in jail for fourteen years in this version, not eight and change. He talks about surviving prison, remaining human, implying that the alternative was to live like an animal. Max keeps Bowden at bay. As Sam pulls out, Cady says in a stage whisper, "You're going to learn about loss." Sam stops for a clarification but Cady is now far in the distance.

1962—The Bowden residence is solid southern-modern gothic style with plenty of acreage and lush landscaping. Peggy (Lori Martin) runs to meet her Dad with her dog running alongside. She is a perky teen, very clear about her traditional role as daughter. Sam's wife Peggy (Polly Bergen) is a stay-at-home-mom, with full but short black hair. They are all set for a bowling outing.

At the bowling alley Peggy rises and takes her turn, revealing her trim, balanced figure. Cady enters and smugly checks out Sam's wife. His attention turns to a pretty waitress (Joan Staley) who he crudely eyeballs from the front. His short-sleeve shirt is a period version of DeNiro's in the movie theater sequence, a retro/deconstructionist take on Mitchum's, which is an open-neck, sport shirt, with a tight graphic pattern of small shapes in contrast to DeNiro's large, imposing, and arrowhead-like pattern. Cady continues to laser in on the Bowden family and watches as his daughter, now dressed in shorts and short-sleeve sports top, bowls. The waitress brings Cady his beer. Max becomes flirtatious, then rude as he asks if her wedding ring means anything. Cady places a twenty-dollar bill down as a proposition. The waitress quickly runs away, as Cady chuckles. As Sam turns the ball into position he sees Cady. The silent exchange is one of concern for Sam and relish for Max. Rattled, Sam totally misses the solo pin and Cady silently mocks him. As Nancy gets up to bowl, Cady takes the opportunity to move down to Sam, sitting alone at the score table. Suspense is created by an angle that watches Cady slowly walking down to tap Sam on the shoulder and make his presence apparent. Max taunts Sam by looking off (into the bowling area) and saying "Nice shot," another Cadyism which is intended as a rude remark, not a compliment on female bowling skills. He tells Sam that he is there to take a "gander" at his family. The daughter comes over to her father and when Sam is distracted, Cady takes the opportunity to slip away.

Sam tells Chief Mark Dutton (Martin Balsam) that eight years earlier he was in Baltimore on a case. As he was walking back to his hotel he heard the sounds of a struggle. When he arrived on the scene a woman was being attacked; Bowden grappled with the assailant. When the man saw the police arriving, he beat the woman savagely, requiring her to be hospitalized. This man was Max Cady. Sam appeared against Cady as a witness. It is perfectly clear that Cady blames Bowden for his troubles. Sam confides that he wasn't concerned when Cady first arrived but the bowling alley appearance troubled him because of the way Cady looked at his family.

Cady is drinking beer at a dive bar giving the eye to an attractive bar girl (Barrie Chase). This character does not appear in the Scorsese film, but Lori Davis has a similar function in the Scorsese plot line. They exchange long looks.

A detective and police officer arrive to pick up Cady, who quickly demonstrates that he is willing to cooperate but only on his own terms. He tells the bartender he'll be back for his change, drains the beer, and goes over to the girl giving her one hour to "get rid of" her friends. She is a tough veteran of the scene, and remains both unperturbed and intrigued.

The Chief brings in Sam Bowden as they begin a strip-search on Cady. When his wallet is examined there are only seven dollars, so the Chief moves to book Cady on vagrancy. Cady, who has thought of everything, points to a bankbook containing $5,400. Sam stares Cady down and warns him to stay off his property. Cady announces he is not leaving and laughs at Sam's admonition.

1991—Sam is at home at the piano picking at the keys, while Danielle tries to concentrate on homework; when she gets his attention she explains her assignment is to read Thomas Wolfe's *Look Homeward Angel*, reminiscence, and to write something in the same style. Danielle has chosen to look back at family life on their houseboat. This links to the opening when Danielle reads reminiscence in her classroom but directly to the viewer. This real time scene with Sam reveals that the opening must be a flash forward because she has not yet written the essay. The theme of reminiscence also amplifies Danielle's passage to adulthood, from the time of innocence to a time of awakening.

Pink and blue bouquets of fireworks explode in the sky and are reflected on the Bowden master bedroom window.

Sam and Leigh undress for bed. It is the third of July. They argue about not having time for vacation and Danni's commitment to summer school until Labor Day. Candy-colored light animates the windows.

Sam brushes his teeth in the foreground as the conversation continues with Leigh in the background. This is no ordinary two shot but taken with a Split Diopter lens, which allows separate focus for the right and left quadrants of the shot. The result is an extreme and heightened example of deep focus. Sam's face fills the left side of the frame, while Leigh is seen in a medium position on the right. This speaks of the tension between husband and wife as they discuss Danielle's problem with smoking marijuana at school. They agree the school was being puritanical; there are now two images of each character because they are both looking into separate mirrors and not at each other. Under the sheets they make love, the camera moves up from their intertwined feet to Leigh's face enjoying the sex, and down to her hand as it intertwines with Sam's so that both wedding rings touch. The camera moves in closer on the hands as the image turns to black and white then negative then dissolves to Leigh's face, skeleton-like, then back to black and white. The black and white is a reference to the medium of the original, but the negative image is an X-ray of the soul and morality of the characters. Cady is not entering the lives of the perfect American family of the early sixties' original, but into a complex relationship of the nineties, filled with dysfunctional behavior and miscommunication. Leigh's eye opens in color then in the tradition of *Vertigo* crossfades during a wash of yellow as she gets out of bed. The windows flash yellow and blue. Leigh examines herself in a three-sectioned boudoir mirror in which we also see her from the back, looking at the three faces which dissolve into themselves, four faces of Leigh, and multiple lamps some real others a mirror illusion. She closes then rubs her eyes as the screen dissolves to an orange/red field and back to a push-in to Leigh applying hot pink lipstick to her open and sensuous mouth— dissolve to red/orange again she moves toward the shuttered windows. Max is sitting on their fence as the fireworks blaze around him. Leigh goes from window to window staring at Max, last seen in a low angle shot with the sky awash in explosive color. She and Sam both go to the shutters. They go down the staircase and out the door with Sam screaming for the intruder to get off his property, but Cady is gone, the fireworks fade,

Leigh is startled by the lipstick she has put on and wipes it off with her fingers.

Inside they talk about Max, first interrupted by the family dog getting on top of the table. Sam tells Leigh he doesn't remember what crime Cady committed fourteen years ago. Leigh gets in a dig about Sam's clientele.

Sam passes Danielle on the steps as he leaves for the office; she tells him he looks tired and he suffers another arrow to his manhood, which he tries to joke off while struggling to be respected. He tells Leigh he doesn't want Danielle to walk the grounds alone until he's looked into things. Leigh suggests having the dog with her but Sam demeans Ben's abilities as a guard dog. Leigh asks for a weapon and then flirts with the now all-serious Sam. Leigh sarcastically accepts the denial for a gun telling Sam, "We'd probably end up using it on each other." Her behavior is all marital subtext.

The camera quickly pushes into Tom Broadbent. Tom puts in a call to a criminal defense lawyer for Sam. Sam then confides to Tom the reasons for Cady's vengeful return. A principal difference between the two films is that in the original Sam was a witness who was responsible for putting Cady in prison. Here, Bowden reveals he was Cady's defense lawyer and that he deliberately buried documented evidence that the victim was promiscuous, in essence becoming Cady's judge and jury. Tom is judgmental about Sam's action reminding him about the Sixth Amendment. Sam's moral view of the law is as complex as the one he takes toward marriage and as complex as Scorsese's struggles concerning Catholicism, sin, and redemption.

Sam walks along the street when Cady drives up in a red convertible wearing a white sports cap and an extreme Hawaiian shirt, screaming with red, yellow, black, and white. Sam tries to be firm asking Max what he wants but Cady is in control, pointing to a group of teenage girls admiring the future they have ahead of them, as he continues to make veiled threats to Sam's family. In a sequence shot in traditional over-the-shoulder, shot/reverse shot, Sam tries to convince Cady he did right by him, and that he could be sitting on death row. Cady explains that he taught himself how to read in prison and now has a firm understanding of the law, acting as his own attorney for several appeals. Sam asks Cady how much he wants but Max wants something beyond money. He quotes the Bible about suffering in vain. Bowden offers ten thousand dollars in cash. Cady tells Bowden that even fifty thousand would only come to ten dollars a day based on the time he spent in jail. He continues to talk about loss.

A secretary comes into Sam's office to tell him his wife is on the phone. It appears that the camera swish-pans from Bowden at his desk, to the secretary in the doorway, then swish-pans back to Sam, all in one shot. In reality these are three separate shots joined by cuts during the quick movement. The purpose is to control the size of each shot. First Sam is in full shot, then the secretary is in a medium shot, and the final back to Sam is a close-up; this control of the size and composition would be impossible to achieve in a single take. By planning the shot structure Scorsese gets the impact of a swish-pan with the added benefit of control over the shot size. It is the action that dictates the composition. Scorsese alternates between traditional Hollywood technique, and expressionistic use of the camera to keep his film connected to the original, while he's taking it apart piece by piece.

Sam picks up the phone and says "Yeah," which is followed by a time cut that begins as an extreme close-up of Sam's face inside his car—only his nose and mouth can be seen. The camera quickly whips back to reveal a tight but full close-up of Sam driving with his eye line on the road ahead of him, just right of the lens.

At home Leigh explains the dog was outside making terrible sounds and has just died; she is crying and Danni is pensive. The dog was poisoned. When Sam criticizes Leigh for letting the dog out, she totally loses control screaming and pulling at Sam; Danni runs into her bedroom.

Sam walks down the corridor of the police station with Police Lieutenant Elgart. Scorsese wanted both Gregory Peck and Robert Mitchum to make cameos in his film as homage. Robert Mitchum is Police Lieutenant Elgart who was Cady in the original. Martin Balsam was the Chief of Police in the original. By going from villain to law officer, Scorsese makes a trenchant comment about the thin line between crime and law. He also demonstrates the art of acting. Mitchum created Cady, DeNiro reinterpreted him, and now Mitchum is inhabiting another character and interpreting a part developed by Balsam.

Cady is brought into a room with a one-way glass. A pan from Cady being strip-searched to the Lieutenant and Bowden watching through the one-way glass becomes another experiment of reflections, in which Cady and the two officers conducting the search appear and reappear blurring the sense of reality. Scorsese is more interested in the postmodern theme of duality as it applied to the multitude of emotions experienced by his characters: divergent feelings that exacerbate the plight and emotional state. Isolated shots of Cady's tattooed body transform him into a subhuman, living Bible, an object of revenge. One arm says, "Vengeance is Mine NT: Romans, XII, 19." The other, "My Time is at Hand NT: Matthew, XXVI." On the side of one arm is written, "I have put my trust in the lord God. In him will I trust, Psalm 91.2." Above that is, "The lord is the Avenger NT:

I Thessylonigin SI7, E," and above that is, "My time is not yet full come
NT: JAYIW, VII6." And still above that is a smiling/crying clown with a
gun that has just been fired, peering out of a jail cell, holding a Bible. On
Cady's back is a wooden cross with the scales of Justice hanging from
them. On his chest are blue/black lighting bolts edged in red, a broken
red heart, and a hooded man labeled, "The Avenger." The detective and
Sam are told by another man that no weapons were found but that they
did find his savings account, which begins at $30,000. His mother died
while he was in prison, the family farm was sold off, and Cady received
the proceeds. Sam is questioned and has no real grounds to hold Cady.
The strip-search continues. He is wearing orange/red bikini briefs dotted
with black leopard spots. Cady stares into the mirror and when intercut
with Sam on the other side. The silent communication is chilling.

1962—Cady is laughing at Sam's warning and is superimposed against
the image of moving through the hedges into the Bowden property. The
dog is barking furiously. Inside the phone rings. Sam has been on edge
waiting. His daughter stands at the back of the room pensively looking
through a magazine.

On the phone Chief Dutton informs Sam he's learned that Cady sold the
old family farm for $5,900, and that he was released a couple of hours ago.
The dog continues to bark, the daughter watches out of the window and
asks what's wrong with "Marilyn." Dutton tries to reassure Sam there are
legal ways to dissuade Cady from living in their town. Sam thanks him.
The dog howls, then there is silence. Sam reminds his daughter that the
dog is gentle, a stark contrast to the way this is imparted in the 1991 film.
Peggy comes running off the property urgently calling for Sam. The dog
is having a fit.

The vet tells Sam the dog was poisoned with strychnine. Nancy is guilty
because she fed the dog. Sam enters and tells them about Cady. Father and
daughter believe Cady poisoned the dog, but Sam firmly states there is
no proof. He tells Nancy never to leave the house or the school grounds
except in her mother's car. He tells them there is nothing to worry about,
the police will watch over them, and Cady is just trying to scare them.

Dissolve to Peggy Bowden sleeping. This scene tangentially relates to
Leigh awakening to the fireworks. As Peggy sleeps her dreams are visualized and pass through the image of Peggy in bed. In these dream ex-
cerpts we learn that Peggy doesn't feel Cady deserves civil rights, which
are defended by Sam. She suggests going away, taking Nancy out of
school. Sam thought of this as well but says Cady can afford to follow
them anywhere. Peggy asks, "What are we going to *do* about that man?"
Sam says they mustn't let him frighten the family—that's his game. Peggy

comes out of her sleep; Sam is not in bed. She goes to find him. She checks on Nancy; she is not in her bed. The house is full of shadows. She descends the steps with dread. At the foot of the steps she sees the silhouette of a man with a hat. She screams and turns on the light to learn it is just a hat and a jacket on a coat hanger. Outside a police officer hypothesizes that Cady probably tossed the meat for the dog onto the Bowden property from outside their grounds. Sam thanks him and the police car drives off. Peggy hugs her husband glad to be in his safe arms.

In the courtroom Sam is given a note that Chief Dutton wants to speak to him immediately. Sam and Chief Dutton enter a meeting with lawyer Dave Grafton (Jack Krushen) at which Cady is present. Grafton explains that his client doesn't want to cause any trouble but wants an end to the persecution. Grafton accuses Dutton of giving special attention to one citizen and concludes by warning Bowden and Dutton to back off. Cady says, "I'll see you around, counselor," to torment Sam. Dutton tells Sam privately that there is nothing else he can do. He does recommend that Sam hire a private detective, Charlie Seviers (Telly Savalas), to dig up anything on Cady the police can act upon.

1991—The Fourth of July Parade. Sam is telling Leigh (with Danni listening) that he has been assured that as an ex-con Cady will get the message and leave town but she is angry, "I'd still like to kill him," in revenge for killing their dog. Wearing mirrored sunglasses, Cady stands in the crowd staring at the Bowden family. Bowden gets angry because Cady is staring at Leigh and charges across the street. Cady tells Sam that Leigh is "hotter than a firecracker on the Fourth of July." Sam hits Cady in front of the large crowd and has to be physically restrained by the onlookers. Cady disappears into the crowd.

Cady is sitting at a bar flirting with Lori Davis. She has told him about getting stuck on a married guy, referring to Sam. He tells her he was arrested at a protest rally held at a nuclear power plant when a sheriff manhandled a woman behind him, so Max hit him and got a little time.

Max is straddling Lori in bed. Lori is so drunk and unaware, she continues to joke and laugh even after Max turns her on her stomach and handcuffs her. Then Max turns crazy with anger telling her what Sam did to him hurt more than what he's about to do. He dislocates her arm and as she continues to scream, he bites a piece of flesh out of her cheek and punches her repeatedly.

Sam is again at the piano but one of the keys is not working. Sam goes into Leigh's studio and asks if she knows why there is a wire missing from the piano when the Lieutenant calls.

In a hospital hallway the Lieutenant tells Sam the victim is scared and would only say she fell down a flight of stairs.

Sam is shocked to see it is Lori; he tells the lieutenant they work together. Lori tells Sam she felt abandoned and wanted to get back by having an affair. Sam tries to convince her to testify against Cady but doesn't tell her who he really is. Working in a legal office Lori knows how victims are *"crucified."* She is emphatic.

The Lieutenant suggests Sam use his wife and daughter as bait to bring Cady out and then for Sam to take care of him. Sam is offended by the coded suggestion and the Lieutenant makes it clear he was misunderstood, and is sarcastic when Sam is offended by the suggestion. Again Sam's credibility is soiled (unlike Peck's Sam who is a paragon of integrity). In the original a lawyer is a respected and honored profession, as is a police officer. In the Scorsese universe everyone is guilty of the sin of corruption.

Sam is in the office of Private Investigator Claude Kersek (Joe Don Baker), the counterpart of Telly Savalas's Charlie Seviers. Kersek is larger and more imposing. He tells Sam the law is slow to deal with a situation where no law has been broken but a constant threat is known. The P.I. agrees to look into Cady and to write up a risk assessment. Both Seviers and Kersek are professionals but the nineties bring a new terminology to an ongoing problem.

The Bowden family is eating dinner. Sam tries to remain in control telling Leigh and Danni he is confident Kersek will resolve their problem. The phone rings, in rapid, successive, single shots; all three react to the ring by jumping out of their skins, highlighting the tension in the household. Sam talks to Kersek who is staked out in front of Cady's apartment. Cady working out with weights is intercut with the talk. A zoom out from the window to Kersek's car visually links the two pursuers.

An extreme low-angle shot of Sam calling Lori at the hospital from the master bedroom emphasizes the secrets Bowden is keeping from his wife and daughter. As he apologizes to Lori for her attack the camera booms up and later reveals that Leigh is watching the whole conversation from the background. She is lit with a white halo around her—an expressionistic sign that she is white-hot with anger and knows about her husband's character flaws. When Sam becomes aware that Leigh is present he changes his tone and makes the call seem like it was business. Sam is full of deception but Leigh is direct. She tells her husband she knows he was talking to Lori and the young coworker was attacked by Cady as an assault on Sam and his family. The bedroom continues to be a sore focal point for Leigh, which represents their damaged marriage. In a fury Leigh lunges toward Sam and begins to beat him with her fists. Danni hears the parental violence. When Sam disingenuously assures her nothing is wrong, the teenager, damaged by the fractured marriage, storms into her room and slams the door. A poster of James Dean, the icon of teenage rebellion, is on the inside of the door.

The Bowdens have been to marriage counseling. Leigh unleashes her anger toward Sam repeating, "Why did you bother?" Referring to their marriage and uprooting the family unit, implying that they moved when Sam's indiscretions made it difficult to maintain their roots.

Leigh tells Sam he didn't have "the balls" to walk out and he retaliates by reminding her that for three months she couldn't work, couldn't fix meals, and only cried day and night, never leaving the bedroom (expanding the symbolism from an unhappy marriage bed to a place of retreat). The room, like the rest of the home, is vulnerable from within and without. Here Scorsese shows his place in the Cassavetes/Kazan universe as characters confront the truth of their own and shared lives. The emotions are raw, the actors being, not acting. Sam tries to convince Leigh that the past should be left alone and that he hasn't been "messin' around" since they moved to New Essex. He tells Leigh, Lori is just a kid who is infatuated with him—the real danger is Cady, an animal who is stalking them. He reveals his hidden fears, but Leigh enjoys the moment telling him, "Somebody finally got to you," implying that Sam's sins have finally caught up with him. Sam continues to try and gain Leigh's shattered confidence, explaining Cady knew that involving Lori would cause a rift between husband and wife, making them even more vulnerable to his vengeful plans.

Kersek sits at a restaurant counter as part of his tail on Cady who is eating at a back table. The waitress approaches the P.I. with a plate of food, telling him it was ordered and paid for by Cady, who is now going out of the door.

Kersek confronts Cady. They trade barbs; Kersek wants Cady out of the State; Cady continues to stress his rights and that all his actions are within the law. He strips Kersek of his power by insinuating the man was not "good enough" to be a police officer, leaving Kersek frustrated.

Leigh is out getting the mail. Cady drives up in his red convertible and hands Leigh their dog's leash. She explains the pet has passed away and Cady enters her psyche by revealing he could picture her with the dog at her feet as she worked on her "pesky little sketches." Knowing it is Cady, she tells him she is calling the police but he explains he is not on her property. Unlike Sam, Leigh is forceful and tells him he is repulsive. Cady is unmoved. He talks about desecrating his flesh and that if it wasn't for what Sam did to the two of them, their lives might have been different, implying they could be lovers. Cady knows how to get at Leigh telling her Sam has betrayed them both. Scorsese is relentless in keeping the relationships and confrontation between Cady and the Bowden family in Old Testament terms. This *Cape Fear* is more than a thriller—it is a morality play. Danni comes out on the lawn and Leigh screams for her to get back in the house. It is too late; Cady takes a long look at the girl and then speeds off.

Kersek suggests Sam let him do a "hospital job" on Cady, hiring men to give him a beating. Sam continues to be high-minded, "I can't operate outside the law—the law is my business." This interesting choice of words implies that law is Sam's vocation, not a belief system.

1962—Cady is driving with Diane Taylor, when he realizes he is being tailed by Charlie Seviers. Taylor tells Max he is an animal, barbaric, and Cady tells her he is turned on by that kind of talk.

Seviers is staked out outside a room where Cady and Taylor are shacked up. He calls the police and tells them they will be able to bust Cady on lewd vagrancy.

Shirtless, Cady approaches Taylor who is lying on a bed in her lingerie. She becomes frightened at his threatening demeanor and tries to run out of the room. As she makes it to the shutter doors, Cady snatches at her; the doors swing back and forth, suggesting an attack is taking place. The transposition from a bar pick up to a colleague allowed Scorsese to continue to erode the Bowden family values. Diane Taylor is an unfortunate victim but a member of the seedier side of life.

The police arrive but Cady has escaped through a back exit. Diane Taylor has been beaten. Seviers is filled in by the police and told that Taylor does not want to press charges.

Seviers explains to Sam that Cady knows he's being shadowed and will always find a way to "shake loose." He suggests Sam get in touch with a contact of his, a man with rough waterfront friends. Sam rejects the idea based on his ideals as a lawyer.

At the marina, Sam and Peggy leave to get supplies as Nancy continues to work on readying the family boat. As he drinks out of an open can of beer—Max glares lasciviously at the teenager. Sam comes back and sees Cady in the act. When confronted Cady remains cool telling the counselor he's just drinking a beer and thinking about renting a boat. Sam becomes hot and accuses Cady of poisoning their dog and attacking Diane Taylor. Cady is getting to Sam who threatens Max not to "push his luck." Cady looks down at Nancy and tells her father, "She's getting almost as juicy as your wife." This is beyond Sam's tolerance; he throws punches at Cady who puts up his arms to block the blows in defense. Cady has Sam where he wants him. A crowd forms around them as he tells Bowden, "You're not going to push me into anything. You've had your innings—I'll make my stroke later."

Nancy gets out of school, walks over to her mom's car, but there is no one there. She looks around nervously—then gets in. Nancy looks out and sees Cady steadily approaching. As fear and panic mount, Nancy gets out of the car and runs to the school, but the main door is locked. Nancy runs through a classroom and into the basement. Cady follows. Feeling Cady's presence Nancy screams and runs into a locker room. Finally she is able to get outside. As she leaves the frame it is revealed that it was the school janitor who was behind her. Outside Nancy flees for the front gate and runs right into Cady. She screams and runs out into the street as an oncoming car brakes just in time. Cady, deed done, casually walks away from the scene. Peggy pushes through a gathering crowd of bystanders and embraces Nancy.

Sam walks out of the bedroom into his office. Peggy follows. As she enters Sam is putting a handgun from his desk drawer into his pant belt, and charges out of the house. She warns Sam that Cady is in control. Sam turns the ignition of his car. Peggy runs back into the office and calls Chief Dutton; as she is waiting for him to come to the phone, Sam has come to his senses, enters the room, takes the phone and tells the chief it was a false alarm. They embrace.

At a restaurant Sam asks Cady how much money he wants to leave his family alone. Sam offers $10,000 and another $10,000 over the next two years providing Cady stays out of the State. Cady toys with Sam asking what the counselor would do if he ran out of money after the first payment and came back into town. Sam quickly answers, "I'll kill you off."

Cady's wife left him as soon as he was incarcerated—he lays the blame at Bowden's feet. When Cady was released he visited his ex-wife, who was remarried. Cady forced her to call her husband to say she was going on a vacation, then made the woman write a love note to Cady with a lot of dirty words. He assaulted her for three days. Finally he forced her to drink until drunk, took off all her clothes, and made her "work her way home." Cady had plotted his revenge for eight years. During his eighth year in prison, Cady arrived at a greater satisfaction than immediate death, which he calls "the Chinese death of 1,000 cuts."

1991—Danni receives a phone call from Cady who says he's her summer school drama teacher. When he says she sounds "down" Danni quickly confesses there is "stuff" going around. The scene switches to Cady's room. The camera slowly gets to Max hanging upside down in his doorway, rocking back and forth. He tells her he is interested in all his students and that everything she is going through is normal. He talks about emerging sexuality, the emotional changes she experiences during her menstrual cycle, the anger she feels toward her parents who don't want her to grow up. He tells her to use her feelings in her work and in her life. Danni listens in her nightie and removes a piece of sucking candy from her mouth; she becomes engaged and curious. Cady, elated that he has captured the girl's interest, tells her the room to the theater has been changed as the camera circles around until Cady's upside-down face is right side up, his hair standing up straight as he rocks back and forth, telling Danielle to draw upon her fears to learn. He puts on the stereo as "Do Right Woman—Do Right Man" sung by Aretha Franklin plays out of the speakers and into the phone. He signs off by telling Danni she can trust in him because he is the do-right man. Danni hangs up, pushes her retainer into her mouth, and is in deep thought.

In the main hall at school Danni talks to a friend about how crowded the summer session is, then leaves to go downstairs to drama; she anticipates meeting her drama teacher with a sly curious look, and skips to the door. The long, empty basement corridor is scary and ominous, much like the original. Danni is now anxious as she goes through another door into the theater. The set is a small old house with large trees surrounding it—the overall impact is of walking into a scary fairytale. Like Little Red Riding Hood, Danielle calls out "Hello," then for her friend Nadine. Cady lights a joint as Danni sees him. Cady knows that Danni was caught smoking pot in school. He asks her if she's been busted to gain her acceptance and explains smoking pot is a privilege of artists to ease inhibitions. He offers her the joint, she takes a pull, seems to relax a bit, and returns it to Cady who puts it out on his tongue telling her it's a little trick he learned, but doesn't reveal that he learned it in prison. Cady pontificates about human truths, inner voice, and self-discovery. They discuss Thomas Wolfe and he suggests she read Miller's trilogy, *Plexus, Nexus, and Sexus*. She tells Cady she's read parts of *Tropic of Cancer*, which she snuck off her parent's bookshelf. He tells Danni her parents don't want her to reach adulthood because of the pitfalls Leigh and Sam know all too well. Danni now realizes this is not her drama teacher but Max Cady. The exchange is presented in single shots, which separate the two physically as their conversation brings them together. He successfully denies that he killed her mom's dog. Cady promises Danni he just wanted to meet her and sees that she is "a nice person." He establishes that Danni is not judgmental but her parents are. They punished their daughter for their sins. He gets Danni to open up about how her parents reacted when she was caught smoking grass. Cady encourages Danni to resent this but to forgive them "for they know not what they do." He assures Danni he doesn't hate her father but prays for him. Cady is here to help him. Cady talks about salvation, a constant theme in Scorsese's work. He gets Danni to confide that she is not happy. When he asks if he can put his arm around her, she consents, after she moves through a series of adolescent emotions. Cady now moves into her space previously captured in various two shots. He caresses her face and runs his thumb over her lips. In a symbolic gesture of felatio, she sucks on his thumb and wraps her fingers around it while looking longingly into his eyes. Cady then moves into her and they exchange a long French kiss. He then walks away leaving Danni breathing heavily off camera. Now alone, Danni feels mixed emotions, then fear as she runs up the stairs and out of the theater. She does not run into anyone as Nancy did in the original, but the sound of Sam yelling, "Kersek" into the phone begins as she reaches the camera lens, creating a cinematic shock.

Sam decides to go ahead with "the hospital job." Kersek explains he'll hire three men and they'll be on for the next night. Sam is in conflict, but agrees.

Sam approaches Cady, sitting in a restaurant booth. This scene parallels the meeting in the original when Sam offers Cady money to leave town, but here the conference is called to issue a final threat. Cady is wearing a loud Hawaiian shirt and his hair is slicked back. Clothes are part of his control. In the scene with Danielle he wore a dark blue Lacoste sweater over a tasteful sport top, and his hair was loose and natural to convey authenticity in posing as a teacher, and to achieve a level of attractiveness that would satisfy Danielle's anticipation of meeting him after their phone conversation. Here Cady has the cigar and is exposing his tattoos to convey the constant threat he's been to Sam. In the original Mitchum achieves this largely through the cult of his personality and his sheer presence. DeNiro shares this ability as an actor and the costume becomes a tool to match his over-the-top performance, one more in common with Jack Nicholson as Jack Torrence in Stanley Kubrick's *The Shining*. Sam presents a clear threat to Cady. If he doesn't leave town he'll "be hurting like you never dreamed." Sam is still hoping he can talk reason. Cady sees through this immediately and tells Sam he wants what he has, "a wife, a daughter." He tells Sam he is here to save him, and as Bowden leaves, Max tells him to go to the Bible and look between Esther and Psalms.

1962—Three hired men beat up Cady under the pier. He quickly gets control of the situation knocking down one of the men. Another one hits him with a thick chain, inflicting a bloody bruise, but Cady gets the chain from the man and chases him away.

Cady phones Peggy. He taunts her saying he wanted to hear her voice again, and that he dreamed of "a chick with a voice like that" for the eight years he was incarcerated. He talks dirty to her; Sam comes into the room, grabs the phone and Cady laughs. Cady tells Sam that he has just put the law into his hands and "I'm going to break your heart with it. 'Ain't nothing can stop me."

Dave Grafton is waiting for Sam in the courtroom. The three men ended up in the hospital; one man talked. The judge wants to see Bowden. Grafton is instituting disbarment proceedings.

Chief Dutton tells Sam if he is implicated, the Chief will have no alternative but to arrest Bowden. Sam reveals his "carefully worked out" plan. There is a houseboat on the Cape Fear River, where he can hide his family. Grafton gave him the solution. Sam must fly to Atlanta the next day to appear in front of an ethics committee. Cady will tail him on his way to the airport. In Atlanta, Sam will hire a car, drive over to the coast, rent a boat, and get to the houseboat with Peggy and Nancy. Sam wants Sievers to lure Cady up to the boat by driving up there, while Max tails him.

1991—Both films are set in the south but Scorsese continually references that Cady is fanatical about his religion and homeland. The character is extreme but based on a prototype. It is the contrast of Cady's pious religiosity and his evil heart and behavior that animates the character and Scorsese's point of view; *Cape Fear* as a meditation in Old Testament revenge and justice. Scorsese's "hospital job" sequence is bloodier and more realistically violent than the original. The three men attack Cady. He is hit with a chain and bleeds from the side as in the 1962 version. Here Bowden is hiding in an alley, watching the dirty deed in progress. Cady crouches on the ground to protect himself as all three whale away at him. Sam, having seen enough, turns to leave. Max, up on his feet, head-butts one of his hired attackers, bloodying his face. He gets the pipe in his possession and begins to beat one of the other men. The man with the chain tries to gain the advantage back but Cady snags the weapon with the pipe. Two of the men run away in fear as Cady bashes the third. Sam turns to run but kicks a can, which signals his presence. Cady stops and repeatedly calls out, "Counselor?" Another allusion to Little Red Riding Hood is made by Cady saying, "Come out, come out wherever you are." Sam continues to hide from the Big Bad Wolf. Cady is a jailhouse philosopher who is only interested in proving himself right by a higher authority than the mortals who put him there. Cady walks toward the garbage dumpster where Bowden is hiding. The irony reduces Cady's moral position even further as he is helpless against his pursuer. Finally Cady backs off, throws the pipe down, and ends the notion of a violent confrontation with Sam.

Sam tells Tom Broadbent he won't proceed as asked on his daughter's divorce case. Desperately trying to hang on to his integrity he tells his boss that would be perjury. Tom calls top criminal lawyer Lee Heller and asks to hire his services to take out a restraining order on Max Cady. The phone voice is immediately identifiable as the rich baritone of Gregory Peck, the original Sam Bowden. Heller explains he cannot be of assistance; he was just hired by Cady to file a restraining order against Sam.

The hearing begins. Unknown to Sam at the time, Cady taped Bowden's threat in the restaurant. Cady is badly bruised and heavily bandaged. The judge is played by Martin Balsam, Chief Dutton in the original. Scorsese's three cameos all pay tribute to the original and make a sardonic comment on shifting moral codes. Mitchum, the pathologically dangerous criminal becomes a law officer. Peck transforms from a righteous lawyer defending his family to a self-righteous criminal rights advocate who has got religion as much as the law on his side. Balsam, the Chief, willing to bend the law to help a friend and to see that justice is really done, is a judge who adjudicates in favor of Cady not Bowden. Heller, like his client, also pronounces quotations, "Just as God rose to judgment to save the meek of the earth . . . " and appeals to the judge to do the same, with his variation of Psalm 76. After Heller's (note the first four letters) Sunday pulpit presentation Sam tries to rationally explain he was set up for the taping but the judge rules against him telling Sam he cannot come within 500 yards of Cady in the "spirit of Christian harmony"—a misapplication of the law, reversing the pursued and the pursuer.

Kersek tells Sam he has to leave his home for two days to attend the disbarment hearing. This will give Cady an opportunity to get to the Bowden women. If Cady breaks into the house he can be killed justifiably. Kersek tells Sam that Cady won't show up unless he is sure that Sam won't be there.

Sam, Leigh, and Danni leave their house, get into the family car and drive off into the night. Cady follows them in his car. They get to the airport. Leigh and Danni say goodbye to Sam as Cady secretly watches them from an upper-level restaurant. Sam turns to board the plane, Danni and Leigh turn to leave.

Cady goes to a ticket counter and tries to get on Sam's plane, when he is told there are no more seats available; Cady cons the attendant into giving him Sam's return flight information using his injuries to gain sympathy. She agrees and tells Cady that Sam will return in two days.

Sam and his family return and slip back into the house undetected. Kersek is inside rigging the house to trap Cady. Danni finds Sam crouching below the window then standing up; infuriated, she yells, "You're not allowed to stand up, Dad," referring to his lack of courage. She storms off to her room. Kersek rigs a monofilament line across all the windows and doors then wraps it around Danni's teddy bear. In another religious allusion, Kersek tells them if the wire around the teddy moves he could tell if even the Holy Ghost is sneaking in.

Kersek waits patiently with a gun. Upstairs Leigh tries to sleep; Sam is reading the Bible. He agrees with his wife that this experience will test how strong or weak they are. Sam finds the passage Cady referred him to; Sam reads that Job was a good man and God tested his faith, then took away every thing Job had, even his children.

In her bedroom, Danni wakes up suddenly; she hears a dog barking.

In the morning Kersek takes down the monofilament line. Outside Danni tells Graciella her father's plan is crazy and barbaric. She sees a large can of Charlie Chips in front of the door. As she picks it up Danni sees a copy of Miller's *Sexus* hidden underneath, a message that Cady has been there. She looks around, then hides the book under her shirt.

Inside Sam tells Kersek the thought of killing Cady really disturbs him. He's not sure that he can deal with it. Sam is tortured by his lawful morality. Murdering Cady would make him an accessory, an abettor to a crime; they are planning to use excessive force. Sam seems less concerned with the Christian morality involved than the one created by the legal system, which he has manipulated to his advantage. Sam is duplicitous, not a clear-cut hero like his counterpart in the original.

Leigh, Danni, Sam, and Kersek watch *All That Heaven Will Allow*, directed by Douglas Sirk. Graciella is cleaning up. Leigh jumps when Graciella drops a magazine. After a short discussion it is decided she should sleep over as she would normally if Sam wasn't at home to drive her.

Outside is a moving camera, presumably Cady moving around the house. The camera pushes into the rigged bear, then to Leigh lying in bed, then Sam, then the clock: a constant moving camera from cut to cut to build the tension. Both J. Lee Thompson, director of the original and Scorsese reference the cinematic grammar of Hitchcock. Scorsese's approach is less traditional and modified with his own nervous, kinetic style. The technique continues, moving into Kersek holding his pistol until the gun fills the screen, then the bear under the P.I.'s careful watch. Finally the wire jerks the bear, Kersek readies his weapon. The camera follows the monofilament as it jerks back and forth leading to a window, moving because of the strong outside wind current. Sam jumps out of his rest, and sees a black-and-white negative image of Cady standing in the doorway. It turns to color. Sam rubs his eyes and the image is gone, the doorway is quiet. Sam wakes up Leigh and tells her he now knows how the dog died. A feeling told him Cady was already in the house. Kersek checks all the windows; he hears a noise and moves into the kitchen with his gun drawn, relieved to see it's Graciella who just can't sleep. Kersek sits at the table with his back toward her and pours his favorite stakeout drink, Jim Beam and Pepto Bismol. In a variation on *Psycho* the camera reveals that it is not Graciella but Cady dressed in a woman's wig and clothes, he strangles Kersek with a garrote. Kersek tries to shoot Cady but the gun goes off blowing a hole in Kersek's neck killing him instantly. He drops to the floor. Sam and Leigh are startled by the shot. Cady is covered with the P.I.'s blood as he calls the dead man "a white trash piece of shit." Sam keeps calling for Kersek. Leigh goes to the shutters and sees Cady running across their property. Leigh runs to her husband, who is in the kitchen; they are both horrified at the bloody sight. Danni comes in and discovers the bloody dead body of Graciella; she screams. Sam slowly approaches Kersek's body and realizes he was killed with the missing piano wire. The scene turns into a grisly dark comedy as Sam and Leigh fall, slip and slide on the pool of blood pouring out of Kersek. Sam, totally out of control, takes the gun, runs outside, and begins firing as Leigh and Danni scream for him to stop.

1962—The Bowden family arrives at the houseboat. Inside the houseboat Peggy and Nancy unpack provisions. Sam says goodbye to his daughter. Outside Peggy reassures Sam that Nancy comes from pioneer stock, they kiss. Sam casts off and heads back.

The Airport. A ramped-up pan (similar to Scorsese's use of a swish-pan in his films) starts on Sam about to board and speeds to Cady sitting in his car, watching. Cady tells the attendant he has a brief for the lawyer. He quickly gets an answer that Sam will be gone for two days. No con was necessary in the original because of a more relaxed policy or the audience's belief that it would be no problem to get that information.

Nancy hears a boat coming closer. Peggy shoots off the lights, takes a gun out of a drawer, and looks around. Through the shadowy interior she moves and hears a boat arriving. Both women are terrified as they hear a person get out of the boat and walk toward the houseboat. Peggy opens the door and sees it is Sam who has arrived with Mr. Kersek, played by Page Slattery (the name Scorsese's version uses for the P.I) of the sheriff's office. Peggy serves coffee. It's decided that the women will sleep on the boat and the men on the shore.

The next day Cady watches from afar as Severs carries Nancy's portable record player to his car. A binocular shot shows Severs get into the car and drive off.

Severs stops on the road at a gas station. He is looking to see if Cady is following. He calls Sam from a pay phone and reports he's halfway and there has been no sign of Cady. Sam tells Severs to come ahead.

Cady comes out of a truck on which he hitched a ride. Severs is also there but unaware of Cady. He rents a motorboat to get to the Bowden houseboat. Cady watches Sievers go down the river.

Sievers arrives at the houseboat and delivers the case to Peggy, then boats away.

Sievers travels down the river. Cady observes him from a boat he has rented.

Cady travels to the houseboat.

Night. Peggy cleans up in the kitchen. Nancy puts a 45 on her record player. Sam keeps watch off the shore with a gun. Kersek is at another vantage point watching out for Cady, his gun ready. Cady comes out of the bushes. He positions himself across from the houseboat. Through a binocular shot, he sees Peggy in the kitchen window. He then finds Nancy and peers at her through his glasses. Cady again looks at Peggy in the window and quickly moves from his position.

Peggy quarters an orange and places it on a dish. Nancy nervously listens to her record player; the source music is blended with the score for an eerie, dreamy, but ominous effect. She bounces a ping-pong ball on a racket to keep busy. Cady changes his position and watches Nancy sitting, an unaware prey. Sam continues to keep watch. Cady takes off his shirt and hat. He carefully lowers himself into the water and swims toward the houseboat. Nancy drops the ball and kicks over a garbage can. Sam is alerted by the sound. Nancy is back in her seat bouncing the ball. Sam sees this and is relieved. Cady slowly makes his way across the water. Kersek, keeps a lookout. Now on the shore Cady quietly approaches the houseboat getting close enough to see Nancy directly. Kersek slaps a bug, calling attention to himself. Cady takes the man by the throat from behind and drowns him. Cady loosens the rope tying the houseboat to its mooring setting it adrift. Sam sees that the boat is starting to move; he runs to the dock but doesn't make it in time. Cady climbs aboard the boat. Sam finds the body of the dead officer. The boat is moving downstream. Peggy watches as the door opens and Cady appears. Sam comes around back and warns Nancy to call the sheriff's office. Sam runs through the glades and sees that the boat gets stuck on the opposite shore. Cady backs Peggy into the stove. She tries to grab for a knife next to a plate of eggs. Cady grabs her and tells her there is nothing to be scared of. Peggy tries to tell Cady if he harms her he will go to jail. Cady crushes an egg in his hand and explains that with consent there will be no charges. He rubs the raw egg over her neck, shoulder, and cleavage. He tells Peggy he has decided to go after her and terrorizes the woman into a state of panic. Sam gets into the boat and searches frantically for Peggy and Nancy. He hears sounds and finds Peggy. She grabs hold of Sam and says that Cady only wanted to get Sam away from Nancy; it's Nancy he is really after.

Nancy tries to get the operator on the phone. Cady is outside the locked door. Nancy tries to hide. Cady breaks the window with his bare hand and lets himself in. They are on either side of the ping-pong table. Cady forces her into the back wall by pushing the table at her. Nancy grabs a poker and threatens Cady with it, but she is too frightened to use it. He pulls the poker out of her hand, grabs her arm, covers her mouth, and pulls her out of the room. Sam charges out of the water but is grabbed by Cady. In the struggle the gun falls to the ground. They fight exchanging blows; Cady eventually knocks Sam into the water. Cady jumps in after Sam and tries to drown him. After a second attempt he holds Sam underwater for a long time and brings him up thinking he is dead. He lets Sam go and he sinks to the bottom. In an underwater shot Sam's hand grabs a big rock. He brings it up and bashes Cady repeatedly then runs out of the water. He gets Nancy and tells her to "run and hide." Cady makes it out of the water. Sam sees him and waits. Cady picks up a heavy stick with a long, thick metal screw and searches for Sam who is hiding in the brush. He finds him; Sam runs but Cady comes at him and misses, plunging the weapon into a tree. They chase through the brush. Sam stops and Cady approaches him as Bowden crawls along the ground toward the gun. Just as Sam is about to get the gun Cady swings at him but Sam gets the gun in time and shoots Cady. Still alive Cady tells Sam to kill him saying a line that aptly defines character and actor, "Go ahead, I just don't give a damn." Sam turns Cady's earlier words about killing too fast and tells him he'll be nursed back to health so he can live a long life in a cage where he belongs. Sam has finally found Cady's weak spot—the fear of being caged in jail. Dissolve to the Bowden family on a boat, and then to a full shot of the craft on the water as the end credits run over.

1991—The Bowden's station wagon speeds down a highway. Leigh looks concerned and worried. They pass a roadside flower stand. Danni looks distraught, Sam very determined. At a roadside stand Danni and Leigh carry out provisions, while Sam is on the phone to Lieutenant Elgart telling him he has Kersek's gun on him and that they will find the piano wire Cady used as a murder weapon in the house. He tells the Lieutenant about force majure, which means an unforeseeable act of god can cancel all obligations. Still a master at using the law he tells the Lieutenant that legally speaking "all bets are off." There is a juicy irony as he ends the phone call saying, "You find Max Cady and we'll come back." Although we never hear Mitchum's voice, in the larger history of the two films, Sam is asking Max Cady to find Max Cady. As the camera follows the Bowdens to their car it reveals that Max is hanging onto the undercarriage undetected.

A wavering reflection in the water shows the road sign "Cape Fear Next Exit," as the string theme notches up the tension level. The Bowdens arrive at the dock. Cady lowers himself from the car undercarriage to the ground. Sam and Leigh enter the houseboat, named the Moara. Cady unbuckles the rig that held him to the body of the car and gets up. He is covered with dirt and grime from head to toe. A woman walking by stops and witnesses Cady's entrance. He glares at her then walks into the men's room. Inside he cleans up and carefully slicks back and darkens his hair. As the Moara starts down river, Cady watches and rents a boat. Sam drops anchor. The camera moves through the swamp toward the Moara, not defining the point of view. Inside, the Bowdens eat dinner. Sam suggests catching some fish; Leigh immediately goes into her emasculating tone saying she has bought enough food for a week. When she sees the hurt expression on Sam's face she says, "But it would be nice," and Sam says, "Good," gaining some respect as the man of the household. They hear a noise. Sam says it's only rain. An exterior shot shows the boat has been cut adrift. Sam takes the gun and goes out to check, telling Danni, who is terribly frightened and now protective of her father, "It's just a squall." Out in the rain Sam checks the anchor rope and stares into the water. Leigh calls to Sam about a cup of tea. He doesn't respond, then finally he say's he can't hear them because of the wind. As he moves around the boat soaked to the skin, Cady grabs Sam by the neck from the top of the boat and pulls him up. Inside the women hear a sound from up above. The audience sees Sam getting hauled up through the window but the women don't see him. Cady continues to apply pressure to Sam's neck until he passes out. He ties Sam's hands behind his back and sets him down on the deck, then pulls up anchor. Inside Leigh feels that the boat is moving and Cady makes a dramatic entrance. She tells Max her husband has a gun; he shows her he has taken it and has it tucked into his pants. He tells Danielle she can't escape her demons by running away from home, tapping into his power over the teenager, who gets shy and girlish saying, "I didn't my parents brought me here." He asks where *Sexus* is and is mock disappointed when she tells him it is back at the house, because he wanted them to read it aloud together. She tells Cady she memorized some for him. She becomes fearful as he presses her to tell him which parts of the book she read, and that she is going to get to know him a lot better, when

Danni throws the pot of hot water at his face. Cady is not affected by the scalding water. He lights a flare and tells the women about his time in jail when he became more than human. He talks about his granddaddy handling snakes in church and drank strychnine. The molten fluid from the flare pours down his arm and Leigh watches in horror and Danni cries. He throws the flare outside by smashing the window with his bare hand. He forgives Danni but tells her to get in the hold. He forces her in, locks it, and says, "Ready to be born again Miss Bowden?" Cady, with threat implied, moves toward Leigh telling her after being carnal with him she'll be "speaking in tongues." The phrase refers to proof that a person has truly been born again. Bible references include Mark 16–17, "He that believeth and is baptized shall be saved; but he that believeth not shall be damned. And these signs shall follow them that believe. In my name shall they cast out devils; they shall speak with new tongues." The ability to speak in tongues with God is a tenet of the Pentecostal church, a sect Cady would be familiar with. Danni's eye inside the hold watches with fear and voyeuristic emotions. Leigh tries to back away; Cady ravishes her, kissing her face and body. Danni lights a match inside the hold and later picks up a tool, throws it down, and puts out the match. Cady lifts up Leigh and backs her up to the wall. Sam's horizontal eye, from outside on the deck, tied up, is staring in horror. The double voyeurism represents Sam's worst fear of losing his wife to Cady, even though he has been unfaithful; and Danni's love for her mother and burgeoning feelings of adolescent sexuality. Being watched heightens Max's thrill as getting revenge and satisfying his distorted religious and sexual longings. Danni lights another match and finds a container of lighter fluid, which she puts down her pants and Cady continues to maul at her mother, building on the metaphor of Max's gun and penis down his pants as weapons. Cady handcuffs Leigh to a pipe announcing he has bigger plans in mind. He opens the door to the cabin, pulls out Danni and spreads her out on the table. Sam begs Cady to let his wife and daughter go, Max answers by stomping Sam in the head repeatedly. Leigh begs Cady to stop, she tells Max she has been thinking of him locked up all those years. She talks about loss time, referring to her unsatisfying marriage. She taps into Danni's fantasy about first meeting Cady and tells Max they have a connection and to "do it" just with me. Cady had been listening intently but is too emotionally sheathed to embrace compassion, especially the manipulative kind. Cady responds verbally with sarcasm and physically by kicking Sam again. Max takes Leigh's cuffs off, bites the end of a cigar off, and spits it into Sam's face. As he lights the cigar Danni seizes the moment and squirts the lighter fluid at Cady who becomes a human torch, runs out of the cabin, and jumps into the water. The boat is adrift. Sam gets free and steers the craft. Cady swims up to the torn rope, which once held the anchor. Sam sees the rope but not Cady, through a series of three ever-closer Hitchcockian shots and beyond as a variation of the master's grammar, Bowden watches the dangling rope and pulls it up. Cady with gun drawn is on deck and gets control over Sam again. As the boat goes off course and out of control Cady has staged a mock trial inside the cabin with Leigh and Danni as the jury, Max as the prosecutor, and Sam as the perpetrator. Max badgers Sam about how he handled his case. When he doesn't like a response he hits Sam and apologizes to the nonexistent judge for being "argumentative." Leigh and Danni scream for Cady to stop but he continues to beat Sam and eventually gets him to admit he buried the report about Cady's victim that may have freed him. He tries to explain to Cady he was a menace, which sets Max off on the injustice done to him, "You were my lawyer." This sends him into a tirade in which Cady turns himself into Virgil from Dante's *Inferno*, guiding Sam through the gates of hell into the ninth circle and traitors. Cady uses information to show his supremacy, asking Sam if he knows the Rules of Professional Conduct Canon Seven. Sam begins to recite but Cady interrupts to vilify Bowden who didn't "zealously represent his client within the boundary of the law" and by the "power invested in me by the kingdom of God," again confusing law, literature, and religion into an Old Testament revenge revival sentences Sam to the ninth circle of hell for his loss of humanity. Cady, still wielding the gun, tells the women to get down on their knees and to take their clothes off. When they won't comply Cady pulls Danni down by her hair as Leigh takes down the straps of her top. Cady handcuffs Leigh and tells her, "Tonight you're going to learn to be an animal." As Max goes to cuff Sam, the boat hits rock and throws Cady to the other side of the cabin. Caught in a maelstrom the boat spins around furiously. Sam gets the women off the boat. Cady comes from behind and grabs Sam by the leg and they fight to get to the gun on the floor as the boat spins in freefall. Cady gets control of the gun and points it at Sam. Scorsese takes the opportunity for another Hitchcock homage, this one from the climax of *Spellbound* when Dr. Murchinson (Leo G. Carroll) reveals himself as the killer to Dr. Constance Petersen (Ingrid Bergman). In a bravura POV shot his arm and gun are in foreground with Bergman in the background. Scorsese doesn't use it as a special but as part of his mise-en-scène. Scorsese's encyclopedic cinematic grammar is so comprehensive the result is the right shot at the right time. He's learned his lessons from the master filmmakers so well their innovations become a part of his highly motion picture literate style. Sam cuff's Cady's foot to a post, Max starts to shoot but the boat hits rock and the gun flies out of his hand. The craft spins out of control and begins to implode. Sam jumps out of the boat just in time and gets to the shore. Still cuffed to the post and a fragment of the deck, Cady makes it to the shore. Sam grabs a rock and smashes Cady who responds with a sarcasm concerning Bowden violating the restraining order against him. Sam hits him again, and Cady laughs. They trade punches. Cady hits Sam with a rock. Bowden looses all semblance of his connection to the law, a system he has well manipulated but stayed within contemporary definition until now—"I'M GOING TO KILL YOU!" Sam picks up a huge stone and brings it down on Cady who has been pulled out by the tide. Cady is in the final stages of his religious conversion on earth, "Who will come with me to the promised land!" He begins to speak in tongues, proving he is now truly born again as his world ends as did the first—by water. Cady and Sam share one last stare, Bowden on the shore, and Cady's head just above water, then after a long enough time to again prove his unearthly strength, goes under. Sam's hands are covered in blood. The realization hits him, and the audience that he has killed Cady. No justice here in sending him back to jail as Gregory Peck so proudly announced to Mitchum at the conclusion of the original film. A point of view of the bloody hands perfectly sums up Scorsese's visual approach to violence and religion. Sam is hunched over on the shore, hands outstretched as the camera pulls back. This is not the ending even though the viewer has been conditioned that most films end with a pulling back. Even when Scorsese doesn't specifically reference a movie, the cinephile sees images from other movies flashing by. Sam looks emotionally destroyed like Zampano on the beach in Fellini's *La Strada*. Leigh gets up from the mud, Danni goes to her, and Sam joins them; the family is reunited. The image of Danni speaking into the camera at the start of Scorsese's *Cape Fear* becomes a bookend, proof that the film has all been in flashback to the present experience and the toll it has taken on the Bowden family. We stay with the Bowdens at the moment of their absolution as Danni, the voice of truth in the family, states the price they paid. "We never spoke about what happened, at least not to each other. Fear I suppose that to remember his name and what he did would be letting him into our dreams, and me, I hardly dream about him anymore. Still, things won't ever be the way they were before he came, but that's all right because if you hang onto the past, you die a little every day and for myself I know I'd rather live. The end." In an extreme closeup of Danni's eyes they transform to black and white negative, referring to the medium of the original film and an X-ray of the character. The Bowdens have been deconstructed, examined through heart and soul. The field containing Danni's eyes turns blood of Christ red, and then fades to black. As the Bowdens continue to live in their personal hell on earth, the theme music plays over the credits. When the credits have played out, the sound of rain is heard over black and then distant blood-curdling female screams, as if it were sounds from the ninth circle of hell. The majority of the audience is gone, but Scorsese continues to portray everlasting hell.

25

Emotional Violence: *The Age of Innocence*

Early in his career Martin Scorsese dreamed of making movies in all the genres he loved from the Hollywood Studio System. One of the genres was the costume picture, also known as the period film, movies such as *Gone with the Wind, Kitty, Marie Antoinette* (1938), *The Private Lives of Henry the VIII, The Scarlet Empress, The Devil is a Woman, Jezebel, Mr. Skeffington, All This, and Heaven Too, Knights of the Round Table, Ivanhoe, Prince of Foxes, Jane Eyre, Lorna Doone,* and *Wuthering Heights*. This genre has endured during the history of film and was especially vibrant in the years Scorsese was growing up during the forties and fifties. The costume picture allowed the viewer to be transported back, either to, gentler, more romantic or turbulent times, and to escape the everyday drudgery of their lives and crises, such as World War II. Women, especially, enjoyed the costume picture, and men related to the history and action aspects. The period film examines our culture at a point in time and is a bridge between the past and the present. The production design and costume design for these films was complex and forefront within the frame. Even in the twenty-first century the majority of films nominated for best costume design and best production design are period works.

Scorsese's decision to make Edith Wharton's novel into a film was based on several factors. Scorsese liked costume epics. His dad was a history buff and as a presser had great interest in clothing of all eras. The film took place in old New York beginning in the 1870s, so it allowed the New York director to investigate his city's roots, specifically the upper class. He would do a 180 degree later in making *Gangs of New York*, which begins in 1846 and focuses on the lower classes. This was a project of choice, not an assignment, so the key to the personal attraction Scorsese found lies within his own psyche.

The Age of Innocence concerns Newland Archer (Daniel Day Lewis) who is set to marry May Welland (Winona Ryder), but when he meets May's cousin, the Countess Ellen Olenska (Michelle Pfeiffer), he becomes obsessed with her. For Scorsese the most painful emotion is passion repressed. Newland is tortured throughout the film never able to fully communicate or physically express his sexual and romantic feelings toward the Countess. This makes the film a moral drama and a familial one as well. The Countess has married richly but without love and is both mysterious and a scandal to the two families.

The many scenes of the suffering Newland and the contorted ones of him and the Countess as he tries without success to physically win her over must have their roots in Scorsese's experiences during aspects of his four marriages. He has developed the theme of the impossibility of sustained intimacy between artists, but here he goes into the inner life of a character who can't communicate with women successfully to achieve happiness. The "violence" of *The Age of Innocence* that Scorsese and many critics refer to is emotional violence—the physicality of repressed passion in the body and its effect on the mind, heart, and soul. The nature of obsession rises again in a Scorsese film. "It seems to be a theme I like a lot, and it's in movies like *Who's That Knocking at My Door* or *Taxi Driver*, where Travis Bickle becomes obsessed with Betsey," Scorsese says in *Scorsese on Scorsese*. "I can identify with those feelings of wanting to take and not taking, of wanting to proceed with something and not proceeding, for many different reasons—shyness, a certain kind of propriety, or deciding that it wasn't such a great idea. I had a late adolescence in a way, I would say even up to the point when I started to make *The Age of Innocence*. It has made me think at the age of fifty, what if I'd been a different type of person. One who could have handled such things easily? Would my life have been very different?"

The production is exquisite, shot mainly on location and in Kaufman Astoria Studios. Scorsese and his team, including production designer Dante Ferretti, director of photography Michael Ballhaus, and costume designer Gabriella Pescucci, meticulously recreated the period researching the film down to the finest detail in décor. Three films by master Italian director Luchino Visconti were key in providing Scorsese with influence and inspiration: *Senso, The Leopard*, and *The Innocents* form a "trilogy of political change and romantic dissolution in the 19th century." *The Leopard*, a film that Scorsese has viewed repeatedly, was a major reference in his historical sweep, lush décor, and "emotional grandeur." *The Innocents*, directed by Jack Clayton, is an adaptation of Henry James's *The Turn of the Screw* and deals with "unspoken, feelings unexpressed

Martin Scorsese gives close direction to Daniel Day Lewis on the set of *The Age of Innocence. Courtesy Photofest.*

and dreams that die in shame with the daylight." Stylistic and aesthetic devices to present the text were rooted in Truffaut's *Jules and Jim*, a film that Scorsese often returns to when beginning a project. Scorsese applied that film's "flutter punch editing," the roving, restless camera, never still; the narration, which broke rules by recounting how characters felt, and even, on occasion, describing what they were doing while they did it; the reliance on letters, notes, and diaries (also borrowed from *Citizen Kane*), and the way they were presented. The fluid camera of Max Ophuls, the major influence on the films of Stanley Kubrick, was inspiration for the use of camera between Scorsese and Ballhaus. *Letter From an Unknown Woman*, and *Lola Montes* "combine worldliness and fabulism with a kind of reflective melancholy: the characters here are creatures of fate whose fates . . . rush them past follow toward doom."

To visualize the film Scorsese once again turned to film history and created a wide range of references to composite the look for *The Age of Innocence*. From *Barry Lyndon* Scorsese was influenced by "the tone: the chill bemused irony of the narration—the lavish but careful use of the novelist's language—turns the drama gradually from shrewd observation of 18th Century English mores into a complex poignant portrait of vanity and ambition." *Carrie*, a William Wyler adaptation of Dreiser's *Sister Carrie*, contained an obsessed man with an "impossible object of desire." The film noir *Detour* gave Scorsese the idea of shooting Archer's eyes with a block of light as he sunk deeper into spiritual ruin over the Countess. *Experiment Perilous*, a Jacques Tourneur film from 1944, provided a dreamy quality "in which he used setting to reinforce atmosphere, not just to establish it." Use of shafts of light in the film also influenced the lighting of Scorsese's film. *Far from the Madding Crowd* is a period film that reflects current time, which gave *The Age of Innocence* the ability to comment on the nineties through a film taking place over a hundred years earlier. In *The Heiress*, "Wyler shoots drawing rooms, ballrooms, and dining rooms as if they were antechambers of the soul, each filled with deep shadow and stalks of light, each holding some possible secret about a mystery that can never be solved." Another "touchstone" for *The Age of Innocence* was the climax of the film in which Olivia de Haviland comes down the steps with a lamp leaving Montgomery Clift pounding on her door, shut out of her life forever. Vincente Minnelli's *Madame Bovary* concerns "Longing and desperation and wrongheaded, hopeless romanticism."

Overall Scorsese's mise-en-scène in *Age of Innocence* is traditional with wide shots, shot reverse shot conversations, and less interscene cutting than in most of his films. But there is another dreamy, expressionistic aspect: dissolves and jump cuts aesthetically comment on the structure, especially in the first half of the picture. Like many of the films he referenced, Scorsese worked with a meticulous period décor but, at times an abstract sensibility of time and space, which gets into the emotional life of the main characters, especially Archer. It's as if the events have altered his way of seeing and moving through space. The fracturing, and restructuring moments through jump cut dissolves Schoonmaker, and Scorsese personalizes *The Age of Innocence* with editorial comments, which augment Ballhaus's expressive and fluid cinematography.

The film's literary voice is maintained with a near constant narration spoken in cool but elegant style by Joanne Woodward. Elmer Bernstein's tragic romantic thematic underscoring gives *The Age of Innocence* a traditional and sophisticated accompaniment reminiscent of the first Golden Age of Hollywood.

A shot of a crowd of men all finely dressed and wearing bowler hats as they walk down a street sums up the era, and like the opening shot of *Raging Bull*, sums up the tone of the film.

Scorsese finds plenty of opportunity for his signature top shot, especially on meticulously prepared tables and plates of food. Information is another theme of *The Age of Innocence*. In addition to the tragic romantic story of love lost, Scorsese imparts layers of information about the traditions of upper-class New Yorkers, often down to the finest detail, the most didactic aspects of what is essentially an emotional film about repression.

The Age of Innocence doesn't quite reach the heights of *Barry Lyndon* as a period film, but Scorsese surprised audiences and critics with his elegant and expressionistic mise-en-scène making the costume picture highly personal. His most violent film emotionally, and one that on the surface may be the least identifiable, but not so from the heart.

The Age of Innocence is dedicated to Luciano Charles Scorsese, who passed away during the making of the film. It is a valentine to the city the director loves unconditionally, and the man who delivered the movies to his son's imagination.

26

Trilogy: *Casino*

The great admiration for *GoodFellas* has overshadowed *Casino* and even provided the groundwork for dislike toward Scorsese's Las Vegas crime epic.

The initial response from Scorsese's admirers was that with *Casino* Scorsese had committed the mortal sin of copying himself. What is often the thrust of the dismissal of *Casino* lies in its shared traits, to the exclusion of the new ground Scorsese breaks with this film.

Both are gangster films and have three main characters at the core of the story. DeNiro plays a non-Italian here, Jewish rather than Irish. Tommy in *GoodFellas* and Nicky in *Casino* are both played by Joe Pesci as psychopaths, often cited as a major *Casino* flaw. Scorsese, like James Joyce, can see a universe in a single block or character. Tommy and Nicky may be archetypes for the out-of-control cowboy hothead, but Nicky is enveloped in a more difficult and dangerous world by the epic structure of *Casino*, which treats old Vegas like an ancient civilization examined. Narrators again shift; a potent mélange of musical styles comment on the narrative.

Released in 1995 *Casino* has slowly been gaining acceptance, and like Kubrick's *Barry Lyndon*, one day it will take its own place as one of Scorsese's strongest films.

With some examination, what is often missed about *Casino*, should be seen boldly on the surface. The principal position of *Casino* in Scorsese's body of work is revealed (not totally by design) from the outset—that Scorsese has completed a gangster trilogy that towers over the popular genre.

Scorsese's earliest plans for a trilogy go back to the dawn of his career. This early concept dealt more with religious and social inner conflicts rather than gangsters.

Who's That Knocking at My Door is acknowledged by Scorsese as an amateur warm-up film for what later would become *Mean Streets*, the beginning of the existing trilogy of *Mean Street, GoodFellas,* and *Casino* was, in fact, the conclusion of the unfilmed trilogy in which it was called *Season of the Witch.*

Scorsese's gangster trilogy is an epic triad. David Lean made films in faraway and exotic places—Scorsese filmed on the streets, but it is the intention and ambition of the director that creates stature in a cinematic work.

Mean Streets is concerned with mob wannabes. Some, like Charlie, the Scorsese on-screen representation and others, such as Michael, are already in the nonrecorded training program for a *made man.*

GoodFellas centers on the foot soldiers and *Casino* completes the triangle by presenting the power players who ran Las Vegas and other carved-out territories that had been muscled over. These men are not kingly like Puzo and Coppola's Don Corleone of the *Godfather* trilogy. Ironically, that most respected Mafia movie, considered an American film classic, was not based directly on research, observation, or reality, but on Hollywood's magical tool—perceived reality.

Scorsese's bosses, the guys back home, the old greaseballs of *Casino* earned their positions of power by working the ranks outlined in Scorsese's trilogy, so they are street guys with the power of attorney over the activities they rule—a commission of Italian-American men with ambition and greed.

Working again with Nicholas Pileggi from a nonfiction book, Scorsese shaped the characters to mirror the men he observed back in Little Italy.

In *GoodFellas* the characters strive to *earn*, the local capos such as Paulie control a small piece of the total enterprise. The guys back home in *Casino* are seen sitting at a long table, a not-so-subtle analogy to Da Vinci's *The Last Supper*. Their purpose is to eat well, live well, and make decisions and not to earn, but to collect, and the heyday of Vegas in the sixties and seventies was the perfect base of operations.

DeNiro presents a different slant on the gangsters. His Ace Rothstein is a gambling professional looked up to as a doctoral scientist in the operation of crap, twenty-one tables, and slot machines. Ace didn't believe in luck, he weighed dice, demonstrated the proper way to put a bet down, and understood the astromathematics of programming slot machines so the house always won. Called "The Jew" by the bosses, the arrangement with Ace running the fictional Tangiers was to keep the flow of money in their pockets.

The first and fascinating third of *Casino* is a fictional representation of how the Vegas gambling system works. Documentary in its detail, the viewer for the first time in movie history gets a thorough schooling on the running of the Vegas Empire. Scorsese's camera, here manned by Robert Richardson, actually enters the holy grail of the counting room where an intricate system of skims, suitcases, and regular trips to the bosses is maintained.

Through Ace's behavior and his meticulous voice-over, casino operations are detailed as well as the human system of payoffs to union and political figures. Cheats are punished with cattle prods and hammer to the hand assaults as a warning. Those who refuse to impart valued information are put into a vice head-first and squeezed until their eye pops.

The conflict between the glamour and violent rule of law of the Tangiers creates a frisson not found in the earlier installments. Scorsese thematically takes advantage of a religious metaphor. The characters speak of Vegas as paradise. As an Old Testament cinematic interpreter, Scorsese follows the sinful behavior of his three main characters and how they destroy everything they have. At the opening Ace has full reign over the Tangiers, Nicky is allowed freedom in carrying out muscle activities while pursuing his own endeavors lorded by violence, mayhem, and destruction. Ginger (Sharon Stone) refuses to be content as Ace's wife and weakens in the hands of her former boyfriend who is a junkie. She gives up all her earthly possessions for him and ends up consumed and obliterated by drugs. Nicky upsets the bosses by too much high-profile trouble, which affects the earning, he is baseball-batted to death and dropped in a hole in the desert. Ace's car is rigged with a bomb. The act of terror commissioned by the bosses is circumvented by a miracle resulting in Ace's survival to continue his gambling expertise into old age. Retribution by the bosses is a godlike condemnation of the sinners losing their divinity. Of course, this is all subtext translated into a gangster narrative.

Trust, and the lack of it, causes the fall of Ace, Ginger, and Nicky in *Casino*. Human nature compels them to take advantage of a good thing and disobey the commandments of the bosses. Ace knows that Nicky and Ginger are in trouble at first glance but his belief in trust and what he perceives as the power to control all around him is his fatal flaw.

Law enforcement is disdained. Nicky's brother shows contempt for a group of officers as he secretly spits onto their comp sandwiches, then telling them to enjoy them. Ace's strict operational rules force him to fire a local's relative, turning the Vegas power brokers against him.

Beauty in *Casino* is garish, flamboyant, tacky, and outrageous. Garish in *Casino* is money. The color palette of Dante Ferretti's production design, features overwrought architecture, and colors that clash and nauseate. The Tangiers is an Overlook Hotel from Kubrick's *The Shining*, but without the ghosts. The costumes are flavored with saturated pure color, pinks, blues, and yellows. Ace's ever-changing wardrobe makes him an untouchable—a man above it all. Ginger is all bling hidden behind a stunning beauty. She is the combination of every whore, B-girl, and glam movie star who survives by taking care of her network of supporters. They, in turn, allow her to function and supply all her needs. Ginger is the rare strong woman in a Scorsese film. She is independent, a class A con artist, and a moneymaker, until she is brought down by Lester (James Woods), her junkie boyfriend and Ace, a reversal of fortunes in dramatic narratives. A reverse noir. Ginger is a femme fatale, an Eve in the Old Testament analogy who goes on a path of destruction far beyond average tolerance.

Sharon Stone is given the role of a lifetime. An actress who struggled to prove she was more than a babe, Stone is gorgeous, but her beauty and drive are not skin-deep. She gives a ferocious performance that climaxes in a screaming match with Ace in front of their home: Stone more than holds her own against the legendary DeNiro, if not steals the scene.

Again the audience has mixed emotions for the brutal demise of a Joe Pesci character. As in *GoodFellas* he is a dangerous and bad man we love to watch. As he is pounded to death with metal baseball bats our sympathy rises, because lying on the ground in his underwear, he is revealed as only human.

Scorsese has no trouble filling the nearly three-hour running time. The story is vast, the history of a great civilization and its fall. Like the biblical epics Marty experienced as a child, he has filled his film with a large cast of characters, scenes that serve the purpose of charting the rise and fall and a bold use of space are revealed in a scene when Ace and Nicky go out into the desert to talk. After the bursting-with-life-and-sin Casino world, Scorsese enters an area alien to a city kid. The existential majesty of the desert seems the sight of revisionist production of Beckett's *Waiting for Godot*. But the mystery of the desert has a purpose for the bosses; it's where all the bodies are buried.

In his first outing with Scorsese, Richardson supplies the epic visual approach *Casino* demanded. He is a fascinating choice because of the director of photography's long association with Oliver Stone. In Stone's films Richardson lights in a signature style that creates a cloud of white light over the images. When asked about the derivation of this visual aesthetic, Richardson, a quiet and mysteriously elusive man, gave all credit to Stone for the style. But history has proven otherwise. As he began working with other directors this lighting glow has been augmented to suit the subject and in *Casino* it is the perfect companion to the hard lines, bright lights, and deeply saturated colors. Like Freddie Young, David Lean's longtime director of photography, Richardson by nature understood the epic frame.

The title sequence by Saul and Elaine Bass imagines Ace passing through a fiery hell. Scorsese's involvement with Bass on several of his films is another example of the film historian paying homage and extending the notions of a cinematic master. Bass is responsible for the contemporary title sequence, which is an integral aspect of the film. He worked with Hitchcock and Preminger and set new standards for graphic design in the cinema.

For all the deserved accolades *GoodFellas* has received for its use of music, *Casino* goes beyond it into the expanse of the universe of its subject. Bach's Saint Matthew's Passion which appears at the opening and closing of the film, gives *Casino* its thunderous Old Testament power. Scorsese layers the track with pop tunes of the era, indigenous music, and themes from the soundtracks of other movies. The most effective use is from Godard's *Contempt*, not because it's a movie about a movie or a film about power and creation but the quiet somber quality of Delure's theme is a contrast to the cacophony—a time of sadness and introspection. Scorsese continues his use of lyrical connection to the action of a scene. When Ginger and Ace meet, "Love is Strange" scores the electric interaction and becomes the mantra of their relationship. Love drives both Ginger and Ace beyond their behavioral bounds.

Casino ends with the end of an era in Vegas, on a grand scale. The dramatic story supports this as well as a montage, which illustrates the physical destruction of the old Vegas and the building of the new Disneyfied one. Viewing *Casino* for nearly three hours, it is at this moment that the film comes together. Scorsese's grand intention is revealed.

27

Zenned In: *Kundun*

During the sixties and seventies celebrities became entranced with spiritual movements from Asia. The Beatles and Mia Farrow followed Maharishi Mahesh Yogi; Guru Maharaj Ji, the fifteen-year-old Indian Lord of Creation and the Perfect Master, took America by storm including Chicago Seven member Rennie Davis; and Sri Chinmoy had followers that included musicians John McLaughlin and Carlos Santana. In the nineties, Tenzin Gyatso, the fourteenth Dalai Lama and head of state and spiritual leader of the Tibetan people, captured the hearts and minds of Hollywood, led by Richard Gere who introduced him to the community. Many observers scoffed at this spiritual movement as the Dalai Lama spoke across the country, wrote books, and promulgated his message of peace. The skepticism grew not out of the Dalai Lama, a courageous spiritual man of great integrity and wisdom, but toward celebrities who morally were less than holy.

In 1989 Scorsese first became cognizant of the plight of the Tibetan people who were in exile, banished from their country by the Chinese government, by Mao Tse-Tung. A script written by Melissa Mathieson (*E.T., the Extra-Terrestrial, The Indian and the Cupboard*) was given to Scorsese who then spent a weekend at Mathieson's Wyoming home during her marriage to Harrison Ford, meeting and talking to the Dalai Lama. By 1993 between ten and twelve drafts had been written with one close enough to go into production, but Scorsese was contractually bound to make *Casino*, the first film in a deal with Universal, and a movie he felt he needed to make then.

In 1996 he was ready to shoot *Kundun*, which was released in 1997.

Kundun is a personal film only in its theme about religion. As a Catholic, Scorsese admired the Buddhist embrace of love, as well as their

Scorsese patiently shows young Tulku Jamyang Kunga Tenzin how he wants him to handle the objects for a scene in *Kundun. Courtesy Photofest.*

determination to fight for their beliefs. He believed love and compassion was important to heal the world after decades of struggling with his spirituality. Scorsese's upbringing on the streets of Little Italy taught him that one must defend against enemies. *Kundun* was "one for them" only in the sense it was not initiated by him and a film he would have to find a way to make. As a history buff he had some background on the plight of the Tibetans, but was not deeply connected or aware of their culture and situation.

As always Scorsese turned to the movies to find his way through *Kundun*. From Ozu's *Floating Weeds* he watched how looking at nature was captured on film. Another influence, Jean Renoir's *The River*, a favorite since childhood, gave him inspiration concerning people, culture, rituals, music, and the awareness of being in love. Satyajit Ray, the Indian master filmmaker played a key role in the *Kundun* research, especially *Panther Panchali*, a film that taught him about Indian village life. Scorsese also ran Ray's *Aparijito*, and *The Music Room*, before embarking on the location shoot. He also looked at the New Chinese films of Yimou Zhang (*Ju Dou, Raise the Red Lantern, Hero* [2002]) and Chen Kaige, (*Ba wang bie, Jing ke ci gin wang, The Promise*), as well as Tian Zhuangzhuang's *The Horse Thief*, which was shot in Tibet.

Scorsese also adopted tropes from his cinematic hero Bernardo Bertolucci's *The Last Emperor*. The spiritual sequences in *Kundun* and those that take place within the world of the Dalai Lama feature warm colors and the light was yellow-based. The sequences concerning the Communist Chinese are bathed in cool, blue light, and the color palette responds accordingly. Both films were production designed by Italians, *The Last Emperor* by Ferdinando Scarfiotti and *Kundun* by Dante Ferretti. Although both pictures are meticulously rendered and accurate, there is an Italianate sensibility, a certain flamboyancy in the intensity and use of color and the grandeur of the architecture.

Kundun is a movie about memory, dreams, and seeing. Scorsese and Thelma Schoonmaker weave a series of dissolves to make time pass, often in small increments, to give the film a mystical aura. Dreams are communicated cinematically by intercutting the sleeping holy man with his thoughts, sometimes nightmares; others, premonitions of what is to come or what he fears will happen. Many shots are POVs or augmented POVs, to get inside the head of the Dalai Lama. The metaphor of cinema is transmitted through a projector he finds and the movies he watches and a telescope used to *see* what is ahead of him as his holiness contemplates how to deal with the takeover of Tibet by the Chinese.

The first movie shown is *La Poulle aux oeufs d'or*, a 1905 short by Gaston Velle. The fantasy film tells an ancient fable concerning a poor man who is given a hen that lays golden eggs. Rather than marvel at the accomplishments the man is focused on getting the gold out of the eggs. Kundun is fascinated and delighted by the film, which fits into his Buddhist convictions that pride and greed are the enemy of a good and enlightened man.

The next film is a newsreel of World War II, which gives Kundun insight into the political wave that will eventually push him into exile.

When the Chinese use violence against his people, Kundun screens the landmark battle scene from Lawrence Olivier's film production of *Henry V*. The references serve the story as well as Scorsese's artistic need to add self-referential qualities to his pictures.

The telescope reminds the viewer of *Rear Window*, and in a late moment in the film transcends the device itself by showing his eye looking out from the front of the lens. This analogy between seeing and optical devices had been brilliantly explored by Dziga Vertov in *Man with the Movie Camera*.

The collaboration between director of photography Roger Deakins and Scorsese created *Kundun*, in which the context is light as a metaphor, for the enlightened Buddhist state of mind. Deakins brings clarity to the images, sharp, at times high contrast at others modeled with light in the chiaroscuro tradition. The interior light is often a yellow amber cast flickering from its source, a campfire or flames coming from a lit urn. The effect is mesmerizing and magical, the true light for spiritual thought and conversations. Dark and light is another theme to illustrate his holiness's struggle between spirituality and the violence, and evil around him.

Scorsese's use of camera is restrained when compared to his body of work (with the exception of *The King of Comedy*), movement follows action, rarely becomes an expressive tool with its own emotional context, a result Scorsese is well-known for. Compositions are either intimate or in the epic tradition, Scorsese has studied his David Lean well, especially *Lawrence of Arabia*, for large tableaus that are heavily peopled. Scorsese makes substantial use of the Kubrick framing, placing a figure in the center of a frame or counterbalancing characters, one centered, the others on opposite sides of the subject.

Scorsese was familiar with minimalist composer Philip Glass from his scores for *Koyannisqatsi* and his longtime collaborator Paul Schrader's *Mishima: A Life in Four Chapters*. A practicing Buddhist, Glass was perfect for the assignment and created a magnificent orchestral score that sings to the drama, mystery, and spiritual aspects of the film.

The signature Scorsese top shot is utilized for an overhead shot of monks on a floor. Utilizing freeze frame and blur techniques a mature Scorsese has found a use for the top shot that goes beyond its unique point of view into a magical realm.

Sand mandalas were created for the film and at one point symbolize the destruction of the sanctity of Tibet by destroying the vibrate patterns with a sword and large brush, intercut with images of the actions that had taken place in Kundun's country.

Sudden violence again appears in a Scorsese picture. When Kundun is told that the Communists are forcing children to kill their parents, he sees the image, filled with pain, blood, and atrocity.

Scorsese additionally channels his admiration for neorealist films in the sequences that depict Kundun and his people. The faces look like real people, not actors, and create a documentary but poetic realism much in the tradition of Vittorio DeSica's work. In contrast with the epic style, *Kundun* is a film of great power and texture.

Kundun has a lot in common with *The Last Temptation of Christ*; both are about persecution and belief. Jesus and Kundun are men of conviction, courage, and purpose. They are also both about religion and Scorsese's conviction that a spiritual life cannot be separated from the world of the people, or god. They form a pair of films directly about religion; one is Catholicism and the other Buddhism, which directly take on their subject. Scorsese has delved into spirituality in many films, *Mean Streets*, *Bringing out the Dead*, *Raging Bull*, and others, but *The Last Temptation of Christ* and *Kundun* are at the other end of the spectrum to Scorsese's gangster pictures. They represent the altar boy who aspired to be a priest but became a filmmaker.

PART 7

Out of Touch/Out of Time, 1999–2007

28

Five Marriages

Martin Scorsese has been married five times. How does this intimate aspect of his life impact on his work? Scorsese is a personal filmmaker who always draws on himself for the content of his films. His relationships with women are complex but clearly defined and determined by factors of his early experience.

His Sicilian heritage was dominated by the principles of the Madonna/Whore syndrome, which was a significant aspect of his first feature, *Who's That Knocking at My Door.* A man must marry a good girl, a virgin, who he idolizes in ways similar to the idolization of the mother in Italian-American culture. A man has sex with bad girls, whores. Any woman who is not a virgin before marriage is a tramp and to be used for sexual desires. A man loves and respects a virgin he intends to marry. The purity is disgraced by a fallen woman. There is no love here only sex. Dealing with the weight of this tradition caused rebellion and confusion in Scorsese's psyche as he struggled to form relationships.

His diminutive and sickly physicality had a strong negative impact on Scorsese's self-image as he was growing up. Self-consciousness about his height, known as a Napoleonic Syndrome, or in street terms, small-man complex, made Scorsese shy around women, and led him to feel and be perceived as someone who was not "good with women."

Catholicism taught Scorsese that marriage is sacred and holy; before two become one they should be pure, then sex is for procreation, and children to be raised as more good Catholics. The Catholic concept of impure thoughts and actions created a constant cloud of shame and guilt within Scorsese as he first experienced natural sexual feelings and began to masturbate to express those emotional forces within. Confession is not the easy way out from sin as often believed by outsiders. Sin represents the eternal pain of Hell. Confessing an act of lust may adjust it in the spiritual ledger, but it does nothing for the guilt of the experience, the act or feelings in question, or for the guilt acquired by thoughts that if an impure act is committed it can always be forgiven through the confessional/act of contrition process. Few Catholics believe that come judgment day they will go to heaven if the tab is paid up; the moral center of the Catholic mind understands that it is sum of the whole that leads to Heaven.

Going to the movies may have been a religious encounter for the young Scorsese but it tempted him and stimulated his emotions of lust and sexuality. He was able to obsess and fantasize over the idealized women he watched in the dark. The distinct female types of the forties and fifties, the femme fatales, the bad girls, the untouchable beauties, the sweater girls, the pointy breasts, and the hourglass figures and peek-a-boo hairstyles aroused his libido. The voyeuristic tendencies of the cinephile are not a healthy grounding for daylight relationships.

Like many parents of the Greatest Generation, Charles and Catherine believed in the sanctity of their wedding vows taken at the altar—"until death do us part." This concept of marriage was not readily embraced by their children, who would run up one of the highest divorce rates in American human history. Watching parents "put up" with each other and "sacrifice" personal dreams for the sake of the family caused a seismic shift in the culture. Gender roles, desires, and needs were shifting. For many boomers marriage became a rebellion against the bedrock institution.

Another emotional conflict was created by the force of the old-world morality on which Scorsese was raised and the sexual revolution around him, perhaps begun in the backseat, in a field, or in a bed, but spread and infused to all of American consciousness: fashion, the media, social behavior, and above all morality. Scorsese lived in an old world surrounded by the biggest social experiment of the twentieth century: free love, wife swapping, nudity, and open expression of love without shame. This collision of mores caused Scorsese to challenge what he had been taught and to explore, if at first in mind only, the Dionysian possibilities confronting and beckoning him.

On the NYU campus Scorsese encountered a new world of feminine beauty. His inhibitions toward women didn't evaporate, but now dating became easier and Scorsese saw carnal possibilities that had been denied him.

It was during this time that a pattern emerged. He would become obsessively in love with a young woman—this invariably led to disillusionment and eventually to boredom, which led to ignite the next liaison.

The tie that would not break was between mother and son—the deep-seated need to be mothered, to be cared for by a woman. He would seek out or orient the women in his life to serve those traditional male needs. A reluctant chauvinist, Scorsese never demonstrated or utilized macho strategies toward women, but he did play the role of the fragile little boy, the artistic genius, who needed the constant motherly care of a woman. His signals were powerful and received by many women who were attracted to his sensitivity and his fragile nature. Those who had a mothering instinct toward men, even though it conflicted with their own growing sense of individuality during the pioneering years of the Women's Movement, also struggled with their conflicts toward traditional American values and gender roles.

Once Scorsese became a celebrity, first locally, then nationally, and eventually internationally, he experienced the magnet of fame—how women were interested in him both for who he was and *who* he was. This position of power also brought indulgence including pursuit of the daughters of his cinematic idols: Liza Minnelli, daughter of Judy Garland and Vincente Minnelli, and Isabella Rossellini, a love child of Ingrid Bergman and Roberto Rossellini.

Scorsese's drive to be mothered and cared for by a woman produced a sixth "marriage" with his longtime editor Thelma Schoonmaker. The relationship has always been totally platonic but in addition to being a major artistic contributor to all of Scorsese's films since *Raging Bull* in 1980, Schoonmaker has also functioned as social secretary, protector, and explainer. Their "marital home" is the editing room, where they spend months slaving over the birth of each film, working right hand, left hand. It is Scorsese's most successful relationship with a woman because by removing romance and sex he has found the secret to coexistence in a male/female relationship, which is based on respect, mutual admiration, dependency, and above all the unconditional dedication to movies.

The voluptuous Black-Irish Laraine Marie Brennan was in the NYU acting program when she met Martin Scorsese during the production of *It's Not Just You Murray!* When it was absolutely clear that Laraine was interested in Scorsese who was a virgin at the time, he made the move to announce his intentions to his parents. The decision represented a rebellion against his family, church, even his anger toward the war in Vietnam, which has grown out of a radicalization at NYU. Most revealing was the beginning of a pattern of dropping one woman only when he was sure another relationship was ready to move into. This emotional self-protection protected

Scorsese from loneliness and an anxiety of being without a female who could be his maternal figure.

Laraine who embraced the hippie culture of numerology and the I Ching, and the Martin Scorsese who wore a suit and tie to hang out on Elizabeth Street and had now discovered the youth uniform of blue jeans and tee shirts, were married in St. Patrick's church, soon after the groom graduated from NYU. Chick, a neighborhood guy saw Scorsese's behavior toward Phyllis, the Sicilian girl he had a long-term relationship with, as a disgrace to the girl's reputation. Incensed at the surprise marriage, Chick pledged a *vendetta* toward Scorsese in the name of Phyllis's honor. Marty's close friend Joey Morale played the dual role of *consigliare* and enforcer by telling Chick in no uncertain terms that if Marty was harmed there would be consequences to be paid. Marty in the grand tradition of Italian-Americans in street trouble—laid low.

Marty moved out of his parents' apartment, the first time he had left the nest, and moved into a Jersey City apartment with his wife. On December 7, 1965, a daughter, Catherine, named after her paternal grandmother was born. Like most new fathers, Scorsese got up in the middle of the night when the baby was crying, but in true form as an obsessed cinephile, would put on the television and watch movies like Hitchcock's *Psycho*, not exactly the lullaby the baby required.

Marital troubles appeared swiftly. Scorsese struggled to get film work of any kind, and tried to save money to further his education. Financial difficulties strained the relationship. Marty and Larraine fought all the time over his inability to make a living. Marty and Mardrik Martin spent days on end at each other's apartments scheming about how to break into the film business. Eventually both spouses were so fed up that the two men were forced to meet in their cars during a cold New York winter.

Scorsese fought off the emotional guilt concerning the principal role of an Italian-American man's responsibility to his family and refused to give up his ambition to be a film director. Ultimately he decided for his career against his wife and young child.

Scorsese met his second wife, Julia Cameron, when, as a freelance journalist, she was on the set of *Taxi Driver* to conduct an interview for *Oui* magazine with screenwriter Paul Schrader. Cameron, a smart and determined young woman, a petite redhead with sharp and captivating features, had been a professional writer since eighteen. As a journalist her impressive resume includes articles on the arts and politics.

After interviewing Schrader, who with the scripts for *The Yakuza, Obsession*, and *Taxi Driver*, was the screenwriter du jour at the time, Cameron met Scorsese and the two immediately connected on romantic and artistic levels. Cameron became Scorsese's girlfriend, even though his four-year relationship with girlfriend Sandy Weintraub was officially still on. She became involved with the work at hand on the *Taxi Driver* screenplay. Scorsese's friends found Cameron to be aggressive and ambitious and resented that she came between his buddies.

Following the production of *Taxi Driver* Martin Scorsese married Julia Cameron on Wednesday, December 30, 1975, six weeks after his thirty-third birthday. The ceremony, with vows personally written by the bride and groom, was held in Cameron's hometown of Libertyville, Illinois.

On the director's next feature film *New York, New York*, Cameron again would be involved in the screenwriting process without credit. A complex and excessive film, *New York, New York* was Scorsese's attempt to work out his conflicted feelings toward Cameron and the turbulent nature of two artists trying to coexist. "I wanted to capture a relationship between two people who were doing creative work and trying to live together.... The film was very autobiographical—it was about my second marriage," Scorsese explained in 1981.

The screenplay for *New York, New York* was written over a two-year period by Earl MacRauch. That draft was rewritten by Mardik Martin. Cameron also worked with MacRauch for approximately a month before shooting began, then the writer left the project. Jealousy erupted between Martin, Scorsese's longtime friend and collaborator, and the director's wife; the competitive atmosphere did not do the script or the participants much good. As the project grew more out of control, Cameron became a scapegoat blamed for Scorsese's descent into the era's drug of choice—cocaine. Scorsese who by nature suffered from bouts of paranoia, but was unable to confront those around him concerning his feelings, told Cameron he was angry at Schrader, now a celebrity in his own right, for comments the *Taxi Driver* scenarist made to the press about him. And if things weren't bad enough Cameron further alienated herself from the *New York, New York* company by telling them and Scorsese's friends that she was principally responsible for the script.

During all this Scorsese became a father for the second time when Domenica Scorsese, named after her paternal grandmother, was born on September 6, 1976. Shortly after the birth the Cameron/Scorsese marriage began to come apart. By January of 1977 Cameron had moved out of the Mulholland Drive house. Scorsese began an affair with his leading lady, Liza Minnelli, who he was also directing in the stage musical, *The Act*, and who was the daughter of Judy Garland and Scorsese's hero and master of the crane shot and lurid saturated color palettes—Vincente Minnelli. At the time Liza was married to Jack Haley Jr., the son of the man who immortalized the Tin Man in *The Wizard of Oz*, and she had a liaison with ballet superstar Mikhail Baryshnikov. It would take an incarnation of Freud to understand Scorsese's motivation for engaging in the affair at this time at all, as well as the psychological associations he may have experienced from this connection with two Hollywood legends he admired from childhood, but it also was consistent with his pattern of setting up a new relationship with a woman when he believed a current one was endangered.

At the end of 1977 as *The Act* was about to open on Broadway on November 29 (but without Scorsese who was fired and replaced by Gower Champion), Cameron filed divorce papers that petitioned for financial support and accused Scorsese of squandering the couple's money as well as endangering his fragile health through excessive cocaine use during his illicit liaison with Liza Minnelli.

In addition to marital problems both Minnelli and Scorsese were heavily under the influence of cocaine and out-of-control drug use. In diary entries from 1977 to 1978 the prince of Pop Art and New York underground society, Andy Warhol, states that Minnelli often carried on about her affair with Scorsese in what is described as a drunken state with her pupils dilated. She confided to Warhol that Scorsese had a severe coke problem, which caused blood poisoning, and which he treated with medication prescribed to "clean himself out." On May 11, 1978, Warhol was lunching with Scorsese and later wrote in his diary that "Marty was shaking like crazy, I guess from coke."

Another player in the seventies' celebrity drug scene was fashion designer Halston. During a strung out moment, Liza appeared at Halston's home (while Scorsese dressed in a white suit stood by shaking) and asked the haberdasher of the rich, famous, and terribly hip if he had any drugs at all to give them. Halston responded by giving them Qualudes, Valium (another seventies' drug of choice), and four joints.

The Minnelli affair of adultery and drug debauchery is one that Scorsese would like to forget. Twenty years later during the planning of a tribute to his directorial achievement Scorsese asked that Liza Minnelli not be invited, cringing at the thought.

The stage was set for Scorsese's third marriage and second encounter of the close kind with the daughter of a film director he revered when Isabella Rossellini, one of the twin female love children of Ingrid Bergman and Robert Rossellini, interviewed him as a television journalist for RAI, Italian television. This occurred during the making of *New York, New York* when Scorsese's love life was chaotic between his marriage to Julia Cameron and the affair with Liza Minnelli. Scorsese has repeatedly listed

Roberto Rossellini, one of the founding architect's of Italian neorealism as the director of *Rome, Open City*, *Paisan*, and *Germany Year Zero* as his favorite Italian film directors. Ironically the Italian-American and Italian directors never met during the brief matrimonial period between Martin and Isabella—Robert Rossellini died just prior, in 1977.

As with any couple myriad reasons and feelings can bring two people together; Rossellini's Italian background, deep and pure beauty, as well as her European ways were certainly factors in winning Scorsese's heart and the two began living together in early summer of 1978.

The period just before making *Raging Bull*, while living with Rossellini, was the height of Scorsese's involvement with cocaine. While at the end of summer Telluride Film Festival with Rossellini, Robert De Niro, and Mardik Martin, Scorsese had snorted what was believed to be "bad coke" and on Labor Day suffered a physical collapse.

In a little more than a year after they began cohabitation, on September 30, 1979, as the shooting of *Raging Bull* began, Marty and Isabella were married in the City Hall of Bracciano, a town near Rome. Rossellini was twenty-seven, Scorsese, ten years older. The nuptials were her first and his third.

Although Rossellini would continue her acting career it was during her period with Scorsese that she began modeling. She became the face of *Lancôme* cosmetics and a supermodel of the first rank. Isabella did her first of many *Vogue* covers while married to Scorsese. When the issue appeared in March of 1982 he was so upset at the thought of strangers lusting over her picture that he refused to leave home for a month until it was no longer on every newsstand.

Rossellini had difficulty watching the violent scenes in her husband's films. "I find them too hard to watch. I close my eyes," she recounted in her memoir. "Yet I once saw Martin pass out at the sight of his own blood. Just a drop of it. It was at the doctor's, and his finger was being pricked to collect a sample for medical analysis. When he was revived, I shouted at him, "See what you do to the rest of us?" The incident was additional proof that the use of blood in violence in a Martin Scorsese film was an avenue for him to express emotions of anger and rage, and his Catholic fever dreams; it had little to do with his actual reaction to the sight of blood, especially his own.

Isabella immediately attained insight into her husband's nature by witnessing his daily routine of waking up in the morning and annunciating in his rapid fire verbal delivery, "Fuck it, fuck it, fuck it, fuck it, fuck it, fuck it, fuck it, fuck it, fuck it!" At first she thought something might be wrong, but when he explained it was a New York version of a mantra, which gave him the strength and energy to get out of bed and face another day, she understood what it took to be Martin Scorsese and to make a ferocious film like *Raging Bull*.

Scorsese executed some of the postproduction work on *Raging Bull* at home. One day Isabella, always fascinated with the artistic process, watched Scorsese edit a sequence from the film. He worked on it meticulously until it was editorially perfect and then as a deliberate act cut out a frame from one of the shots explaining, "This way I know it's not *perfect*, so its soul can flow through it."

From November of 1981 through March of 1982, during the making of Scorsese's next film, *The King of Comedy*, his marriage to Isabella began to dissolve. During the marriage Isabella had an affair with Jonathan Wiedemann, a handsome very American type who was a Bruce Weber model. She became pregnant by Wiedemann and after divorcing Scorsese, Rossellini and Wiedemann became the parents of a baby girl they named Elettra. Rossellini claims Scorsese didn't mind but he wanted the marriage to continue so he wouldn't run the temptation of marrying for a fourth time. When asked about this fact by Dinitia Smith for the *New York Times* Scorsese answered, "If that's how she remembers it. I don't think she's telling a lie." Scorsese and Rossellini divorced in 1983. Isabella felt that Scorsese resented her independence and really wanted a traditional American wife, circa 1950. She ended the marriage to Scorsese and married Wiedemann.

In February of 1985, less than two years after his divorce to Isabella Rosselini, Martin Scorsese married for a fourth time to Barbara De Fina, a producer who worked in the world of low-budget filmmaking. De Fina was born in New Jersey on December 28, 1949. The couple met during the making of *After Hours* and formed a solid working producer/director relationship. At least for a brief time, Scorsese seemed to achieve a harmony in a relationship with another artist, which had failed so miserably in the past. Beginning with his next film, *The Color of Money*, De Fina would produce eight feature films, two documentaries, a short, a music video, and two commercials for Scorsese, even though the marriage officially ended earlier.

Barbara De Fina, a slender brown-eyed woman did not possess the allure of wife number one, the physical dynamism of number two, or the incandescent beauty of number three. Her looks were familiar to an Italian-American man, a neighborhood girl, discreet, properly dressed, her shoulder-length hair slowly lightened as she gracefully aged. De Fina was well-spoken and down-to-earth, the perfect antidote to her emotional, passionate, and obsessive husband.

Scorsese and De Fina were married on February 8, 1985, the bride was thirty-six, the groom forty-three, and the New York production veteran of almost fifteen years made the transition to producer on Scorsese's next film, *The Color of Money*. Professionally, De Fina and Scorsese were the perfect match. Scorsese had started as a no-budget New York guerrilla filmmaker, exercised his American New Wave status to the limits of excess, was confronted with the inability to realize his dream project, and then got back in the game through a low-budget New York based film. De Fina steadily rose up the ranks reaching the point of making the next step to producer. For Scorsese having a wife and a producer in the house was the ideal situation. De Fina offered the companionship he couldn't live without and immediately became an integral component in the creation of a Martin Scorsese Picture. De Fina would be the constant producer of one of America's most important film directors and make a critical contribution in keeping the films fiscally sound, so that Scorsese could get back to making the personal films he needed to make. They were cinematically compatible; she enjoyed the preproduction and production process, he, the editing. De Fina was able to set the projects up to give the director what he wanted, but for the price the project could afford. By defining her role to getting the project off the ground, planned, and shot De Fina didn't infringe on the sanctity of the Schoonmaker/Scorsese relationship in the editing room where the intimacy had all to do with giving birth to a Scorsese picture, a shot at a time.

With De Fina as his producer Scorsese learned a valuable lesson in gaining more control of his films and developing discipline to work within his means without compromising his expressive desires. De Fina found Scorsese to be reasonable as a director who allowed her to make the decisions that would ensure a responsible and successful result. As a couple who worked together Martin and Barbara found it easier to maintain their personal life, an issue that had plagued Scorsese all his adult life.

When Scorsese had a second chance to make *The Last Temptation of Christ*, De Fina helped him do the impossible—make a low-budget religious epic. De Fina constantly combed over the budget for solutions such as telling Scorsese she would only authorize a small crane, not a large one, but he still got his beloved crane shots. Although they continued to work compatibly, Scorsese's marriage to De Fina dissolved in 1991.

Their director/producer relationship continued on many significant projects for another decade.

On July 22, 1999, Scorsese took the matrimonial plunge for the fifth time marrying Helen S. Morris, a Random House book editor. They had met when Morris was developing a companion book to *Kundun*. Morris is five years his junior. The day before his fifty-seventh birthday on November 16, 1999, he became the father of a baby girl for the third time; the parents named the baby Francesca, after Scorsese's maternal grandmother. Like some older divorced men Scorsese began to have a more substantive relationship with his daughters later in life, and Francesca provided him with the opportunity to raise the child as the marriage has lasted long enough for him to be home as the child progressed through her formative years— a paternal redemption of sorts. Both Catherine Scorsese, who played the role of Delores in her dad's *The King of Comedy*, assistant director in *Men of Respect*, and worked her way in the prop department of Scorsese's *Casino*, *Night Falls on Manhattan*, *Picture Perfect*, *Just the Ticket*, *The Tic Code*, *The Emperor's Club*, and HBO's *The Sopranos*, from assistant props to property master; and Domenica Cameron-Scorsese, who has gone on to an acting career, which includes roles in her father's *Cape Fear* and *The Age of Innocence*, as well as *Straight Talk, Bullfighter*, and *Au Pair Chocolat*, and one of the actresses to play Valentina Vitale-Nunzio in the interactive stage hit, *Tony n' Tina's Wedding*, were raised by their mothers. In recent years Morris has developed a serious neuromuscular disease, which has affected her motor coordination, apparent at televised industry events when she has accompanied her husband.

Will five be the magic number for Martin Scorsese? Age changes emotional needs. Whether Scorsese has found marital bliss only time will tell. Marriage is an affair of the heart and Scorsese is an emotional man who is steadfast. The demands and commitments he has made to his work have complicated his marriages. They say a man can't serve two masters, but the need for companionship, the fear of being alone, and acceptance and maturity may be a Martin Scorsese life lesson.

29

Taxi Driver Lite: *Bringing Out the Dead*

It's been said film directors make one continuous film throughout their career. Themes, visual signatures, character traits, and myriad narrative elements can be reordered or applied to the endless fascination of the viewer.

The new work must have distinction, a greater purpose for its existence. The director must be in the moment of the story, and in the time period and place that it occurs.

There were many reasons for Martin Scorsese to direct *Bringing Out the Dead*. It is a New York street story about a man, a paramedic, whose soul is in danger. He is in search of redemption.

Bringing Out the Dead is graced with Scorsese's touches and signatures. It looks and sounds like a Scorsese film, but it is missing its heart. The great observer was out of his league. Scorsese had found himself out of touch with his time, residing in movie history and ancient worlds, which he loved to read about. He stopped walking the streets, spent most of his time in the seclusion of his home, a movie set, or in the editing room.

The Joe Connelly novel tracked the contemporary story of Frank Pierce, based on the author's actual experience as an EMS worker (Emergency Medical Services). Paul Schrader adapted the book, a perfect choice for a portrait of a man unhinged, caught in a spiritual crisis. Schrader, the scenarist of *Taxi Driver*, was aware of the parallels, but it is the director's job to translate a script into its proper time and place through sound and image. *Bringing Out the Dead* proclaims at the opening to take place in the nineties, but that announcement is immediately betrayed. The city is dirty, ungentrified, and void of Giuliani's Disneyfication. In look, atmosphere, and attitude, *Bringing Out the Dead* spiritually takes place in the seventies, a time period Scorsese knows well. His time out in the

Big Apple streets is not an exhilarating release as *After Hours*, which refreshed the director, looking to the streets to reclaim him. In *Bringing Out the Dead* Scorsese seems trapped in a time warp with no exit in sight.

The plots of *Taxi Driver* and *Bringing Out the Dead* are different but watching *Bringing Out the Dead* gives the impression that Travis and the other characters and happenings occurring in *Taxi Driver* are not far away, just off in a different part of the neighborhood. Scorsese does little to introduce the nineties' culture to *Bringing Out the Dead* and the mélange of outrageous characters seem out of place, out of time. At moments the viewer experiences déjà vu as in the sequence when Frank meets his boss. The small room, the positioning of the desk, and the blocking of the characters channel Travis's interview scene in the cab office.

The music selections are far fewer in *Bringing Out the Dead* than in *Mean Streets, GoodFellas,* and *Casino* and Scorsese relies heavily on Van Morrison's "T.B. Sheets," which barely captures the mood of the narrative as it is used as a recurring theme.

Nicholas Cage gives a haunting performance as a man in search of redemption, plagued by the image of a young woman he couldn't save. Patricia Arquette, as the woman whose father was revived by Frank and his partner, is vocally flat. She is only in the present moment of the character, unable to reveal her past as a drug user with loose morals, which has a significant impact on the story.

Scorsese figures his significant color red into the movie in ample doses. There is plenty of blood and enough violence to suit the situations of life on the street as encountered by EMS workers.

Scorsese contracted the wizards at Industrial Light & Magic (ILM) to make the dead girl appear, reappear, at times, in multiple images, and to produce shots of the dead coming out of the ground. Scorsese has little feel for the technology, unlike his contemporaries Steven Spielberg and George Lucas, to integrate these moments into the live action sections of the movie. Conventional film special effect treatment would have allowed Scorsese more control over this central aspect of his film.

Bringing Out the Dead has a vivid street style owned by Scorsese and the film generously taps into the director's sense of black humor.

Scorsese's selection of projects is determined by a number of factors. Beloved personal projects have taken decades to realize. *Bringing Out the Dead* lies in a netherworld and it is an auteurist critic's wet dream: it is a film packed with Scorsese references to early work and stamped on every frame by its maker. It is unlikely to be rediscovered by general audiences and takes a lowly position in the Scorsese canon. What's evident in the making of *Bringing Out the Dead* is Scorsese's demonstrated passion for the sheer act of making movies. When this passion connects with content and style—a masterpiece emerges. But for Scorsese, a man in search of his own redemption, making *Bringing Out the Dead* was just another bead on the Rosary.

30

New York Stories: *Gangs of New York*

In 1970 Martin Scorsese, while visiting at a friend's house, began looking through the titles on a bookshelf and came upon a volume titled, *The
Gangs of New York* by Herbert Asbury. He read the book, part of a series
of informal histories of American cities and life, and immediately felt the
passion to adapt the loosely documented, nonfiction book into a film.

That this occurred in 1970 is audacious and reflects Scorsese deep romance with New York City. The notion of how the area known as the five
corners led to the creation of one of the world's most vital and exciting
cities was important to Scorsese, who has long been a history buff. But
how could Scorsese have made this movie in 1970? He had only one feature film to his credit, *Who's That Knocking at My Door*. The project could
not be shot on location and the massive scale would turn the project into a
megaproduction reminiscent of old Hollywood. If done on the cheap, the
historical value would evaporate. An adaptation of *The Gangs of New York*
was more likely to be made during Hollywood's original Golden Years,
not in a time of transition and reinvention of the industry experienced in
the early seventies.

Scorsese believed in tribal life and tended to see society as a series of
tribes, as in Italy and Little Italy. The gangs outlined in Asbury's book
were the harbingers of both the modern-day tribe as well as the core of
American government.

At the turn of the twenty-first century, nearly thirty years after his first
encounter with *The Gangs of New York*, Scorsese received a green light to
turn Asbury's book into a movie with Harvey Weinstein and Miramax
footing the bill.

The production had to be built from scratch in and on a studio and its
back lot. It was decided that production designer Dante Ferretti would
construct old New York at the legendary Cinecittà Studios in Rome.

The sets for *Gangs of New York* are a monument of production design as they recreate in meticulous detail the Five Corners and its environs.

Gangs of New York's greatest asset is also its greatest burden. The production is so vast and yet detailed that it appears more out of a museum than a functioning movie set. It becomes a character in the film, but not to its advantage. What it lacks as compared to Kubrick's *The Shining* in which the Overlook Hotel is also entirely built on a stage, is the ability to come alive and breathe, to interact with the story and the characters.

Scorsese has taken the Hollywood studio period film to the next level, but he and Ferretti never lose the artifice of the sets. Like *Gone with the Wind*, the viewer is always aware movie artistry is as large as the totality of the human story. The form and content balance is tipped.

When boiled down to basics the close to three-hour epic is a revenge picture. A son returns to kill the man who in battle took the life of his father. Rather than detail the inner workings of this society as successfully rendered in *Casino*, Scorsese opts for the pageantry of the times.

The battle scene in the film's opening is a recreation of Welles' *Chimes at Midnight*, also borrowed by Mel Gibson for *Braveheart*. In *Gangs of New York* physicality of action dominates behavior. There's no better example of the phenomenon than the central character of Bill the Butcher played by Daniel Day Lewis. The talented and dedicated actor gives a flat out brilliant performance, digging into the psychology and essence of the violent, greedy, racist, powerbroker, and gang leader. He is a dandy, sporting stovepipe hats and brightly colored attire, but then, there is the matter of the manner of his hairstyle—jet-black, greasy, long bangs plastered to his forehead. Looking like an even more maniacal Captain Hook, Bill the Butcher exudes slime, but his repulsive looks are a major distraction. His very presence is an unfortunate choice that dominates a large percentage of the movie in which the Butcher appears. Bill the Butcher nauseates the audience with his brutality and crude manner as he should, given Bill's outlandish and violent behavior, but over the course of the epic-length film, Lewis' locks become an increasing distraction and, like the surrounding sets, Lewis doesn't make himself a part of the fabric of *Gangs of New York*. Lewis plays Bill full steam so the flamboyant costumes and crank oil-grease hair are so overstated they become an exaggeration of historical accuracy.

Leonardo Di Caprio, as male muse, the new DeNiro having starred in three Scorsese films (*Gangs of New York, The Aviator,* and *The Departed*), gives a strong leading man performance but the weight and length of *Gangs of New York* is too much for the young actor to survive. Cameron Diaz attempts to give a strong leading lady performance but her coquettish demeanor destroys the character's integrity.

Leonardo DiCaprio, Scorsese's new DeNiro, both point off in concentration on the set of *Gangs of New York. Courtesy Photofest.*

Gangs of New York is a triumph of period film effort. Scorsese put so much of his vision into recreation that the story, far too little for a long-form film, gets lost in the beauty and mayhem of a fire scene and a concluding battle scene in which Di Caprio succeeds in avenging his father.

Scorsese's encyclopedic memory of every film he's ever seen is part of the assault on the narrative. *Gangs of New York* is old-fashioned filmmaking influenced by models of countless period epics, good and bad in Scorsese's all-encompassing attitude toward movies. This guilty pleasure along with the scholarly understanding of great epics often fuels *Gangs of New York's* overbearance.

In spite of these criticisms, many expressed by Scorsese followers, the fact remains that Martin Scorsese realized a thirty-year dream. His tenacity and driven nature are the stuff of legends in today's Hollywood.

Although not by design, *The Gangs of New York* is a fitting prequel for Scorsese's crime trilogy of *Mean Streets, GoodFellas,* and *Casino.* The style of *Gangs of New York* bears no resemblance to the other three. There are no substantial narrative links, but the film is a starting point for what's to come, a structure, a moral code, and a conviction to take what one can on the streets and as a member of a tribe. We belong to something and that has meaning. The universe of the tribe contains the DNA of human nature, power, self-preservation, and destruction. The gangs who built New York handled a legacy of vitality, tragedy, and the pursuit of the American spirit.

31

My Voyage to Spielberg/Lucasland: *The Aviator*

Martin Scorsese directed *The Aviator* as part of his one for them, one for me philosophy. *The Aviator* was for *them*. Of course the one and one concept can't be taken literally, but at times when a proposed project was ready to go and suited Scorsese, he would put that project on the front burner as he continued to develop personal projects. Some like *The Last Temptation of Christ* and *Gangs of New York* have taken decades to reach the screen.

Scorsese and Leonardo DiCaprio not only enjoyed working together on *Gangs of New York*, both men sensed a substantive collaboration had been forged. DiCaprio had long been fascinated with Howard Hughes as had Warren Beatty and many before him. After developing the project DiCaprio brought the John Logan screenplay to Scorsese.

Through an auteurist schemata *The Aviator* is a film with Scorsese's stylistic and thematic fingerprints on every frame. On the surface this is a plausible argument. *The Aviator* is about compulsion, inner demons, redemption, old Hollywood, and the difficulty of two artists surviving a serious relationship. Stylistic elements are present, the exploding flashbulbs, and the top shots. *The Aviator is* a Martin Scorsese picture because he did direct it, but as Scorsese moved into a new phase of his career (that of professional film director more than personal filmmaker), his approach changed radically. A close look at *The Aviator* reveals why this is not in the tradition of his best work, *Mean Streets, Taxi Driver, Raging Bull*, and *Goodfellas*—films in which Scorsese totally committed his personal and emotional life.

The Aviator is a great entertainment. Focusing on the young Howard Hughes the epic biopic traces his foray into the movies, his business life, romantic life, his aviation triumphs, and his struggle with compulsive disorders that attacked his mental health and endangered his ability to function. In the end Hughes heroically overcomes all his challenges, but the ground is laid for what was to come for the older Hughes who died unkempt and in seclusion. The film has a happy ending with just the slightest edge of foreshadowing—a good compromise for a commercial film.

The megabudget project was underwritten by the Weinsteins for Miramax. An unlikely choice for *The Aviator* for a director not particularly fond of flying, Scorsese's name and Leo's star power guaranteed a safe box office bet.

Scorsese is a great film director for his gangster and personal films, but it can be easily overlooked that he is a masterful filmmaker. As a hired hand he needed to find a way to make the film the studio wanted, be true to the subject, yet make it his own, or *appear* to make it his own. In his best films Scorsese connects form and content and his personal inner-workings. *The Aviator* did not provide the latter so he would have to find a way to make the film. As a cineaste of the highest nature Scorsese approaches every film by looking for reference, influence, and inspiration from film history. As a lion of the seventies' generation of filmmakers Scorsese has long been part of a group, which includes Spielberg, Lucas, Coppola, Brian DePalma and others who are less active or out of action. Spielberg and Scorsese are as different as red and white clam sauce but they have remained good friends for over thirty years. Their differences as film directors, which are legion, are less important than the most significant quality they share—they both love movies unconditionally.

Pondering how to approach *The Aviator* Scorsese came up with a brilliant ploy: he would apply the Spielberg and Lucas styles to this film, which relied heavily on Computer Generated Imagery (CGI) effects for the many flying sequences. It's unfair to say that Scorsese "sold-out" by making *The Aviator*. With this film Scorsese proved he could make a commercial picture, succeed as a hired hand on a high stakes project, and manage to embrace his elders like Hitchcock, Ford, Hawks, and others to find how to "smuggle" himself into the film, a concept he outlines in his documentary and companion book on the American Cinema.

In the great majority of period films color comes out of the décor, costumes, and photography of the era. Scorsese decided to structure *The Aviator* by application of a specific color process. Long a champion and admirer of the old Technicolor process, Scorsese made a bold aesthetic decision. The first section of *The Aviator*, approximately fifty-seven minutes, with the exception of a few scenes toward the end, which act as a transition, were digitally color-corrected to look as if they were shot in the two-strip Technicolor process in which the color scheme is largely blue and red and devoid of other colors in the spectrum. His reasoning was that after a prologue the film takes place in 1927, a time when two-strip Technicolor was in use. After this section a transition occurred in a scene taking place in Juan Trippe, the head of Pan Am's office, a futuristic room that resembles a planetarium. Other scenes begin to introduce a wider color palette. The second major section of the film begins when Howard and Katherine Hepburn drive to her family estate. The color palette via digital color alteration becomes full three-strip Technicolor with vivid, saturated color. Again Scorsese stated that this time frame was when three-strip was in use. Gradually the film expands its color range until it becomes the more traditional palette.

In fairness, the majority of viewers aren't actively aware of this color approach so it becomes part of the period fabric. From a cinematic and objective position Scorsese's idea is flawed. As a historic reference it is a fascinating idea, but the reality is that for nearly an hour the viewer is watching what is largely an unpleasant, limited, and out-of-place color schema. This is most noticeable in a scene taking place at the legendary Coconut Grove, whose glamour is spoiled by the limitation of color. Movies are a complicated experience. Audiences will buy outrageous conventions such as rear screen projection, painted backdrops, and other common techniques from the classical studio era just as they will go along with computer-generated characters and environments of today, if they believe in it. The danger of Scorsese's two-strip ploy is *if* the viewer becomes aware they are watching color designed for a purpose or effect they may only see the blue and red and not the wholeness of the image. The idea also lacks the personal and emotional connection Scorsese can conjure in his best films, in which his obsession and personal emotions are shared by the audience. The three-strip section works to evoke memories of viewing old, lush, color movies but the two-strip only can truly excite a film historian, buff, or scholar such as Scorsese.

These choices are representative of a surface approach to a film in which the director has little personal connection. Scorsese's triumph in *The Aviator* is his ability to pull off complicated special visual effects and an extravagant design.

Although there are previously recorded songs used in the classic Scorsese methodology to influence and heighten the narrative, *The Aviator* has a traditional thematic score composed by Howard Shore. Again, entering the notion of how a viewer watches (and in this case listens to) a film many complicated factors are involved. Music is the most abstract of mediums, also the most emotional and universal. Most listeners will hear the totality of a musical composition; the specialist will hear that as well as all the parts that make up the whole. For reasons only known to Shore and Scorsese, a large part of the music has a constant rhythmic accompaniment by clicking castanets. This percussion instrument (which consists of two wooden shells that are manipulated by the fingers to produce its highly recognizable effect) has largely been used for Latin genre music as well as experiments in rock and roll conducted by producer Phil Spector and others. There is no Latin content in *The Aviator*. There is talk about international flight but no solid grounding for the castanet backgrounds. They do succeed in creating tension, which combines with the orchestra to bring majesty and power to the flying sequences, but a snare drum would have accomplished the purpose and been less perverse and distracting.

The flying sequences executed by special effects wizard Rob Legato (*Apollo 13*, *Titanic*, and *Harry Potter and the Sorcerer's Stone*) are masterful in a movie/movie tradition but it is here where Scorsese temporarily loses his identity as a director. Although heavily involved in the planning and storyboarding, he could not shoot these sequences like a street movie. Special effects work is meticulous, time consuming, and done in minute stages. Here is where Scorsese relies on the work of Spielberg and Lucas. Images reminiscent of *Star Wars* and countless Spielberg films take their place over the visualization of a gritty personal filmmaker. Scorsese, the consummate professional, helmed this aspect of the production with confidence, but without a true connection to what flight meant to Hughes— the way he presents the purpose of boxing in Jake LaMotta's life in *Raging Bull*. The connection is on the surface from a visual standpoint, more "boys and their toys" than getting inside Hughes' head, which would stamp the film with the director's character.

Echoes of *Citizen Kane* resonate throughout *The Aviator*. Brassy music similar to the score for a scene between Susan Alexander and Kane in their dark days is used for a Howard and Hepburn sequence. Hughes' home and business empire is his Zanadu. These touches are effective and are as successful as when this linking approach was used by Oliver Stone for *Nixon* and Todd Haynes in *Velvet Goldmine*. One of the downsides of reverential referencing is the unfortunate choice of placing a rosebud substitute to explain Hughes demons and manias, which turned him into a germaphobe as well as a man with enormous mental illness issues. Welles called the sled, which represented Kane's lost childhood, a "dollar-book Freud." In *Kane* the sled becomes part of his mythology. *The Aviator* opens with a scene in which Hughes (as a boy) is bathed by his mother who teaches him how to spell "quarantine," and instills in the child a fear of germs, the unclean, and in a larger sense the outside world. The scene is effective in a movie, movie way, but falls short of explaining the radical behavior witnessed throughout the body of the film. Hughes's mother may have been the cause of his neurosis, but one moment in time isn't enough to understand his complex psychology as an adult.

Stylistically Scorsese's camera, manned in collaboration with Robert Richardson, is surprisingly static. Gone are the signature dolly moves and constant nervous camera movements, which give most of Scorsese's movies lifeblood. The choice, as he also applied to *The King of Comedy* for different reasons, is a wise one. Scorsese also applies the Kubrick center focus framing, in which a subject is centered and counterbalanced on the right and left. The emphasis on composition and camera angles is appropriate to a popular entertainment like *The Aviator* and Scorsese is a disciplined artist. Throughout his career he always has found the right way to shoot a film, but the price paid here is a lack of making it his own. There is a sense that he has studied his masters of this style along with the blockbuster giants Spielberg and Lucas and largely suppressed other impulses except for some deft smuggling.

Thematically Scorsese brings common knowledge from past film and life experiences to the many scenes documenting Hughes' phobias. The scenes are harrowing and relentless as Hughes washes his hands incessantly, labors over the process of preparing food, making planes, anxiety attacks, and a tour de force breakdown in which a naked Hughes would not leave his screening room for days upon end, peeing into empty milk bottles. The scenes are both clinical and visceral. Intercut with the flying, and romantic adventures, as well as the sweep of Hughes' young life, the scenes are self-contained, narratively linked, a cause and effect of reaction to his life, but so intense they could be short films like *The Big Shave*. Watching *The Aviator* the viewer senses Scorsese was captivated with parts of the film and less so with others, the latter receive a professional and craftsmanlike execution.

Scorsese makes the Hepburn/Hughes love affair another of his stories concerning two artists who can't find a way to make a marriage, or in this case a relationship, work. This aspect of the film emits some emotional heat because of its personal connection to Scorsese's earlier life experiences with women.

Biopics demand selection. Even a 170-minute film on the early life of Howard Hughes can't portray every aspect of his life. A curious choice is to emphasize the Hepburn romance, which was substantial over the well-known image of Hughes as a playboy who dated and bedded every actress and starlet in Hollywood. There is mention of it in character dialogue from Ava Gardner and others, but it is primarily disposed of in a short magazine montage and voice over that shows Hughes with many of the famous women he has been linked to. Also curious is that a man so obsessed with breasts that he made a movie about them (*The Outlaw*), who had his engineers design Jane Russell's brassiere for maximum torque and exposure, would fall head over heals in love with the slim Hepburn, who's body type was the polar opposite of the center of his attention. Not portraying the womanizing to a greater balance to reality deprives Hughes of fully revealing his obsession with women. Ironically, for many years Warren Beatty developed an unrealized Hughes film in which the actor, equally known for his amorous adventures, was to portray him. One would imagine Beatty would have adjusted the balance between Hughes' romantic life and his business one, because Beatty saw a connection between the eccentric billionaire and himself. *The Aviator* strikes a perverse chord in downplaying Hughes' philandering. Scorsese would seem an unlikely director to explore the sexual side, as this aspect of human behavior is so devoid in his body of work, which may be part of the result here.

DiCaprio gives an electrifying performance, capturing the young Hughes outside and in. In a true star turn DiCaprio centers the film with the manic energy of his character, successfully rendering the wily Hughes, the paranoid Hughes, the maverick businessman, the aviator, the man crippled by obsession, and the one looking for love in a multifaceted acting feat. As the film progresses DiCaprio looks more and more physically like Hughes not because of makeup, hair, or costume, but due to inhabitation of the character. The only element missing from the DiCaprio/Scorsese collaboration is the level of intimacy and oneness of artistic intent Scorsese achieved with DeNiro. DiCaprio is a good actor who is a movie star. Robert DeNiro is a great actor who becomes his characters and becomes one with the cinematic elements, like the sound design, editing, and cinematography of *Raging Bull*. DiCaprio is just shy of this total immersion into the film.

Much attention lauded on Scorsese concerns his filmmaking abilities. In addition he is one of the finest directors of actors in the tradition of his hero, separated at birth spiritual cinematic father, Elia Kazan. Scorsese loves and encourages actors. He is their greatest audience, gleefully reacting behind the camera as they work, always ready for a conference after a take.

The Aviator has a fine supporting cast. Cate Blanchett pulls off the impossible task of inhabiting and not impersonating Hollywood icon Katherine Hepburn, an actress so larger than life on and off screen, she seems larger than life and impossible to portray without the trap of parody. Alec Baldwin, Danny Huston, Alan Alda, and John C. Reilly give solid character performances. Kate Beckinsale is less successful at bringing Ava Gardner to life, a part that Gina Gershon was born to play.

What is to be made of the popping flashbulbs? How can they not be compared to the use of flashbulbs in *Raging Bull*? If directors other than Scorsese would use this device they would be roundly criticized for cribbing from the master. Can a filmmaker borrow from himself? Can they repeat an image, a device and have it work in a new project? The answer is not only certainly yes but is the essence of directorial style. This applies to signatures like the Kubrick dolly shot, and the Spike Lee glide shot, but does it apply to a metaphor? In *Raging Bull* the flashbulbs were both part of the environment, news cameramen photographing a boxing match, a winner being crowned champion, the agony of defeat as well as a visual and especially aural element that attacked LaMotta like guns firing at his very self. The explosions pierce the verisimilitude of the moment. Those who remember the flash cameras could literally smell the unmistakable odor of a burning object.

The flashbulbs in *The Aviator* serve a similar metaphorical purpose. Hughes is a private man and the flash of the bulbs aggressively pierce his demeanor, and like Jake, violently show the price of fame. The aesthetic answer here is not whether the flashes belong in *The Aviator* but whether they express the story and atmosphere of the film in an organic way. If they immediately remind a viewer of *Raging Bull* they become less powerful, less a natural choice to express what's going on inside the head of Howard Hughes. *Raging Bull* took place inside of Jake LaMotta's head. *The Aviator* takes place in the world of Howard Hughes. Scorsese was pleasuring himself in applying the flashbulbs from *Raging Bull* to *The Aviator*. Rather than to find *the* solution for the specificity of *The Aviator*, he went into his aesthetic toolbox, again fair game for a top shot or dolly shot, but not a largely lifted sequence from an earlier movie. To be fair, not everyone who sees *The Aviator* has seen *Raging Bull*, so all viewers won't make the same connection, but it's there for the picking, for the analyst trying to understand Scorsese the professional director as opposed to the personal filmmaker.

Production designer Dante Ferretti brings old Hollywood and the world of Hughes' aviation to life with richly detailed and historically accurate sets. Robert Richardson delineates this world through sharp and epic compositions. His signature halo-glow lighting is effectively applied to Hepburn flying Hughes' plane on their first date as he looks on at her beauty and independent spirit.

Scorsese indulges in an inside reference by casting three members of the Wainright family, father Loudon, son Rufus, and daughter Martha as Coconut Grove singers at different points in the film. Rufus and Martha present the period music of the day. Loudon is given a larger purpose. When a fight breaks out suddenly Loudon goes into a dancing frenzy that is a "fiddling while Rome burned" metaphor so obtrusive and overbearing that the film temporarily threatens to cave under the weight of the excess. In *Raging Bull* there is a sudden riot after a boxing match and the organist is signaled to play the "Star Spangled Banner" to stop the proceedings—a humorous touch that emphasizes the absurdity of the moment. Loudon's episode, encouraged by Scorsese, is simply frivolous and obvious.

There is one moment of sudden inexplicable violence in *The Aviator* and it ranks with similar signature moments in Scorsese's works such as *Mean Streets*, *Raging Bull*, *GoodFellas*, and *Casino*. It occurs in a night scene in which Howard and Ava Gardner are on a date driving in a car. Suddenly, without warning, Faith Domerque (Kellie Garner), the fifteen-year-old starlet under a Hughes' personal contract, rams them in the side with her car repeatedly in a furious rage over Howard's relationship with Gardner. The moment is unnerving like the scene in *Raging Bull* when Joey LaMotta repeatedly slams Salvy's head with a car door. In *The Aviator* Domerque's outburst makes Howard vulnerable to outside forces previously in his control. In a larger sense, Scorsese is indicating that anything can happen at any time, a constant theme in his films. Scorsese's early life experiences proved violence had no timetable. It also had no prelude or epilogue like in a Hollywood movie—it occurred with brutal human honesty and intense emotion—then it's gone.

The Coconut Grove bathroom in which two manic handwashing episodes occur is predominantly green to suit the jungle motif of the club. Bathrooms are usually decorated without personality or to comfort the user there to relieve bodily pressures. Ferretti's set is off-putting and not at all comforting or private. The green is more sickly than lush like vegetation. Somehow it appears to agitate Howard even further although he mainly focuses on the sink, towels, and the door handle, elements that can contain the unclean. It is Hughes's presence in this environment that communicates to the viewer a larger sense of panic—he is not in a safe place. The atmosphere of these scenes recalls the blood-red and stark white bathroom of *The Shining* when Jack Torrance talks to Grady, the caretaker who murdered his family. This kind of comparison is fair to apply to Scorsese, a director who is half realist, half cinematic expressionist. Also, Scorsese's encyclopedic knowledge of films and the cinema is so vast; it seems plausible he sees every connection from his films to those he has viewed, especially those that resonate within him.

During a DVD interview for *The Departed* Scorsese talks about placing X's everywhere in homage to Hawks's *Scarface*, a film that places a graphic form of an X in the frame every time a murder was to occur. Toward the end of *The Aviator* after Hughes has left his screening room meltdown, he is visited at his home by Ava Gardner who is troubled to see red tape cordoning off all unsafe areas all over the rooms. Knowing the deliberate act of placing X's in *The Departed* (Scorsese's next film) the crisscross pattern of the Red tape clearly seems to form many X's throughout the house. No murder occurs but Howard's sanity is rapidly dying.

The color red applied to the tape stands for danger and is a hue significantly present in most Scorsese films. Red is dramatically present during the breakdown scene, presumably coming from a red light in the screening. The pulsing and flashing of the red light heightens Howard's descent into his own private hell.

Expression of sexuality is rare in a Scorsese picture. *The Aviator* sports a symbolic scene through which Scorsese can express Howard's virility. During the flight in which Howard broke all current aviation speed records he grasps a phallic-looking throttle stick, a deliberate finger at a time as if he was grasping his member. In the next scene when he tells Hepburn he's "The fastest man on the planet," Howard's spread, outreached hands resemble the crude gesture used to indicate the size of a penis, like the scene in *The Godfather* in which Sonny's wife is showing a group of women the girth of her husband, before turning to see him walk off for a tryst with another woman.

Scorsese's finest contribution to *The Aviator* is the relentless depiction of Hughes's mental illness. The attacks are visceral, visual, and disturbing. Transcending the clinical they examine the manifestation of paranoia and mania without judgment and with florid energy never downplaying the sum total of the illness, which is valiantly fought by Hughes, who ends the film by defeating the corrupt Senator Brewster (Alan Alda) out to destroy Howard's TWA intercut with the flight of the Hercules, the world's largest plane. This achievement is Howard's redemption, the most sacred theme in all of Scorsese's films.

Analogy can be made to Scorsese's lifetime dealings with asthma and the pathology of *Taxi Driver*'s Travis Bickle, *Bringing Out the Dead*'s Frank Pierce, and of course, Scorsese's finest creation the Jake La Motta of *Raging Bull*, making *The Aviator* a film more personal than the average work-for-hire project.

Scorsese's passion for filmmaking and ability to share his inner self make him a rarity in contemporary cinema—a film director incapable of selling out or leaving his psyche totally out of all of his work.

Scorsese's voyage to Spielberg/Lucasland resulted in a successful and popular film that kept him moving forward, his own private smuggler, until the next opportunity to make a full-blown Martin Scorsese Picture.

32

Tribal Rites of the Irish: *The Departed*

The director-actor teaming of Scorsese/DiCaprio was the perfect evolution of the Scorsese/DeNiro collaborations. It was DeNiro (who worked with kid DiCaprio on *This Boy's Life*) who told Scorsese of this enormously talented youngster. DiCaprio was steadfast in his commitment to serious acting in the tradition of his elders like DeNiro, although the public viewed him with mixed signals due to his startling good looks and megafame after starring in James Cameron's *Titanic*.

Scorsese remembered DeNiro's recommendation and cast DiCaprio in *Gangs of New York*. A List names remain important to the business of film; even Stanley Kubrick cast stars Nicole Kidman and Tom Cruise in *Eyes Wide Shut*. Working with DiCaprio also gave Scorsese a wider audience and kept him current. *The Aviator* was a cherished DiCaprio project, and the actor also suggested their third movie together, *The Departed*.

The Departed is an American version of Hong Kong's *Mou Gaan Doc* (*Infernal Affairs*), ironically the first part of a gangster trilogy, directed by Eai Keung Lau and Siu Fai Mak and released in 2002. William Monahan, a former editor of *Spy* magazine and screenwriter of Ridley Scott's *Kingdom of Heaven*, was hired to transpose the story from Hong Kong to Boston. Monahan had good credentials; he was born and raised in Boston, and understood the world of spies and informants critical to the story.

Scorsese approached *The Departed* as a crime film, more a genre piece than a personal film like those in his gangster trilogy. As a hired hand he was functioning much like his beloved William Wellman, Howard Hawks, and the line of directors who were responsible for the Warner crime series. Ironically *The Departed* is a Warner Brothers' film.

The strength of *The Departed* is its cast including Matt Damon, Leonardo DiCaprio (who was interested in an American version of the Hong Kong film and the motor of the project), Mark Walhberg, Martin Sheen, Jack Nicholson, and Alec Baldwin, as well as a fine supporting cast of character actors. The story revolves around the knowledge of an informant in the special units department as well as one in the Frank Costello mob.

For some inexplicable reason, the Nicholson character, loosely based on Whitey Bulger, a real Boston Irish mobster who ran operations for years and was beloved by the people, is named after the legendary Frank Costello—Francesco Castiglia an Italian crime boss. Costello was internationally known to control gambling in the United States and was eventually the leader of the Genovese crime family. To those familiar with the gangster known as the "Prime Minister of the Underworld," the character name is puzzling and distracting. For those who aren't, the surname is clearly Italian, although he is called Francis by some (predominantly an Irish name but then there's Francis Albert Sinatra). The name Costello works against the Irishness of the character, who celebrates his heritage throughout the film.

Scorsese plays the story, an intricate interweaving of deception, lies, and survival, with tight reins on the plot with little emphasis on set pieces. Two inspired by Jack Nicholson, one concerning a dildo in a porno theater and the other a fragment of a three-way sex scene that begins at the opera and ends in a avalanche of cocaine, were shortened to the bone and move swiftly through the main story.

The teaming of Nicholson and Scorsese was as audacious as Nicholson and Kubrick for *The Shining*. An actor with enormous gifts and range, Nicholson gives a nearly over-the-top "Jack" performance that delighted Scorsese. DiCaprio, in his third outing with Scorsese, proves his skills as an ensemble player and gives a solid character, not star, performance.

Scorsese, who has dealt with Irish culture and characters in *GoodFellas* and *Gangs of New York*, gets under the skin of the Boston neighborhood known as Southie and applies his gangster acumen to the environment and action. The concept of a rat arose in *GoodFellas* as Henry Hill was schooled never to rat on his friends, but ends up giving up all of them to save himself. The informer lies deep in Irish culture as well as Italian: both nationalities abhor the practice. Scorsese utilizes a clip of Ford's classic *The Informer* and the heartbreaking last line, "Frankie, your mother forgives me." Scorsese grew up with the *omerta*, constantly told you don't say nothing, you don't see nothing, by his father as well as the neighborhood wiseguys and good citizens.

In his mature work Scorsese has begun to utilize his signature grammar in new ways. There are many top shots in the film but unlike the earlier ones that linger and are dwelled upon to great effect, the ones in *The Departed* are swiftly paced part of the mise en scene.

The cinematography by Michael Ballhaus captures the verisimilitude of story and environment, as does Kristi Zea's (*New York Stories, Life Lessons, GoodFellas*) production design.

The legend between Martin Scorsese and the Oscar has preyed over his career. Fans and admirers as well as industry insiders (who vote in the Academy!) could not fathom why Scorsese never won the statue for best director. There have been plenty of opportunities. Scorsese has been nominated for Best Achievement in Directing for *Raging Bull, The Last Temptation of Christ, GoodFellas, Gangs of New York, The Aviator*, and *The Departed*. He has been nominated for the Director's Guild of America award, usually with few exceptions, a guarantee of the Oscar, seven times. *Raging Bull, GoodFellas, Gangs of New York, The Aviator*, and *The Departed* gave him five opportunities at the double as well as for *Taxi Driver* and *The Age of Innocence*, for which he was not Oscar nominated. Hitchcock and Welles never received Oscars. It took Spielberg until *Schindler's List* to win.

Always gracious, Scorsese kept about his business of making movies as the sentiment grew against this injustice by the Academy. Then came *The Departed*. Not one of Scorsese's finest accomplishments, but a professional and superbly directed film, the buzz grew that his time had come. Scorsese won the Director's Guild Award for *The Departed*, his first. During the Oscar ceremony the cameras picked up the presence of Francis Coppola, possibly there because of his daughter, George Lucas who rarely goes beyond the confines of his empire, and Steven Spielberg who was there for his association with Clint Eastwood.

Toward the end of the long and tedious telecast, the presenters for Best Achievement in direction were announced—Francis Ford Coppola, George Lucas, and Steven Spielberg, longtime friends and associates of Scorsese and fellow representatives as lions of the seventies' generation of filmmaking. Spielberg, a close Scorsese friend, read the winner's name. The moment was magical—seeing these four gray-haired eminences together on stage celebrating the win of the long-suffering *paisan*. Scorsese gave a gracious speech thanking all the regular people who constantly stopped him on the street, in restaurants, and in public places wishing him well on his quest to Oscar gold.

The nagging ghost that the Academy gave him the award for payback was defeated when *The Departed* went on to win the big prize, the Best Picture of the year. The press and public now relieved, celebrated for weeks, feeling justice had finally been done, and for Scorsese his honor is due. To him winning the Oscar linked him to Old Hollywood, an accomplishment that overwhelmed him. He never felt worthy of these comparisons; the historian in him knew better, but then Scorsese has always been in it for the love of the movies, not the fame, money, or celebrity. There are still many, many projects to do as time grows short, and making movies is not just all-important to Scorsese: it's the *raison* of his existence.

EPILOGUE

How does one conclude a biography when the subject continues to live and work? Often, the solution is to sum up, while letting the reader know the subject continues to work and grow. When I finished my biography of Stanley Kubrick, he was still at work on *Eyes Wide Shut*. I thought about appropriate summing up sentences and decided to conclude by emphasizing the impact Kubrick had on my adult life. I recalled patiently waiting for each Kubrick film to make its way to the screen and was comforted by the knowledge that the artist Stanley Kubrick was always "out there" making movies and that his artistry had inspired and motivated me. The biography ends by recognizing that "Stanley Kubrick is out there making movies. He'll be out there making movies, and international audiences will be waiting to see what he has to reveal with his cinematic imagination—until he isn't out there anymore."

Now I find myself closing the biography of another great filmmaker who has motivated and inspired audiences and made unique contributions to the evolution of cinema.

This I know. Martin Scorsese is out there. At the zenith of his career, he will pursue personal projects that are dear to his heart and reflect his honesty and humanity. He will make documentaries about subjects that represent his emotional and physical life. He will take assignments from studios, producers, and actors and make those films his own because he is always a personal filmmaker. He will make films that reflect his deep convictions concerning religion, spirituality, his ethnicity, and his roots and traditions. Scorsese will make films in which music plays a significant narrative role and produces a wellspring of memories and feelings that interact with the characters and stories. He will continue to explore the struggles of the outsider, the artist, and of men trying to communicate and find love and to examine the fundamental realities of human sin and redemption. He will utilize his vast knowledge of the cinema to tell stories that are true to life as he knows and experiences it. Martin Scorsese will be out there making movies and we will all wait to see them and be thrilled and humbled by the experience.

Writing a biography of Martin Scorsese has been another odyssey, not through my own version of Kubrick's *Star Gate* in 2001, but a personal journey. There was some wisdom in my apprehension about this project. It has taken me back to my own childhood, to an examination of my shared ethnicity with Scorsese; Catholicism, the violence and cruelty of the mean streets of New York, the epic story of the sixties and seventies, the search for self, and the search for truth in art. In my work as a writer, I had not attempted to probe areas that crossed over to my personal life. I promised to do this just one time and then close the door and move on to other challenges.

Writing this book became my *Raging Bull*. It forced me to confront truths about myself, to seek my own redemption. At times it possessed me and influenced my thoughts and behavior. Mostly, it made me admire Martin Scorsese even more than when I began. Martin Scorsese is a filmmaker of incredible honesty and commitment. Scorsese has reinforced within me that art is important, the cinema is holy and real, and that we are here for a purpose. I have no answers—only that when we realize and accept that purpose, in the most positive sense—we have no choice.

APPENDIX A: FILMOGRAPHY AS DIRECTOR—FICTIONAL WORKS

1963   *What's a Nice Girl Like You Doing in a Place Like This?* (short)

1964   *It's Not Just You Murray!* (short)

1967   *The Big Shave* (short)

1969   *Who's That Knocking at My Door*

1972   *Boxcar Bertha*

1973   *Mean Streets*

1974   *Alice Doesn't Live Here Anymore*

1975   *Taxi Driver*

1977   *New York, New York*

1980   *Raging Bull*

1982   *The King of Comedy*

1985   *After Hours*
         Mirror, Mirror (*Amazing Stories*, television series episode)

1986   *The Color of Money*
         Commercial for Giorgio Armani

1987   *Bad* (music video)

1988   *Somewhere Down the Crazy River* (music video)
         The Last Temptation of Christ
         Commercial for Giorgio Armani

1989   *New York Stories* ("Life Lessons" episode)

1990   *GoodFellas*

1991   *Cape Fear*

1992   *The Age of Innocence*
1995   *Casino*
1997   *Kundun*
1999   *Bringing Out the Dead*
2002   *Gangs of New York*
2004   *The Aviator*
2006   *The Departed*

APPENDIX B: FILMOGRAPHY AS DIRECTOR—NONFICTION

1969   *Street Scenes*

1970   *Italianamerican*

1977   *The Last Waltz*
American Boy: A Profile of Steven Prince

1990   *Made in Milan*

1995   *A Century of Cinema—A Personal Journey with Martin Scorsese through American Movies*

2001   *My Voyage to Italy*
The Neighborhood

2003   *The Blues*

2005   *No Direction Home: Bob Dylan*

APPENDIX C: FILMOGRAPHY AS ACTOR

1967   *Who's That Knocking at My Door?* (Gangster)

1969   *Boxcar Bertha* (Client in brothel)

1970   *Mean Streets* (Shorty)

1971   *Alice Doesn't Live Here Anymore* (Diner patron)

1972   *Taxi Driver* (Man in the backseat of a cab)
         Cannonball (Mafioso)

1980   *Raging Bull* (Barbizon Hotel stagehand)

1981   *Il Pap'occhio* (*In the Eye of the Pope*) (Television director)

1982   *The King of Comedy* (Television director)
         Pavlova—A Woman for All Time (Gatti-Cassaza)
         After Hours (Spotlight operator)
         Round Midnight (Goodley)
         Dreams (Vincent Van Gogh)

1990   *Guilty By Suspicion* (Film director Joe Lesser)

1992   *Age of Innocence* (Photographer)

1994   *Quiz Show* (Sponsor)

1995   *Search and Destroy* (IRS accountant)

1998   *With Friends Like These* (Himself)

1999   *The Muse* (Himself)
         Bringing Out the Dead (Voice of Dispatcher)

2002   *Gangs of New York* (Wealthy homeowner)

2004   *Shark Tale* (Voice of Sykes)
         The Aviator (Projectionist) (Voice of the man on the red carpet)

APPENDIX D: FILMOGRAPHY AS EXECUTIVE PRODUCER AND PRODUCER

1989   *The Grifters*—producer

1992   *Mad Dog and Glory*—producer

1994   *Naked in New York*—executive producer

1995   *Search and Destroy*—executive producer
Clockers—producer
In the Spotlight: Eric Clapton—Nothing but the Blues—executive producer

1994   *Grace of My Heart*—executive producer

1995   *La Tregua (The Truce)*—executive producer
Kicked in the Head—executive producer

1996   *The Hi-Lo Country*—producer

2000   *You Can Count on Me*—executive producer

2001   *Rain*—executive producer

2003   *The Soul of a Man*—executive producer

2004   *Something to Believe in*—executive producer
Brides

APPENDIX E: FILMOGRAPHY AS PRESENTER

1992   *The Golden Coach*
Rocco and His Brother
Intervista

1993   *Les Orgueilleux (The Proud Ones)*
La Strada
El Cid

1995   *I Am Cuba*
Mamma Roma
A Matter of Life and Death
Belle de Jour

1997   *Plein Soleil (Purple Noon)*
Rough Magic

1999   *Le Mépris (Contempt)*
Peeping Tom
The Saragossa Manuscript
Les Amants du Pont Neuf

2000   *Love's Labour Lost*

2005   *Brooklyn Lobster*

APPENDIX F: INTERVIEW WITH MARTIN SCORSESE

(November 2006)

By Vincent LoBrutto

Published in an altered form in *CinemaEditor* magazine; Courtesy of *CinemaEditor*.

VL: Congratulations on The Departed, *it just hit one hundred million.*

Martin Scorsese: Yes, it's amazing, a gangster picture. We just made it as kind of a reaction against other films being made these days and just put it out there and let it be it's own worth. I didn't think in terms of the picture making a lot of money.

It doesn't really look like a Scorsese movie. Your use of editing grammar was interesting in The Departed. *You've built up all this grammar over the decades and that's what you used for this film. The famous Scorsese top shots are cut very quickly.*

Martin Scorsese: Yes, they're very quick. The big experiment for me was doing a film with a very strong plot, which I've rarely done, and still enriching the picture, enriching the characters. For me, the thing I kept going back to every time I complained about doing the movie or difficult problems, I said, "Why am I doing..." I would get excited about doing these scenes, and these characters and the sense of betrayal—the whole idea of betrayal, trust, and betrayal, and particularly in family situations. In making the film, around the time I was doing the scenes with Jack Nicholson and Leo DiCaprio in the restaurant when Jack pulls a gun on him, I realized that I had similar scenes in *Gangs of New York*. I realized I had been doing similar scenes in all of my movies and it's pretty much about fathers and sons in the family and betrayal, tradition, and the obligation to the father. I still get excited about not analyzing—but working out of the scene with the actors in which the characters are trusting each other, but one is betraying the other, and one knows it but can't be sure about it; I find this fascinating. I guess it's something I grew up with.

It's very Italian, isn't it?

Martin Scorsese: It is. It's very Sicilian actually; my father every night would expound on this whole issue, every night and day, all kinds of issues: he would bring up stories, things that were happening, always about loyalty and betrayal.

It means very much to us as Italian-Americans.

Martin Scorsese: Yes, it really does and I think it's because coming from my father's background, he was born on Elizabeth Street in 1913, he was more Sicilian than American; my grandparents didn't even speak English, they weren't even citizens, and so I've always talked about this; they didn't have the trust in government or the church or any kind of institution. The only trust that you could rely on or that you had to nurture was in the family. So this was a key issue; it's almost tribal in a way.

We're all part of a tribe one way or another.

Martin Scorsese: Yes, we are, but as you know being an Italian-American, you can go downtown, Elizabeth Street was mainly Sicilian, the Neapolitans were on Mulberry Street—you had different types of cooking, different types of cuisines. I mean it was a major difference and everything was a melting pot in America—it's all mixed together. But when I go to Italy, it's still that way. Everything below Rome is considered not Italian, only the North is the good thing.

What I found was that we started to cut *The Departed* to the plot points, but basically, the real trick to the cutting that we were still into only a week or two before the picture opened, was balancing the character to the plot and how much time was given to each character—when you intercut the characters and, could you follow the characters and could you follow the plot. I had a lot of trouble, quite honestly, when I was putting it together. I found that one always learns from the nature of what you are doing; images teach you so much, and they have their own nature. So you may think you may be communicating something so simple to an audience and it could be just the opposite.

The top shots in Taxi Driver *that are so memorable are long and slow. Here, in* The Departed, *they are quick.*

Martin Scorsese: Yes, they're just touchstones, based on, I do feel I want to see the image from above, but I'm no longer interested in holding on them.

Isn't that interesting. And they are probably shot differently in a certain way.

Martin Scorsese: Very differently. I just don't feel the same weight is there. I think the weight of the picture is somewhere else and it's the accumulation, a mosaic of images, like a cubist kind of imagery, and the images that I keep in my mind are the looks in the eyes of Leo and Matt when they shift back and forth. Whenever they are asked a question they are always working on something else in the back of their heads to save their lives.

So The Departed *was really a character movie. Did you make as many drawings as you usually do? I would think as much.*

Martin Scorsese: I just did my notes on the side of the script and I certainly designed a lot of it, but part of the enjoyment was designing a scene, let's say, where Leo DiCaprio is harassed by Dignam and Queenan is just sitting there. If you look, the shots are very clearly designed, if you look at each one of those intercut sequences—and that was enjoyable, it was almost like a one-act play. What I mean by enjoyable was that the camera was restrained to a certain extent and the composition was very important and the camera moves were very important; they all meant something. I carried that through a lot of the picture, sometimes the more slack the image was, the better it was, because there was so much going on with the people, I felt that if you pull the camera back and make it *seem* objective, you could be just as uneasy as the characters, because you don't know which way the camera is going to go, you don't know which way the story is going to go, you don't know which way the character is going to go.

It's interesting. It's not like The King of Comedy *where you said you were going back to the early cinema style of William S. Porter.*

Martin Scorsese: That was a conscious effort to almost imitate a television style, it was hard to do right; it was very tight. That was a conscious effort to stop all kinds of cinematic flash. I mean coming off *Raging Bull*, you could probably feel that. In *Raging Bull* we had just done it all. Not that we did it all—meaning what everybody else had done—I mean for myself, what I had come out of. I thought it was my last film. I put it all up there and said, "Okay, let's start again." *The King of Comedy* was a good example, a good opportunity to take that advantage.

Do you think a lot of people took you seriously at the time, with all the things that were going on in your life?

Martin Scorsese: Exactly, I was just working it through, but *The King of Comedy* was a picture DeNiro wanted me to do, but it took me eight or nine years to get to understand it.

I'll tell you the truth I'm not so sure I understand it and I've watched it over and over.

Martin Scorsese: It's about celebrity and that need for celebrity. When a person finally does get your autograph and does get you over to their house for dinner, what is it they want? They want you to place your hands over them, almost like a religious thing, and create a miracle in their lives. And we put this onto stars and our television personalities and our culture, and we can't do that for them.

I really had put everything I knew into *Raging Bull*. I was also very concerned about the well-made film, the perfect film, and I wanted to mar the picture somehow, to mark it, maybe to injure the movie in a way—the images, maybe the frames themselves. Eventually, I did that on the home movies. I wrote on them, I scratched them myself, the negatives.

I spent a whole day watching the home movie opening of Mean Streets. *I know what's on that leader.*

Martin Scorsese: Oh, you do!

It says Charlie Cappa—Season of the Witch. I also found a frame of you and Harvey Keitel—the director and his on-screen persona.

Martin Scorsese: You're right, it's in there. "Season of the Witch" was a wonderful song by Donovan and when I was working on that story, the mood of "Season of the Witch"—the song—permeated the whole picture. Also, on the script, we used to have a quote from *Subterranean Homesick Blues*, which was "Twenty years of schooling and they put you on the day shift." But I knew we were not acting out what Bob Dylan was saying. They didn't want to go on the day shift; they behaved in a different way about the day shift, my guys.

The way you used songs in Mean Streets *is amazing—Be My Baby, The Stones. Did you ever play an instrument?*

Martin Scorsese: No. My brother played guitar (that's what I wanted to play). I'm obsessed with the guitar. My father played the mandolin, but

I never saw him play. In those home movies that are in the Italian documentary, I never saw it. I listened to Django Reinhardt; my father had those records.

My father played guitar and I got him a Django Reinhardt record; he listened to it all night. My father didn't take me to the movies, but we had this thing with music.

Martin Scorsese: My father took me to the movies when I was living in Corona in Queens until 1949. My mother took me to see *Duel in the Sun*, "He likes Westerns." She marred me for life; I was hysterical, I was totally terrified. The old story, I was hiding under the seat. But then my father took me a few times into New York after we moved back to the old neighborhood where he was born. He took me to the Lowe's and the Academy and RKO theaters and the Warner Brothers theaters that had the MGM, Columbia, and Paramount pictures. And so I saw a lot of film, my early film history was with him in New York. Back then I called Manhattan— New York. Queens to me is different; it's like the country. That was nice. It was like being in the country for us.

With my father I saw *The Bad and the Beautiful. Sunset Boulevard* was the first film I saw about Hollywood. I saw tons of movies with him, extraordinary experiences—*Rear Window, The Day the Earth Stood Still*, and *The Thing*—that was the real bond there.

You are talking about this as an adult. In some cases it must have taken years to realize what you saw with him.

Martin Scorsese: Yes, totally yes.

I remember being at the old New York Cultural Center watching Bigger than Life *and all of a sudden I got the chills because I said, "Oh yes God, I saw this with my mother as a little boy.*

Martin Scorsese: Oh, my God. That must have done something.

It was when they put him behind the X-ray machine— that image.

Martin Scorsese: That's terrifying, the whole film. I was on Prednisone for eleven years because of asthma. I saw that film with my friends and I remember loving James Mason in it—Jekyll and Hyde, the perfect American family. The image of sitting at dinner at the table and the undercurrent of destructiveness and madness in what seems to be a very healthy image. This to me was a big thing, because everybody thought about suburbia, "Wouldn't it be great?" because we were living in tenements; but then these stories started to come out. Then we said, "Thank God we were living in the tenements!"

You have said that Citizen Kane *was the first film that made you aware of the director.*

Martin Scorsese: I think you could really see the hand at work—it's a showy kind of filmmaking. I began to realize there's a director, too. The first director's name I remember on films that I liked was John Ford.

Those were all your favorite movies.

Martin Scorsese: Yes, as a kid, as a boy, I liked them. Now I've kind of changed my opinion on some of them; still I think Ford and Welles are the key men. Welles, you can see the work—it's not that you can see it— it's you can enjoy it, you can see that somebody had an idea of where to put the camera—a certain place—and move the camera a certain way, and shoot with a lens that kept everybody in focus; something special in the way that it was visualized, came across. That meant there were people whose process you could see and it also opened up ways to open up stories with different visual techniques as opposed to the seamless editing style, the classical style of Ford and William Wyler. That's not a criticism of Ford and Wyler, but it's a different way of looking at it. After you get through that period of being excited by Welles and Carol Reed's *The Third Man*, then it's getting back to *not* editing, *not* cutting the shot, its getting back to that.

When you talk to an editor that's what they talk about—that's the grand level—to be able to achieve with long takes.

Martin Scorsese: Long takes, but that's in the visualization and the narrative. In other words, you have to visualize a shot that tells a story and that is complete in and of itself—that you can't cut—but there are two schools of thought. Is one better than the other? I don't necessarily think so, to say that Ford is better than Eisenstein? I don't think so.

And I know you love Antonioni. It's a different almost religious experience.

Martin Scorsese: It really is. It's a different thing I had to learn watching Antonioni films. I had to learn about them, but it becomes another kind of experience, a meditative experience and that's good—that's a good thing.

What's the very first cutting that you did? You did some films with your friends, right?

Martin Scorsese: I did some things in 8mm. I borrowed my friend's camera: he had a Dejur. He had this little 8mm camera; I guess they had a little money. I really didn't know how to use it and I shot it with black-and-white film, I shot some stuff on a roof up on Mott Street. It was very silly, but I remember having to cut and tell the story in images. I kind of relied upon the drawings I did as a kid, as a younger person, when I was doing storyboards. The traditional way of editing and composition, I just picked it up from seeing so many films.

So how did you cut the film?

Martin Scorsese: I used a little 8mm viewer I had to borrow from somebody else. It was fun.

How about in 16mm? Was it the student shorts while you attended NYU?

Martin Scorsese: Yes, the first editing I did were some short films. They were little film exercises in the first class in sophomore year. The sophomore class was just one course called Sight and Sound and you did little exercises. I remember editing 16 mm there. I think it was 1962.

For the shorts how did you come up with the name Eli Bleich.

Martin Scorsese: He was a real person who helped edit the picture.

Oh he's a real person! I thought he was a name you came up with.

Martin Scorsese: No, and he came up with the little special effect that we did to bring the blood up in *The Big Shave.*

I show that film to my students. They go crazy!

Martin Scorsese: It's insane, I know.

I hope you know how much film students love you.

Martin Scorsese: It's amazing. And it is fun. It's so hard; you can't learn how to make a movie in school. The big thing is the inspiration. That's the whole thing. I had a teacher who was able to inspire me. If you have a spark and there is someone there who believes in you, it makes you go ahead and try different things because you can learn everything. The old Orson Welles story, you can learn everything you need to know about making a movie in four hours. It depends on how you use the technique.

Talk about how you and Thelma Schoonmaker work. You realized early on this was someone that you really wanted to work with.

Martin Scorsese: She knows me. She wasn't a film student; she comes from political science and she took a six-week workshop class where I met her. Basically, we edited documentaries together and she helped me edit *Who's That Knocking.* I did *Boxcar Bertha* and *Mean Streets.* I had to give the credit to someone else because I wasn't in the union. Sid Levin actually came in and made two or three cuts for me in the end, in the last scene. Sid was Marty Ritt's editor and I called him. He was a nice guy, so I put his name on it and the poor guy got a negative comment in the Variety review. You do someone a personal favor and that's what happens. I did *Alice Doesn't Live Here Anymore* with Marcia Lucas and myself, *Taxi Driver, New York, New York,* and *The Last Waltz* with other people. By the time we got back together, I felt I needed someone like Thelma because she knew me. What I mean by that is, she has very strong feelings about a personal voice in movies. She supports that. I have had problems with people over the years when the allegiances line up differently. So that's a key element in a relationship in editing. I've found her to be a key collaborator since 1980.

What are you doing next?

Martin Scorsese: There are two or three projects I would like to do. There's *Silence* that I'm aiming to do next. A story on the music business that I'm working on with Mick Jagger as one of the producers. I wish I could get those two projects up right away, but something comes your way like *The Aviator,* which was really fun to do, and *The Departed.* There are so many books I've read and things I would like to do, but there's not that much time left.

Sidney Lumet is what, 82? You're a kid!

Martin Scorsese: Yes, so I look toward Lumet, and Clint Eastwood who is in his seventies.

I can imagine working with Jack Nicholson.

Martin Scorsese: Oh, it was extraordinary, extraordinary. We worked about twenty-five days together on the picture but . . .

He's Jack.

Martin Scorsese: He's Jack.

He worked with Kubrick . . .

Martin Scorsese: That's what I wanted. I wanted Jack; I wanted something special.

That's what Kubrick said. If you say, "Walk through the door" he's going to do it the way that no one else has done it.

Martin Scorsese: And a lot of the times you don't know, and, quite honestly, no matter how arduous it might be, the proof is when you watch the rushes and you're getting excited watching the rushes—that's the proof.

BIBLIOGRAPHY

Abbott, John S. C. *Italy: And the War for Italian Independence*. New York: Dodd, Mead, and Company, n.d.

Abel, Richard, and Rick Altman, eds. *The Sounds of Early Cinema*. Bloomington: Indiana University Press, 2001.

Aberdeen, J.A. *Hollywood Renegades: The Society of Independent Motion Picture Producers*. Los Angeles, CA: Cobblestone Entertainment, 2000.

Abramowitz, Rachel. *Is That a Gun in Your Pocket? Women's Experience of Power in Hollywood*. New York: Random House, 2000.

Ackerman, Kenneth D. *Boss Tweed: The Rise and Fall of the Corrupt Pol Who Conceived the Soul of Modern New York*. New York: Carroll & Graf Publishers, 2005.

Aftab, Kaleem, and Spike Lee. *Spike Lee, "That's My Story and I'm Sticking to It."* New York: W.W. Norton & Company, 2005.

Alleman, Richard. *New York: The Movie Lover's Guide*. New York: Broadway Books, 2005.

Alpert, Hollis. *Fellini: A Life*. New York: Atheneum, 1986.

Alter, Robert. *The Five Books of Moses: A Translation with Commentary*. New York: W.W. Norton & Company, 2004.

Andbinder, Tyler. *Five Points: The 19th-Century New York City Neighborhood That Invented Tap Dance, Stole Elections, and Became the World's Most Notorious Slum*. New York: The Free Press, 2001.

Andrew, Geoff, ed. *Film: The Critics' Choice: 150 Masterpieces of World Cinema Selected and Defined by the Experts*. New York: Billboard Books, 2001.

Anger, Kenneth. *Hollywood Babylon*. New York: Straight Arrow Books, 1975. Originally published in French, 1958.

Arnheim, Rudolf. *Film as Art*. Berkeley: University of California Press, 1969.

Asbury, Herbert. *The Gangs of New York*. New York: Thunder's Mouth Press. Originally published in 1928, New York: Alfred A. Knopf, Inc.

———. *All Around the Town: Murder, Scandal, Riot and Mayhem in Old New York*. New York: Thunder's Mouth Press, 2003.

————. *Sucker's Progress: An Informal History of Gambling in America*. New York: Thunder's Mouth Press, 2003. Originally published by Dodd, Mead, and Company, Inc., 1938.

Attwater, Donald, general ed. *A Catholic Dictionary*, 3rd ed. The Macmillan Company, 1958. Rockford, IL: Tan Books and Publishers, Inc.

Aulier, Dan. *Hitchcock's Notebooks: An Authorized and Illustrated Look Inside the Creative Mind of Alfred Hitchcock*. New York: Avon Books, 1999.

Bandy, Mary Lea, and Antonio Monda. *The Hidden God: Film and Faith*. New York: Museum of Modern Art, 2003.

Barlett, Donald, and James B. Steele. *Howard Hughes: His Life and Madness*. New York: W.W. Norton & Company, 1979.

Barone, Arturo. *Italians First! An A-to-Z of Everything First Achieved by Italians*, revised 3rd ed., 1994. Folkstone, Kent: Renaissance Books, 1989.

Barreca, Regina, ed. *The Penguin Book of Italian American Writing*. New York: Penguin Books, 2002.

Bart, Peter, and Peter Guber. *Shoot Out: Surviving Fame and (Mis)Fortune in Hollywood*. New York: G.P. Putnam's Sons, 2002.

Barthes, Roland. *Image—Music—Text*. New York: Hill and Wang, 1977.

Bartunek, John. *Inside the Passion: An Insider's Look at The Passion of the Christ*. West Chester, PA: Ascension Press, 2005.

Barzini, Luigi. *The Italians*. New York: Touchstone, 1996. Originally published in 1964.

Basten, Fred, E. *Glorious Technicolor: The Movies Magic Rainbow*. Camarillo, CA: Technicolor, 2005.

Battcock, Gregrory, ed. *The New American Cinema: A Critical Anthology*. New York: E.P. Dutton & Company, Inc., 1967.

Baxter, John. *Fellini: The Biography*. New York: St. Martin's Press, 1993

————. *De Niro: A Biography*. London: HarperCollins Publishers, 2002.

Begleiter, Marcie. *From Word to Image: Storyboarding and the Filmmaking Process*. Studio City, CA: Michael Wiese Productions, 2001.

Behlmer, Rudy. *Inside Warner Bros (1933–1951)*. New York: Simon & Schuster, Inc., 1985.

Bell, Dale, ed. *Woodstock: An Inside Look at the Movie that Shook Up the World and Defined a Generation*. Studio City, CA: Michael Wiese Productions, 1999.

Belton, John. *Widescreen Cinema*. Cambridge, MA: Harvard University Press, 1992.

Bergman, Ingmar. *The Magic Lantern: An Autobiography*. New York: Penguin Books, 1988.

————. *Images: My Life in Film*. New York: Arcade Publishing, 1990.

Bertellini, Giorgio, ed. *The Cinema of Italy*. London: Wallflower Press, 2004.

Biskind, Peter. *Seeing is Believing: How Hollywood Taught Us to Stop Worrying and Love the Fifties*. New York: Pantheon Books, 1983

————. *Easy Riders, Raging Bulls: How the Sex-Drugs-and-Rock 'n' Roll Generation Saved Hollywood*. New York: Simon & Schuster, 1998.

———. *Down and Dirty Pictures: Miramax, Sundance, and the Rise of Independent Film.* New York: Simon & Schuster, 2004.

———. *Gods and Monsters: Thirty Years of Writing on Film and Culture from One of America's Most Incisive Writers.* New York: Nation Books, 2004.

Bitzer, G.W. *Billy Bitzer: His Story.* New York: Farrar, Straus, and Giroux, 1973.

Blake, Richard A. *Street Smart: The New York of Lumet, Allen, Scorsese, and Lee.* Lexington: The University of Kentucky Press, 2005.

Blanchard, Paul. *Blue Guide: Southern Italy*, 10th ed. New York: W.W. Norton, 2004.

Blatty, William Peter. *The Exorcist.* New York: Harper & Row, Publishers, 1971.

Bliss, Micheal. *The Word Made Flesh: Catholicism and Conflict in the Films of Martin Scorsese.* Lanham, MD: The Scarecrow Press Filmmakers Series No. 45, 1998.

Bluestone, George. *Novels into Film: The Metamorphosis of Fiction into Cinema.* Berkeley: University of California Press, 1957.

Bogdanovich, Peter. *John Ford.* Berkeley: University of California Press, 1970.

———. *Pieces of Time: Peter Bogdanovich on the Movies.* New York: Arbor House/Esquire Books, 1973.

———. *Who the Devil Made It: Conversations with Robert Aldrich, George Cukor, Allan Dwan, Howard Hawks, Alfred Hitchcock, Chuck Jones, Fritz Lang, Joseph H. Lewis, Leo McCarey, Sidney Lumet, Otto Preminger, Don Siegel, Josef von Sternberg, Frank Tashlin, Raoul Walsh.* New York: Alfred A. Knopf, 1997.

Bokenkotter, Thomas. *A Concise History of the Catholic Church.* New York: Image Books, Doubleday, rev. and exp. ed., 1990.

Bondanella, Peter. *Italian Cinema: From Neorealism to the Present*, 3rd ed. New York: Continuum, 2003. New York: Frederick Ungar Publishing Company, 1984.

———. *Hollywood Italians: Dago, Palookas, Romeos, Wise Guys, and Sopranos.* New York: Continuum, 2004.

Boorman, John, and Walter Donohue, eds. *Projections 7.* Includes *Martin Scorsese: A Passion for Films.* London, Boston: Faber and Faber, 1997.

Booth, Wayne, C. *The Rhetoric of Fiction*, 2nd ed., 1983. Chicago: The University of Chicago Press, 1961.

Bordwell, David: *The Way Hollywood Tells It: Story and Style in Modern Movies.* Berkeley: University of California Press, 2006.

Bordwell, David, Janet Staiger, and Kristin Thompson. *The Classical Hollywood Cinema: Film Style & Mode of Production to 1960.* New York: Columbia University Press, 1985.

Borg, Marcus J. *Reading the Bible Again for the First Time: Taking the Bible Seriously but Not Literally.* New York: HarperSanFrancisco, 2001.

Bouwsma, William J. *The Waning of the Renaissance 1550–1640.* New Haven, CT: Yale University Press, 2002.

Bouzereau, Laurent. *The DePalma Cut: The Films of America's Most Controversial Director.* New York: Dembner Books, 1988.

Boyd, Herb, with Ray Robinson II. *Pound for Pound: A Biography of Sugar Ray Robinson.* New York: Amistad, an imprint of HarperCollins, 2004.

Brady, Frank. *Citizen Welles*: A Biography of Orson Welles. New York: Charles Scribner's Sons, 1989.

Brassco, Donnie (AKA Joseph D. Pistone) *The Way of the Wiseguy*. Philadelphia, PA: Running Press, 2004.

Breslin, Jimmy. *The Church That Forgot Christ*. New York: Free Press, 2004.

Brodsky, Alyn. *The Great Mayor: Fiorella La Guardia and the Making of the City of New York*. New York: Truman Talley Books, St. Martin's Press, 2003.

Brophy, Philip. *100 Modern Soundtracks*. London: BFI publishing, 2004.

Brouwer, Alexander, and Thomas Lee Wright. *Working in Hollywood: 64 Film Professionals Talk about Moviemaking*. New York: Crown Publishers, Inc., 1990.

Brown, Alison. *The Renaissance. Seminar Studies in History Series*, 2nd ed. Essex, England: Longman, 1999. First published in 1988.

Brown, Dan. *The Da Vinci Code*. New York: Doubleday, 2003.

Browne, Nick, ed. *Cahiers du Cinéma: 1969–1972. The Politics of Representation*. Cambridge, MA: Harvard University Press, 1990.

Brownlow, Kevin. *The Parade's Gone By* . . . New York: Alfred A. Knopf, 1968.

———. *Behind the Mask: Sex, Violence, Prejudice, Crime: Films of Social Conscience in the Silent Era*. New York: Alfred A. Knopf, 1990.

Brunette, Peter. *Roberto Rossellini*. New York: Oxford University Press, 1987.

Bruno, Giuliana and Maria Nadotti, eds. *Off Screen: Women and Film in Italy*. London: Routledge, 1988.

Burckhardt, Jacob. *The Civilization of the Renaissance in Italy. Modern Library Classics* series. New York: Modern Library, 2002.

Burke, Frank. *Fellini's Films: From Postwar to Postmodern. Twayne's Filmmaker Series*. New York: Twayne Publishers, 1996.

Burns, Rick, and James Sanders, with Lisa Ades. *New York: An Illustrated History*. New York: Alfred A. Knopf, 1999.

Burrows, Edwin G., and Mike Wallace. *Gotham: A History of New York City to 1898*. New York: Oxford University Press, 1999.

Burstein, Dan, ed. *Secrets of the Code: The Unauthorized Guide to the Mysteries Behind the Da Vinci Code*. New York: CDS Books, 2004.

Buscombe, Edward. *The Searches. BFI Film Classics*. London: BFI Publishing, 2000.

Caldiron, Orio. *Italian Directors: Mario Monicelli*. Rome: National Association of Motion Pictures and Affiliated Industries, Institute for the Promotion of Italian Motion Pictures Abroad, under the Auspices of the Ministry of Tourism and Entertainment, n.d.

Cameron, Julia. *The Artist's Way: A Spiritual Path to Higher Creativity*. New York: Jeremy P. Tarcher/Putnam, 1992.

———. *Walking in This World: The Practical Art of Creativity*. New York: Jeremy P. Tarcher/Penguin, 2002.

———. *The Sound of Paper: Starting from Scratch*. New York: Jeremy P. Tarcher/ Penguin, 2004.

Cannato, Vincent J. *The Ungovernable City: John Lindsay and His Struggle to Save New York*. New York: Basic Books, 2002.

Cantwell, Anne-Marie, and Diana de Zerega Wall. *Unearthing Gotham: The Archaeology of New York City.* New Haven, CT: Yale University Press, 2001.

Capeci, Jerry. *Jerry Capeci's Gang Land.* New York: Alpha, a Member of the Penguin Group (USA), Inc., 2003.

Capeci, Jerry, and Gene Mustain. *Gotti: Rise and Fall.* New York: Onyx, 1996.

Capra, Frank. *The Name Above the Title: An Autobiography.* New York: The Macmillan Company, 1971.

Card, James. *Seductive Cinema: The Art of Silent Film.* New York: Alfred A. Knopf, 1994.

Cardiff, Jack. *Magic Hour: The Life of a Cameraman.* Foreword by Martin Scorsese. London: Faber and Faber, 1996

Carey, Gary. *Lenny, Janis & Jimi.* New York: Pocket Books, 1975.

Carney, Raymond. *American Dreaming: The Films of John Cassavetes and the American Experience.* Berkeley: University of California Press, 1985.

———. *American Vision: The Films of Frank Capra.* Cambridge: Cambridge University Press, 1986.

———. *The Films of John Cassavetes: Pragmatism, Modernism, and the Movies. Cambridge Film Classics.* Cambridge: Cambridge University Press, 1994.

———. *Cassavetes on Cassavetes.* London: Faber and Faber, 2001.

Carr, Caleb. *The Alienist.* New York: Random House, 1994

Catechism of the Catholic Church. New York: Doubleday, 1995.

Changler, Charlotte. *I, Fellini.* New York: Random House, 1995.

Charity, Tom. *John Cassavetes: Lifeworks.* London: Omnibus Press, 2001.

Charyn, Jerome Charyn. *Gangsters & Gold Diggers: Old New York, The Jazz Age, and the Birth of Broadway.* New York: Four Walls Eight Windows, 2003.

Christopher, Nicholas. *Somewhere in the Night: Film Noir and the American City.* New York: Henry Holt and Company, 1997.

Ciment, Michel. *Kazan on Kazan.* New York: The Viking Press, 1974.

Clarens, Carlos, *Crime Movies: The Story of the Gangster Genre in Film from D.W. Griffith to The Godfather and Beyond.* New York: W.W. Norton, 1980.

Clooney, Nick. *The Movies That Changed Us: Reflections on the Screen.* New York: Atria Books, 2002.

Cochran, David. *America Noir: Underground Writers and Filmmakers of the Postwar Era.* Washington, DC: Smithsonian Institution Press, 2000.

Cohen, Hubert I. *Ingmar Bergman: The Art of Confession. Twayne's Filmmakers Series.* New York: Twayne Publishers, 1993.

Cohen, Rich. *Tough Jews: Fathers, Sons, and Gangster Dreams.* New York: Simon & Schuster, 1998.

Connelly, Joe. *Bringing out the Dead.* New York: Vinatage Contemporaries, 1998.

Connelly, Marie Katheryn. *Martin Scorsese: An Analysis of His Feature Films, with a Filmography of His Entire Directorial Career.* Jefferson, NC: McFarland & Company, Inc., 1993.

Cook, Pam. *I Know Where I'm Going BFI Film Classics.* London: BFI Publishing, 2002.

Cooper, Stephen, ed. *The John Fante Reader.* New York: William Morrow, 2002.

Corey, Melinda, and George Ochoa, eds. Includes an essay on Film Preservation by Martin Scorsese. *The American Film Institute Desk Reference*. London: DK, 2002.

Corman, Roger, with Jim Jerome. *How I Made a Hundred Movies in Hollywood and Never Lost a Dime*. New York: Random House, 1990.

Cott, Jonathan. *He Dreams What Is Going on Inside His Head: Ten Years of Writing*. San Francisco, CA: Straight Arrow Books, 1973.

Coughlan, Robert, and the editors of *Time-Life* Books. *Time-Life Library of Art. The World of Michaelangelo 1475–1564*. New York: Time Incorporated, 1966.

Cousins, Mark. *The Story of Film*. New York: Thunder's Mouth Press, 2004.

Cowie, Peter. *Revolution! The Explosion of World Cinema in the Sixties*. New York: Faber and Faber, 2004.

Crabb, Kelly Charles. *The Movie Business: The Definitive Guide to the Legal and Financial Secrets of Getting Your Movie Made*. New York: Simon & Schuster, 2005.

Cramer, Richard Ben. *Joe DiMaggio: The Hero's Life*. New York: Simon & Schuster, 2000.

Cronin, Paul, *On Film-Making: An Introduction to the Craft of the Director*. Foreword by Martin Scorsese. New York: Faber and Faber, 2005.

Cross, Milton, and Karl Kohrs. *The New Milton Cross' Complete Stories of the Great Operas*, revised and enlarged ed. New York: Doubleday & Company, 1957.

Cullen, Jim. *Catholics and the American Dream: Portraits of a Spiritual Quest from the Time of Puritans to the Present*. Franklin, WI: Sheed & Ward, 2001.

Dalai Lama, The. *The Way to Freedom: Core Teachings of Tibetan Buddhism. The Library of Tibet series*. New York: HarperSanFrancisco, 1994.

———. *Awakening the Mind, Lightening the Heart. The Library of Tibet* series. New York: HarperSanFrancisco, 1995.

D'Angelo, Pascal. *Son of Italy*. New York: John Day Co., 1924.

Dannen, Fredric. *Hit Men: Power Brokers and Fast Money Inside the Music Business*, updated ed. New York: Vintage Books, 1991.

Davis, Clive, with James Willwerth. *Clive: Inside the Record Business*. New York: William Morrow & Company, 1974.

Davis, John H. *Mafia Dynasty*. New York: HarperCollins, 1993.

Decherney, Peter. *Hollywood and the Culture Elite: How the Movies Became American*. New York: Columbia University Press, 2005

Delaney, John J. *Pocket Dictionary of Saints*. New York: Image Books, Doubleday, 1983.

Delaney, Samuel R. *Times Square Red, Time Square Blue*. New York: New York University Press, 2001.

D'Epiro, Peter, and Mary Desmond Pinkowish. *Sprezzatura (The Art of Effortless Mastery): 50 Ways Italian Genius Shaped the World*. New York: Anchor Books, 2001.

DeSalvo, Louise. *Breathless: An Asthma Journal*. London: Faber and Faber, 1994; Boston, MA: Beacon Press, 1997.

De Stefano, George. *An Offer We Can't Refuse: The Mafia in the Mind of America*. New York: Faber and Faber, 2006.

Dick, Bernard F. *The Merchant Prince of Poverty Row: Harry Cohn of Columbia Pictures*. Lexington: The University Press of Kentucky, 1993.

Dickie, John. *Cosa Nostra: A History of the Sicilian Mafia*. New York: Palgrave Macmillan, 2004.

Dickos, Andrew. *Street with No Name: A History of the Classic American Film Noir*. Lexington: The University Press of Kentucky, 2002

de Toth, Andre. Foreword by Martin Scorsese. *Fragments: Portraits From the Inside*. London: Faber & Faber, 1996.

di Donato, Pietro. *Christ in Concrete*. Indianapolis, New York: Bobbs-Merrrill Company, 1939.

di Lampedusa, Gieuseppe Tomasi. *The Lepoard*. New York: Everyman's Library, Alfred A. Knopf, 1991. Originally published in Italy as *Il Gattopardo* by Giangiacomo Feltrinelli Editore, 1958.

Dorsky, Nathaniel. *Devotional Cinema*, 2nd ed. Berkeley, CA: Tuumba Press Books, 2005.

Dostoevsky, Fyodor, translated by Richard Pevear and Larissa Volokhonsky. *Notes from the Underground*. New York: Vintage Books. 1999.

———, translated by Constance Garnett. *The Gambler*. New York: Modern Library, 2003.

Dougan, Andy. *Martin Scorsese Close Up*. New York: Thunder's Mouth Press, 1998.

———. *Untouchable: The Unauthorized Biography of Robert De Niro*, 2nd ed. New York: Thunder's Mouth Press, 2002.

Drazin, Charles. *Korda: Britian's Only Movie Mogul*. London: Sidgwick & Jackson, 2002.

Duncan, Paul; *Martin Scorsese*. Harpenden Hertz: Pocket Essentials, 2004.

Dunn, Brad, and Daniel Hood. *New York: The Unknown City*. Vancouver, Canada: Arsenal Pulp Press, 2004.

Durgnat, Raymond. *Durgnat on Film*. London: Faber and Faber, 1976.

Dworkin, Susan. *Double De Palma: A Film Study with Brian De Palma*. New York: Newmarket Press, 1984.

Dylan, Bob. *Chronicles Volume One*. New York: Simon & Schuster, 2004.

Ebert, Roger. *The Great Movies*. New York: Broadway Books, 2002.

Ebert, Roger, and Gene Siskel. *The Future of the Movies: Interviews with Martin Scorsese, Steven Spielberg and George Lucas*. Kansas City, MO: Andrews and McMeel, 1991.

Ehrenstein, David. *The Scorsese Picture*. New York: Birch Lane Press, 1992.

Ehrman, Bart D. *Truth and Fiction in The Da Vinci Code: A Historian Reveals What We Really Know about Jesus, Mary Magalene, and Constantine*. Oxford: Oxford University Press, 2004.

Eisner, Will. *Comics & Sequential Art*. Tamarac, FL: Poorhouse Press, 1985.

———. *Graphic Storytelling & Visual Narrative*. Tamarac, FL: Poorhouse Press, 1996.

Elasaesser, Alexander Horwath, and Noel King, eds. *The Last Great American Picture Show: New Hollywood Cinema in the 1970s*. Amsterdam: Amsterdam University Press, 2004.

Eliot, Marc. *Down 42nd Street: Sex, Money, Culture, and Politics at the Crossroads of the World*. New York: Warner Books, 2001.

Ellis, Edward Robb. *The Epic of New York City: A Narrative History*. New York: Kodansha International, 1997. Originally published, New York: Coward-McCann, 1966.

Ellroy, James. *Destination Morgue! L.A. Tales*. New York: Vintage Books, 2004.

Endo, Shusaku. *Silence*. New York: Taplinger Publishing Company, New York, 1980. First published in 1969 by Momunmenta Nipponica, Tokyo.

English, T. J. *The Westies: Inside New York's Irish Mob*. New York: G.P. Putnam's Sons, 1990.

———. *Paddy Whacked: The Untold Story of the Irish American Gangster*. New York: HarperCollins, 2005.

Epstein, Edward Jay. *The Big Picture: The New Logic of Money and Power in Hollywood*. New York: Random House, 2005.

Estrin, Mark, ed. *Orson Welles: Interviews. Conversations with Filmmakers Series*. Jackson: University Press of Mississippi, 2002.

Ettedgui, Peter. *Production Design & Art Direction. Screencraft* series. Woburn, MA: Focal Press, 1999.

Evanier, David. *Making the Wiseguys Weep: The Jimmy Roselli Story*. London: Methuen Publishing Ltd., 2002.

Eyman, Scott. *Five American Cinematographers: Interviews with Karl Struss, Joseph Ruttenberg, James Wong How, Linwood Dunn, and William H. Clothier. Filmmakers* Series, No. 17. Metuchen, NJ: Scarecrow Press, 1987.

———. *The Speed of Sound: Hollywood and the Talkie Revolution 1926–1930*. New York: Simon & Schuster, 1997.

———. *Print the Legend: The Life and Times of John Ford*. New York: Simon & Schuster, 1999.

Feder, Sid, and Joachim Joesten. *The Luciano Story*. New York: Da Capo, 1994. Originally published in New York, 1954.

Fell, John L. *Film and the Narrative Tradition*. Berkeley: The University of California Press, 1974.

Film Comment. 34(3) (May/June, 1998). Special Issue on Scorsese on the Occasion of His Receiving The Film Society of Lincoln Center Honor in 1998.

Fine, Marshall. *Harvey Keitel: The Art of Darkness* New York: Fromm Int'l, 2000.

Fischer, James A. *Priests: Images, Ideals, and Changing Roles*. New York: Dodd, Mead & Company, 1987.

Fleishman, Avrom. *Narrated Films: Storytelling Situations in Cinema History*. Baltimore, MD: The Johns Hopkins University Press, 1992.

Fonda, Peter. *Don't Tell Dad: A Memoir*. New York: Hyperion, 1998.

Fordham, Joe. "Angels and Demons." *Cinefex* 101 (April 2005): pp. 54–85.

Forgacs, David, and Robert Lumley. *Italian Cultural Studies: An Introduction.* Oxford: Oxford University Press, 1996.

Forster, E.M. *Aspects of the Novel.* New York: Harcourt Brace & Company, 1927.

Fox, Ted. *In the Groove: The People Behind the Music.* New York: St. Martin's Press, 1986.

Frazer, James. *The Golden Bough*, abridged edition. New York: Penguin Books, 1996, first published in 1922.

Freud, Sigmund. *An Outline of Psycho-Analysis.* New York: W.W. Norton, 1949.

Friedman, Lawrence S. *The Cinema of Martin Scorsese.* New York: Continuum, 1997.

Friedman, Lawrence S., and Brent Notbohm. *Steven Spielberg: Interviews. Conversations with Filmmakers Series.* Jackson: University Press of Mississippi, 2000.

Friedrich, Otto. *City of Nets: A Portrait of Hollywood in the 1940s.* New York: Harper & Row, 1986.

Frolick, Billy. *What I Really Want to Do Is Direct: Seven Film School Graduates go to Hollywood.* New York: Dutton, 1996.

Frommer, Myrna Katz, and Harvey Frommer. *It Happened in Manhattan: An Oral History of Life in the City during the Mid-Twentieth Century.* New York: Berkley Books, 2001.

Fuchs, Cynthia, ed. *Spike Lee: Interviews. Conversations with Filmmakers Series.* Jackson: University Press of Mississippi, 2002.

Fuller, Samuel, with Christa Lang Fuller, and Jerome Henry Rudes. *A Third Face: My Tale of Writing, Fighting, and Filmmaking.* Introduction by Martin Scorsese. New York: Alfred A. Knopf, 2002.

Fulton, A.R. *Motion Pictures: The Development of an Art from Silent Films to the Age of Television.* Norman: University of Oklahoma Press, 1960.

Gabler, Neal: *An Empire of Their Own: How the Jews Invented Hollywood.* New York: Crown Publishers, Inc., 1988.

Gado, Frank. *The Passion of Ingmar Bergman.* Durham, NC: Duke University Press, 1986.

Gallagher, Tag. *John Ford: The Man and His Films.* Berkeley: University of California Press, 1986.

———. *The Adventures of Roberto Rossellini: His Life and Films.* New York: Da Capo Press, 1998.

Gambino, Richard. *Blood of My Blood: The Dilemma of the Italian-Americans*, 2nd ed. Canada: Guernica editions (Picas Series No. 7), 2002. New York: Doubleday & Company, Inc., 1974.

———. *Bread and Roses.* New York: Seaview Books, 1981.

Gazzara, Ben. *In the Moment: My Life as an Actor.* New York: Carroll & Graf Publishers, 2004.

Gelmis, Joseph. *The Film Director as Superstar.* New York: Doubleday & Company, 1970.

Gentry, W. Doyle. *Anger-Free: Ten Basic Steps to Managing Your Anger.* New York: William Morrow and Company, Inc., 1999.

George-Warren, Holly, Patricia Romanowski, and Jon Pareles, eds. *The Rolling Stone Encyclopedia of Rock & Roll*, 3rd ed. New York: Fireside, A Rolling Stone Press Book, 2001.

Gerard, Fabien S., T. Jefferson Kline, and Bruce Sklarew, eds. *Bernardo Bertolucci: Interviews. Conversations with Filmmakers Series*. Jackson: University Press of Mississippi, 2000.

Gibbon, Edward. *The Decline and Fall of the Roman Empire*. New York: Modern Library, 2003.

Gilbey, Ryan. *It Don't Worry Me: The Revolutionary American Films of the Seventies*. New York: Faber and Faber, Inc., 2003.

Ginsborg, Paul. *Italy and Its Discontents: Family, Civil Society, State 1980–2001*. New York: Palgrave Macmillan, 2003.

Giovino, Andrea, with Gary Brozek. *Divorced from the Mob: My Journey from Organized Crime to Independent Woman*. New York: Carroll & Graf, 2004.

Gitlin, Todd. *The Sixties: Years of Hope, Days of Rage*, revised ed. New York: Bantam Books. Originally published, New York: Bantam Books, 1987.

Gomery, Douglas. *Shared Pleasures: A History of Movie Presentation n the United States*. Madison: The University of Wisconsin Press, 1992.

Goodwin, Michael, and Naomi Wise. *On the Edge: The Life & Times of Francis Coppola*. New York: William Morrow and Company, 1989.

Gottlieb, Sidney, ed. *Hitchcock on Hitchcock: Selected Writings and Interviews*. Berkeley: University of California Press, 1997.

———. *Roberto Rossellini's Rome Open City*. Cambridge: Cambridge University Press, 2004.

Grady, Ellen, *Blue Guide: Sicily*, 6th ed. New York: W.W. Norton, 2003.

Grant, Barry Keith, ed. *Film Genre Reader*. Austin: University of Texas Press, 1986.

Grant, Michael. *History of Rome*. London: Faber and Faber, 1979.

Gray, Beverly. *Roger Corman: An Unauthorized Biography of the Godfather of Indie Filmmaking*. Los Angeles, CA: Renaissance Books, 2000.

Gregory, Mollie. *Women Who Run the Show: How a Brilliant and Creative New Generation of Women Stormed Hollywood*. New York: St. Martin's Press, 2002.

Grieveson, Lee, Esther Sonnet, and Peter Standfield, eds. *Mob Culture: Hidden Histories of the American Gangster Film*. New Brunswick, NJ: Rutgers University Press, 2005.

Grist, Leighton. *The Films of Martin Scorsese 1963–77: Authorship and Context*. New York: St. Martin's Press, 2000.

Groia, Philip. *They All Sang on the Corner: A Second Look at New York City's Rhythm and Blues Vocal Groups*. Port Jefferson, New York: Phillie Dee Enterprises, Inc., 1983.

Guralnick, Peter, Robert Santelli, Holly George-Warren, and Christopher John Farley, eds. *Martin Scorsese Presents the Blues*. New York: Amistad, an imprint of HarperCollins, 2003.

Hack, Richard. *Hughes: The Private Diaries, Memos and Letters: The Definitive Biography of the First American Billionaire.* Beverly Hills, CA: New Millennium Press, 2001.

Haden-Guest, Anthony. *The Last Party: Studio 54, Disco, and the Culture of the Night.* New York: William Morrow and Company, Inc., 1997.

Haines, Richard W. *Technicolor Movies: The History of Dye Transfer Printing.* Jefferson, NC: McFarland & Company, 1993.

Hamblett, Charles. *The Hollywood Cage.* New York: Hart Publishing Company, Inc., 1969. Originally published as *Who Killed Mariyln Monroe?* 1966.

Hamill, Pete. *Why Sinatra Matters.* Boston, MA: Little Brown and Company, 1998.

———. *Downtown: My Manhattan.* New York: Little, Brown and Company, 2004.

Harpole, Charles, general ed. *History of the American Cinema, Vol. 1: The Emergence of Cinema: The American Screen to 1907.* Charles Musser. Berkeley: University of California Press, 1990.

———. *History of the American Cinema, Vol. 2: The Transformation of Cinema 1907–1915.* Eileen Bowser. Berkeley: University of California Press, 1990.

———. *History of the American Cinema, Vol. 3: An Evening's Entertainment: The Age of the Silent Feature Picture, 1915–1928.* Richard Koszarski. Berkeley: University of California Press, 1994.

———. *History of the American Cinema, Vol. 4: Talkies: American Cinema's Transition to Sond, 1926–1934.* Donald Crafton. Berkeley: University of California Press, 1999.

———. *History of the American Cinema, Vol. 5: Grand Design: Hollywood as a Modern Business Enterprise, 1930-1939.* Tino Balio. Berkeley: University of California Press, 1996.

———. *History of the American Cinema, Vol. 6: Boom and Bust: American Cinema in the 1940s.* Thomas Schatz. Berkeley: University of California Press, 1999.

———. *History of the American Cinema, Vol. 8: The Sixties: 1960–1969.* Paul Monaco. Berkeley: University of California Press, 2001.

———. *History of the American Cinema, Vol. 9: Lost Illusions: American Cinema in the Shadow of Watergate and Vienam, 1970–1979.* David A. Cook. Berkeley: University of California Press, 2000.

———. *History of the American Cinema, Vol. 10: A New Pot of Gold: Hollywood under the Electric Rainbow, 1980–1989.* Stephen Prince. Berkeley: University of California Press, 2000.

Hart, John. *The Art of the Storyboard: Storyboarding for Film, TV, and Animation.* Boston, MA: Focal Press, 1999.

Harvey, Stephen. *Directed by Vincente Minnelli.* New York: The Museum of Modern Art, Harper & Row Publishers, 1989.

Hay, James. *Popular Film Culture in Fascist Italy: The Passing of the Rex.* Bloomington: Indiana University Press, 1987.

Hayes, Dade, and Jonathan Bing. *Open Wide: How Hollywood Box Office Became a National Obsession.* New York: Miramax Books, 2004.

Hedin, Raymond. *Married to the Church*. Bloomington & Indianapolis: Indiana University Press, 1995.

Hendler, Herb. *Year by Year in the Rock Era*. New York: Praeger, 1983.

Hess, Herman. *Mafia & Mafiosi: Origin, Power and Myth*. New York: New York University Press, 1998.

Heuring, David, and Nora Lee. "This Is the City: New York Stories." *American Cinematographer* 70(3) (March 1989): pp. 54–62.

Hickenlooper, George. *Reel Conversations: Candid Interviews with Film's Foremost Directors and Critics*. New York: Citadel Press, 1991.

Higham, Charles. *Hollywood Cameramen: Sources of Light*. *Cinema One* series. Bloomington: Indiana University Press, 1970.

Hill, Gregg, and Gina. *On the Run: A Mafia Childhood*. New York: Warner Books, 2004.

Hill, Henry, as told to Gus Russo. *Gangsters and Goodfellas: The Mob, Witness Protection, and Life on the Run*. New York: M. Evans and Company, Inc., 2005.

Hillier, Jim, ed. *Cahiers du Cinéma: The 1950s. Neo-Realism, Hollywood, New Wave*. Cambridge, MA: Harvard University Press, 1985.

———. *Cahiers du Cinéma: The 1960s. New Wave, New Cinema, Reevaluating Hollywood*. Cambridge, MA: Harvard University Press, 1986.

Hirsch, Foster. *Film Noir: The Dark Side of the Screen*. New York: Da Capo,1981.

———. *A Method to Their Madness: The History of the Actor's Studio*. New York: W.W. Norton and Company, 1984.

Hoberman, J. *The Dream Life: Movies, Media, and the Mythology of the Sixties*. New York: The New Press, 2003.

Hogan, Ron. *The Stewardess is Flying the Plane! American Films of the 1970s*. New York: Bulfinch Press, 2005.

Holden, Amanda, with Nicholas Kenyon, and Stephen Walsh. *The Penguin Opera Guide*. London: Penguin, 1996.

Hollywood Reporter, The. "New York Special Issue: Specs and the City" (June 2003).

Holy Bible, The: King James Version. New York: Ballantine Books, 1991.

Hoobler, Dorothy, and Thomas. *Lost Highways: A Map of Neo-Noir*. New York: Limelight Editions, 1991.

———. *The Italian American Family Album*. New York: Oxford University Press, 1994.

Horton, Andrew. *Henry Bumstead and the World of Hollywood Art Direction*. Austin: University of Texas Press, 2003.

Hoskyns, Barney. *Across the Great Divide: The Band and America*. New York: Hyperion, 1993.

House, Adrian. *Francis of Assisi: A Revolutionary Life*. Great Britain: HiddenSpring, 2001.

Hunter, Jack, ed. *Moonchild: The Films of Kenneth Anger*. New York: Creation Books, 2002.

Imago: The Federation of European Cinematographers. *Making Pictures: A Century of European Cinematography*. New York: Harry N. Abrams, Inc., 2003.

Isacoff, Stuart. *Temperament: The Idea That Solved Music's Greatest Riddle*. New York: Alfred A. Knopf, 2001.

Jacobs, Diane. *Hollywood Renaissance*. South Brunswick and New York: A.S. Barnes & Company, Inc., 1977.

Jackson, Kenneth T., ed. *The Encyclopedia of New York City*. New Haven: Yale University Press, New York, The New York Historical Society, 1995.

Jackson, Kenneth T., and David S. Dunbar eds. *Empire City: New York Through the Centuries*. New York: Columbia University Press, 2002.

Jackson, Kevin, ed. *Schrader on Schrader & Other Writings*. London: Faber and Faber, 1990.

James, David E., ed. *Jonas Mekas & The New York Underground*. Princeton, NJ: Princeton University Press, 1992.

Janson, J.W., and Anthony F. Janson. *History of Art*, 6th ed. New York: Harry N. Abbrams, Inc., Publishers, 2001

Jenkins, Philip. *Decade of Nightmares: The End of the Sixties and the Making of Eighties America*. New York: Oxford University Press, 2006.

Johnson, Paul. *A History of the American People*. New York: HarperPerennial, 1997.

Johnson, Paul. *The Renaissance: A Short History*. New York: A Modern Library Chronicles Book, The Modern Library, 2000.

Jones, David Richard. *Great Directors at Work: Stanislavsky, Brecht, Kazan. Brook Books*. Berkeley: University of California Press, 1986.

Kashner, Sam, and Jennifer MacNair. *The Bad & the Beautiful: Hollywood in the Fifties*. New York: W.W. Norton & Company, 2002.

Katz, Robert. *The Battle for Rome: The Germans, the Allies, the Partisans, and the Pope September 1943–June 1944*. New York: Simon & Schuster, 2003.

Katz, Steven D. *Film Directing Shot by Shot: Visualizing from Concept to Screen*. Studio City, CA: Michael Wiese Productions, 1991.

Kaufman, Lloyd, with Adam Jahnke, and Trent Haaga. *Make Your Own Damn Movie! Secrets of a Renegade Director*. New York: St. Martin's Griffin, 2003.

Kazan, Elia. *A Life*. New York: Alfred A. Knopf, 1988.

Kazantzakis, Nikos. *The Last Temptation of Christ*. New York: Simon & Schuster, 1960.

Kazin, Alfred. *A Walker in the City*. Orlando, FL: Harcourt, 1997.

Kelly, Mary Pat. *Martin Scorsese: The First Decade*. New York: Redgrave Publishing Company, 1980.

———. *Martin Scorsese: A Journey*. New York: Thunder's Mouth Press, 1991.

Kelly, Sean, and Rosemary Rogers. *Saints Preserve Us! Everything You Need to Know about Every Saint You'll Ever Need*. New York: Random House, 1993.

Kertzer, David. *Prisoner of the Vatican: The Pope's Secret Plot to Capture Rome from the New Italian State*. Boston, MA: Houghton Mifflin Company, 2004.

Keyser, Les. *Martin Scorsese*. New York: Twayne Publishers, 1992.

Kezich, Tullio. *Federico Fellini: His Life and Work*. New York: Faber and Faber, 2006.

King, Geoff. *New Hollywood Cinema: An Introduction*. New York: Columbia University Press, 2002.

King, Ross. *Michelangelo and the Pope's Ceiling.* New York: Penguin Books, 2003.

Kitses, Jim. *Horizons West: Anthony Mann, Budd Boetticher, Sam Peckinpah: Studies of Authorship within the Western. Cinema One* series. Bloomington: Indiana University Press, 1970. New edition: *Horizon's West: Directing the Western from John Ford to Clint Eastwood.* London: BFI Publishing, 2004.

Kline, T. Jefferson. *Bertolucci's Dream Loom: A Psychoanalytic Study of Cinema.* Amherst: The University of Massachusetts Press, 1987.

Knapp, Laurence F., ed. *Brian De Palma: Interviews. Conversations with Filmmakers Series.* Jackson: University Press of Mississippi, 2003.

Knickerbocker, Diedrich. *A History of New York from the Beginning of the World to the End of the Dutch Dynasty.* Philadelphia, PA: Lea & Blanchard, 1839.

Knight, Arthur. *The Liveliest Art: A Panoramic History of the Movies.* New York: The Macmillan Company, 1957.

Kodak. *Basic Production Techniques for Motion Pictures.* Rochester, NY: Eastman Kodak Company, 1971.

Kolker, Robert. *A Cinema of Loneliness: Penn, Stone, Spielberg, Scorsese, Spielberg, Altman,* 3rd ed. Oxford: Oxford University Press, 2000.

———. *Bernardo Bertolucci.* New York: Oxford University Press, 1985.

Kotkin, Joel. *The City: A Global History.* New York: The Modern Library, 2005.

Kouvaros, George. *Where Does it Happen? John Cassavetes and Cinema at the Breaking Point.* Minneapolis: University of Minnesota Press, 2004.

Kozloff, Sarah. *Invisible Storytellers: Voice-Over Narration in American Fiction Film.* Berkeley: University of California Press, 1998.

———. *Overhearing Film Dialogue.* Berkeley: University of California Press, 2000.

Krämer, Peter. *The New Hollywood: From Bonnie and Clyde to Start Wars.* London: Wallflower Press, 2005.

Krohn, Bill. *Hitchcock at Work.* New York: Phaidon, 2000.

Kubly, Herber, and the editors of *Life. Italy.* New York: Time Incorporated, 1965.

Lamb, Wally. *I Know This Much Is True.* New York: Regan Books, 1998.

La Motta, with Joseph Carter, and Peter Savage. *Raging Bull: My Story.* New York: De Capo Press, 1997.

Landy, Marcia. *Italian Film.* Cambridge, UK: Cambridge University Press, 2000.

Lanzoni, Rémi Fournier. *French Cinema: From Its Beginnings to the Present.* New York: Continuum, 2002.

Laskin, Emily J., editorial director, William Horrigan and Greg Beal, eds. *The American Film Institute Guide to College Course in Film and Television,* 8th ed. Introduction by Martin Scorsese. New York: Arco, 1990.

Laura, Ernesto G. *Comedy Italian Style.* Rome, Italy: National Association of Motion Pictures and Affiliated Industries.

Laurino, Maria. *Were You Always an Italian? Ancestors and Other Icons of Italian America.* New York: W.W. Norton & Company, 2001.

Lazar, David, ed. *Michael Powell Interviews. Conversations with Filmmakers Series.* Jackson: University Press of Mississippi, 2003.

Leaming, Barbara. *Orson Welles: A Biography.* New York: Viking, 1985.

Leider, Emily W. *Dark Lover: The Life and Death of Rudolph Valentino*. New York: Faber and Faber, 2003.

Lev, Peter. *American Films of the '70s: Conflicting Visions*. Austin: University of Texas Press, 2000.

Levi, Carlo. *Christ Stopped at Eboli*. New York: Farrar, Straus, and Giroux, 1963.

Levy, Shawn. *King of Comedy: The Life and Art of Jerry Lewis*. New York: St. Martin's Press, 1996.

Lewis, C.S. *The Screwtape Letters*. New York: HarperSanFransisco, 2001. Originally published in 1942.

———. *Mere Christianity*. New York: HarperSanFransisco, 2001. Originally published in 1953.

Lewis, Jerry. *The Total Film-Maker*. New York: Warner Paperback Library, 1973.

Lewis, Jon. *Whom God Wishes to Destroy: Francis Coppola and the New Hollywood*. Durham: Duke University Press, 1995.

Liehm, Mira. *Passion and Defiance: Film in Italy from 1942 to the Present*. Berkeley: University of California Press, 1984.

Lindgren, Ernest. *The Art of the Film*. New York: The Macmillan Company, 1963.

Lindsay, Vachel. *The Art of the Motion Picture. Modern Library: The Movies*, Martin Scorsese, Series Editor. New York: The Modern Library, 2000. Originally published, New York: Macmillan, 1915.

Lippy, Tod, ed., John Boorman, and Walter Donohue, exec. eds. *Projections 11: New York Film-Makers on New York Film-Making*. London: Faber and Faber, 2000.

Lipton, Lenny. *Independent Film-Making*. San Francisco, CA: Straight Arrow Books, 1972.

Lloyd, Norman. *Stages: Of Life in Theatre, Film and Television*. New York: Limelight, 1993.

LoBrutto, Vincent. *Selected Takes: Film Editors on Editing*. New York: Praeger, 1991.

———. *By Design: Interviews with Film Production Designers*. Westport, CT: Praeger, 1992.

———. *Sound-On-Film: Interviews with Creators of Film Sound*. Westport CT: Praeger, 1994.

———. *Stanley Kubrick: A Biography*. New York: Donald I. Fine, 1997.

———. *Principal Photography: Interviews with Feature Film Cinematographers*. Westport, CT: Praeger, 1999.

———. *The Encyclopedia of American Independent Filmmaking*. Westport, CT: Praeger, 2002.

———. *The Filmmaker's Guide to Production Design*. New York: Allworth Press, 2002.

———. *Becoming Film Literate: The Art and Craft of Motion Pictures*. Praeger: Westport, CT: Greenwood Press, 2005.

Logan, John. *The Aviator: A Screenplay*. New York: Miramax Books, 2004.

Lopate, Phillip. *Totally Tenderly Tragically: Essays and Criticism from a Lifelong Love Affair with the Movies*. New York: Anchor Books, 1998.

———. *Waterfront: A Journey around Manhattan*. New York: Crown Publishers, 2004.

Lopez, Donald, Jr., ed. *Buddist Scriptures*. New York: Penguin Books, 2004

Lourdeaux, Lee. *Italian and Irish Filmmakers in America: Ford, Capra, Coppola and Scorsese*. Philadelphia, PA: Temple University Press, 1990.

Lowes, John Livingston Lowes. *The Road to Xanadu: A Study in the Ways of the Imagination*. Boston, MA: Houghton Mifflin Company, Sentry edition. First published in 1927.

Lunn, Martin. *Da Vinci Code Decoded*. New York: The Disinformation Company Ltd., 2004.

MacCabe, Colin. *Godard: A Portrait of the Artist at Seventy*. New York: Farrar, Straus, and Giroux, 2003.

MacCann, Richard Dyer, ed. *Film: A Montage of Theories*. New York: E.P. Dutton & Company, Inc., 1966.

MacDonald, Scott. *Cinema 16: Documents toward a History of the Film Society*. Philadelphia, PA: Temple University Press, 2002.

Macgowan, Kenneth. *Behind the Screen: The History and Techniques of the Motion Picture*. New York: A Delta Book, 1965.

Mackendrick, Alexander, ed. Paul Cronin. *On Film-Making: An Introduction to the Craft of the Director*. New York: Faber and Faber, 2004.

MacLusky, Julie. *Is There Life After Film School? In Depth Advice from Industry Insiders*. New York: Continuum, 2003.

Magid, Ron. "Visualizing a Vintage Vegas." *American Cinematographer* 76(11) (November 1995): p. 43.

Magueijo, João. *Faster than the Speed of Light: The Story of a Scientific Speculation*. New York: Perseus Publishing, 2002.

Makower, Joel. *Woodstock: The Oral History*. New York: Doubleday, 1989.

Mangione, Jerre, and Ben Morreale. *La Storia: Five Centuries of the Italian-American Experience*. New York: HarperCollins, 1992.

Mannoni, Laurent. *The Great Art of Light and Shadow: Archaeology of the Cinema*. Exeter, Devon: University of Exeter Press, 2000.

Manoogian, Haig P. *The Film-Makers Art*. New York: Basic Books, Inc., 1966.

Marchus, Greil. *Lipstick Traces: A Secret History of the Twentieth Century*. Cambridge, MA: Harvard University Press, 1989.

Marco, Phil. "Honoring the Ceremony of the Sand Mandala." *American Cinematographer* 79(2) (February 1998): pp. 50–51.

Marcus, Millicent. *After Fellini: National Cinema in the Postmodern Age*. Baltimore, MD: The Johns Hopkins University Press, 2002.

Marwick, Arthur. *The Sixties: Cultural Revolution in Britain, France, Italy, and the United States, c.1958–c.1974*. New York: Oxford University Press, 1998.

Marx, Arthur. *Everybody Loves Somebody Sometimes (Especially Himself): The Story of Dean Martin and Jerry Lewis*. New York: Hawthorn Books, Inc., 1974.

Mascelli, Joseph V., *The Five C's of Cinematography: Motion Picture Filming Techniques*. Los Angeles, CA: Silman-James Press. First published in 1965.

Mason, Fran. *American Gangster Cinema: From Little Caesar to Pulp Fiction*. Hampshire: Palgrave Macmillan, 2002.

Mast, Gerald. *Howard Hawks: Storyteller.* New York: Oxford University Press, 1982.

McBride, Joseph. *Hawks on Hawks.* Berkeley: University of California Press, 1982.

———. *Frank Capra: The Catastrophe of Success.* New York: Simon & Schuster, 1992.

———. *Searching for John Ford: A Life.* New York: St. Martin's Press, 2001.

McCarthy, Todd. *Howard Hawks: The Grey Fox of Hollywood.* New York: Grove Press, 1997.

McCarthy, Todd, and Charles Flynn, eds. *Kings of the B's: Working within the Hollywood System: An Anthology of Film History and Criticism.* New York: E.P. Dutton & Company, Inc., 1975.

McCloud, Scott. *Understanding Comics: The Invisible Art.* New York: HarperPerennial, 1994.

McFarlaine, Brian. *The Encyclopedia of British Film.* London: Methuen Publishing, 2003.

McGinn, Colin. *The Power of Movies: How Screen and Mind Interact.* New York: Pantheon Books, 2005.

McGilligan, Patrick. *Alfred Hitchcock: A Life in Darkness and Light.* New York: Regan Books, 2003.

McKay, Keith. *Robert De Niro: The Hero Behind the Mask.* New York: St. Martin's Press, 1986.

McKee, Robert. *Story: Substance, Structure, Style, and the Principles of Screenwriting.* New York: Regan Books, 1997.

McManus, James. *Positively Fifth Street: Murderers, Cheetahs, and Binion's World Series of Poker.* New York: Farrar, Straus, and Giroux, 2003.

McNeil, Legs, and Gillian McCain. *Please Kill Me: The Uncensored Oral History of Punk.* New York: Grove Press, 1996.

Medavoy, Mike, with Josh Young. *You're Only as Good as Your Next One: 100 Great Films, 100 Good Films, and 100 for Which I Should be Shot.* New York: Pocket Books, 2002.

Mekas, Jonas. *Movie Journal: The Rise of a New American Cinema, 1959–1971.* New York: The Macmillan Company, 1972.

Meltzer, Richard. *The Aesthetics of Rock.* New York: Da Capo Press, 1987. First published New York: Something Else Press, 1970.

Middleton, Darren J. N. *Scandalizing Jesus? Kazantzakis's The Last Temptation of Christ Fifty Years On.* New York: Continuum, 2005.

Miles, Barry. *Hippie.* New York: Sterling Publishing, 2005.

Miles, Jack. *Christ: A Crisis in the Life of God.* New York: Vintage Books, 2001.

Miliora, Maria T. *The Scorsese Psyche on Screen: Roots of Themes and Characters in the Films.* Jefferson, NC: McFarland & Company, 2004.

Miller, James. *Flowers in the Dustbin: The Rise of Rock and Roll 1947–1977.* New York: Simon & Schuster, 1999.

Milne, Tom, translator and commentator. *Godard on Godard.* New York: The Viking Press, 1972.

Monaco, James. *American Film Now: The People, the Power, the Money, the Movies.* New York: Oxford University Press, 1979.

Moramarco, Federico and Stephen. *Italian Pride: 101 Reasons to Be Proud You're Italian*. New York: Citadel Press, 2000.

Mordden, Ethan. *The Hollywood Studios: House Style in the Golden Age of Movies*. New York: A Fireside Book published by Simon & Schuster, Inc., 1989.

———. *Medium Cool: Movies of the 1960s*. New York: Alfred A. Knopf, 1990.

Morgan, David. "A Remake that Can't Miss: *Cape Fear*." *American Cinematographer* 72(10) (October, 1991): pp. 34–40.

Morris, Charles R. *American Catholic: The Saints and Sinners Who Built America's Most Powerful Church*. New York; Vintage Books, 1997.

Morrissey, Jake. *The Genius in the Design: Bernini. Borromini, and the Rivalry That Transformed Rome*. New York: William Morrow, 2005.

Morthland, John, ed. *Mainlines, Blood Feasts, and Bad Taste: A Lester Bangs Reader*. New York: Anchor Books, 2003.

Mowbraly, Jay Henry, compiler. *Italy's Great Horror of Earthquake and Tidal Wave*. No publishing or date information available.

Naremore, James. *The Films of Vincente Minnelli*. Cambridge: Cambridge University Press, 1993.

National Film Preservation Foundation. *The Film Preservation Guide: The Basics for Archives, Libraries, and Museums*. San Francisco, CA: The National Film Preservation Foundation, 2004.

Nelson, Al P., and Mel R. Jones. *A Silent Siren Song: The Aitken Brothers' Hollywood Odyssey, 1905–1926*. New York: Cooper Square Press, 2001.

Nyce, Ben. *Scorsese Up Close: A Study of the Films. Filmmakers Series, No. 105*. Lanham, MD: Scarecrow Press, 2004.

O'Brien, Geoffrey. *The Phantom Empire*. New York: W.W. Norton & Company, 1993.

———. *The Times Square Story*. New York: W.W. Norton & Company, 1998.

Oliver, Paul. *Screening the Blues: Aspects of the Blues Tradition*. New York: Da Capo, 1989. Originally published, London: Cassell, 1968.

Orlando, Leoluc. *Fighting the Mafia and Renewing Sicilian Culture*. San Fransisco, CA: Encounter Books, 2001.

Oumano, Ellen. *Film Forum: Thirty-Five Top Filmmakers Discuss Their Craft*. New York: St. Martin's Press, 1985.

Pagels, Elaine. *The Origin of Satan*. New York: Vintage Books, 1995.

Palahniuk, Chuck. *Stranger than Fiction*. New York: Doubleday, 2004.

Papaleo, Joseph. *Italian Stories*. Chicago, IL: Dalkey Archive Press, 2002.

Pasolini, Pier Paolo, Louise K. Barnett, ed. *Heretical Empiricism*. Bloomington: Indiana University Press, 1988.

Pavlus, John (interview with Robert Richardson). "High Life: Robert Richardson, ASC Exploits a Modern Method to Craft a Classic Look for *The Aviator*, an Epic that Details the Ambitions that Drove Howard Hughes." *American Cinematographer* 86(1) (January 2005): pp. 38–53.

Pellegrino, Frank. *Rao's Cookbook: Over 100 Years of Italian Home Cooking*. New York: Random House, 1998.

Perkins, Roy, and Martin Stollery. *British Film Editors: "The Heart of the Movie."* London: BFI Publishing, 2004.

Perry, Charles. *The Haight-Ashbury: A History.* New York: Vintage Books, 1985.

Phillips, Gene D., ed. *Stanley Kubrick: Interviews. Conversations with Filmmakers Series.* Jackson: University Press of Mississippi, 2001.

———. *Godfather: The Intimate Francis Ford Coppola.* Lexington: The University Press of Kentucky, 2004.

Phillips, Julia. *You'll Never Eat Lunch in This Town Again.* New York: Random House, 1991.

Pierson, John, with Kevin Smith. *Spike, Mike, Slackers & Dykes: A Guided Tour Across a Decade of American Independent Cinema.* New York: Hyperion, 1995.

Pileggi, Nicholas. *Wise Guy: Life in a Mafia Family.* New York: Pocket Books, a division of Simon & Schuster, 1987.

———. *Casino.* New York: Pocket Star Books, a division of Simon & Schuster, Inc., 1996.

Pileggi, Nicholas, and Martin Scorsese. *Casino* (screenplay). London: Faber and Faber, 1996.

Pincus, Edward. *The Filmmaker's Handbook.* New York: New American Library, 1969.

Pizzello, Stephen. "Ace in the Hole: Director Martin Scorsese Recruits a Crack Production Team, Including Academy Award-Winning Cinematographer Robert Richardson, ASC, to Help Create His Complex Las Vegas Crime Epic, "Casino." *American Cinematographer* 76(11) (November, 1995): pp. 34–46.

———. "Kundun: A Kinder, Gentler Scorsese Film." *American Cinematographer* 79(2) (February 1998): pp. 58–66.

———. "Raising Tibet in the Desert. *American Cinematographer* 79(2) (February 1998) pp. 38–57.

Poland, Larry W., *The Last Temptation of Hollywood.* Redlands, CA: Mastermedia International: Redlands, 1988.

Powell, Michael. *A Life in the Movies: An Autobiography.* New York: Alfred A. Knopf,1987.

———. Introduction by Martin Scorsese. *Million Dollar Movie.* New York: Random House, 1995.

Prada, Fondazione. *Tribeca Talks.* Milan, Italy: Progetto Prada Arte, 2004.

Premiere. Special Issue, *New York and the Movies*, 1994.

Price, Richard. *Three Screenplays: The Color of Money, Sea of Love, Night and the City.* New York: Grove Press, 1993.

Pugliese, Stanislao G., Editor. *Frank Sinatra: History, Identity, and Italian American Culture*, New York: Palgrave Macmillan, 2004

Puzo, Mario. *The Fortunate Pilgrim.* New York: The Ballantine Publishing Group, 1997. Originally published, New York: Atheneum Books, 1964.

———. *The Godfather.* New York: G.P. Putnam's Sons, 1969.

————. *Inside Las Vegas*. New York: Grosset & Dunlap, 1977.

————. *The Last Don*. New York: Ballantine, 1996.

————. *Omerta*. New York: Ballantine Books, 2000.

————, completed by Carol Gino. *The Family*. New York: Regan Books, 2001.

Pye, Michael, and Lynda Myles. *The Movie Brats: How the Film Generation Took Over Hollywood* New York: Holt, Rinehart, and Winston, 1979.

Raab, Selwyn. *Five Families: The Rise, Decline and Resurgence of American's Most Powerful Mafia Empires*. New York: St. Martin's Press, 2005.

Rabinovitz, Lauren. *Points of Resistance: Women, Power & Politics in the New York Avant Garde Cinema, 1943–71*. Urbana: University of Illinois Press, 1991.

Rainsberger, Todd. *James Wong How, Cinematographer*. San Diego, CA: A.S. Barnes & Company, Inc., 1981.

Randall, Stephen, ed., and the editors of *Playboy Magazine*. *The Playboy Interviews: The D Directors*. Milwaukee, OR: M Press, 2006.

Rawlence, Christopher: *The Missing Reel: The Untold Story of the Lost Inventor of Moving Pictures*. New York: Atheneum, 1990.

Reitman, Dr. Ben. *Sister of the Road: The Autobiography of Boxcar Bertha*. Edinburgh, Scotland: AK Press/Nabat, 2002.

Repeppetto, Thomas. *American Mafia: A History of It's Rise to Power*. New York: Henry Holt and Company, 2004.

Riley, Robin. *Film, Faith, and Cultural Conflict: The Case of Martin Scorsese's The Last Temptation of Christ*. Westport, CT: Praeger, 2003.

Riordan. James. *Stone: A Biography of Oliver Stone: The Controversies, Excesses, and Exploits of a Radical Filmmaker*. New York: Hyperion, 1995.

Robb, Peter. *Midnight in Sicily*. New York: Vintage Books, 1996.

Robinson, David, Foreword by Martin Scorsese. *From Peep Show to Palace: The Birth of American Film*. New York: Columbia University Press, 1996.

Rosenbaum, Jonathan. *Moving Places: A Life at the Movies*. New York: Harper & Row, 1980.

Rosenbaum, Ralph, and Robert Karen. *When the Shooting Stops . . . the Cutting Begins*. New York: The Viking Press, 1979.

Rossellini, Isabella. *Some of Me*. New York: Random House, 1997.

————. *In the Name of the Father, the Daughter and the Holy Spirits:Remembering Roberto Rossellini*. Munich, Germany: Schirmer/Mosel, 2006.

Rossellini, Roberto, with Aprà, Adriano, ed. *My Method: Writings & Interviews*. New York: Marsilo Publishers, 1992.

Rotha, Paul, Richard Griffith. *The Till Now: A Survey of World Cinema*. Hamlyn House, London: Spring Books, 1967. Originally published by Jonathan Cape, London, 1930.

Roud, Richard. *Godard*. *Cinema One* series. Bloomington: Indiana University Press, 1967.

————. *A Passion for Films: Henri Langlois and the Cinémathèque Francaise*. New York: The Viking Press, 1983.

Sanders, James. *Celluloid Skyline: New York and the Movies.* New York: Alfred A. Knopf, 2001.

Sangster, Jim. *Scorsese.* London: Virgin Books, 2002.

Sanowski, Jeffrey A. *Italian Cuisine: The Gourmet's Companion.* New York: John Wiley & Sons, Inc., 1997.

Saramago, José. *The Gospel According to Jesus Christ.* San Diego, CA: Harcourt Brace & Company, 1994.

Sante, Luc. *Low Life.* New York: Vintage Books, 1992.

Santelli, Robert. *The Bob Dylan Scrapbook 1956–1966: The Companion Volume to No Direction Home: Bob Dylan, A Martin Scorsese Picture.* New York: Simon & Schuster, 2005.

Santini, Loretta. *Vatican City.* Italy: Plurigraf Narmi-Temi, 1983.

Sarris, Andrew. *The American Cinema: Directors and Directions* 1929–1968. New York: Da Capo Press edition with original dates and deaths amended, 1996. Originally published in 1968.

———. *Interviews with Film Directors.* New York: Avon Books, 1969.

———. *Confessions of a Cultist: On the Cinema, 1955/1969.* New York: Touchstone, 1971.

Savage, Jon. *England's Dreaming: Anarchy, Sex Pistols, Punk Rock, and Beyond.* New York: St. Martin's Press, 1992.

Schaefer, Dennis, with Larry Salvato. *Masters of Light: Conversations with Contemporary Cinematographers.* Berkeley: University of California Press, 1984.

Schaefer, Eric. *"Bold! Daring! Shocking! True! A History of Exploitation Films, 1919–1959.* Durham & London: Duke University Press, 1999.

Schatz, Thomas. *The Genius of the System: Hollywood Filmmaking in the Studio Era.* New York: Pantheon Books, 1988.

Schickel, Richard. *D.W. Griffith: An American Life.* New York: Limelight Editions, 1984.

———. *Elia Kazan: A Biography.* New York: Harper Collins, 2005.

Schirripa, Steven R., and Charles Fleming. *The Goomba's Book of Love: How to LOVE like a Guy from the Neighborhood.* New York: Clarkson Potter Publishers, 2003.

Schrader, Paul. *Transcendental Style in Film: Ozu Bresson, Dreyer.* New York: Da Capo Press, 1988. First published Berkeley: University of California Press, 1972.

———. *Taxi Driver* (screenplay). London: Faber and Faber, 1990.

———. *Bringing Out the Dead* (screenplay). London: Faber and Faber, 2000.

Schulberg, Budd. *Waterfront.* New York: Donald I. Fine, Inc., 1955.

———. *On the Waterfront: The Final Shooting Script.* Hollywood: Samuel French, 1980.

Schulman, Bruce J. *The Seventies: The Great Shift in American Culture, Society, and Politics.* New York: The Free Press, 2001

Schumacher, Michael. *Francis Ford Coppola: A Filmmaker's Life.* New York: Crown Publishers, 1999.

Schwam, Stephanie, ed. Martin Scorsese Series Editor Modern Library: *The Movies. The Making of 2001: A Space Odyssey.* New York: The Modern Library, 2000.

Scorsese, Catherine, with Georgia Downard. *Italianamerican: The Scorsese Family Cookbook.* New York: Random House, 1996.

Scorsese, Martin. *Gangs of New York: Making the Movie: Including the Complete Screenplay.* New York: Miramax Books, 2002.

Scorsese, Martin, and Jay Cocks. *The Age of Innocence: A Portrait of the Film Based on the Novel by Edith Wharton.* New York: Newmarket Press, 1993.

———. *The Age of Innocence: The Shooting Script.* New York: Newmarket Press, 1995.

Scorsese, Martin, and Nicholas Pileggi. *GoodFellas* (screenplay). London, Boston: Faber and Faber, 1990.

Scorsese, Martin, and Michael Henry Wilson. *A Personal Journey with Martin Scorsese through American Movies.* New York: Miramax Books, Hyperion, 1997.

Scottoline, Lisa. *Killer Smile.* New York: HarperCollins Publishers, 2004.

Sean. *The Cinema Effect.* Cambridge, MA: The MIT Press, 2004.

Segal, Gillian, Zoe. *New York Characters.* New York: W.W. Norton & Company, 2001.

Seltzer, Sallie. "Cutting Kundun." *American Cinematographer* 79(2) (February 1998): p. 48.

Sennett, Robert S. *Setting the Scene: The Great Hollywood Art Directors.* New York: Harry N. Abrams, Inc., 1994.

Sennett, Ted. *Warner Brothers Presents: The Most Exciting Years—From the Jazz Singer to White Heat.* New Rochelle, NY: Arlington House, 1971.

Shannon, Bob, and John Javna. *Behind the Hits: Inside Stories of Classic Pop and Rock and Roll.* New York: Warner Books, 1986.

Shapiro. *Shooting Stars: Drugs, Hollywood and the Movies.* London: Serpent's Tail, 2003.

Shelton, Robert. *No Direction Home: The Life and Music of Bob Dylan.* New York: Ballantine Books, 1986.

Shipman, David. *The Story of Cinema: A Complete Narrative History from the Beginnings to the Present.* New York: St. Martin's Press, 1982.

Shorris, Sylvia, and Marion Abbott Bundy. *Talking Pictures: With the People Who Made Them.* New York: The New Press, 1994

Siciliano, Enzo. *Pasolini: A Biography.* New York: Random House, 1982.

Sigoloff, Marc. *The Films of the Seventies: A Filmography of American, British and Canadian Films 1970–1979.* Jefferson, NC: McFarland & Company, 1984.

Silet, Charles L.P., ed. *Oliver Stone: Interviews: Conversations with Filmmakers Series.* Jackson: University Press of Mississippi, 2001.

Silfkin, Irv. *Video Hound's Groovy Movies: Far-Out Films of the Psychedelic Era.* Detroit, MI: Visible Ink Press, 2004.

Silver, Alain, and Elizabeth Ward. *Film Noir: An Encyclopedic Reference to the American Style*, 3rd ed. New York: The Overlook Press, 1992. First published in 1979.

Simon, Mark. *Storyboards: Motion in Art*, 2nd ed. Boston, MA: Focal Press, 2000.

Sitney, P. Adams, ed. *Film Culture Reader*. New York: Cooper Square Press, 2000. First published New York: Praeger, 1970.

———. *Visionary Film the American Avant-Garde, 1943–2000*, 3rd ed. Oxford: Oxford University Press. 2002. First published in 1974.

Sklar, Robert. *A World History of Film*. New York: Harry N. Abrams, Inc., 1993.

Smith, Steven C. *A Heart at Fire's Center: The Life and Music of Bernard Herrmann*. Berkeley: University of California Press, 1991.

Snyder, Robert W. *The Voice of the City: Vaudeville and Popular Culture in New York*. Chicago, IL: Ivan R. Dee, 2000. First published in 1989.

Solnit, Rebecca. *River of Shadows: Eadweard Muybridge and the Technological Wild West*. New York: Viking, 2003.

Sontag, Susan. *Where the Stress Falls*. New York: Picador USA, 2001.

Special Issue on Scorsese on the Occasion of His Receiving The Film Society of Lincoln Center Honor in 1998. *Film Comment* 34(3) (May/June, 1998), 16–77.

Spignesi, Stephen. *The Italian 100: A Ranking of the Most Influential Cultural, Scientific, and Political Figures, Past and Present*. Secaucus, NJ: A Citadel Press Book, published by Carol Publishing Group, 1998.

Stendhal. *The Charterhouse of Parma*. New York: The Modern Library, 2000. Written in 1839.

Stephens, Michael L. *Gangster Films: A Comprehensive, Illustrated Reference to People, Films and Terms*. Jefferson, NC: McFarland & Company, 1996.

Sterling, Kate Anna, ed. *Cinematographers on the Art and Craft of Cinematography*. *Filmmakers* series, No. 18. Metuchen, NJ: The Scarecrow Press, 1987.

Stern, Lesley. *The Scorsese Connection*. London: British Film Institute, 1995. Bloomington: Indiana University Press, 1995.

Sterritt, David, ed. *Jean-Luc Godard: Interviews*. *Conversations with Filmmakers Series*. Jackson: University Press of Mississippi, 1998.

Stevens, George, JR. *Conversations with the Great Moviemakers of Hollwood's Golden Age at the American Film Institute*. New York: Knopf, 2006.

Summers, Anthony, and Robbyn Swan. *Sinatra: The Life*. New York: Knopf, 2005.

Talese, Gay. *New York: A Serendipiter's Journey* (Horace Walpole's coinage in allusion to a fairytale *The Three Princes of Serendip* who in their travels were constantly finding valuable or agreeable things they did not seek.) New York: Harper & Brothers, 1961.

———. *Honor Thy Father*. New York, World Publishing, 1971.

———. *Unto the Sons*. New York: Alfred A. Knopf, 1992.

Taubin, Amy. *Taxi Driver BFI Film Classics*. London: BFI Publishing, 2000.

Tevis, Walter. *The Hustler*. New York: Warner Books, 1984.

Thomas, Tony. *Howard Hughes in Hollywood*. Secacus, NJ: Citadel Press, 1985.

Thompson, David ed., and Ian Christie. *Scorsese on Scorsese*. London, Boston: Faber and Faber, 1989, updated edition, 1996. Updated edition, 2003.

Thompson, Kristin, and David Bordwell. *Film History: An Introduction.* New York: McGraw-Hill, Inc., 1994.

Thomson, David. *The Whole Equation: A History of Hollywood.* New York: Knopf, 2005.

Thurman, Robert A.F. *Inside Tibetan Buddhism: Rituals and Symbols Revealed.* San Francisco, CA: Collins Publishers, 1995.

———. *Anger.* Oxford: Oxford University Press, 2005.

Tirard, Laurent. *Moviemakers' Master Class: Private Lessons from the World's Foremost Directors.* New York: Faber and Faber, 2002.

Tobias, Michael, ed. *The Search for Reality: The Art of Documentary Filmmaking.* Studio City, CA: Michael Wiese Productions, 1998.

Tonelli, Bill, ed. *The Italian American Reader.* New York: William Morrow, 2003.

Tonelli, Bill, ed. *The Italian American Reader: A Collection of Outstanding Fiction, Memoirs, Journalism, Essays, and Poetry.* New York: William Morrow, 2003.

Tonetti, Claretta Micheletti. *Bernardo Bertolucci: The Cinema of Ambiguity. Twayne's Filmmakers Series.* New York: Twayne Publishers, 1995.

Tosches, Nick. *Dino: Living High in the Dirty Business of Dreams.* New York: Doubleday, 1992.

———. *King of the Jews.* New York: HarperCollins, 2005.

Trager, James. *The New York Chronology: The Ultimate Compendium of Events, People, and Anecdotes from the Dutch to the Present.* New York: Harper Collins, 2003.

Trevelyan, Raleifh, ed. *Italian Short Stories: Penguin Parallel Text.* London: Penguin Books, 1965.

Truffaut, Francois. *Hitchcock/Truffaut.* New York: Simon & Schuster, 1967. Revised ed. *Hitchcock.* New York: Simon & Schuster, 1985.

Turim, Maureen. *Flashbacks in Film: Memory and History.* New York: Routledge, 1989.

Turner, George. "Lighting for Drama: *The Color of Money.*" *American Cinematographer* 67(11) (November 1986): pp. 52–58.

Usai, Paolo Cherchi. *Silent Cinema: An Introduction.* London: BFI Publishing, 2000.

Vaughn, Dai. *Portrait of an Invisible Man: The Working Life of Stewart McAllister: Film Editor.* London: BFI Publishing, 1983.

Vincent, Frank, and Steven Priggé. *A Guy's Guide to Being A Man's Man.* New York: Berkeley Books, 2006.

Vollman, William T. *Rising Up and Rising Down,* vols. I–VI. San Francisco, CA: McSweeny Books, 2003.

Walker, Alexander. *Hollywood, England: The British Film Industry in the Sixties.* London: Harrap, 1986. First published in Great Britain, 1974.

———. *The Shattered Silents: How the Talkies Came to Stay.* New York: William Morrow and Company, Inc., 1979.

———. *National Heroes: British Cinema in the Seventies and Eighties.* London: Harrap, 1986.

Walker, Joseph, and Juanita Walker. *The Light on Her Face.* Hollywood: The ASC Press, 1984.

Wallace, Robert, and the editors of *Time-Life* Books. *Time-Life Library of Art. The World of Leonardo 1452–1519.* New York: Time, Inc., 1966.

Ward, Ed, Geoffrey Stokes, and Ken Tucker. *Rock of Ages: The Rolling Stone History of Rock & Roll.* New York: Rolling Stone Press/Summit Books, 1986.

Warshow, Robert. *The Immediate Experience: Movies, Comics, Theatre and Other Aspects of Popular Culture.* Cambridge, MA: Harvard University Press, 2001.

Weegee. *Naked City.* New York: Da Capo Press. Originally published, New York: E.P. Dutton, 1945.

Weinberg, G. Herman. *Saint Cinema: Writings on the Film 1929–1970,* revised edition: New York: Dover Publications, Inc., 1973. First published, New York: DBS Publications, Inc., 1970.

Weiss, Marion. *Martin Scorsese: A Guide to References and Resources.* Boston, MA: G.K. Kahll & Co., 1987.

Wetzsteon, Ross. *Republic of Dreams: Greenwich Village: The American Bohemia, 1910–1960.* New York: Simon & Schuster, 2002.

Wharton, Edith. *The Age of Innocence.* New York: Collier Books, a reprint from *Novels* by Edith Wharton published by Library of America, 1986. Originally published in 1920, copyright, D. Appleton and Company.

White, E.B. *Here Is New York.* New York: A New York Bound Book, The Little Bookroom, 1991. Originally published, New York: Harper & Bros., 1949.

Whitehead, Colson. *The Colossus of New York.* New York: Anchor Books, 2003.

Willis, Clint, ed. *Crimes of New York: Stories of Crooks, Killers, and Corruption from the World's Toughest City.* New York: Thunder's Mouth Press, 2003.

Wills, Garry. *Venice: Lion City: The Religion of Empire.* New York: Simon & Schuster, 2001.

———. *Why I Am A Catholic.* Boston, MA: Houghton Mifflin Company, 2002.

Winegardner, Mark. *The Godfather Returns.* New York: Random House, 2004.

Wolfe, Tom. *The Kandy-Kolored Tangerine-Flake Streamline Baby.* New York: Bantam Books. Originally published in hardcover, Farrar, Straus, and Giroux, June 1965.

———. *The Electric Kook-Aid Acid Test.* New York: Farrar, Straus, and Giroux, Inc., 1968.

Wood, Robin. *Rio Bravo BFI Film Classics.* London: British Film Institute, 2003.

Woods, Paul A., ed. *Scorsese A Journey through the American Psyche.* London: Plexus, Ultrascreen series, 2005.

Young, Freddie, as told to Peter Busby. *Seventy Light Years: A Life in the Movies.* London: Faber and Faber, 1999.

Zinman, David. *Saturday Afternoon at the Bijou.* New Rochelle, New York: Arlington House, 1973.

Zucker, Carole. *Figures of Light: Actors and Directors Illuminate the Art of Film Acting.* New York: Plenum Press, 1995.

INDEX

About the Author

Vincent LoBrutto is an instructor of editing, production design, and cinema studies for the Department of Film, Video, and Animation at the School of Visual Arts, where he is a thesis advisor and member of the Thesis Committee. He is the author of *Selected Takes: Film Editors on Editing* (Praeger, 1991); *By Design: Interviews with Film Production Designers* (Praeger, 1992); *Sound-on-Film: Interviews with Creators of Film Sound* (Praeger, 1994); *Stanley Kubrick: A Biography* (1997); *Principal Photography: Interviews with Feature Film Cinematographers* (Praeger, 1999); *The Filmmaker's Guide to Production Design* (2002); *The Encyclopedia of American Independent Filmmaking* (Greenwood, 2002); and *Becoming Film Literate: The Art and Craft of Motion Pictures* (Praeger, 2005). A member of the American Cinema Editors (ACE), LoBrutto is the editor of *CinemaEditor* and is a contributing author to *American Cinematographer, Film Quarterly*, and *Films in Review*. His frequent media appearances include *Entertainment Tonight*, National Public Radio's *All Things Considered*, and CNN.